KING COWBOY

King Cowboy

Tom Mix

And The Movies

Robert S. Birchard

Riverwood Press • Burbank, Calfornia

Dedicated to the memory of
Sid Jordan, Ted French, and
the other riders of the purple sage
who made their last stand in Hollywood

Robert S. Birchard
    KING COWBOY - Tom Mix and the Movies
ISBN: 1-880756-05-6

    Copyright (c) 1993 by Robert S. Birchard

    FIRST EDITION

Cover: Les Leverett
Graphics: Business Graphics, Hollywood, California
Typesetting production: Michael Bifulco

Photo Credits:

Academy of Motion Picture Arts and Sciences Margaret Herrick Library: 12, 37, 40, 42, 43, 48, 50, 54, 55, 57, 60 (top)
Richard W. Bann: 69 (bottom), 143 (top), 173 (bottom), 210 (top-right), 238, 241, 249, 252 (top), 254, 255, 257 (bottom), 261 (bottom)
Critt Davis: 2, 185 (top), 194 (top), 199 (top), 201 (top), 205 (top), 211 (top), 224 (top), 225 (top)
Mike Hawks: 156 (top), 168 (top), 177 (top), 182, (bottom), 190 (bottom), 192 (top), 206 (bottom),
Dave Holland: Frontispiece, 121, 143 (bottom), 145 (bottom), 181 (top-right)
Hollywood Studio Museum: 192 (bottom), 194 (bottom), 196
Richard F. Seiverling: 70, 222
Marc Wanamaker/Bison Archives: 6, 7, 116, 120, 237, 272, 281
Bob Wolter: 133, 190 (top)

CONTENTS

INTRODUCTION

When I told Riverwood Press that I was interested in doing a book on Tom Mix, my editor tempered his fondness for the subject with a question: "How will yours be different from everyone else's?"

A fair challenge, especially since books about the cowboy star have become a minor industry in recent years. To answer the question properly, it is useful to explain how the present volume came about.

My own interest in Tom Mix dates back to 1961 when I was eleven years old and first became curious about silent movies. My young mind deemed it a miracle of no small proportion that motion pictures provided a time machine that made it possible to see people and events that occurred long before I was born, a proposition I find no less miraculous as time goes by. My childhood interest in Gene Autry, Roy Rogers, Hopalong Cassidy, the Cisco Kid, and other cowboy stars of the 1950s translated into a curiosity about Hoot Gibson, William S. Hart, Buck Jones, and the greatest of them all—Tom Mix.

That is—everyone said Tom Mix was the greatest, but there was no way to be sure. Although movies made a retrospective appraisal possible—for all practical purposes it was highly unlikely. As late as 1966, 20th Century-Fox Television Executive Vice-President William Self answered an inquiry by saying: "As far as I can determine, most of the Mix films were destroyed and I have been unable to find any prints. Even if the prints did show up, we have no plans to release them to television at this time, nor do we plan any prints for the collectors' market."

A few of Mix's early one-reelers were around, but they offered only a hint of the Mix magic that long-ago movie fans remembered. While screening one of these shorts for a small audience, Natalie Jordan Pavani introduced herself and said: "My father-in-law used to work with Tom Mix." The father-in-law turned out to be Sid Jordan, a friend of Tom's from his days in Oklahoma who worked with him on screen throughout the silent era.

Sid and his wife, Alice, were pleased at my young interest in their old friend, and they shared memories and still photographs with me. They also helped break the ice for me to meet Tom's former wife Olive Stokes Mix, George O'Brien, and other members of the Mix stock company including Jim Rush, Rocky Cline, and Lucinda Ruffner. I also came to talk with others who knew and worked with Tom Mix, including his daughter Thomasina Mix Gunn, director George Marshall, producer Stanley Bergerman, leading lady Ruth Hall, cowboy Ted French, circus clown and stage hand Gypsy Joe Bowers, and Jodie Eason Frame.

In the late 1960s, producer and film historian Alex Gordon was hired by Fox to undertake an inventory of its studio vaults and he managed to turn up prints of nearly a dozen Mix films that were thought to be lost. Not all of these rediscovered treasures were classics, but *The Untamed* (1920), *The Great K & A Train Robbery* (1926), and *The Last Trail* (1927) confirmed Tom's reputation for fast-paced, well-produced Western entertainments and made one yearn to see the other missing Fox Mix pictures. One of my first jobs was patching up some of these battered nitrate prints so that they could be copied and preserved.

I wrote a number of articles about Tom Mix and other early movie cowboys for publications like *Frontier Times, Westerner,* and *Westways,* and along the way I corresponded with Mix fans throughout the world including Robert Cotton, Harold J. Triem, Bob Wolter, Richard F. Seiverling, Leo Riemens, Sam Henderson, Janus Barfoed, and famed Western writer Walt Coburn.

One thing we all had in common was a desire for a comprehensive Tom Mix filmography. We combed our limited research resources and traded lists with each other in an effort to develop the most complete index possible, but our work was hampered by several factors.

Since no two sources seemed to agree on just how many films Tom Mix made (figures like "over 200" and "nearly 400" offered only vague targets), compiling a filmography was doubly difficult because many of Tom's pictures were made in the nickelodeon era when cast listings were rare and often incomplete. It helped that Mix made all his early films for the Selig Polyscope Company, but, because Selig was notoriously poor about advertising its films in the industry trade magazines, the studio often received short-shrift in the film review columns of the time. As a result, some researchers assumed that virtually every Selig Western was a Tom Mix film. Titles changed for theatrical and home movie reissue also added to the confusion.

Living in Los Angeles, I had one tremendous advantage—the Margaret Herrick Library at the Academy of Motion Picture Arts and Sciences. I spent many an afternoon paging through *Moving Picture World, Motion Picture News,* and the Academy's large collection of Selig Polyscope bulletins covering the years 1911 through late 1915. I managed to develop a listing that was complete enough to satisfy my curiosity, and after helping Darryl Ponicsan with research for his 1975 biographical novel *Tom Mix Died For Your Sins,* I put my notes in my file cabinet and pursued other interests.

In 1992 I was asked to write an essay about silent Western stars and another about the real cowboys who worked in movies for the Riverwood Press expanded reissue of *Don Miller's Hollywood Corral.* In going through my twenty year old notes and interviews, I became reacquainted with old friends—many long since gone to their reward. I missed having early morning coffee with that "man of a few thousand words" George O'Brien, meeting Ted French around the campfire at the Chuck Wagon Trailers cookouts, and trying to draw out the more taciturn Sid Jordan, who rivaled Gary Cooper when it came to "yep" and "nope." I also renewed my interest in the life and films of Tom Mix.

Around the same time I picked up a copy of *The Tom Mix Book* by Merle G. "Bud" Norris and *Tom Mix: Portrait of a Superstar* by Dr. Richard F. Seiverling, and I re-read Paul E. Mix's *The Life and Legend of Tom Mix.* All three books contained filmographies, but all three differed in substantial ways from the one I had compiled so many years before. Bud Norris's book presented a special challenge. Like others, Bud had compiled his list with the help of fellow enthusiasts, and he listed dozens of titles that I did not have, but there were also titles on my list that were not on his. My curiosity was aroused, and I dusted off my notes and returned to the Academy Library for a new round of research.

In the intervening years, the Academy had acquired the Charles G. Clarke collection which filled in many holes in the Selig collection. Now the Academy has a nearly uninterrupted sequence of Selig bulletins from mid-1910 to late 1915, supplemented with Selig British release pamphlets for 1911 through 1913. I started from scratch, going through all these original sources as if approaching the task for the first time. Where before I was content merely to list titles, release dates, directors and cast members, now I was determined to compile the most complete possible record of Mix's film work, including character names, production numbers and still codes, contemporary synopses and critical reaction. I wanted all this information in one place for myself, and I thought other collectors and enthusiasts would enjoy such a volume as well. I checked the disputed titles in other Mix filmographies—confirmed some, denied others, and managed to add a few that none of us had come up with before.

With he help of Karl Thiede, a tireless researcher, I consulted microfilm of such early obscure trade publications as *The Nickelodeon, Harrison's Reports,* and *Exhibitors Herald,* and when all efforts failed in finding published information on some of Mix's early Foxfilm shorts, I called on David Pierce to pull copyright deposit materials from the files of the Library of Congress. Aside from minor silent corrections of typographical errors and lapses in continuity, the synopses and reviews are presented as originally published. The copy written by the Selig publicity department is naive, windy, and stilted; while the often illiterate prose of *Harrison's Reports* concentrates on whether the films are "suitable for Sunday showing." Reviewers from *Variety* are New York hip, while those from the other trades balance real criticism with a desire not to offend their advertisers.

The stories are here as well as vivid descriptions of the stunts performed by Mix. They will reward the patient reader with a fascinating insight into how the films were viewed by audiences in the teens, twenties and thirties, and provide a ready reference for the more casual reader who may be interested in finding out about specific films. Throughout his career Tom Mix appeared in dozens of promotional shorts, including numerous issues of *Screen Snapshots, Hollywood on Parade, Voice of Hollywood,* as well as various special trailers and newsreels. Some of these have been mentioned in the text, but because they are not specifically Tom Mix titles, they have been ignored in the filmography.

For illustrations I relied heavily on my own collection, but Richard Bann, Dave Holland, Marc Wanamaker/Bison Archives, Mike Hawks, Critt Davis, Bob Wolter, and Richard F. Seiverling and the Hollywood Studio Museum have also generously contributed photos. The most unique pictures are frame enlargements from the Selig collection at the Academy of Motion Picture Arts and Sciences covering a number of titles in the years 1913-1914. These frame enlargements are all that is known to survive on many of these early films, and I want to thank Linda Mehr and Robert Cushman for their help and for granting permission to print them. Sam Gill of the Academy special collections deserves special thanks as well. Although some of the photos will be familiar, most have never been published before now.

Biographical essays introduce each section of the filmography and highlight Mix's tenure at each of the five studios where he worked. Tom's days with his own ill-fated circus are also detailed. These essays are filled with the first-hand reminiscences of many who worked with Mix, and Tom also speaks for himself, through letters, published writings, and court reports. Eugene Hilchey of Century Archives offered details of Tom's studio locations in the Teens. I have attempted to offer a well-rounded word portrait of the cowboy star without relying on oft-repeated legends dished out over the years by Tom and an army of Hollywood press agents.

It is my opinion that *King Cowboy - Tom Mix and the Movies* offers the first truly reliable index to the films of Tom Mix, although I make no claim to infallibility and I would appreciate hearing from anyone who can add pieces to the puzzle.

Robert S. Birchard
Los Angeles, California
1993

I hope my loved
gets fat hoff the
I rate that grows
from the grass I throw
that shut like me

Sincerely
Tom Mix

KING COWBOY

TOM MIX

THE REAL THING IN COWBOYS

For a cowboy out of work in 1910 the possibilities were few and the prospects were bleak. The romance of the West as depicted by the likes of Zane Grey and Owen Wister bore little relation to reality. There were fences to mend and manure to shovel, but ranch work was often irregular and the pay was poor. An occasional contest or rodeo might bring a chance for extra money and short-lived local fame; or, with real luck, a top hand might land with a circus or Wild West show and play at being a fabled knight of the range; but for the most part being a cowboy meant back-breaking work and an uncertain future. An adventurous soul like Tom Mix, however, found the drudgery of the "wild" West more appealing than a life of boredom at a regular job back home.

Tom Mix was born January 6, 1880 at Mix Run, Cameron County, Pennsylvania, the son of Ed and Elizabeth Mix. The family moved to Driftwood, Pennsylvania when Tom was four. In 1888 Ed Mix gave up his work as a lumberman to take a position as stablemaster for lumber baron John E. DuBois, and the family settled in the town of DuBois in Clearfield County, Pennsylvania.

At the age of three, Tom rode his first animal—not a horse, but a cow. However, his father's work in the stables gave him ample opportunity to learn about horses, and he took a strong interest in becomming a cowboy. Making a lasso from his mother's clothesline, he practised roping the local farm animals, much to the disgust of the Mix's neighbors.

"When he was twelve years old," his mother recalled in a 1935 interview, "he made his own first cowboy suit. He sewed some old rick-rack lace along the

legs of his trousers. Then he cut off his coat and made a jacket which he trimmed with fringe from a red broadcloth table cover. With the money he earned from the care of the [neighbor's] cows he bought himself an old revolver and a [rifle]."

The whole world seemed to be just beyond Clearfield County, and at age eighteen Tom Mix set out to conquer it. He would later say (with tongue in cheek, no doubt) that he left home because he couldn't stand the smell of the animals in his father stable, but he was indentured to a DuBois foundry and the prospects of factory life did not appeal to him. Troubles with Spain were brewing in 1898, so Tom signed up for a hitch in the Army. There were no campaigns to sooth his thirst for adventure, however, and he sat out the ten-week war at Montchanin and Pea Patch Island on the Delaware River with the Coast Artillery, never seeing battle action.

After his first three-year hitch Tom was honorably discharged, but he immediately re-upped. On July 18, 1902 he married Grace I. Allin, a school teacher from Louisville, Kentucky. Apparently, Grace had no desire to be an army wife, and in October, 1902 Tom took a furlough from Fort Hancock, New Jersey, and never returned to the service of Uncle Sam. Listed first as AWOL, and finally as a deserter, the government made no attempt to catch up with him. Tom and Grace made their way to Guthrie, Oklahoma Territory, where she resumed her work as a teacher and he took whatever work he could find—nothing too exciting, and nothing too remunerative.

He worked as a wrangler, taught physical culture, and served as Drum Major to the Oklahoma Cavalry Band at the St. Louis Exposition in 1904. He even managed to work as a peace officer in a couple of construction camps. Along the way he became a crack shot and a pretty fair bulldogger. But mostly he tended bar before landing with the Miller Brothers 101 Ranch Show in 1906. The Miller outfit was one of the great Wild West shows of the day, and Tom Mix became a leading performer. While working for the 101, Zack Miller accused Tom of borrowing a horse to enter a rodeo. The horse was injured and the Millers filed suit for horse embezzlement—a charge that would continue to haunt Mix for years after the alleged offense.

Tom's first marriage ended in annulment shortly after he came to the Oklahoma Territory. On December 20, 1905 he married Jewell "Kitty" Perrine, daughter of an Oklahoma City hotel owner. The union lasted little more than a year, although locals remembered that Tom paid visits to Jewell Perrine whenever he returned to Oklahoma in later years.

In 1908 Tom married Olive Stokes, daughter of an Oklahoma rancher. Their first months as man and wife were spent with Olive's parents, but soon they were on the road working for several Wild West shows and even mounting their own short-lived show.

Opposite page: Hats off to Mom. Tom's cowboys lift their hats as Elizabeth Mix visits her son during production of *The Texan* (1920).

In early 1910 the Chicago-based Selig Polyscope Company signed a deal with Will A. Dickey and his Circle D Ranch Wild West Show and Indian Congress to provide stock and wranglers for a series of movies to be made on location in the West. Dickey was an old friend of the Stokes family and had seen Tom perform with the Miller Brothers' show. He wrote to ask if the couple would be interested in appearing in moving pictures. The reply was affirmative, so Dickey asked Tom and Olive to meet the Selig Western unit at Flemington, Missouri.

Col. William N. Selig was a pioneer in the picture business. A former stage magician, he began making and marketing films before the turn of the century, and by 1907 he was able to build a large studio on Randolph Street in Chicago. That same year he set up a second production unit in Los Angeles. The West coast unit began humbly with makeshift stages atop Deardon's Department Store and in the backyard of a Chinese laundry, but by 1909 the company occupied a beautiful mission style studio facility near Echo Park on Allesandro Street (now Glendale Boulevard) in the Edendale district of Los Angeles.

In 1908 Selig joined with Thomas A. Edison, Inc., the Biograph Company,

Opposite page: A former stage magician, Colonel William N. Selig founded the Selig Polyscope Company before the turn of the century and by 1910 controlled a far-flung motion picture empire with studios in Chicago, Los Angeles, Florida, and Arizona.

Below: The Selig Polyscope Studio in Chicago where Mix made a few pictures between engagements at Selig's satellite studios. The facility became something of a white elephant when Selig moved most of his operations to California in the mid Teens.

the Vitagraph Company of America, and several other leading producers to form the Motion Picture Patents Company. The object was to create a monopoly based on patent rights to discourage other producers from entering the market. The Patents Company forced theatre owners to pay a two-dollar weekly license fee for the right to use a film projector. Under threat of losing their access to Patents Company product, exhibitors were also prohibited from running any non-licensed film in their theatres, effectively eliminating competition from upstart independent producers.

Exhibitors grumbled but complied. Then in 1910, the Patents Company formed the General Film Company to distribute the films of the member companies. General Film bought out or shut down competing independent film exchanges, and created the first national film distribution system. General agreed to buy all the product produced by its member producers with a guaranteed sale of sixty-five prints for each film at a price of twelve cents a foot. The average one-reel subject could be produced for a few hundred dollars and offered a return of over $7,500! Soon the Patents Company was challenged by independent producers and distributors like Carl Laemmle and William Fox, but for nearly a half dozen years Selig and his fellow film trust barons had a license to mint money.

While other producers in the Patents Company (notably Vitagraph, Biograph, and Kalem) made an effort to produce films of real quality, Selig seemed content to grind out stodgy, unimaginative, cheaply made pictures. However, Selig did send units throughout the country from time to time to obtain picturesque locations for his films.

The company that Tom Mix and his wife met at Flemington was one of Selig's many travelling units, and the month they spent in Missouri and Oklahoma resulted in at least a half dozen films including *The Trimming of Paradise Gulch, The Range Riders* (both released in June of 1910), and *Ranch Life in the Great South-West* (released in August, 1910). The films were directed by Otis Turner, who entered the picture business as early as 1906 and was affectionately known as "the dean of motion picture directors."[1]

According to Olive Mix, Tom was not impressed with his image on the screen, but Otis Turner obviously was. When Turner returned to Chicago, he brought Tom and Olive Mix with him. Olive Mix also recalled that Tom made at least one film at the main Selig studio in the windy city playing support to Margarita Fischer, Harry Pollard, and Wallace Reid in a society drama. The title of this film has not been determined, and the Selig release bulletins of the period offer no clues to what the film may have been.

It was not Mix's intention to remain in films. He signed to help organize Zack Mulhall's Wild West Show for the Appalachian Exposition in Knoxville,

Tennessee, which was scheduled to run from September 12 to October 12, 1910. Olive Mix remembered that the Selig company went to Knoxville with Tom and made a film before the Exposition opened. The best available evidence suggests that the picture was *Two Boys in Blue*, released in late October, 1910, and remade in 1915 as *Pals in Blue*.

On September 21, 1910, Colonel Selig wrote Mix and advanced him $250 to organize a troupe of cowboys and Indians to make Western pictures.

"... I know of desirable places where western films could be produced along the cowboy lines," Tom replied on September 26th, "but as to the Indians desirable for that purpose I would have to go and look the situation over before giving you an answer. The Indians employed with the Mulhall show would not do for picture purposes as they are mostly short haired and young and do not look the part. I can gather at any time all the typical real cowboys at a remarkably low salary—they to furnish their own horses if necessary but would suggest that in order to cover the Indian proposition either send a man to the reservation and secure good picture workers or get them from some show that is just closing, the latter would be rather hard as the Indians all like to go home after closing season.

"I am at liberty to leave here at any time as my contract with Mulhall was only to organize and get the show in shape for the opening and if you wish me to come to Chicago and work the proposition up from that end let me know as I am

"The Dean of motion picture directors," Otis Turner (right) with another early Western star, J. Warren Kerrigan, at Universal in 1915. While working at Selig in 1910, Turner discovered Tom Mix while the cowboy was with the Will Dickey Wild West show troupe which he had hired to perform for a series of Western pictures to be made on location in Missouri and Oklahoma. After their initial pictures, Turner brought Mix back to Chicago and introduced him to Col. Selig. Later, Mix worked with Turner in St. Augustine, Florida, and Silver City, Colorado, for the Selig Company.

in touch with all the men that you would require we could get together at any place you would designate. The securing of suitable Indians is the only drawback that I can see to organizing a company at once."

While Mix assured Selig that he was free to leave Zack Mulhall's employ at any time, Mulhall saw things differently. His Wild West show was in desperate straits, and he tried to maneuver Mix into using his connection with Selig to bail out the show.

Tom Mix did arrange to hire the Indians working in Mulhall's show, and Mulhall promptly sought to have the Appalachian Exposition officials hold them in order to recover the $400 deposit he had made at Valentine, Nebraska for their return. Mix also arranged with the Chancery Court to buy six steers and two bucking horses for $35 a head from Mulhall's bankrupt show, but the Colonel managed to get an extension postponing the sale. Mix then traveled to North Carolina and arranged to contract "a fine bunch of picture Indians" from a fellow with the handle of California Frank, but Mulhall moved to thwart the cowboy by dredging up the 1908 charge for horse embezzlement against Mix while he had been with the 101 Ranch.

Although Tom managed to clear himself of the charges, the nature of Mulhall's harassment finally became clear. Mix wrote Selig on November 1, 1910 that Mulhall "wanted me to recommend that you advance $1,000 to spring [Mulhall's] outfit and ship same to Jacksonville [Florida]. [Mulhall's associate] Autto was to receive a bill of sale for said stock, provided I could prevail upon the company to advance the money. Certainly I would not enter into any such deal, and they attempted to crowd me out and brought this Oklahoma charge against me. . ."

The delays and legal disputes apparently led Selig to let Mix's contract lapse, and Tom rejoined the Miller Brothers 101 Ranch Show. He appeared in Mexico City with the Miller-101 troupe in late 1910, but by the spring of 1911, Mix had again joined the Selig company at Dixieland Park in Jacksonville, Florida, trading in his Stetson for "Bolemany" and a pith helmet. He wore the pith helmet in the jungle picture *Back to the Primitive* (released May 11, 1911) and darkened his skin with Bole Armenia to play a Seminole Indian in *The Rose of Old St. Augustine* (released June 1, 1911) and the "good Indian" in *Captain Kate* (released July 13, 1911). After these non-Westerns, the unit pulled up stakes and moved west to Colorado where Tom made a strong impression as the rider in *Saved by the Pony Express* (released July 29, 1911). When Otis Turner moved on to work at Universal in Los Angeles, the direction of the Colorado unit passed first to Joseph A. Golden, then to William Duncan and Otis B. Thayer.[2]

Wanderlust struck again, and in early 1912 Tom joined his former 101

Ranch associate Guy Weadick in Alberta, Canada to help stage the first Calgary Stampede. The inital Stampede was not a major success, and while Weadick persisted and built the event into one of the great rodeos, Tom and Olive signed with the Buffalo Ranch Wild West Show to tour the eastern provinces of Canada.

Olive left the show and returned to her family's Oklahoma ranch to await the birth of their daughter, Ruth, born July 13, 1912. When the Buffalo Ranch Show closed, Tom rejoined his family and settled into domestic life. Through his friend Mayor Earl Woodard, Tom was appointed night marshal of Dewey, Oklahoma, by Washington County Sheriff John Jordan, father of his friend and fellow deputy Sid Jordan.

The job of night marshal leant credibility to Tom's later claims of having been a genuine Western lawman; however the glamour was all in the title. For all practical purposes Tom was a small town cop, dealing mostly with drunks, vagrants and an occasional disturbance of the peace. The town jail was a wasp-infested concrete bunker with an open-grate door of strap iron. It could "comfortably" hold no more than two evil-doers. Dewey's facilities did not allow for a major crime wave, and Tom's tenure was brief and uneventful.

Sid Jordan and Tom Mix in an unidentified Selig film. Jordan and Mix became friends in Oklahoma and worked together on the 101 Ranch and as deputies under Sid's father John Jordan, first Sheriff under statehood of Washington County, Oklahoma. Sid Jordan joined Tom in pictures in 1913 and worked with the cowboy star throughout the silent era.

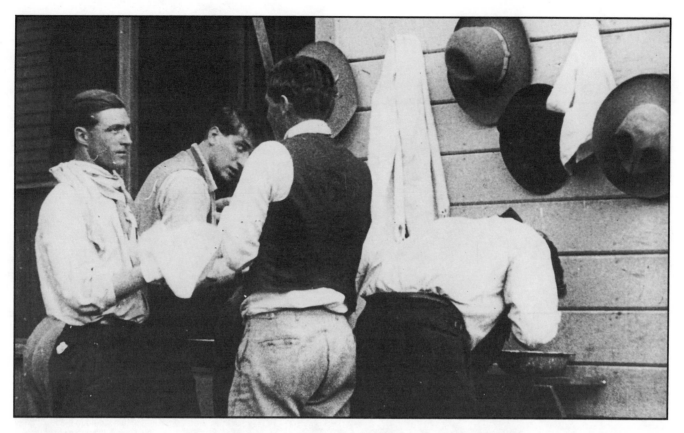

The Mix Selig films generally followed simple, dime-novel story formulas, which offered documentary glimpses of life on the ranch in the last days of the old West, as in this moment from *Buster's Little Game* (1913) when Tom and his fellow cowboys hang up their hats and wash for dinner.

In mid 1912, Romaine Fielding of the Lubin Mfg. Co.'s Southwest unit came to Prescott, Arizona to make Westerns. In his grand manner, Fielding told the people of Prescott that he intended to put the town on the map with his films, but the colorful actor-writer-filmmaker, who signed everyday business correspondence with a rubber stamp and saved his rounded sprawling autograph for personal letters, quickly moved on to Las Vegas, New Mexico; Glen Eyre, Colorado; Phoenix, Arizona; Galveston, Texas and other points of interest after giving the good people of Prescott a taste of movie money and glamour. The Prescott Chamber of Commerce moved quickly to persuade another film producer to bless their fair city, and the Selig Western unit, under the supervision of actor-director William Duncan, moved from Colorado to fill the void.

As the Duncan unit became established at Prescott, William Selig sent a brief note to Tom Mix: "If at present you are not doing anything, would be glad to have you write me."[3]

With a child to feed and clothe, the movies offered a steady pay envelope with a semblance of the gypsy life that Tom Mix seemed to prefer, so Tom wrote the Colonel and was offered a job with the Duncan unit. The Mixes arrived at Prescott in January, 1913. The year Tom Mix spent with William Duncan in Prescott served as his real apprenticeship in the picture business.

Although Tom took an occasional lead in films like *Religion and Gun*

The Selig Polyscope Studio was located in Edendale on Allesandro Street (now Glendale Boulevard) near downtown Los Angeles. Built in 1909, this was the primary Selig studio in Los Angeles until the company built the Selig Zoo and Studio at Eastlake Park. Selig leased this studio to the Fox Film Corporation in late 1916. Although he was Selig's top star, Mix rarely set foot in this studio, making his films in other facilities.

Practice and *The Law and the Outlaw,* he generally played supporting roles to Duncan and leading lady Myrtle Stedman. Born in Scotland, William Duncan was raised in the United States, and shared Mix's enthusiasm for physical culture. Like the cowboy, he had taught exercise and body building. The two men got along well, and Duncan gave Mix an occasional opportunity to try his hand at writing scenarios. *The Sheriff and the Rustler* (released November 13, 1913) offered a hint of the type of film Tom would become noted for in the '20s. The plot, written by Mix, can be stated in one brief sentence: The sheriff chases a cattle thief. It served merely as an excuse for staging a series of wild stunts.

At the end of 1913, the Selig Western unit was placed under the direction of Marshall Farnum, brother of William and Dustin Farnum, when Tom Mix and William Duncan were called to Chicago. Mix was then assigned to Selig's West Coast studio to work with the company's top filmmaker, the taciturn Scotsman Colin Campbell, who had directed Selig's ambitious nine reel feature, *The Spoilers.* Known to his friends and associates as Jim, Campbell was entrusted with most of Selig's big pictures in the Teens, but this is not to say he was one of the better directors of the period. Campbell's style was leaden and stodgy, and his surviving films have not aged well.

The films Tom Mix made with Campbell were mostly two and three-reel specials based on stories by leading writers of the day like James Oliver Curwood, Gilbert Parker, B. M. Bower (pseudonym of Bertha Muzzy Sinclair), and Cyrus Townsend Brady, and they attracted more attention than the average Selig release. The majority of these films were set in the snow country of the great Northwest, and were probably filmed in Truckee, California, a favorite location for "snow stuff." These pictures were released at intervals from late June to late September, 1914. The lack of any Mix releases between February and June suggests that all of the snow pictures were completed before the first, *In Defiance of the Law*, was released. Two straight Westerns, *When the Cook Fell Ill* (released July 31, 1914) and *Chip of the Flying U* (released August 29, 1914), were produced after the location trip to the snow country.

Following his stint with Campbell, Mix was promoted to director and given his own unit. He moved his operation to the Bachmann Studio, a small rental lot located at 831 9th Street (now Windsor Road) in a residential district of Glendale, California, owned by a dentist who liked to dabble in the picture business. It offered an open air stage and a modest Western street.

The Mix unit was virtually self-contained, and Tom had no interference from the front office. He had little contact with the studio at all, in fact. While he was pleased with his success, he also wondered how his efforts were being received, and he cautiously broached the subject to William Selig in a letter dated September 28, 1914, just a day before the release of his first directorial effort.

"Hope my pictures meet your approval," he wrote. "I am not making excuses but I am sure handicapped here [in Glendale, California] for real atmosphere . . . Everything has been going fine and I have turned out over a picture a week at a total cost of $500 a week counting everything, horses and all. I find it easy enough and my only worry is do you think I am making good? I could easy take. . . what books and stories I have in mind and lay out a years work if I could get into the ranch country again. Outside of the cowboys I only have [my leading lady] Miss [Goldie] Colwell—my payroll is but $300 a week.

"I never see anyone from the other plants [Selig maintained two other Los Angeles studios, one in the Edendale district and another at the Selig Zoo on Mission Road] as I live in Glendale, but I guess everything is going fine and I guess Mr. Persons [West coast production head] thinks I am doing O.K. as he has never been out—I call him up once in awhile to find out something. I send my pictures to Edendale when finished—"

The Tom Mix series was much less ambitious than the Colin Campbell specials. Tom's first film was a single-reeler appropriately titled *The Real Thing in Cowboys* (released on September 29, 1914). It set the pattern for all the Selig-Mix Westerns that were to follow in the next two and a half years. His pictures proved to be popular enough with audiences and their bargain-basement budgets made them highly profitable with the guaranteed returns provided by the General Film Company.

As Mix prospered in the picture game he built a stock company of hand-picked cowboys which at various times included Hoot Gibson, Leo Maloney, Joe Ryan, and Floyd (Wally Wales) Alderson, who later became Western stars themselves. Others in the group were Dick Hunter, Boss and Goober Glenn,

George Panky, Pat Chrisman (who served as Tom's foreman and horse trainer), and "Dopey" Dick Crawford.

According to Sid Jordan, Mix found Crawford in Arizona. He was an exceptional Western artist, but he was also a dope fiend. Tom got Crawford "likkered up," and kept him drunk for three weeks to get him over the withdrawls. After the "cure," Tom gave Crawford a job, and he was never known to take drugs again.

Pat Chrisman was a veteran of the American branch of the French-owned Lux Motion Picture Company, and was noted for his ability as a horse trainer. One day in 1914 Olive Mix noticed a chicken wagon trailing a colt behind as it rolled along Glendale Boulevard. Olive called Pat, who lived several blocks down the road, and suggested he look at the colt. Chrisman took her advice and paid the driver fourteen dollars for the animal that was to become known the world over as Tony, the Wonder Horse.

Sid Jordan, a cousin of Will Rogers and a friend from Tom's days in Oklahoma, was another member of the unit. With little cowboying to be done in Oklahoma, Sid decided to take a ranch job in South America in 1913.

"I read in the papers that Tom Mix was making pictures with the Selig

In many ways working in pictures was little different from punching cattle. The cowboys in Tom's company gathered around the chuck wagon for their meals. The above photo was taken at Newhall, California in 1916. Sid Jordan is on the ground behind Mix at left, Ed 'Pardner' Jones (in black hat) and George Panky are at right. Boss Glenn is foreground right with five air holes punched in his Stetson.

Company," Sid remembered. "I went out to see him, and he got me a job. I never did get to South America."

Sid went on to say that despite the popular conception that early filmmakers worked off the cuff, "Tom always worked from a script. Sometimes he'd just jot it down on the back of an old still picture—they weren't too complicated, but we never just made it up as we went along. Sometimes, though, we'd add something to make the pictures more daring."

A publicity release published in *Motion Picture News* gives a harrowing glimpse of Tom's efforts to bring daring stunts to the screen:

"Tom Mix, manager and director of the Selig company at Glendale, making western drama, has been advised to curb his attempts for realistic scenes, and in the future not to endanger the lives of his people or himself," the story related. "Recently, Mix, with a steel plate inside his shirt, had one of the men shoot a hole in a star he was wearing while playing the role of a western sheriff.

"In another instance he had bullets shot past his head in order that pictures could be secured of the missiles raising his hair. His latest stunt resulted in painful injury. He rolled down a very steep incline and a dozen or more deep gashes were cut in his legs by the sharp rocks."[4]

With all the other tall tales about Tom Mix's exploits, it would be easy to

Tom demonstrates his skill with a lasso by roping Sid Jordan for an unidentified Selig film, circa 1915. For the still cameraman, Tom and Sid had to do the stunt twice (as evidenced by the hat off as Tom tosses his loop, and hat on when it lands). The negatives in the 5'x7' glass plate still camera could not be changed quickly enough to capture the action in one pass.

dismiss this story as a press agent's pipe dream, but Sid Jordan confirmed the story of shooting Tom's hat off, with the bullet passing so close to his skull that Mix's hair raised up through the the hole in his Stetson.

In November, 1914, Selig released Mix's first five-reel feature film, *In the Days of the Thundering Herd.* The film was directed by Colin Campbell and was probably completed before Mix started work on his own series. It was staged on a large scale, but with little skill. Filled with wagon trains, Indian attacks, and buffalo hunts, *In the Days of the Thundering Herd* lacked only characterization and plot. It was primitive indeed when compared to feature films produced by other studios at the time. Two years would pass before Mix made another feature for Selig.[5]

In 1915, Mix returned to the Arizona ranch country to make pictures. Eventually, leading lady Goldie Colwell was replaced by a blue-eyed, straw hair blonde named Louella Maxam. Also joining the company was a veteran actress named Eugenie Forde, who had been on stage since 1898 and in pictures since 1911. "Fordie" was first seen with Mix in *The Outlaw's Bride,* released in March, 1915, and she made only a handful of pictures with Tom before leaving the unit, but her brief tenure had a lasting impact.

Sid Jordan remembered that Tom took a fancy to Eugenie Forde, who was about his age, and Olive Mix was understandably upset by her husband's roving

William Brunton, as dress heavy Hiram Flint, announces that he is about to foreclose the mortgage of Widow Wilson (Eugenie Forde) and her daughter (Louella Maxam) in *The Conversion of Smiling Tom (1915).* Old timers in the Mix unit recalled that Tom took a shine to Eugenie Forde before he ever met her daughter Victoria Forde.

eye. It is uncertain when Mix met Eugenie's daughter, Victoria Forde, who was the leading lady with Al Christie's Nestor unit at Universal while her mother was working with Tom. However, about the time Eugenie left the Mix unit, the eighteen year old Victoria was signed as the new leading lady for the Mix pictures. One of the reasons Vicky was hired was to give Eugenie Forde a reasonable excuse to visit Tom.

In later years, Olive Mix bitterly remembered Vicky Forde as a wild girl who was a ward of juvenile court. Whether this is true or not is unknown, but her status with the court may have related to the fact that she was a working minor from 1910 until she reached her majority. What is known, however, is that Eugenie Forde joined the American Film Company Flying "A" Studio in Santa Barbara, California, and Victoria Forde quickly became Tom's leading lady off-screen as well as on. Olive Mix returned to California, while Tom remained on location in Arizona. He came to Los Angeles to spend the 1915 Christmas holidays with his wife and daughter, but it was becoming clear that their marriage was on the rocks.

Victoria Forde was not a beautiful woman. She made her screen reputation playing eccentric comedy roles. However, she did project her personality in a way that had eluded Mix's other leading ladies. Tom's constant re-workings of simple comic and dramatic tales of love and rivalry seemed fresher with Vicky in the female lead. Unlike Tom, she had worked with several film studios, including Nestor, Universal, and the Albuquerque Film Mfg. Company, and had a better sense of the state of the film business than did Mix.[6] She took an active interest in Tom's work, and helped build his confidence as the fortunes of the Selig Polyscope Company began to decline.

Throughout 1915 the output of the various Selig studios remained constant with the release of some two hundred pictures, but disputes with the General Film Company led Selig to join with several other dissident producers of the "film trust" to form V-L-S-E (Vitagraph-Lubin-Selig-Essanay) to distribute its feature-length productions. Mix's one and two-reel pictures, and Selig's other short subjects, stayed with General Film. As a result of the breakup there was steady decline in the fortunes of General Film, and with World War I cutting into foreign sales, Selig trimmed his production schedule.

In 1916 Mix and the Selig Company received an invitation from the Commercial Club of Las Vegas, New Mexico, to make pictures in that town. The club had been instrumental in bringing Lubin's Romaine Fielding to Las Vegas in 1913 and, since Fielding's departure, they had actively sought another film company to spend dollars in the community and tout the virtues of Las Vegas on screen. Tom Mix seemed an ideal substitute for the flamboyant Fielding, and he welcomed the opportunity to work in the last remaining area of open range in the West.

Sometime after June, 1916, Tom Mix and his company came back to California. Rather than working at either of the Selig studios or his old Glendale facility, Mix moved the unit to Newhall, north of Los Angeles, in an effort to escape the jealous rampages of Olive Mix.

On August 19, 1916, Selig announced that E. A. Martin would direct a feature-length version of Zane Grey's *The Light of Western Stars* to star Tom Mix, Kathlyn Williams, and Frank Campeau. Williams signed with the Pallas-Morosco Company shortly after the announcement, and Bessie Eyton was assigned to replace her. A dispute over the rights to Grey's 1914 novel forced Selig to change the character names, re-cut and re-title the film, which finally became known as *The Heart of Texas Ryan.*

The Heart of Texas Ryan might have marked the beginning of a feature career for Tom Mix at Selig, but there were problems brewing between the star and his producer. By the end of 1916 the Tom Mix Westerns were the only short subjects regularly produced by Selig, and the cowboy star faced heavy pressure to cut costs. Unfortunately, Selig's longer films were faring poorly at the box office, and the V-L-S-E combine collapsed as Lubin ceased producton and Vitagraph sought to distribute its superior product apart from the indifferent productions of its partners. Selig joined with distriutor George Kleine, the Edison Company, and Eassanay to form the K-E-S-E service. It was evident that the end was near for the Selig Polyscope Company.

In October, 1916, Selig leased his Edendale studio to the Fox Film Corporation, and moved all of his operations to the Selig Zoo studio at Eastlake Park. Then, according to Sid Jordan, Selig sent an efficiency expert to the Mix unit to suggest ways to trim production costs. Tom told the story that the only cost-cutting measure the "expert" could find was to withhold oats from the horses that did not work in the day's shooting, keeping the animals on a thrifty ration of hay. No doubt he suggested trimming several cowboys from the payroll, and charging for the stabling of Mix's horses. There is evidence to suggest that the studio wanted to dictate a change in Tom's leading ladies as well.

The Motion Picture News trade review for *Twisted Trails* (released December 11, 1916) offered the hope that leading lady Bessie Eyton would continue to play opposite Tom Mix. Since such observations were often planted by the producing companies, it is not unreasonable to assume that Selig was attempting to break up the Tom Mix/Victoria Forde team. In addition to the two pictures with Eyton, Selig also brought Louella Maxam back from a stint with the Keystone Film Company to play opposite Tom in *The Saddle Girth* and released *The Luck That Jealousy Brought,* a film with Mix and Maxam that was produced in early 1915 but withheld from distribution.

Tom and his troupe are vexed when their auto goes off the road near Newhall, California in 1916. The boxes on the ground above the car contain the camera and film for the day's work.

Although he felt great personal loyalty to William Selig, Mix resented the intrusion on his independence and, with the suport of Victoria Forde, he guaranteed the wages of the entire company while he sought a new producer.

In 1933 William Fox remembered that when he visited his West Coast studio in 1916, "Every morning for a week this . . . figure was waiting always in a different [cowboy] costume, each one louder than the last, until my curiosity was arroused. One day he approached me and said: 'My name is Tom Mix. I made up my mind I wouldn't work for any other company until I saw you, Mr. Fox.'

"He was very picturesque," Fox continued," and I interviewed him and decided to engage him. When the subject of salary was broached, he said that the thing he was interested in was the provision for the care and feeding of his horses. We agreed on $350 a week, including feed and stables for his horses. . ."[7]

When one considers that William Fox was leasing Selig's studio and that Tom Mix was a Selig player, it is not surprising that the cowboy signed with the Fox Film Corporation. It is difficult to believe that Fox would not have known who Mix was, and he was certainly the most convenient producer Tom could have approached. However, Fox's recollection that Tom was interested in the care of his animals, is consistent with Sid Jordan's memory of the unit's last days at Selig.

Almost immediately after Mix joined Fox, William Selig sought to exploit the Mix films in his vaults. In July, 1917 Selig released a two-reel compilaton of scenes from Mix productions titled *Movie Stunts by Tom Mix*, and in 1918 he made arrangements with Exclusive Features, Inc. to re-cut and reissue the cowboy star's Selig Polyscope films.

Today it is difficult to judge the impact of Tom Mix's Selig films. Although he made nearly 170 pictures in his six years with the company, fewer than 20 of them are known to survive in established film archives. Several others are in private collections, but nearly all of these survive in reissue versions with remade titles and recycled footage. Prints of *An Arizona Wooing*, for example, contain footage from *Weary Goes a Wooing*. The 1913 two-reeler *The Law and the Outlaw*, is a heavily re-titled three-reel pastiche of the original film, with additional footage from other shorts. *The Heart of Texas Ryan* exists only in its 1923 reissue version under the title *Single Shot Parker*. The film contains a saloon fight lifted from the 1915 version of The *Tell-Tale Knife*. Hoot Gibson and Leo Maloney are clearly recognizable in the footage, and Goldie Colwell is seen working behind the bar, although she plays an entirely different role in the body of the film. It is unknown whether this footage was incorporated when Selig was forced to re-work the abortive version of *The Light of Western Stars* or added for the reissue.

What is evident from the few that have survived is that whether directed by William Duncan, Colin Campbell, E. A. Martin, or Mix himself, the Selig films were crude affairs and not on a par with the average releases of other companies at the time. The Broncho Billy one-reelers produced by G. M. Anderson for Essanay have stronger stories and better production values. The 101 Bison Westerns produced by Thomas Ince in 1912, although lacking in character development, are staged with a dynamic sense of filmmaking, and the two-reelers William S. Hart made for Ince in 1914-1915 are far better than anything Mix produced during the period.

Production notes among the Selig records at the Academy of Motion Picture Arts and Sciences suggest that Tom had a tendency to overshoot his films. *Sage-Brush Tom* (released March 16, 1915), for example, contained 1,196 feet of picture and 81 feet of titles, for a one reel 1,000 foot subject. The home office sent Tom a notice to "Ship at once—[the film] can be cut down [to release length] in Chicago." *Tom's Strategy* (released September 2, 1916) came in at 1,312 feet before cutting. However, not every film was overly long. Selig asked Tom to shoot a hundred feet of additional material to bring *The Taking of Mustang Pete* (released August 3, 1915) up to length, and the studio also ordered him to shoot a different ending for the picture.

Although he had talent as an organizer of scenes, Mix tended to maintain

Sid Jordan and Tom Mix in *The Conversion of Smiling Tom (1915)*. Movie audiences in the East were fascinated at seeing real-life cowboys on screen.

the "front-row-center" point of view evident in so many early films, and details of action were often lost because he did not move his camera closer to the action. In *Bill Haywood, Producer* (released February 16, 1915) Tom plays Haywood, a cowboy who takes over the direction of a stranded motion picture troupe. Haywood explains the scene to his actors, and fires a shot in the air to start the action. The bang scares the ranch animals and they wreak havoc with the set. Mix staged the scene in one long shot, and the humor was lost in the overall chaos.

However, it can be said that Tom Mix's work improved as he gained experience as a filmmaker. *Roping a Bride* (released February 9, 1915) suffers from the same static treatment evident in *Bill Haywood, Producer*, but in *Roping a Sweetheart*, a remake released 18 months later, the camera seeks the most interesting parts of the action, with close-ups and traveling shots used to bring life to this little comedy.

Tom Mix's greatest success lay ahead. His slick, tongue-in-cheek romps for Fox in the '20s created a new type of Western picture; but rough as they are, the Selig films offer a unique picture of ranch life seen through the eyes of a cowboy. Certainly there is exaggeration in the melodramatic plots, but there are also moments that give the films an interest beyond their dramatic content.

An enthusiastic Selig press agent touted *Ranch Life in the Great South-West* by writing that "The people and pastimes of the great west are depicted. Historic and accurate in every detail. Every element has been combined to present to an admiring public an ethnological subject, the equal of which has never before been approached, and can never be duplicated."

Although this anonymous wordsmith over-stated his case in 1910, his words have become true with the passage of time. *Ranch Life in the Great South-West* is thought to be a lost film, but the handful of Tom Mix's other Selig films that do survive are like amber preserving the life of a vanished age and in their own way, valuable documents of our Western past.

NOTES

1. A number of accounts have suggested that Francis Boggs directed the first Tom Mix films, but this is incorrect. Boggs worked at the Selig studio in Los Angeles during this period, and the traveling Western unit was under the direction of Otis Turner.

2. Otis B. Thayer spent most of his motion picture career in Colorado, working for the Colorado Film Company, the Pike's Peak Film Company, and the Art-O-Graf Film Company after his association with Selig.

3. Olive Mix remembered Selig's note and recited it from memory in 1966. The exact wording of Selig's letter may have been different.

4. *The Motion Picture News*, October 17, 1914, p. 41.

5. It may be unfair to characterize *In the Days of the Thundering Herd* this way, because it only survives in a three-reel reissue version re-titled *The Wagon Trail*. However, the fact that Aywon, the company that re-issued the film in the '20s, decided to cut footage and release it as a short suggests that the film could not successfully sustain its original five-reel length.

6. Vicky worked with Otis Turner at Universal, and it may have been Turner who recommended the Fordes to Tom Mix. Despite its name, the Albuquerque Film Mfg. Company was based in Los Angeles, and was headed by former American Film Mfg. Company executive Gilbert P. Hamilton.

7. Sinclair, Upton, *Upton Sinclair Presents William Fox*, Los Angeles (West Branch), 1933.

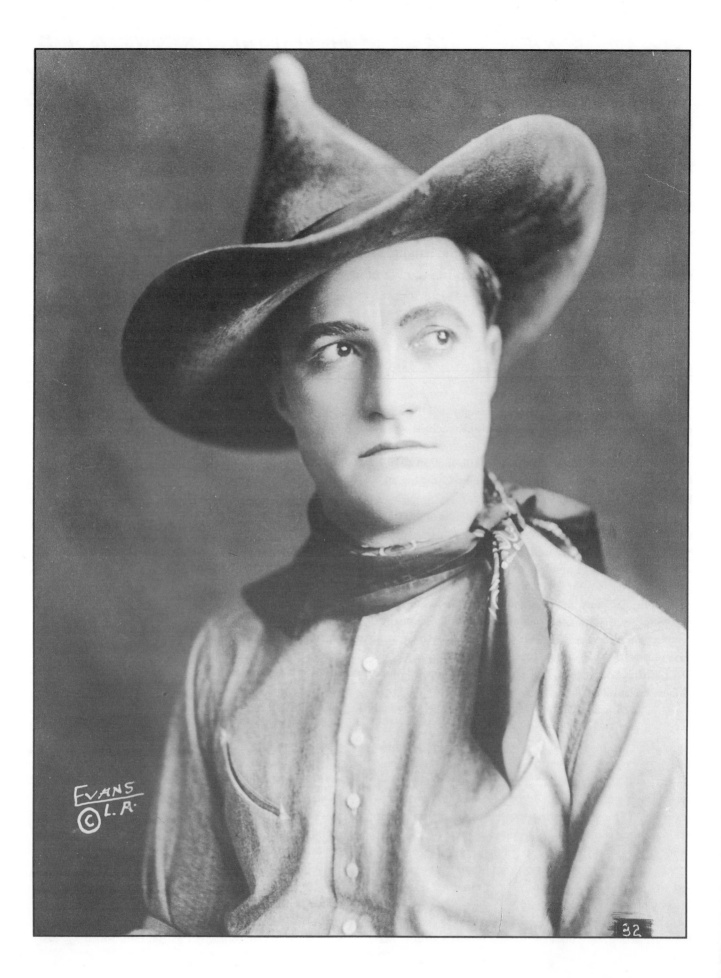

Evans
© L.A.

32

THE SELIG POLYSCOPE FILMS
1910-1917

On May 28, 1910, the New York Dramatic Mirror announced that "The Selig regular annual offering of Western pictures begins with 'The Trimming of Paradise Gulch' to be released on June 2nd and about fifteen days apart for the next four months." From contemporary trade ads and articles it is certain that Tom Mix appeared in two of the films produced by Selig's traveling Western unit that season, *The Range Riders* and *Ranch Life in the Great South-West.*

The Selig Polyscope Company did not formally list actors' credits until mid-1911, so there can be no precise listing of all the Tom Mix credits during his first year in films. Photos published in Selig trade ads of mid-1910, although small and lacking precise detail, suggest that Tom Mix was in several other films produced by the Western unit. Without additional corroborating evidence it can only be assumed that he appeared in these films.

The only first hand account of Tom's early film career comes from his former wife, Olive Stokes Mix, in her book *The Fabulous Tom Mix*, written with Eric Heath, and published in 1957. She claimed that Tom Mix's first film was *The Range Rider* made in 1909. Other published accounts suggested that Olive's reminiscences were faulty. For example, in his pioneering film history *A Million And One Nights*, published in 1926, Terry Ramsaye stated that 1910's *Ranch Life in the Great South-West* was the first Tom Mix film . Because he was writing only a few years after the event, other historians took Ramsaye's citation as gospel.

When I interviewed Olive Mix in 1966 I was skeptical of her version of events, but after further research most of her

assertions checked out. However, there were some inconsistencies in her account.

Tom Mix definitely appeared in *The Range Riders* (plural) before *Ranch Life in the Great South-West*, but the film was made in the spring of 1910, and *The Trimming of Paradise Gulch* was released before either of them. Olive recalled that Tom made only one picture on his first sojourn with the Selig Polyscope Company, and that he left films for a time to work on a round-up in Medora, North Dakota. It is possible, therefore, that Tom made his film debut in 1909 in some other Selig film, but it appears more likely that Olive Mix's chronology became slightly jumbled with the passing years.

Several researchers have suggested that Mix appeared in at least three Selig releases in 1909—namely *Briton and Boer*, *Up San Juan Hill*, and *On the Little Big Horn; or, Custer's Last Stand*, and it has been suggested that Tom's tales of his service with the Rough Riders and in the Boer War were based on his work in films rather than from actual experience. However, although Tom's claims of service in these two campaigns were largely fictitious, the films *Briton and Boer* and *Up San Juan Hill* were California productions starring Hobart Bosworth and Tom Santschi. Because of a tubercular condition, Bosworth refused to leave California for film work, and since Tom Mix did not arrive in the Golden State until 1914, these titles cannot be Tom Mix credits. There is no solid evidence that Mix appeared in *On the Little Big Horn; or, Custer's Last Stand*, so one must assume that Tom made his film debut in 1910 rather than 1909.

Olive wrote that Tom Mix's second film, which she said

was made sometime later, ". . . involved Tom leaping on horseback down thirty feet into a lake . . ."

Trade stories on *The Range Riders* noted that the film included ". . . a most thrilling encounter between cowboys and cattle rustlers, part of the fight being in a running stream of water on horseback . . ." Since none of the other possible Tom Mix Westerns of 1910 were described as having water stunts, it seems likely that *The Range Riders* was the second film and *The Trimming of Paradise Gulch*, the first film produced by the Selig Western unit in 1910, marked the film debut of Tom Mix.

According to Olive Mix, Tom made a dozen films in 1910. At least one of these films was produced at the main Selig studio in Chicago and starred Margarita Fischer and her husband Harry Pollard. The film also featured Mary Mannering and Wallace Reid. Olive described it as " a drawing room drama, the only film of that type Tom ever appeared in." The Pollard-Fischer film was made after his Western work that season, and it is almost certain that Tom and Olive worked in such a picture, however in the absence of actor's credits for the bulk of Selig's 1910 output, there is little way of knowing what the title was.

Mix's former wife also remembered that "By the time the drawing-room drama was completed, the script for Tom's next film was ready; so we went to Tennessee for the filming." It is known that Tom Mix appeared with Col. Zack Mulhall's Wild West Show at the Appalachian Exposition in Knoxville, Tennessee, from September 12 to October 12, 1910. The Wild West show background, and an admittedly murky photo in Selig trade ads, suggest that the Tennessee film was TWO PALS IN BLUE, which was released October 20, 1910.

Photographic evidence in a surviving Selig release bulletin strongly suggests that Tom Mix also appeared in *The Rustlers*, but the date of release and the lack of any other confirmed credits immediately before or after *The Rustlers* makes this an unlikely title.

Except for the two undisputed films, this list for 1910 can only represent an educated guess, based on best available evidence, of Tom Mix's film work during his first season in pictures.

1910

THE TRIMMING OF PARADISE GULCH

Selig Polyscope Company. Released June 2, 1910 through General Film Company. *Length:* 1 reel

Director: Otis Turner.

Cast: Tom Mix (One of the Paradise Gulch cowboys).

"Spirited Western farce based on a humorous idea and acted with an excellent show of sincerity is presented in this film. It tells the story of a captivating young woman who enters the Western town of Paradise Gulch, where the men become infatuated with her to the extent that they give up card playing and drinking and become her ardent pupils in studying painting. When a traveling dealer in jewelry arrives, they buy out his stock and each man gives the charmer a valuable present. When she has accepted all the jewelry bought from the peddler, she pulls up and leaves with him archly introducing him as her husband by way of a parting shot. The consternation of the sting victims is the best part of the film."

New York Dramatic Mirror, 6/11/10

THE RANGE RIDERS

Selig Polyscope Company. Released June 9, 1910 through General Film Company. *Length:* 1 reel

Director: Otis Turner

Cast: Tom Mix, Myrtle Stedman, William V. Mong

Note: Cast and director credits come from Olive Stokes Mix, who was working from memory. Tom Mix is mentioned by name in a review of the film in *The Nickelodeon*, but there appears to be no contemporary confirmation for the other credits.

"A real ranch with cattle in large number and a most thrilling encounter between cowboys and cattle rustlers, part of the fight being in a running stream of water on horseback, is well presented in this picture. There is not much, however, to the plot, and in fact a plot is hardly needed in this class of film. The foreman of the ranch becomes revengeful because a woman who, with her sister, owns the ranch, will not have him, and he is discharged, becoming the leader of a gang of cattle thieves. But the young woman has a better admirer in the person of the sheriff, who with his men, comes to the rescue of the sisters and their property. The picture has serious elements of reality, and is highly satisfactory for one of its class."

New York Dramatic Mirror, 6/18/10

"Can you imagine a more exciting or sensational picture than a great cattle stampede—curbed by fearless cowboys and dauntless riders of the western range horse? The roping and throwing of the long horns, the invasion of the camp by the notable red skins—an ensemble picture of unusual merit, carrying with it a theme of love, hatred and revenge—making a picture so true to nature—simple in plot and construction, that its advent will be a feature on any program.

"Two sisters own a large western ranch. Mary the elder is in love with Tom Mix, the county sheriff, and the foreman of the ranch is displeased with her attentions to him and his actions make it necessary to discharge him; he then becomes a cattle rustler and arch enemy of the sheriff. A raid is made on the ranch one night and a number are wounded. The sheriff swears vengeance and organizes a posse to rid the country of the outlaw element."

The Nickelodeon, 6/1/10

GO WEST, YOUNG WOMAN, GO WEST

Selig Polyscope Company. Released July 4, 1910. through General Film Company. *Length:* 1 reel

Note: Remade as MRS. MURPHY'S COOKS in 1915.

"This famous motto [sic] is the title of another humorous Western story. It is a narration of the love affaires of the various cooks that reign in the kitchen of Mrs. Kelly's select boarding house for cattle punchers. Two cooks elope with insistent young Lochinvars. A Chinaman [who is hired as a replacement cook] is quickly ejected by the offended cattlemen, and Miss Lizzie Whiz arrives. Being an athlete of no mean ability and resourcefulness, she disposes of eight men who attempt to win her only to fall before the dreamy eyes of one who's afraid of her. In despair, Mrs. Kelly finally employs a stranded actor whom she can marry herself. The best points in the picture are the arrival and departure of Lizzie Whiz. The ensemble work by the cowboys is above reproach."

New York Dramatic Mirror, 7/16/10

THE WAY OF THE RED MAN

Selig Polyscope Company. Released July 7, 1910 through General Film Company. *Length:* 1 reel

Note: The working title for this film was THE RED MAN'S WAY

"An Indian farmer and his wife protect and secrete a gambler who has injured a cowboy in a fight over a game of cards. The gambler repays the Indian by stealing the affections of his wife, a beautiful Indian woman of eighteen. Great is the dismay of the Indian on finding his wife in the arms of the white man whom he has befriended. His first thought is

to kill the destroyer of his home. But he decides to give the squaw to the gambler and when she attempts to take her infant the Indian interposes. 'You take the squaw, the child stays with me.' Five years later we see the effects of the union between the gambler and the squaw. He has become a confirmed drunkard and the squaw, through abuse, neglect and hardship, is dying. The Indian learns of this and his manner of vengeance is unique and gives this picture story its name, 'The Red Man's Way.'"

The Nickelodeon, 6/15/10

THE COWBOY'S STRATEGEM

Selig Polyscope Company. Released July 28, 1910 through General Film Company. *Length:* 1 reel

Note: Remade as TOM'S STRATEGY in 1916.

Production Number: 368

"Bob loves Mab and his love is returned, but as usual, the course of true love fails to run smooth. Bob and two of his cowboy friends go on a fishing and hunting trip in the Platte River bottoms. On their way they stop at the Post Office. An eastern lady out horseback riding stops to ask Bob for directions, Mab sees Bob, apparently paying marked attentions to the lady. Her jealousy is aroused . Bob follows her home, explains, and the cloud blows over. Bob pops the question, Mab accepts and the ring is given.

"The Eastern lady's horse runs away with her, Bob makes a heroic rescue and Mab for the second time in one day finding cause for jealousy, returns Bob's ring and goes away in anger. Bob's companions come upon a bear, and as Steve's gun fails to work, the boys return to camp and find Bob in good humor to vent his anger on a bear or anything else that will prove an outlet for his feelings.

"After finding and shooting the bear, Bob hits on a happy scheme to square matters with Mab and it is this plan that gives our story its name, 'A Cowboy's Strategem.' 'It's a corker' and for genuine merit and scenic environment will be found a true Selig, consequently in a class by itself."

The Polyscope News, Vol. 1, No. 9, 7/15/10

RANCH LIFE IN THE GREAT SOUTH-WEST

Selig Polyscope Company. Released August 9, 1910 through General Film Company. *Length:* 1 reel

Cast: Tom Mix, Henry Grammar, Pat Long, Johnny Mullins, Charles Fuqua

#14. Dewey Okla.
Tom Mix Bulldogging a Steer. Copyrighted by Drum & Griggs 7-12-11

Tom Mix developed his cowboy skills as a member of the Miller Brothers 101 Ranch Show. He was primarily a show cowboy rather than a working cowpuncher. Although others may have been individually better at roping, trick riding or shooting, Mix was a better than fair hand at all these skills, and therefore a valuable Wild West Show performer.

Above: On July 12, 1910 Tom Mix bulldogged a steer for the Selig Polyscope Company production *Ranch Life in the Great South-West.* The film was a tremendous hit, and brought Mix to the attention of William N. Selig in Chicago.

Left: After his first season in pictures, Mix signed on with Colonel Zack Mulhall's Wild West Show for the Appalachian Exposition at Knoxville, Tennessee (September 12-October 12, 1910). He is seen here standing by a downed steer after a team roping exhibition. From 1910 to late 1912 Mix's film career was interrupted several times as he returned to Rodeo or Wild West show appearances. Mix helped organize the first Calgary Stampede with Guy Weadick in 1912.

Note: This film was extremely popular with exhibitors and audiences. Selig's trade ad in the *New York Dramatic Mirror* for September 9, 1910, only a month after the picture's release, states that a third shipment of posters, numbering five thousand units, was ordered by Selig to satisfy the demand. The initial Selig poster run was usually 8,000 units. With two follow-up orders, there would have been between 18,000 and 20,000 posters in circulation for this film.

Production Number: 367

"Selig now contributes to the world his distinctive feature RANCH LIFE IN THE GREAT SOUTH-WEST a combined picture of surpassing interest—celebrities of unquestioned superiority. The people and pastimes of the great west are depicted. Historic and accurate in every detail. Every element has been combined to present to an admiring public an ethnological subject, the equal of which has never before been approached, and can never be duplicated. In the moving picture [one] witnesses varied exhibitions of skill and daring dexterity, wherein the maddened bulls of the plains vie with the American Cowboy—'The Kings of the prairie.'"

The Polyscope News, 8/15/10

[UNIDENTIFIED FILM]

Selig Polyscope Company. Released 1910 through General Film Company. 1 reel.

Cast: Margarita Fischer, Harry Pollard, Wallace Reid, Mary Mannering, Tom Mix, Olive Stokes Mix.

Note: According to Olive Mix, she and Tom made a society drama at the Selig Polyscope studio in Chicago after completing their first season's work with the traveling Western unit. The title has not been determined. The cast is according to Olive's reminiscences in her book *The Fabulous Tom Mix.*

TWO BOYS IN BLUE

Selig Polyscope Company. Released October 20, 1910 through General Film Company. *Length:* 1 reel

Note: Remade as PALS IN BLUE in 1915.

"The lure of the white-top and the music of the band is food for the bronco buster and he is happy with plaudits of the gathered throng. The grand entre is on and all is agog with excitement as Tom and Jerry cut their capers. Just then Sheriff Ketchem rudely announces he has an attachment for an unpaid feed bill at Hebron, Ind., and proceeds to 'sew' the

show up. So Bronco Bill's congress of celebrities are busted—broke and hard on the rocks.

"Tom and Jerry retire gracefully with their tools in trade—two saddles. But as the cook tent was one of the things Sheriff Ketchem had planted on, there was no sign of the forthcoming bean soup, coffee and—as well as other delicacies usually accompany [sic] the cook tops repast. So the poor man's friend—the pawnshop—holds out its welcoming hand to Tom and Jerry's saddles. The loan made—the boys are out to see the sights. But they cost money and soon the two are on the breakers again—when they are attracted to Uncle Sam's sign calling for recruits.

"This seems to hold the key to the best excitement outside the rag and blue inclosure and accordingly they are assigned to a detachment that is detailed to put down an Indian uprising. The officer in charge soon finds he has found two real knights of the saddle and decides to send them scouting to locate the hostile tribe—they are soon surprised and find more real excitement than Bronco Bills ever dreamed of. The old water hole is destined to figure in operation, a message is received by the commander of the post that the men are surrounded and can only hold out six hours longer, signed by Capt. Jim Wells. Upon receipt of the message the scouts are to lead the cavalry against the Indians' stronghold —desperate fighting and final victory, one that has resounded through the pages of history and has made the army post memorable and even today Standing Rock has become a landmark of the great northwest reservations. When Tom and Jerry are decorated with honors they plainly show that this world isn't so bad after all."

Selig release bulletin

1911

It is probable that Tom Mix appeared in a number of films in early 1911 produced by the Selig unit in Florida without being named in studio release bulletins, but there is no way to confirm this. The following are his credited appearances for 1911.

BACK TO THE PRIMITIVE

Selig Polyscope Company. Released May 11, 1911 through General Film Company. *Length:* 1 reel

Director: Otis Turner

Cast: Kathlyn Williams, Charles Clary, Tom Mix, Joseph Gerard

"John Wilton cables his sister Helen in London to leave for South Africa via S. S. China and apprises her of the fact that Lord Thurlow sails on the same ship and is to act as her escort. At the same time telling her he will meet them at Cape Town. After a hurried preparation for the departure the long journey is begun. Lord Thurlow is attentive to his charge that he may fulfill the wishes of his friend and conndent [sic] John Wilton. Will Carson, a fellow passenger aboard, much admires the young and handsome Helen and seeks an introduction through the ship officer. The admiration becomes mutual and they are seen on the promenade deck enjoying fresh sea air. Their action causes much uneasiness on the part of Lord Thurlow who interferes in the discharge of his duty and is in return insulted by Will, much to the disgust of Helen, who regrets the publicity of the incident.

"The approaching storm rivets the attention of all on board and for a time the unfortunate affair is forgotten. When 500 miles off Cape Town the vessel is wrecked and all are struggling in the treacherous waters of the sea. After two days' time famine and starvation made the occupants of the improvised raft almost welcome death as a relief. On the third day they are washed ashore and when sufficiently revived wend their way to the jungle in search of civilization. A deserted hut furnished them shelter—but must be guarded night and day, for the country around swarms with wild beasts and life in these parts is all but pleasant. Helen, secure on the top of the thatched hut, is startled to see lions and leopards prowl around almost within hand reach. Thurlow is at their mercy and meets his fate stoically. Two years elapse and the brother who had mourned his sister as dead has his attention called to an article in the press referring to the wreck and suggesting that it was possibly the China. An expedition by elephant train was organized and John, trusting in kind providence sets out to find the party. After many vigilant days and nights the signal flag and the remains of the fire is found, their hopes were soon realized and amid the greatest rejoicing brother and sister are reunited over the dead body of a savage African lion that the party were compelled to kill in the rescue."

Selig release bulletin

THE ROSE OF OLD ST. AUGUSTINE

Selig Polyscope Company. Released June 1, 1911 through General Film Company. *Length:* 1 reel

Director: Otis Turner.

Cast: Kathlyn Williams (Dolores, The Rose of St. Augustine), Charles Clary (Capt. Lafitte, The Privateer), W. H. Stowell (Lieut. Dalroy, His second in command), Tom Mix (Black Hawk, a Seminole Indian), Frank Weed (Commandant of Fort, Father of Dolores), True Boardman (Senor Alicante, Suitor of Dolores), Vera Hamilton (Duenna, Her Chaperon, old woman), Harrison Gray (Jailor).

"Captain Lafitte receives word that Alicante a young Spaniard is to wed Dolores, the Rose of St. Augustine—whom he has not seen since childhood. She objects to the wedding. Lafitte captures Alicante, dresses in his clothes, and with Dalroy his Lieutenant dressed as his valet and Black Hawk, a Seminole Indian of his band, goes to St. Augustine and poses as the suitor Alicante. Dolores falls in love with him as Alicante. Dalroy, madly in love with her, is refused and betrays Lafitte to her father the commandant. Lafitte is made prisoner and while Dalroy leads her father and soldiers to capture the camp of the Privateer, Black Hawk and Dolores rescue Lafitte from the dungeon. Black Hawk kills the jailor and they escape. The privateers are attacked by Dalroy and Spanish soldiers and after a fight most of them escape by boats to their schooner which is at anchor off the shore.

"Alicante is rescued and news is brought of the escape of Lafitte and Dolores by a soldier sent by the Duenna. The fugitives are followed by the Commandant and soldiers, who use a bloodhound to track them. They are fired on as they float down the bay on an improvised raft—are rescued by the privateers and taken aboard the ship. Lafitte determines to capture Dalroy—the returning party is ambushed on the shell road—all are released except the traitor and return to the vessel. The closing incident is of a very sensational nature—Dalroy being forced to walk the plank—'the reward of treachery.'"

Selig English release bulletin

CAPTAIN KATE

Selig Polyscope Company. Released July 13, 1911 through General Film Company. *Length:* 1 reel

Director: Otis Turner.

Cast: Kathlyn Williams (Captain Kate), Charles Clary (Chas. Clancy), Frank Weed (John Howell), Frank Smith (Samuel Desmond, African Trader), Tom Mix (the good native), Tom Anderson (Ali Ben).

"Two caravans meet on the desert—one headed by Howell and Clancy, two New York men, who are gathering animals for Circus purposes—the other is lead by an old animal

Tom with his first movie horse, *.45*, about the time he appeared in *Saved By The Pony Express*. Even in 1911, bat-wing chaps and fancy embroidered shirts were Tom Mix trade marks. He designed most of his own Western costumes.

trader named Desmond and his beautiful daughter, whom the natives have nicknamed Capt. Kate. After exchanging cards, the caravans go their separate ways.

"Desmond is stricken and dies leaving Kate alone. She assumes her father's business, leading her party of native hunters after big game. Later, one of the hunters is stricken and superstitious followers of Capt. Kate, recognizing the nature of the disease, abandon the hunt and their leader, one servant alone remaining faithful to his mistress.

"Kate, realizing that she can go no further without assistance, calls a halt and they erect a crude hut in which she is to live, while the servant goes in search of Clancy.

"Scenes of Kate's isolated life and her dangers follow. She is besieged by wild animals who make her life a long nightmare of peril. Her only companions during this period are a pair of pet leopards. One scene shows an attack on the heroine's home by a lioness and the leopards are liberated to give the intruder combat. The leopards finally overcome the lioness after a thrilling battle.

"Meantime, the servant who was dispatched with Kate's message meets death on the desert. His body is found long afterwards by Clancy and with it, the message. Of course, the hunter makes all haste to rescue the isolated girl and succeeds. . . .

Selig release bulletin

SAVED BY THE PONY EXPRESS

Selig Polyscope Company. Released July 29, 1911 through General Film Company. *Length:* 1,015 feet (1 reel)

Cast: Tom Mix (the Pony Express Rider)

NOTE: Remade as THE PONY EXPRESS RIDER in 1916.

"This story is laid in the period before the railroads entered the West, when important mail was carried by horsemen riding the fleetest ponies, which were relieved by others at relay stations. The best riders did not even stop to re-mount, but vaulted from their exhausted beast, to the waiting fresh horse.

"Our first scene shows cowboys and their sweethearts, enjoying a quadrille on horseback. 'Happy' Jack, a practical Joker, rides off with Belle Archer, the sweetheart of Jim. Jim, furiously angry, attacks Happy, and the cowboys, taking Jim's pistol away from him, hustle him out of the bunk-house. Later the pistol falls to the floor and explodes, the bullet striking and killing 'Happy,' who is alone. The brave fellow writes on a piece of paper before he dies. 'I shot myself accidentally, Jack Moore.'

"A gust of wind blows the note into a corner. Jim entering, is discovered examining his revolver over the dead man, and is accused of murder.

"Later, we see Jim on trial for his life, and a dramatic Court Room scene and amusing scenes in the Jury room follow. "A Lame cowboy finds the last message of 'Happy' Jack. He limps out to the road and hands the paper to Jim's friend, the Pony Express rider.

"Then follow thrilling scenes by this wonderful rider. His horse goes lame. He lassoes and mounts an unbroken broncho and is on his way again, in a wild dash to save the life of his friend.

"The Jury foreman is about to pronounce the verdict of 'Guilty,' when the heroic rider dashes into the court room still mounted, and delivers the message that proves Jim's innocence. Then a big hurrah for Jim and the Pony Express Rider.

"The mounting and riding at full gallop of Western horses, and an unbroken broncho by Tom Mix, are some of the most thrilling feats of horsemanship ever exhibited in a motion picture."

Selig English release bulletin

LIFE ON THE BORDER

Selig Polyscope Company. Released August 22, 1911 through General Film Company. *Length:* 1 reel

Director: Otis Turner. *Scenario:* M. L. Patterson

Cast: Charles Clary (A Pioneer), Kathlyn Williams (his wife), Lynette Griffin (Dora, their child), Thomas Mix (Indian Chief).

"LIFE ON THE BORDER is a true story of life in the early days of America.

"It is the terrible experience of a young pioneer mother left alone for the day in her wilderness home with only a five year old child as company.

"The mother is accidentally imprisoned in a woodshed near the cabin by her child. The little one tries in vain to lift the heavy latch, and while the mother is thus imprisoned, a bear being pursued by a band of prowling Indians, arrives upon the scene.

"Frightened nearly to death, the child hides near a pile of logs.

"The imprisoned mother, thoroughly frightened, becomes frantic as the pursuing Indians come upon the scene. The Indians explore the grounds and ransack the empty cabin finding the 'fire water' and medicine chest.

"In their subsequent hilarity they set fire to the cabin and out-buildings, among them the shed in which the terrified mother is imprisoned.

"The drunken Indians, suddenly remembering the bear, depart in search of the animal.

"The flames are rapidly accomplishing their deadly work, when the father sights the band of marauding Indians as they pass through the woods after the bear. . . His fears are instantly aroused and he makes all haste for his crude home and dear ones.

"He arrives just in time to save his wife from the burning shed."

Selig release bulletin

DAD'S GIRLS

Selig Polyscope Company. Released September 12, 1911 through General Film Company. *Length:* 1 reel

Director: Otis Turner. *Scenario:* Otis Turner.

Cast: Kathlyn Williams (Rose), Olive Stokes [Mix] (Madge), Frank Weed (Dad), Charles Clary (Sam Gleason, the Sheriff), Tom Mix (Tom Rolston, the Gambler), Stan Twist (Andy Thomas, an assayer), William Stowell (One Feather, an Indian renegade), Louis Fierce (Dr. Beech).

"Dad, a likable old pioneer Character, lived among the hills of the western mining region on a ranch with his two daughters, Rose and Madge. He had been doing a little prospecting, and about the time the story starts we see him carrying some of his quartz to Andy Thomas, a young assayer.

"Andy is a good hearted chap who has fallen into the clutches of a local card sharp who holds his I. O. U. for a large gambling debt. The gambler has offered to cancel this debt if the assayer will put him next to some good nearby claim and report unfavorably on its value to the real owner.

"Andy's opportunity comes when Dad brings in his new found quartz for assay. [Tom] goes to Dad and tries to buy the property. Dad refuses to sell.

"Rose and Madge have gone to town to purchase supplies and while there they meet Sam Gleason, the young cowboy Sheriff, who is in love with Rose. [Tom] attempts to make love to Rose hoping thereby to get in on a portion of the mine. He is rebuffed by the Sheriff, but follows the girls on their return to the claim.

"[Tom] decides to kidnap the girls with the aid of a nearby band of renegade Indians, and does so.

"The girls however effect a thrilling escape, and in the getaway, Rose is slightly wounded. In the meantime, the Sheriff

has been notified of the girls non-return by the anxious Dad. Gathering a Posse, the Sheriff goes in search of the girls and rescues them after a thrilling combat with the Indians.

"The crowd are for lynching the card sharp, and his accomplice Andy, but the girls intercede and the pair are given an hour to get across the county line on a balky buro [sic]."

Selig release bulletin

TOLD IN COLORADO

Selig Polyscope Company. Released October 10, 1911 through General Film Company. *Length:* 1 reel

Director: Joseph A. Golden. *Scenario:* Joseph A. Golden.

Cast: William Duncan (John Hunter), T. J. Carrigan (Percy DeYoung), Myrtle Stedman (Edythe Bellaires), Otis B. Thayer (Papa Bellaires), Tom Mix (Bill Higgins, a miner).

Note: Filmed in Colorado.

"Edythe Bellaires, a guest at the Colorado Hotel, is engaged to be married to Percy DeYoung, a wealthy Eastern fop who is given to flirting. John Hunter, a mining engineer, loves Kate Dawson, a dashing Western belle. Edythe's horse runs away, and she is saved by John Hunter.

"Kate Dawson sees Edythe and John walking together and becomes very jealous. She determines to teach John a lesson and flirts with Percy. John sees his sweetheart flirting and determines to teach her a lesson; he flirts with Edythe.

"John meets Percy on top of a cliff. Words lead to a fight, and in a thrilling scene Percy falls over the cliff. John, believing Percy dead, runs away. Percy has fallen into a clump of bushes and is rescued. John returns, and coming face to face with Percy, believes that he is seeing a ghost, and he runs away, followed by Kate, who captures him. Kate explains and the lovers are happy.

Selig release bulletin

WHY THE SHERIFF IS A BACHELOR

Selig Polyscope Company. Released October 24, 1911 through General Film Company. *Length:* 1 reel

Director: Joseph A. Golden. *Scenario:* Joseph A. Golden.

Cast: Tom Mix (Joe Davis, the sheriff), Myrtle Stedman (Alice Craig), T. J. Carrigan (Billy Craig), Otis B. Thayer (Levi Cohen), William Duncan (Dorley), George Hooker (Mex),

Olive Stokes [Mix] (Shorty), George Allaine (Benistein, a bank clerk)

Note: Filmed in Colorado. Remade in 1914.

"Joe Davis, the sheriff, loves and is loved by Alice Craig. Billy Craig, her brother and the town loafer, is induced to join Dorley's Gang, and they hold up and rob the Eagle City Bank. The sheriff leads his posse in pursuit of the bandits and after a thrilling chase in which the riders accomplish many dare devil, risky feats of horsemanship, he dismounts and goes after Billy Craig. The bullets—real bullets—fly thick and fast. They strike the sheriff's drinking cup, stones are shattered, and a piece of tree is shot away by Craig in his attempt to escape. The sheriff finally gets his man and is horror stricken to find in him the brother of his sweetheart.

"On the return to town Alice meets the sheriff and pleads for her brother's release, assuring him that if he jails Billy, all is over between them. He wavers but a moment between love and duty, and then takes the boy to jail."

Selig release bulletin

WESTERN HEARTS

Selig Polyscope Company. Released November 4, 1911 through General Film Company. *Length:* 1 reel

Director: Joseph A. Golden. *Scenario:* Joseph A. Golden.

Cast: T. J. Carrigan (Sam Long), Tom Mix (Sheriff Strong), Otis B. Thayer (Dr. Lane), William Duncan (a gambler), Myrtle Stedman (Mrs. Long), Ralph Kennedy, Dick Trethwick (a miner), Ralph Kennedy ("Slick" Hoover).

"Sam Long leaves his invalid wife to seek work in a neighboring town. He is unsuccessful in his quest and being penniless and his wife in need of food and medicine he steals a wallet of money from Dr. Lane. While returning home he loses the wallet on the road. It is found by some of the boys who return it to the doctor. Sam meantime has reached home and finds his wife in a serious condition screaming for help. Sam now learns of his loss but cannot leave his wife to look for the wallet. The Sheriff hears Mrs. Long scream and rides to the town and brings Dr. Lane. The Doctor recognizes Sam but repays good for evil by showing deserved mercy."

Selig British release bulletin

THE TELL-TALE KNIFE

Selig Polyscope Company. Released November 25, 1911 through General Film Company. *Length:* 1 reel

Director: William Duncan.

Cast: Tom Mix (Tom Mason, a rustler), Charles Tipton (Tip, his side partner), William Duncan (Will Wright, the Sheriff), Myrtle Stedman (Mabel Madden), Rex de Rosselli (bartender), Leon Watson (Line Rider).

Note: Title reused in 1915.

"Tom Mason and Will Wright are both in love with Mabel Madden, owner of the Prospect Saloon and Gambling House. Will is the County Sheriff, but Tom, although always supplied with money has no visible means of support. Mabel cannot make up her mind as to which of the men she prefers. One evening Tom makes Mabel a present of a bracelet. Next day Mabel gives Tom a pocket knife. A few nights later Tom and Tip, his partner, are seen by a line rider, rustling cattle. In his hurry to escape, Tom leaves his knife. The line rider gives the knife to the Sheriff. While trying to find the owner of the knife, the Sheriff enters Mabel's saloon. Tom and Tip are drinking at the bar. The Sheriff asks Mabel if she recognizes the knife. Mabel says that she gave the knife to Tom. The Sheriff covers Tom and orders him to hand over his pistol. Tom presents the gun, butt foremost, to the Sheriff. Suddenly he spins his gun and covers the Sheriff. Tom and Tip then make their escape. The Sheriff immediately organizes a posse and goes in pursuit. The rustlers lead the posse on a merry chase. Finally they are cornered on the brink of a steep hill, and being out of cartridges decide not to be taken alive, Tom and Tip shake hands and leap over the edge."

Selig British release bulletin

A ROMANCE OF THE RIO GRANDE

Selig Polyscope Company. Released December 12, 1911 through General Film Company. *Length:* 1 reel

Director: Otis B. Thayer. *Scenario:* Otis B. Thayer

Cast: Tom Mix (Tom Wilson, a Texas Ranger), William Duncan (Smith, an old settler), George Hooker (Pedro, a Mexican bootlegger), Myrtle Stedman (Nellie Smith, Tom's sweetheart).

"The Texas Rangers, led by Tom Wilson, are hot on the trail of the Mexican bootleggers who have been smuggling whiskey into American territory and supplying it to the Indians. Pedro, the bootlegger, sells his whiskey to a band of Indians and they go on a drunken rampage, first tying and gagging Pedro. Tom Wilson has just bid goodby [sic] to his sweetheart, Nellie Smith, who with her father are [sic] starting on a long trip overland. He runs into the Mexican who advises him that the Indians are on the warpath. Gathering a posse of cowboys he starts after the Indians. The Indians overtake Smith's wagon and Smith is bound to the burning wagon. Nellie is tied to a horse and led away. Tom rescues Smith and they continue after Nellie's captors. A running fight ensues in which the Indians are killed, and finally Tom rescues the nigh dead girl. Smith decides that Tom has earned his right to Nellie's hand."

Selig release bulletin

THE BULLY OF BINGO GULCH

Selig Polyscope Company. Released December 26, 1911 through General Film Company. *Length:* 1 reel

Director: Otis B. Thayer. *Scenario:* Otis B. Thayer.

Cast: William Duncan (Wild Jim, the bad man of Bingo Gulch), Tom Mix (Pop Lynd, owner of Bingo Gulch Ranch), Myrtle Stedman (Jess Lynd, his daughter), Charles Ferra (Hiram Hughes, ranch foreman), Rex de Roselli (Easy Thompson, Cowboy Bicycle King).

"Hiram Hughes, foreman on 'Pop Lynd's' ranch in Bingo Gulch, has quit his job. He has had enough of 'Wild Jim,' the pest of the ranch; lazy, generally intoxicated, and a bully. Pop places a sign on the Post Office, advertising for a new foreman. 'Easy' Thompson, the star of the 'Circle Bar Ranch' show, resigns his job. 'Easy' is a small man but has a reputation as a weight lifter and as the 'Cowboy Bicycle King.' He reads Pop Lynd's sign, and decides to tackle the job. At the ranch, Pop tries to make Jim go to work, but is knocked down. Jim then attempts to caress Jess. At this moment 'Easy' rides in, rescues Jess, and knocks the bully down. Pop discharges Wild Jim and 'Easy' gets the job as foreman, and, incidentally, falls in love with Jess. Later, Wild Jim sends a note saying that he is on the way to 'get' the foreman. 'Easy' starts off alone to meet Jim. Pop and Jess organize a rescuing party, but find 'Easy' has made Jim a tame bully indeed."

Selig release bulletin

1912 _____

THE COWBOY'S BEST GIRL

Selig Polyscope Company. Released January 16, 1912 through General Film Company. *Length:* 1 reel

Director: Otis B. Thayer. *Scenario:* Everett McNeil.

Cast: Rex de Rosselli (Glen Arnold, just out of college), Robert Perry (Percy Summers, his college chum), William Duncan (Carl Graham, his best friend, a young rancher), Tom Mix (Bull Strokes, a rough cowboy), Frances Carroll (William Marson, Alice's Uncle), Olive Stokes Mix (Belle Thomas, Bull's best girl), Myrtle Stedman (Alice Marson, the real best girl), Charles Canterbery (Big Bill, floor manager of the dance), Florence Dye (Lucy Starr, Alice's friend).

"Alice Marson becomes engaged to Glen Arnold. Girl-like, she tells her friend, Lucy Star, of the engagement. Lucy, who also had designs on Glen, determines to break up the match. Lucy takes Alice's photograph from Glen's pocket and substitutes one of a pretty actress. Alice finds the photograph and accuses Glen of deceiving her, and breaks off the engagement. Glen receives a letter from Carl Graham, asking him to be his partner on a ranch in Wyoming. Glen gladly accepts and goes West. Some three years later Carl is invited to a cowboy open-air dance. The invitation says, 'yourself and best girl are invited.' As Carl has no 'best girl,' he persuades Glen to dress as a girl an accompany him to the dance. Alice Marson is visiting at her Uncle's ranch, which is only a few miles away from Carl's ranch. Alice is also invited to the dance; but her Uncle will only let her go if she agrees to dress as a cowboy. Alice agrees. Alice pays attention to 'Bull' Strokes's girl. Overcome by jealousy, Bull attempts to teach Alice, whom he thinks a man, a lesson. Glen interferes, and during the scuffle loses his wig. Alice's hat is knocked off by Bull, letting her hair fall about her shoulders, thereby disclosing her identity. Alice and Glen recognize each other. Explanations follow and the lovers are reunited."

Selig British release bulletin

THE SCAPEGOAT

Selig Polyscope Company. Released January 30, 1912 through General Film Company. *Length:* 1 reel

Director: Otis B. Thayer.

Cast: Tom Mix (Tom Mason, the scapegoat), C. Perry (Harry Mason, his brother), Frank Carrol (Mr. Mason, his father), Olive Mix (Mrs. Mason, his mother), Florence Dye (Alice Mason, his sister), Myrtle Stedman (Nellie Wright, Tom's sweetheart), William Duncan (Jack Wright, her brother), Olive Stokes (Rose Wright, her sister), Kenneth D. Langley (Jim Woods, Rose's sweetheart).

Note: Olive Stokes Mix played two roles in this film, in age make-up as Tom's mother billed as Olive Mix, and also as Rose Wright under the name Olive Stokes. This was the first use of this title, and is different from the 1915 film of the same name.

"Harry Mason, a young New Yorker of good family, tries to borrow money from his brother, Tom. One afternoon Tom collects $5,000 for his father. As it is after banking hours, Mr. Mason puts the money in his house safe. He is overseen by Harry, who breaks into the safe and steals the money. Tom enters the room just as Harry is closing the safe. As Harry exits with the money, Mr. Mason enters and finds Tom bending over the open safe. Tom is accused of the theft and sent from home by his outraged father.

"Three years later, during which time Tom has met and fallen in love with Nellie Wright, he is elected sheriff of his county. Jack Wright, Nellie's brother, is a cowpuncher. He falls in with evil companions and is persuaded to give up cowpunching and take to the road for a living. Shortly after Tom is elected sheriff, Jack and his companions rob the Logan bank of a large sum of money. On the day of the bank robbery, Tom rescues Nellie from a runaway horse. As he brings her home after the rescue he is told of the robbery, and hurriedly assembling a posse, starts in pursuit of the outlaws. Finally, the outlaws separate and Jack, wounded, plunges into a river in an effort to elude his pursuers. Tom rides into the river and ropes Jack, thereby rescuing him from drowning.

"While on his way to town with his prisoner, Tom meets Nellie. Nellie is thunderstruck at finding her brother an outlaw. She pleads with her sweetheart for her brother's release. Tom finally turns over to Jack the stolen money, and the key to the handcuffs and his sheriff's star over to Nellie. Then he mounts his horse and rides out of the story."

The Moving Picture World, 1/27/12

THE "DIAMOND S" RANCH

Selig Polyscope Company. Released February 29, 1912 through General Film Company. *Length:* 1 reel

Director: Otis B. Thayer.

Cast: Tom Mix, Frank Maish, Olive Stokes Mix

Note: The correct title of this subject, according to the Selig release bulletin is THE "DIAMOND S" RANCH. Selig trade advertisements cite LIFE ON THE DIAMOND S as the title, and an article in *Moving Picture World* cites both WITH THE BOYS OF THE DIAMOND S and WITH THE BOYS ON THE DIAMOND S. The Diamond S Ranch was a fictitious location. The name was derived from the Selig Polyscope Company logo of an "S" superimposed in a diamond. Later,

however, Selig's satellite studio in Prescott, Arizona, became known as the Diamond "S" Ranch.

"A companion to Selig's well known feature film 'Ranch Life in the Great Southwest,' will be released Tuesday Feb. 27. The first named subject was the most striking of its kind up to the time of its release, as the most expert cowboys in the world were engaged in its making; the second, entitled 'With the Boys on the Diamond S,' has even still more thrills and daredevil exploits, as our old friend, Tom Mix, the man of steel muscles and rock-ribbed torso, and Frank Maish, world's champion lassoer and rough rider, are to the fore in some amazing feats of skill, strength and horsemanship.

". . .Some remarkable bulldogging feats are performed by Tom Mix. . . .While his horse is at full gallop, in pursuit of the steer, at the proper moment, Mr. Mix jumps from his mount and lights on the neck of the steer, or on the ground to one side of the animal. . . . He then twists the animal's neck and forces the creature to the ground. In one instance we see Mr. Mix light on the neck of the steer, causing the animal to turn a complete somersault its full length. The spectator expects to find him crushed and limp, but he emerges from the dust a victor and body whole, while the steer gets up and trots off none the worse for the rough experience.

"But there is an additional thrill in these bulldogging feats, and it is furnished by Mrs. Mix. She seizes a monster steer and after a tremendous tussle, which lasts several minutes, succeeds in throwing him.

"There is another big surprise in store for everyone who views this film. For the first time they will see an automobile used instead of a horse in lassoing, roping and tieing steers on the plain. This is done most successfully, and in one instance we see Tom Mix bulldog a steer from the machine, while it is going at high speed. . ."

James McQuade, *The Moving Picture World, 2/10/12*

1913 _____

JUGGLING WITH FATE

Selig Polyscope Company. Released March 12, 1913 through General Film Company. *Length:* 1 reel

Director: William Duncan. *Scenario:* Edward McWade.

Cast: Tom Mix (Andrews, the Marshal/Morgan, the outlaw), Myrtle Stedman (Dolores), Lester Cuneo (Wallace), Rex de Rosselli (Manuel).

Above: Tom Mix and Lester Cuneo in *The Sheriff of Yavapai County.*

Below: Tom's mug on a wanted poster for *His Father's Deputy.* Despite oft-repeated legends to the contrary, Tom Mix was not always cast as a white-hatted hero in his early film appearances.

ED. HANLEY

Committed to Texas State Penitentiary, Rusk, Tex., from Abilene, T
June 8th, 1904, for holding up a train.
One-eighth Apache Indian, straight black hair, black eyes,
weight 180 pounds, height 5 feet, 10½ inches.

Production number: 332

"Dare devil Tom Wallace, so called because of his seeming lack of fear while riding in the stage is held up and robbed by a masked desperado named Morgan, a type of Western bad-man now rapidly disappearing. Wallace finds the trail of the robber and follows it to the face of a cliff where it seemingly ends in solid rock. After some reconnoitering he discovers that the bandit has been hoisted to the top of the cliff by his two confederates, Manuel and Dolores. He returns to town only to find that other depredations have been committed during his short absence. Sheriff 'Bill' Andrews is much vexed over the turn of affairs and implores the further aid of Wallace. By a series of exciting and successful ruses the foxy Morgan is finally captured. When unmasked, the bandit proves to be a combination of marshal and road agent, a daring double."

Selig release bulletin

THE SHERIFF OF YAVAPAI COUNTY

Selig Polyscope Company. Released March 19, 1913 through General Film Company. *Length:* 1 reel

Director: William Duncan. *Scenario:* William Duncan.

Cast: William Duncan (Bud O'Neill, the sheriff), Myrtle Stedman (Nellie Bowen, his sweetheart), Rex de Rosselli ("Fatty" Bowen, her father), Tom Mix ("Apache" Frank, a crooked gambler), Lester Cuneo ("Frisco Kid," his partner).

Production number: 335

"Big 'Bud' O'Neill, the sheriff of Yavapai County, is in love with Nellie Brown, daughter of a wealthy rancher. This individual, long on cattle, is easy and short on gambling, and is regarded as a bird of a 'come on' class by the sporting fraternity. The foolish old rancher flushed with 'fusil oil,' is locked in the back room of the Spread Eagle saloon, where he is being systematically fleeced by a precious pair of rascals when he is discovered by the sheriff. The sheriff forces the gamblers to refund; but they are sore and soon manage to trap old Bowen. They hold him up, getting back their own money with compound interest. The sheriff again intervenes, and shooting commences. The gamblers get away with whole skins, but the daring and persistent officer follows them to their mountain roost and after a desperate hand-to-hand encounter brings them back to justice."

Selig release bulletin

THE LIFE TIMER

Selig Polyscope Company. Released March 26, 1913 through General Film Company. *Length:* 1/2 reel

Director: William Duncan. *Scenario:* William Duncan.

Cast: William Duncan (Steve), Myrtle Stedman (Mona), Lester Cuneo (Tom), Florence Dye (Mother), Tom Mix (Sheriff).

Production number: 333

Note: Released on a split-reel with the actuality film SHANG-HAI, CHINA

"Steve and Tom are rivals for the hand of Mona. She prefers Steve, so they become engaged and are later married. On the night of the wedding, Tom in a jealous rage, is about to kill Steve, but changes his mind when he see how slim his chances are for a get-a-way. He decided however, to waylay Steve the next day. He ambushes himself in the rocks above the trail that Steve is traveling, and, at an opportune time fires three shots at his enemy. His shots all miss their mark, and Steve, turning quickly, sees Tom and fires back. Steve's bullet is fatal and Tom, in falling, drops his gun, which becomes lodged in a crevice a hundred feet or so below the body. Later Tom's body is found and no weapon discovered. Steve is convicted of having deliberately killed his former rival. He is sentenced to life imprisonment and the shock nearly kills his wife. She becomes very ill and in delirium sees a vivid picture of the shooting. In a state of somnambulism she walks to the spot where Tom's gun is hidden, recovers it and returns to the house. With this new evidence she manages to secure Steve's freedom."

Selig release bulletin

THE SHOTGUN MAN AND THE STAGE DRIVER

Selig Polyscope Company. Released April 9, 1913 through General Film Company. *Length:* 1 reel

Director: William Duncan. *Scenario:* William Duncan.

Cast: William Duncan (The Shot-Gun Man), Tom Mix (The Stage Driver), Myrtle Stedman, Florence Dye (The Girls).

Production number: 334

". . .The stage-coach, having the precious freight of two fair girls, and much of Uncle Sam's mail, goes through on scheduled time, despite the fact that a band of outlaws have leagued to capture the mail coach. The shot-gun man and the driver manage to thwart the plans of the bad men without blood-shed. The company gives them ample reward for bringing the mail on time, but, more surprising and acceptable is the reward of the fair ones whose lives were saved by their brave guardians."

Selig release bulletin

THAT MAIL ORDER SUIT

Selig Polyscope Company. Released April 18, 1913 through General Film Company. *Length:* 1/2 reel

Director: William Duncan. *Scenario:* J. Edward Hungerford

Cast: Lester Cuneo (Steve), Myrtle Stedman (Betty), Tom Mix (Slim).

Production number: 331

Note: Released as the second subject on a split-reel with CURED OF HER LOVE.

"Steve, ambitious to outstrip his rivals, 'Slim' and 'Tex,' in a race for Betty's hand, orders a dress suit by mail. The spike-tail is an awful fit and Steve retires from Betty's inspection anything but pleased. He give the 'fixins' to a Mexican, who, in turn, suffers from the hands of the populace when he makes his appearance in public. He is finally suspiciously pursued by a posse. As they all fly past Betty's window, she believes Steve to be the man in the dress suit and sends 'Slim' and 'Tex' to guard him. In the interim Steve comes in propria personna and wins the girl."

Selig release bulletin

HIS FATHER'S DEPUTY

Selig Polyscope Company. Released May 19, 1913 through General Film Company. *Length:* 1 reel

Director: William Duncan. *Scenario:* William Duncan.

Cast: William Duncan (Jim Carter, The Deputy), Rex de Rosselli (Tom Carter, The Sheriff), Lester Cuneo (Sam Marvin, a crook), Tom Mix (Ed Hanley, his partner), Marshall Stedman (John Wilson, a mine superintendent).

Production number: 340

". . .John Wilson goes to the mountain-town bank to draw out the pay-roll. Sam Marvin and Ed Hanley 'pike' this proceeding and ride on ahead, up the road, to await the coming of the superintendent in his auto. Jim Carter, son of Sheriff Carter, also his deputy, observes their actions and

finds their pictures in prison records. In the interim Sam and Ed, well-muffled in their slickers, capture the coin and hide it at a road-house. The deputy tells his father his suspicions. The latter cannot arrest the men, as the superintendent cannot identify them; but he finds his son, the deputy, drinking in company with them. He raises a commotion, takes away his [son's] star, and discharges him for drunkenness. This puts him 'strong' in the confidence of the desperadoes, and he rides away with them to their mountain fastness. The deputy takes advantage of Ed's absence to slip the 'bracelets' on his partner, but Jim, returning, opens fire. They leave their ex-friend for dead and ride away with the money. When he recovers consciousness, he takes up their trail and locates their quarters in a road-house. Jim has another hand-to-hand fight that bests both men, handcuffing them together. He also secures the bag of coin. When he comes back with his prisoners his father gives him his star, and then explains the joke to Sam and Ed in the seclusion of their jail cells."

Selig release bulletin

RELIGION AND GUN PRACTICE

Selig Polyscope Company. Released May 26, 1913 through General Film Company. *Length:* 1 reel

Director: William Duncan. *Scenario:* A. W. Corey.

Cast: Tom Mix (Kill Kullen), Rex de Rosselli (Wesley Judell), Myrtle Stedman (Winona Judell), Lester Cuneo (Finley Overmeyer).

Production number: 345

"Wesley Judell, as a missionary, finds a futile but puzzling field for work in the far wild west. In the temporal rush and struggle for existence, spiritual affairs are not as deeply pondered as he would wish, and life seems cheap and feverish. He has a wide territory to cover in his parish rounds, and in his absence his comely daughter looks after the shack which serves for a parsonage. She converts Kill Kullen, who has wandered from the straight and narrow path, but despite this dereliction, he is the straightest shot in that section. The young people fall in love with each other and the firm, fearless, yet gentle Winona succeeds in thoroughly reforming the redoubtable Kill Kullen. The missionary objects to this marriage, but she persists, and gives Kill spiritual advice while he, in return, instructs her in riding and shooting. By following this uplift plan, she wisely wins out. Instead of taking life, he secures a good, honorable position, and is a useful member of the community. Eventually, through the

Left: Tom waves as he enters a Prescott, Arizona saloon in *The Shotgun Man and the Stage Driver*. The self-conscious attitude of the bartender suggests he was the real thing and not an actor.

Bottom: As Kill Kullen, Tom Mix got religion after an appointment for a necktie party, and then taught the preacher's daughter how to use a six-shooter.

Below: Trade ads and copyright records all indicate *Religion and Gun Practice* was the correct title of this 1913 film, but the original main title shows the alternate spelling *Practise*.

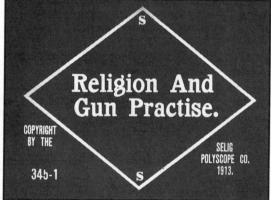

result of her teaching, the girl is enabled to save his life. Her good old father in time relents and consents, so all ends well through the interchange of religion and gun practice."

Selig release bulletin

THE LAW AND THE OUTLAW

Selig Polyscope Company. Released June 4, 1913 through General Film Company. *Length:* 2 reels

Director: William Duncan. *Scenario:* Tom Mix and J. Edward Hungerford.

Cast: Tom Mix ("Dakota" Wilson), Lester Cuneo (Monty Ray), Myrtle Stedman (Ruth Watson), Florence Dye (Betty Watson), Marshall Stedman (Buffalo Watson), Rex de Rosselli (Sheriff Mathers)

"'Dakota' Wilson. . .escapes from the Deer Lodge penitentiary and is swallowed up by the earth for a period. Eventually, . . . he hops into a job on the Diamond S Ranch, the property of the doughty Buffalo Watson. . . . Ruth Watson observes 'Dakota' breaking horses and instantly admires him for his wizardly horsemanship. . . . the cowboys are following the drifting cattle for a round-up, and the chuck wagon follows to cheer them on their way. Ruth Watson, an accomplished horsewoman, thinks nothing of a twenty or fifty mile gallop and happens down that way. . . [the young woman] draws the malignant attention of an outlaw steer. . . 'Dakota' . . .rides in pursuit at top speed and dives from the hurricane-deck of his broncho onto the back of the steer. Fastening his muscular hands on the frenzied beast's horns he never lets go, in what is technically known as 'bulldogging,' until the frenzied animal is brought to a bewildered standstill and finally thrown to the ground. . ."

. . .'Dakota' Wilson is at once the envy and admiration of his cowboy associates—the hero of the minute. Just then a keen-eyed sheriff happens that way. . . and recognizes 'Dakota' as a jailbird wanted by the law. Sheriff Mathers slips the steel wristlets on 'Dakota' and starts for the grim gray walls of Deer Lodge.

"When the sheriff's party are riding along a mountain roadway. . .'Dakota' . . . jumps over the cliff . . . rolls down the steep incline . . . [and] at the bottom he rolls behind a sheltering rock . . .

"The prisoner, free, is still burdened with his manacles. . . He comes across a drowsy shepherd. . . and manages to get away with a revolver and a horse [and he manages to shoot the handcuff chain by holding the gun between his knees and

pulling the trigger with the aid of his teeth and a leather thong].

". . .A long distance rifleman observes him and. . . stuns the fleeing outlaw with a brain-bruise so severe that it tumbles him from his saddle. His foot gets caught in the hickory stirrup and 'Dakota' is dragged across the prairie in view of the camera . . . Eventually 'Dakota's' boot comes off and he is left, bruised and battered, as his horse races away leaving him at the mercy of his pursuers.

"When he recovers consciousness after his rough experience he finds himself a prisoner once more . . . [but] before he is incarcerated, to serve out his short term, he sees Ruth Watson . . . 'Dakota' tells her that the new light that has come into his life has truly changed him, so that after a time he will come to her again with sound heart and clean hands. . ."

Motography, 5/31/13

TAMING A TENDERFOOT

Selig Polyscope Company. Released June 17, 1913 through General Film Company. *Length:* 1 reel

Director: William Duncan. *Scenario:* Cornelius Shea.

Cast: Lester Cuneo (Willie B. Clever), Tom Mix (Bud Morris), Myrtle Stedman (Jessie Reardon), Florence Dye (Mrs. Reardon).

Production number: 344

"Willie Clever, city-born and bred, having been spoiled with plenty of money, thinks he knows it all, or nearly all. His father buys a ranch in Arizona and sends Willie out to run the business. He comes with 'all the fixin's,' and has not been on the place an hour before he tries to run, or reform the outfit. The cowboys decide he needs some experience and proceed to put him through 'the third degree.' He is persuaded to mount an outlaw and he is bucked higher than the price of wheat, then colliding with the uprising earth with emphasis. They put a bearskin on a burro to complete his scare. As soon as he recovers he discharges all of them; but, as he cannot run the ranch without them, he hires them back at advanced wages. They pretend to fall in with his plans, and urge him to show them how to handle a bunch of wild steers. He has a run for his life in this adventure, and faints from fear. As a result, he concludes that he knows nothing about the cattle business, and would rather brave the risks of the boulevards than the broad plains. He leaves for the far East amid universal rejoicing of all concerned."

Selig release bulletin

In his highly colored studio biographies, Tom Mix often made claim to being part Indian, but his Irish mother was always quick to point out that this was not the case. Still, Tom traded on his imaginary heritage in numerous roles for Selig.

Above: The title tells it all, Tom Mix is *The Good Indian* who comes to the aid of a doctor (William Duncan) and his wife (Myrtle Stedman) when their cabin is attacked by renegades.

Above-opposite page: Mix was a half-breed kidnapper in *The Taming of Texas Pete* . Here he tries to fend off capture at the hands of Texas Pete.

Below-opposite page: Lester Cuneo (left) played the Sheriff's hardcase brother-in-law in *The Marshal's Capture*, and Tom was his half-breed accomplice.

Right: Tom as the claim-jumping, sneaking rascal 'Injun' Sam in *Sallie's Sure Shot.*

Films like these were shot in a day or two for a few hundred dollars and offered guaranteed profits for the Selig Polyscope Company.

THE MARSHAL'S CAPTURE

Selig Polyscope Company. Released June 24, 1913 through General Film Company. *Length:* 1 reel

Director: William Duncan. *Scenario:* Elizabeth Frazer

Cast: William Duncan (The Marshal), Myrtle Stedman (his wife), Lester Cuneo (her brother), Tom Mix (The half-breed).

Production number: 347

"The marshal is compelled to arrest his brother-in-law for accidentally shooting a Mexican. His brother's wife pleads for his release, but it is ineffectual. When the marshal is asleep she takes the calaboose keys from his pocket, but on arriving at the jail finds that the prisoner has been helped out by a half-breed. The marshal is awakened by her return [sic] and discovers that his keys are gone. He finds them in her possession and concludes that she has released her brother. He follows the trail into the desert, but the half-breed 'gets the drop' on the marshal, and is about to finish him when the prisoner intervenes and saves the marshal from fatal injury. The half-breed then steals all the horses and leaves them marooned in the desert. The prisoner proves true blue and finally gets the marshal back to his wife and friends. As a climax, he eventually gets the half-breed that perforated him while he was performing his duty."

Selig release bulletin

SALLIE'S SURE SHOT

Selig Polyscope Company. Released July 4, 1913 through General Film Company. *Length:* 1 reel

Director: William Duncan. *Scenario:* Cornelius Shea.

Cast: William Duncan (Fred), Tom Mix ("Injun" Sam), Lester Cuneo ("Coyote" Jim), Myrtle Stedman (Sally).

Production number: 351

"Rob Ralston is forced to go to town for supplies, and 'Injun' Sam, a sneaking rascal, announces that he proposes to jump his claim. This arouses the official ire in Fred, 'the star wearer,' and he soundly trounces the half-breed rascal. Now, Fred has an intrepid sweetheart, Sally, who is a well-spring of information and is naturally hated by law-breakers. 'Injun' Sam gets reinforcements and carries off the girl as a hostage.

Fred senses they are making for the mine, so he girds on his guns and goes in the same direction. The desperadoes arrange to 'dynamite' Sally, but she cuts the fuse in two by a well aimed shot after they have sought safety at a distance. This saves her sweetheart, Fred, who rushes to her rescue and they both retreat to a cabin. The dynamiters are obstinate and place another cartridge so that the cabin will be blown to pieces. The daring Fred picks up the keg of powder and rushing out and rolls it down on 'Injun' and his fellow mischief makers. They are so dazed from the effects of the explosion that they find themselves in 'irons' when they recover consciousness, and Fred single-handed delivers them to authorities."

Selig release bulletin

MADE A COWARD

Selig Polyscope Company. Released July 10, 1913 through General Film Company. *Length:* 1 reel

Director: William Duncan. *Scenario:* A. W. Collins.

Cast: William Duncan (Bud Harris), Lester Cuneo (Tom Jones), Tom Mix (Pete), Rex de Rosselli (Sheep Rancher), Myrtle Stedman, Florence Dye (The Girls).

Production number: 348

"Bud Harris, a young miner with a reputation for courage, goes prospecting in the desert with Tom Jones in an attempt to locate a turquoise mine. Their water gives out and their horses die on the way. Bud thinks that Tom has water in his canteen and strikes him down. Then the terrible, haunting thought of murdering his friend and the loneliness of the desert posses him with such fear that he flees the spot in terror, an abject coward. Tom revives, finds water and discovers a rich mine. Bud, after dragging himself out of the sandy wastes, is laid low with fever, and when he comes to himself seems to be a nervous wreck. He becomes the butt on a ranch, where he finds employment, and is beaten and kicked about—never resenting these humiliations. One day he meets his old partner, Tom, who comes as one from the dead to tell him of his fortune. Tom exonerates Bud and tells him he has a share in the mine. Then the coward of his conscience undergoes a complete regeneration and he goes back to the ranch and thrashes the fellows who had enjoyed insulting him. He next joins his partner and buys a full line of supplies—including an ample quantity of water to serve them en route to their mine."

Selig release bulletin

THE ONLY CHANCE

Selig Polyscope Company. Released July 14, 1913 through General Film Company. *Length:* 1 reel

Director: William Duncan. *Scenario:* C. Chester Wesley.

Cast: William Duncan (Charley West, a lineman), Lester Cuneo (a train dispatcher), Rex de Rosselli (Superintendent), Tom Mix (engineer).

Production number: 350

"Charley West, a lineman, complains about his rickety old hand-car, and is given one that is up-to-date. He tries it out and finds he can send it sixty miles an hour. The train dispatcher, forgetting an on-coming special freight, allows a passenger train to leave the yard before he discovers his mistake. The trains are rushing toward each other, and there seems to be no way of avoiding the collision. Charley hears of this from the line operator, and decides to catch the passenger train. After a thrilling chase, he catches up with the train, twists the shut-off of the air line at the rear of the last coach, brings the train to a stand-still and averts the imminent tragedy."

Selig release bulletin

THE TAMING OF TEXAS PETE

Selig Polyscope Company. Released July 30, 1913 through General Film Company. *Length:* 1 reel

Director: William Duncan. *Scenario:* Joseph F. Poland.

Cast: William Duncan (Texas Pete), Tom Mix (The half-breed), Betty Kastner (Baby Betty), Myrtle Stedman (Her mother).

Production number: 352

"Texas Pete, a gun-man, is 'extra' bad when in liquor. This, however, does not terrify the ranch foreman, who discharges him for drunkenness. Pete laces on his hardware and lurches off, with the intention of shooting up the town where he pumped in his original trouble. On his way he comes across Baby Betty, the imperious pride of the ranch, who has strayed from home and is lost. She demands that he give her his gun, and he obeys her childish caprice. Then she orders him to take her home, and he obediently leads the way for further orders. When they arrive at the ranch she tells her father, the owner, that Pete is a real man and must be given work. The interest and astuteness of the child, tenders the tough westerner and changes him, so that he cuts the liquor, and

becomes a man again. When Baby Betty is abducted by a half-breed as revenge for some fancied wrong, Pete takes the trail like a blood hound, and rounds up the sneaking villain after a desperate fight. He returns the little girl to her parents, showing gratitude for his own reclamation as a respectable member of society."

Selig release bulletin

THE STOLEN MOCCASINS

Selig Polyscope Company. Released August 7, 1913 through General Film Company. *Length:* 1 reel

Director: William Duncan. *Scenario:* Cornelius Shea.

Cast: William Duncan (Jack), Myrtle Stedman (Belle), Lester Cuneo (Harden), Tom Mix (Swift-Foot).

"Harden, a typical border tough, professes love for Belle, but she heroically repulses him in a way that infuriates. Jack, her sweetheart, hears of this and tells Harden to 'vamous.' Harden with several choice spirits, after 'irrigating' freely, goes to an Indian camp and steals several pairs of moccasins. They then, soft-footed, go to the cabin of Belle's father and in his absence carry away the girl. Jack is not slow in learning of her disappearance. He inquires of the Indians about her, but they deny knowledge other than of their own losses at the hands of Harden. Swift-Foot, a trailer, offers his services, and they trail the trio to a lonely cabin. Harden and his confederates put up a desperate defense, but Jack and his crowd out-class them as gun-men. The girl is rescued and Harden much the worse for wear, is taken back to the settlement 'to get his.'"

Selig English release bulletin

AN APACHE'S GRATITUDE

Selig Polyscope Company. Released August 14, 1913 through General Film Company. *Length:* 1 reel

Director: William Duncan. *Scenario:* William Duncan.

Cast: William Duncan (Bob Huntley), Tom Mix (Tonto), Myrtle Stedman (Marion Wilson), Rex de Rosselli (Tom Jones).

"Bob Huntley, U. S. mail rider, while in the performance of duty through a dangerous territory, comes across an Apache Indian who has been thrown from his horse and had his leg broken. Like a good Samaritan, he takes him to camp and earns his gratitude. Later the Indian witnesses a murder and secures evidence by getting possession of the gun which fired the fatal shot. Still later Huntley is accused of the crime and is about to be hung on flimsy evidence, when the grateful and acute Apache dashes on the scene, describes the murder, names the real culprit and frees Huntley, evening up the score of friendship."

Selig release bulletin

THE GOOD INDIAN

Selig Polyscope Company. Released August 22, 1913 through General Film Company. *Length:* 1 reel

Director: William Duncan. *Scenario:* Ethel C. Unland.

Cast: William Duncan (The Doctor), Myrtle Stedman (The Wife), Tom Mix (The Indian).

Production number: 357

"A frontier doctor gets a night call, but regrets leaving his young wife alone in their exposed shack. She insists that he accept the service, so he loads up a revolver and leaves another for her and goes on his mission of mercy and medicine. He has hardly got well away before the young woman looking up discovers to her alarm, the face of an Indian peering through the window. She is reassured, however, of his friendly intention and he begs her to come immediately to his tepee as his child is dying. She gathers from him the nature of the complaint, takes some medicine, picks up the gun and goes with him and applies herself so assiduously to the task that she saves the life of the child. In the interim her husband returns, finds her gone and starts on the search, eventually rounding her up at the tepee. The Indian is very grateful for their service and offers them his choicest treasures which they refuse, but accept his friendship. Some time later, there is an Indian uprising—the cabin of the doctor is burned and he and his wife are in imminent danger when the Indian they defended comes to the rescue, takes them to his own tepee and sees that they are protected and restored to comfort."

Selig release bulletin

HOW BETTY MADE GOOD

Selig Polyscope Company. Released August 27, 1913 through General Film Company. *Length:* 1 reel

Director: William Duncan. *Scenario:* Ethel C. Unland.

Cast: Lester Cuneo(Jim), Myrtle Stedman (Betty), Tom Mix (The Foreman), Rex de Rosselli (The Store Keeper), Howard Farrell (The Minister), Sid Jordan, Vic Frith.

"Blithesome Betty concludes that farming is pretty hard work for a girl all alone in the world and rides to town on a fine Kentucky thoroughbred to look up employment. The proprietor of the 'General Store' is in bad health and desires to live in the country. He meets Betty and offers to trade his store for her horse—and she accepts his proposition.

"The next day a bunch of drunken cattle punchers are 'irrigating' at the saloon next door, when one of them carelessly lets off his gun at a card on the wall, and the bullet passes through, barely missing Betty. She goes immediately into the saloon to remonstrate. Some of the drunkards insult her; but Jim, the one who fired the shot, protects her and promptly falls in love with her. Later she tells him that if he will stop drinking, she will give him a job. He accepts and she puts him in charge of her quarter section. After a year of good behavior, Jim prevails upon Betty to marry him. His old friends prepare a surprise feast for the happy couple when they return from the minister's house and so the dinner is ready and all hands are in for a good time. As they are lifting their glasses of "Ohio champagne" [water] to drink to the bride, Jim says oracularly: 'Boys, if you want to drink to the health of Mrs. Jim, you'll shore have to drink water." Later, Jim buys back the horse that was the means of bringing about their happiness. So Betty made good, likewise Jim."

Selig release bulletin

HOWLIN' JONES

Selig Polyscope Company. Released September 4, 1913 through General Film Company. *Length:* 1 reel

Director: William Duncan. *Scenario:* O. H. Nelson.

Cast: William Duncan (Howlin' Jones), Rex de Rosselli (Jim Thorpe), Florence Dye (Mrs. Thorpe), Myrtle Stedman (Sallie Thorpe), Tom Mix (Robledo), Sid Jordan, George Panky, Vic Frith.

Production number: 364

". . .Howland-Jones (who is in reality Lord Howland), comes to America, incognito, and slides down into the great lone land of Arizona, to try out himself, get next to the people, and incidentally a lot of other 'varmints'. . .

. . . the cowboys on the Diamond S Ranch. . . try him out as a joke by putting him unwittingly on a bucking horse, but he turns the tables on them as he directs the bucker their way and keeps his seat in the fashion that surprises the most hardened broncho buster. They find out that although he is a lord 'a man is a man for a'that,' for he manages to outdo them at most of their athletic stunts and takes to the country like one to the born, and although he is the stature of a man, he settles down to grow up with it, for the love of the new land he has found so congenial."

Selig release bulletin

THE REJECTED LOVER'S LUCK

Selig Polyscope Company. Released September 19, 1913 through General Film Company. *Length:* 1 reel

Director: William Duncan. *Scenario:* Cornelius Shea.

Cast: Lester Cuneo (Ben), Rex de Rosselli (John), Tom Mix (The Indian), Myrtle Stedman (Sadie), Vic Frith (The Mexican).

Brothers Ben and John are in love with the same girl, Sadie (not owing to the scarcity of girls, but matter of choice). Sadie is not the least fussed, rejects Ben's offer of marriage, but accepts the proposal of brother John. Ben disgusted and disappointed, quarrels with the lucky man and then leaves for the West in a huff, hoping to forget his love and trusting that he will find fairer fortunes elsewhere.

"John and Sadie marry and experience three years of happiness when death snatches him from her arms and leaves her penniless with a baby at her breast. She is so poor that she is forced to take in washing. During this interim, Ben has had varying fortunes in the wilds. He saves an Indian from the hands of vigilants about to lynch him for horse-thievery. After stirring adventures they make a get-a-way; the Indian is shot, but under the skilled nursing of Ben, eventually recovers. The Aborigine is so grateful that he reveals to Ben the site of a rich placer mine and the latter washes out a fortune. He goes back to the old town, a sadder but a wealthy man with forgiveness in his hart. He finds his sister-in-law bending over a wash-tub as her chubby infant wails an accompaniment from the floor. These things move honest Ben mightily and he wonders if the days of might-have-been cannot come back. He speaks to her in the old voice, woos her with the old words. She listens to his suit as he persuades her that he should take his brother's place and provide a father for the helpless. So all's well that ends well."

Selig release bulletin

THE CATTLE THIEF'S ESCAPE

Selig Polyscope Company. Released October 1, 1913 through General Film Company. *Length:* 1/2 reel

Director: William Duncan. *Scenario:* R. E. Hicks.

Cast: William Duncan (Rev. John Morrison), Rex de Rosselli (Joe Craig), Myrtle Stedman (Rose Craig), Lester Cuneo (Charley Pointer), Tom Mix (Pete Becker, a half breed).

Production number: 338

Note: Released on a split-reel with the actuality film RANGOON, INDIA.

"John Morrison, educated for the ministry is all the true stature of a real man, goes West to preach the gospel in the cattle country. He likes the men, the cowboys and the country, and at the same time he has a hankering for the fair sex; in fact, he falls in love with Rose Craig, the daughter of a ranchman. This last move is not so highly relished by the male members of the congregation, as girls in that section are really rare, and he, picking the choice, consequently wins the enmity of many horny-handed, green-eyed men, who felt they had the right of prior claim, but lacked the very manly qualities that made him stand first in the esteem of Rose Craig. A bunch of disappointed suitors plan to thrash the successful preacher, but much to their astonishment, he trounces the entire crowd, and their falsely thumping hearts are nothing to the thumpings they got on other parts of their anatomies, and their emergence from the fray with black eyes and bothersome bruises testify to the sincerity of their mourning. The cowards sneak off ingloriously, but one plans to 'fix' the stigma of 'cattle-rustler' upon him. However, the real cattle thief is discovered just in time and 'with the goods.' Again the parson takes the initiative and persuades the revengeful parties that having recovered their property, they can afford to allow the thief a minute's leaway to get out of sight. The rustler takes advantage of the situation to drop over a cliff, and the parson is reinstated as the master of the situation."

Selig release bulletin

SAVED FROM THE VIGILANTES

Selig Polyscope Company. Released October 9, 1913 through General Film Company. *Length:* 1 reel

Director: William Duncan. *Scenario:* Malcolm Douglas.

Cast: William Duncan (Bud Lee), Hugh Mosher (Jeff Lee), Myrtle Stedman (Pearl Tollifer), Olive Stokes Mix (Mrs.

A pair of split-reel Western dramas that each ran barely six minutes of screen time. Above: Tom played Pete Becker, another half-breed, in *The Cattle Thief's Escape*.

Below: Tom's motorcycle was shot out from under him in *A Muddle in Horse Thieves*.

Bludsoe), Rex de Rosselli (Davids), Tom Mix (Squire Beasley).

Production Number: 358

"Two husky westerners, Bud Lee and Curt Bludsoe, have formed an attachment for the. . . daughter of the stage agent, Pearl Tollifer. The men conclude to settle the difficulty of debate by fists and have a fight behind the station, in which Bludsoe has his name illustrated at the hands of the more skillful foe. Disgruntled over the 'claret' effusion on his hickory shirt, Bludsoe bribes a tramp to steal a horse and drive it into Lee's corral. In the interim, the defeated lover has been very busy giving information to the head of a Vigilante committee whose specialty is horse thieves. The victorious, but unfortunate Lee is taken prisoner and is about to be launched in a lynching bee, when his younger brother, Jeff Lee, who is an amateur telegrapher, shins up a pole, attaches an instrument and sends a message to Pearl. She is a 'live wire' and immediately gets in touch with the sheriff, who wrings a confession from the tramp, who was thrown from the top of a moving freight train after stealing the horse, which exonerates Curt. The sheriff, the girl and the tramp join the Vigilantes just in time to save the good man from an air dance."

Selig release bulletin

THE SILVER GRINDSTONE

Selig Polyscope Company. Released October 14, 1913 through General Film Company. *Length:* 1 reel

Director: William Duncan. *Scenario:* Eugene P. Lyle.

Cast: William Duncan (David Stratton), Myrtle Stedman (Mrs. Stratton), Florence Dye (Grace Stratton), Lester Cuneo (Harry Custer), Rex de Rosselli (Slade), Tom Mix (Saloon Keeper).

Working Title: THE SILVER KING

Production number: 367

"David Stratton, the Camp Hope drunkard, has sunk so low he will do almost anything for a slug of fusil oil. His poor wife bends by day over a washtub to secure a little money which he frequently coaxes from her to spend by night in the saloon. Although the only work that the bibulous Stratton will essay is sharpening the tools of miners, who reward him with drinks at the bar. One day, Slick Slade, a gambler, shoots Harry Custer, a miner, and in the melee which ensues, Slade rushes out the door of the saloon, knocks Dave over his grindstone, breaking this only instrument of his occupation.

Dave has been accumulating thirst for at least thirty minutes and is very wroth over the destruction of further opportunity to satisfy it, picks up the broken pieces of the grindstone and is about to hurl them through the saloon window at the group lined up along the counter of the thirst parlor, when he hesitates and finds that it is rich in traces of silver. Some flash of the old keenness comes into his sodden cranium and he starts a sober search to find where that grindstone came from. He ascertains that the saloon-keeper bought it from a farmer, who made it by hand. Dave seeks out the husbandman, strikes a silver bonanza, and handles it right. He returns to hopeless old Camp Hope, finds things in a bad way; but, makes everybody happy in the boom of the new golgonda, Camp Grindstone. Stratton becomes wealthy and likewise a sober and enterprising citizen.

"Twelve years after, Slade slinks back and tries to rob Mayor Stratton's house, but is balked by the timely interference of Custer, whom he had shot years before. The case comes before Senator Stratton, who at first concludes to send Slade to prison, but relents, furnishes him with money and sends him on his way a free man, rewarding Custer even more generously.'

Selig release bulletin

DISHWASH DICK'S COUNTERFEIT

Selig Polyscope Company. Released October 21, 1913 through General Film Company. *Length:* 1/2 reel

Director: William Duncan. *Scenario:* B. L. Williams.

Cast: Rex de Rosselli (Dishwash Dick), Lester Cuneo (Dick Mason), Myrtle Stedman (Caroline Synder), Tom Mix (The Rustler).

Production number: 363

Note: Released on a split-reel with SURF AND SUNSET ON THE INDIAN OCEAN.

"A natty individual, known as Dishwash Dick, obtains a job by mail-order in the grub department of the 'N. Y. Ranch.' On the same train that he takes for the wilds, is Dick Mason, whose father owns the ranch, but who is unknown and who has never been West. The cowboys who are hilarious and likewise impetuous over the arrival of the new knight of the kitchen, go to the train and lay violent hands on young Mason, as a candidate for the third degree; while the ranchman's daughter meets Dishwash Dick, and mistaking him for their guest, drives him home in her runabout, and he is installed in state as the honored visitor. In the interim, Dick Mason, is whirled about so fast that he has no time to explain

Above: Tom Mix (left) was Gray, Lester Cuneo (center) was Brown, and Hugh Mosher (right) was White--members of the school board of trustees out to make time with the new teacher in *The Schoolmarm's Shooting Match*.

Left: Tom Mix and Florence Dye with *The Child of the Prairies*. It was a common practice for Selig to remake their past successes on a regular basis. Little more than a year after this late 1913 film was released Tom made a second version of the story titled *A Child of the Prairie* which hit nickelodeon screens in March, 1915.

his real status and has one awful time, between the perils of the kitchen and the trials and tribulations that the mischievous cowboys put upon him.

"The ranch people are stirred to their uttermost depths by the presence of cattle rustlers, and everybody rushes to the saddle to scour the range and bring the bad men to grass. This brings out the true colors of Dishwash Dick as a coward and poltroon and he is glad to let his horse run away toward the railway, while Dick Mason develops unexpected trepidity which wins him the esteem and regard of the cowboys; in fact, he settles several of the most truculent with neatness and dispatch that commands the highest regard of all."

Selig release bulletin

A MUDDLE IN HORSE THIEVES

Selig Polyscope Company. Released October 29, 1913 through General Film Company. *Length:* 1/2 reel

Director: William Duncan. *Scenario:* Elizabeth Frazer.

Cast: Tom Mix (the horse thief).

Production number: 369

Note: Released as the second half of a split reel with TWO SACKS OF POTATOES.

"A breezy, little Western drama introducing the champion cowboy, Tom Mix, as a light-riding individual with a fancy for other folks' horses. He picks up a horse, but being hard pressed and finding the animal is giving out, he passes a cowpuncher who has dismounted to take a drink, and takes possession of the fresh mount and gets away, despite the fact that he is fired at. His last victim follows after him, but is himself overtaken by a posse, who accuse him of being the thief. The real villain, however, riding forward, passes an old man driving a team, who recognizes the horse as the property of his son, so he joins in the pursuit. The horsethief, now closely pressed, takes to a motorcycle, but the old man looks keenly over the heavy barrel of his Winchester and brings him out of the saddle while the machine is going at full speed."

Selig release bulletin

THE SCHOOLMARM'S SHOOTING MATCH

Selig Polyscope Company. Released November 7, 1913 through General Film Company. *Length:* 1/2 reel

Director: William Duncan. *Scenario:* Cornelius Shea.

Cast: William Duncan (Bill Swift), Myrtle Stedman (Mollie), Lester Cuneo (Brown), Rex de Rosselli (Black), Tom Mix (Gray), Hugh Mosher (White), William Jones (Green).

Production number: 353

Note: Released on a split-reel with VIEWS ALONG THE RHINE.

"When a pretty school teacher comes to the settlement to teach the young ideas how to shoot, where the older ones have been doing it with such deadly accuracy that the graveyard is almost as well tenanted as the town, it causes some sensation. Pretty women, brainy beauties and marriageable opportunities are so rare in the thinly populated wild western districts, that a candidate having the two former attributes, is sure to arouse admiration that will bring about the conflicts of rivals. When dainty Mollie puts her foot over the threshold of the schoolroom, the entire board of School Trustees conspire to propose to her. While they are united in this determination, they are generous enough to individualize and allow her the privilege of choosing between them. She has a sense of humor, cleverness and sentiments all her own, and her sweetheart, Bill Swift, has outdistanced all rivals without their knowing it. She puts up a job with him on them and arranges a shooting match, the best marksman to be the winner. Bill supplies her with blank cartridges, so that the only sensation registered by the shooting upon the Trustees is the recoil of their guns upon their own shoulders. They are but slightly sore over the results—honors being even—but are real hurt when Bill tells them that he is the real one and has arranged to marry Mollie. They are still doubtful, and follow the pair to the preacher's house and witness the ceremony through the window. At the conclusion they 'shoot up' the air in disgust and disappointment and retire to their shacks, vowing to continue their bachelorhood."

Selig release bulletin

THE CHILD OF THE PRAIRIES

Selig Polyscope Company. Released November 13, 1913 through General Film Company. *Length:* 2 reels

Director: William Duncan. *Scenario:* Tom Mix.

Cast: Tom Mix (Fred Watson), Lester Cuneo (Ed Dillon), Florence Dye (Alice Watson), Myrtle Stedman (Jane Watson), Vic Frith (George Jordan), Hugh Mosher (James Jordan), Sid Jordan (Sheriff).

Production number: 373

"Fred Watson and his wife, Alice, attend a dance given on a neighboring ranch. The exertion of the dance is so thirstful that Watson goes out with a friend and irrigates for fair. During his absence, Dillon, a gambler, smooth as the cards he deals, engages Alice in conversation and invites her for a stroll. They meet Watson returning, and he remonstrates with her in bitterness and at length. A few days later Dillon visits the Watson ranch and persuades Alice to promise to elope with him. Shortly thereafter he encounters Watson, and both unlimber artillery, and the unfortunate ranchman goes down. The gambler, thinking he has killed the husband, hurries back to the ranch and persuades Alice to leave with him at once. She insists upon taking her little girl—a child of two—with them. While they are making camp the baby wanders off in the brush and is lost. They make a futile search, and then Dillon, who is now in dread of pursuit, forces the unfortunate mother to go on with him down the now broken trail of her life.

"Two ranchmen, the brothers Jordan, hunting stray cattle, find the little one, and after fruitless inquiries adopt it as their own. Fifteen years later, Watson, who escaped death, heartsore and weary after a long, fruitless hunt for his own, happens to hit that range and rescues a young lady at the risk of his life by snatching her from the back of a runaway horse. He is given employment at the ranch of her foster parents. Through some strange whirligig of fate Dillon, who has given up gambling for horsethieving, comes into that corral, and Watson suspicions him, but is not sure. He compels Dillon to shave, and this discloses a tell-tale scar that makes his identification complete. The latter unworthy then tells how he abandoned Alice, who died years ago, and that the child was lost. The Jordans, hearing this, by comparing dates and localities, restore their ward to Watson's arms as his daughter. As for Dillon, the all-around bad man, he gets his a-plenty."

Selig release bulletin

THE ESCAPE OF JIM DOLAN

Selig Polyscope Company. Released November 17, 1913 through General Film Company. *Length:* 2 reels

Director: William Duncan. *Scenario:* Tom Mix.

Cast: Tom Mix (Jim Dolan), Lester Cuneo (Ed Jones), Nip Van (John Wellington), Vic Frith (Tom Wellington), Myrtle Stedman (Grace Wellington), Rex de Rosselli (Brown), Sid Jordan, Hugh Mosher.

Production Number: B-370-371

"Jim Dolan, an ideal type of cowboy, is the reigning favorite at the Wellington's party and his attentions to the beloved daughter, Grace, appear to be relished not only by the young lady, but her stalwart brothers. Ed Jones, the husky, cheeky foreman of the Brown ranch, tries to 'butt in,' and steal Grace from Jim. Jim is seen in his own 'back' cabin by the spring on his little claim. Brown, the neighboring ranch owner, and Jones, his foreman, ride in, the former insisting that Jim sell out to him, which Jim refuses. Thereupon, the bulldozing Brown points out to him that he can make it hot for him. Jones attempts to join in with his master, but is quickly silenced. This adds fuel to his flame of hate , and he concludes to get good and even with Jim, and put him out of the running. He picks several hides conspicuously branded from a bale of green ones back of the Brown corral. He secretly takes them out along Jim's fence line by night, finds a loose post which he lifts up, places the hides in a hole and replaces the earth. The next move is to report 'cattle missing.' The Sheriff is summoned and the ranch owner directs his foreman to help track the rustler. They find recent hoof marks about Jim's premises, and observing the fence post suspiciously loose, lift it up and discover the 'planted' missing pelts.

"Jim is about to leave the Wellington home when the Sheriff and Jones come upon the scene. The Sheriff handcuffs Jim in spite of the protestations of Grace and her relatives. The Western court gives him a ten years' sentence. He is confined in the town calaboose. Grace and her family are sure that Jim has been imposed upon through some malign motive and is absolutely innocent. With a woman's will she plans his escape from the calaboose, by planting a saw in a bottle of olives, the luxury of a luncheon she has prepared for her lover. She is alowed to deliver it without question. This includes a note which tells him when and where relays in horses will be waiting to carry him over the border, as soon as he can saw his way through the bars of the jail. Jim is quick to avail himself of this information and the bars of the calaboose soon yield to the little saw.

"The second reel shows him leaving in the shadows of the night, finding the horse concealed and speeds away on his desperate ride for liberty. Soon the Sheriff discovers that his prisoner has flown and the alarm in the settlement becomes general as the villainous Jones eggs on pursuit, knowing the local antipathy against 'rustlers.' Jim rides on, finds his second relay and again spurs forward. The posse presumably follow him all night, and through superior arrangements have a relay of fresh horses in the morning. In the interim, Jim's last mount goes lame, but Jim Dolan is game, leaving his faithful steed limping he goes on. Weary as he is, he drags his rifle from the holster and takes it with him. He hears the hoofbeats of the approaching posse as he nears a water course. Knowing that they will find his footprints he walks into the water close to the ford. He breaks his rifle, discards the butt of the piece, submerges himself in the water and breathes through the barrel of the gun. The posse come, pass over the ford and then ride back again through the water as Jim resorts to his former ingenious tactics, effectually escaping observation. He emerges unarmed and is captured by Apaches. They have a choice amusement that consists of tying a man to the tail of a wild horse and dragging him, outdoing the treatment of the fabled Mazeppa at the hands of the Cossacks. Happily Jim is rescued by a prospector, who nurses him back to health.

"In the interim, the treacherous foreman, Jones, is mortally wounded in a saloon brawl and he confesses his crime against Jim Dolan. But Jim Dolan has seemingly disappeared. The local papers tell at length of the confession, establish beyond doubt the innocence of Jim Dolan. Jim Dolan, away off in the mountains, lives with the lone prospector who comes to town for supplies, and carries back among other essentials a newspaper, which has the confession. Jim rewards the prospector for all his kindness and tells him he must make for the settlement at once, explaining that he was the wrong man who has been righted by a tragedy. Jim, footsore and travel-stained, comes back into the game of life for good and Grace Wellington becomes his chiefest treasure."

Selig release bulletin

THE SHERIFF AND THE RUSTLER

Selig Polyscope Company. Released November 13, 1913 through General Film Company. *Length:* 2 reels (1,700 feet)

Director: William Duncan. *Scenario:* Tom Mix

Cast: Lester Cuneo (The Sheriff), Tom Mix (The Rustler), George Panky (The Cattleman), Rex de Rosselli (The Gambler), Neil Broaded (The Blacksmith), Vic Frith (The Foreman), B. L. Jones (The Range Rider).

"Joe Wood, a cattle rustler, has grown rather careless and particularly bold in playing his mischievous and sinful vocation. He is about to brand a maverick when he is surprised at his task, abandons it quickly and rides away. Unfortunately for him, his horse sheds a shoe close by the scene of the branding, which is picked up by the sheriff. This horse-shoe has the initials of the bad 'J. W.' stamped in the metal and when the sheriff rides to the town blacksmith shop with his good-luck symbol and finds Joe, he just having had the shoe replaced, the rustler sniffs a rat, jumps into the saddle without touching the stirrups, and is away like the wind. The sheriff drops the horse-shoe, and unlimbers his artillery; but, ineffectually, for the rustler not only gets away scot free, but sends a bullet back that clips the sheriff in the shoulder and sends him down for the count. Joe, with his usual shiftiness, jumps into a job, and is next seen on a ranch doing some dare-devil stunts with frenzied steers and outlawed horses. These acts are far away from the conventional in originality and daring, and the reel closes with the loud approval of all the rival, but admiring cowboys.

"The sheriff has recovered from the leaden compliment sent by the rustler, is again on the trail, and happens to get a sight of the much wanted individual, who is driving a lot of stock to the roundup. Again, Joe gets away. Subsequently he sees the sheriff at the spring taking a drink, and just to show him there is no ill-feeling, and that he has not forgotten how to shoot, he sends a bullet through the cup, knocking it out of the sheriff's hands. This starts something. The outlaw, finding that he is closely pursued, rides toward the railroad, and seeing a freight train moving along, rides close enough to clasp the rungs of the iron side ladder, and abandoning his pony, swings onto the train and climbs up to the top of the cars. The sheriff, not to be outdone in this specie of agility, also catches the same moving train. Then commences the duel proper over the tops of the cars as both empty their guns until the last cartridge is gone. They then close in and have an exciting and desperate fight on the top of the running cars. The train is crossing a river, and the men, clasped in each others arms fall into the water below. The bath apparently cools them off, and each man starts to swim for himself. Singularly enough, the cowboy in heavy chapergos reaches the shore first, and although almost exhausted, he struggles up the bank to a place of concealment; and, the sheriff having providentially secured a horse, starts in pursuit.

"Joe, the rustler, in a frantic effort to escape, rushes into a bed of quicksand (the real thing by the way), finding himself in a most dangerous and desperate predicament. He is being slowly engulfed in the soft sands when the sheriff comes upon the little bluff and sees his man who has given him such a chase, gallantly struggling against the seeming inevitable. He takes his trusty lasso and by a skillful cast, he loops it about the outlaw's shoulders. Then giving it a turn about the cantle of the saddle, he hauls the victim of the quicksand out and these two game men shake hands at last on firm ground, face to face, and the outlaw gives himself up at last."

Selig release bulletin

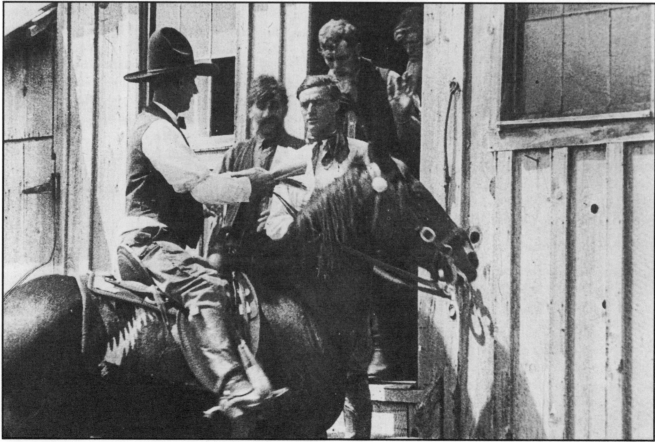

Above: Tom reads a book in one of the less strenuous moments of *Physical Culture on the Quarter Circle V Bar*. Among his many jobs when he first came West, Tom Mix was a physical culture instructor.

Above-opposite page: Buster Holmes (William Duncan) gets some good news and bad news. The bad news is that a rich relative has passed away, the good news is that Bill will receive an income for life if he will only go east for a college education. His cowboy pals in *Buster's Little Game* are Lester Cuneo (left) and Tom Mix.

Below-opposite page: Disappointed lovers Lester Cuneo, Sid Jordan, and Vic Frith surround Tom as a cowboy brings word that the lonely hearts club that offered mail-order brides is a fraud in *Cupid in the Cow Camp*.

Right: Hugh Mosher (left), Lester Cuneo (center) and Sid Jordan (right) in *The Escape of Jim Dolan*. Jordan was a friend of Tom's from Oklahoma. They worked the 101 Ranch show and served together as peace officers before Sid joined Tom in the picture business in 1913.

CUPID IN THE COW CAMP

Selig Polyscope Company. Released November 26, 1913 through General Film Company. *Length:* 1 reel

Director: William Duncan. *Scenario:* J. A. Dunn.

Cast: Tom Mix (Bud Reynolds), Myrtle Stedman (Katie Manners), Lester Cuneo (Arizona Bob), Vic Frith (Limpy Jim), Sid Jordan (Soda Water Sam), Rex de Rosselli ("Cupid" Dick Benton), Art Cook (The "Widow"), Marshall Stedman (Joe Manners).

Production number: B-372

"Bud Reynolds, the king of his class, applies at the Diamond 'S' ranch for a job and promptly falls in love with the ranchman's daughter. They all contest at the County Fair, when Bud captures all the trophies in sight for his prowess, including the hand of fair Katie. Arizona Bob, Soda Water Sam and Limpy Jim are disconsolate thereat and take to reading openly and in secret, the small 'ads' in the crumpled paper from Omaha. They all strike a 'plant' of two confidence men: 'A wealthy widow desires to make the acquaintance of a Westerner.' Each unknown to the other, writes, and are requested to send a sum of money as evidence of good faith. After several weeks of waiting for the return sign of the widow, their mutual secret becomes open and they conclude, both as individuals and syndicates they have been stung. Arizona volunteers to mosey up to Omaha and try to get back the original heartbalm investment. He sends the coy widow an important check, and goes on the same train with the letter. He visits the newspaper office and lays for the 'Con' who gets the letters, and then trails him to the lair of his confederates. As they are about to split the proceeds of the check he pops up serenely, and covering them with his trusty irons, 'persuades' them to pay his bill which includes his traveling expenses and the original investment of his partners, together with divers 'extras' in the form of heart damages—in a naive western way that takes starch and unearned increment out of the swindlers. Then he buys a handsome wedding present for Bob and Katie. His partners are reimbursed, but conclude that the risks of matrimony are too complicated for their simple calculation."

Selig release bulletin

PHYSICAL CULTURE ON THE QUARTER CIRCLE V BAR

Selig Polyscope Company. Released December 11, 1913 through General Film Company. *Length:* 1 reel

Director: William Duncan. *Scenario:* Edwin Ray Coffin.

Cast: William Duncan (Jack), Rex de Rosselli (Bill), Lester Cuneo (Pete), Myrtle Stedman (Alice Moore), Tom Mix (Williams), Florence Dye (Mrs. Williams), Hugh Mosher (Reginald Van Sant).

Production number: 366

"A natty girl from the East, bearing the latest hints from Paris in her costume and get-up, arrives at the Diamond 'S' ranch and immediately becomes the cynosure of all eyes. Three cow-punchers of the wild and wooly order fall desperately in love with her in a minute. They are surprised to find that she is inordinately fond of athletics, and decide to go into training, sending to a mail-order house for a full lot of apparatus. They saw off their pants, make them into athletic costumes, and start madly into muscle-making on hickory horses, Indian clubs and other sweat producers. They meet with many mishaps, but grow strong and eliminate fat. After they think they are very fit, the athletic girl introduces them to a flat-chested, anemic- looking young man, and tells them that he is to be her future husband. They sadly go out behind the bunk- house, build a fire and resignedly consign their training outfits to the flames."

Selig release bulletin

BUSTER'S LITTLE GAME

Selig Polyscope Company. Released December 17, 1913 through General Film Company. *Length:* 1 reel

Director: William Duncan. *Scenario:* C. W. Vansant

Cast: William Duncan (Buster Holmes), Lester Cuneo (Art Robins), Myrtle Stedman (Helen Blake), Florence Dye (Mrs. Blake), Rex de Rosselli (Joe Blake), Tom Mix (Pete Wilson).

Production number: 365

"Buster Holmes, who is 'some lively boy' on a ranch, receives a letter from his late uncle's attorney in the East, stating that he has inherited an income for life if he will take a course through the university. Owning nothing but his spurs, boots and saddle, he concludes to favor the education. Six years after the old spell of the West urges him back again; but the East has so bleached him out that, disguised in store clothes, he goes back to the ranch looking like a true tenderfoot. All the boys naturally take advantage of the callow newcomer, but the ranchman's daughter is much disgusted by what she considers their cruelties, and her interest presently ripens into affection. One day at the corral the boys are saddling up an outlaw, and Buster Holmes manages to get

Right: Lester Cuneo and Tom Mix played a pair of thieves out to steal the wealth that others have dug from the ground in *Mother Love vs. Gold*, one of Mix's last pictures with the William Duncan unit at Prescott, Arizona.

Below: In *By Unseen Hand*, released in early 1914, Tom was on the other side of the law. Here an amateur detective (William Duncan in grey suit) explains the mystery to Chief Jackson (Tom Mix with handle-bar mustache).

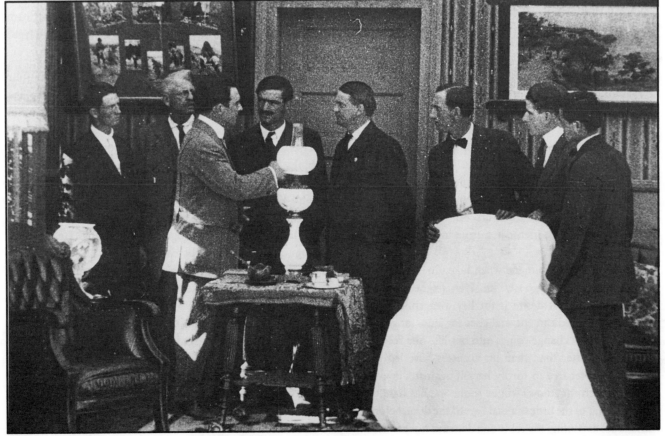

from the girl a promise that she will marry him if he can ride the bad horse. She would have married him without that, if he had only known, but she laughingly agrees. He gets firmly upon the hurricane back of the 'bronc,' who does all the stiff-legged and hunch-back stunts his wild and vicious brain can conjure, but Buster sticks to his mount like a centaur. This makes the other shame-faced cowboys hide behind the fences of the corral, and the girl is angered because the dude has been deceiving her. Presently she stops her pouting, flaunting and protesting as she finds him, after all, a better man than she thought, and is happy with him heart and hand."

Selig release bulletin

MOTHER LOVE VS. GOLD

Selig Polyscope Company. Released December 23, 1913 through General Film Company. *Length:* 1 reel

Director: William Duncan. *Scenario:* John M. Kiskadden.

Cast: William Duncan (Dick Mackey), Myrtle Stedman (Mrs. Bryson), Lester Cuneo (Jim Sykes), Tom Mix (Pete Jackson), Florence Dye (Sallie McKim), Rex de Rosselli (Dave McKim).

Production number: 376

"A pair of precious loafers in a mining town learn from one of their 'kidney' that Dick Mackey's partner, Bill Bryson, has died and that his gold dust is cached in Dick's cabin. They get sober and conclude to rob Mackey, but find that he is too quick on 'the draw,' and give it up. They then put their experience from a correspondence school, in operation and write Bill Bryson's wife, telling her that Dick has killed her husband, stolen his gold and jumped his claim, offering to help her if she will come to Black Butte and abide by their advice. She comes soon, bringing her infant. They plan to have her feign illness at Mackey's cabin door, and when he goes for the doctor, to let them in and they will share the gold concealed in the cabin. She demurs, but they emphasize the enormity of Mackey's offense in murdering her husband, so she finally consents.

"She goes to his cabin and when taken in, she finds that her own baby is seriously ill. Her feigned illness is forgotten—her great desire is for her own child. Mackey recognizes her predicament, and goes for a doctor. With his departure, a new change comes into her life. She recognizes that he is a better man than his accusers have led her to believe, and prepares to fortify herself against the villains' coming, which she knows will be soon. She has hardly had time to attend to the little one and barred the door, before the ruffians are assaulting the cabin and demanding that she find

the gold. She parleys with them through the closed door and finally puts up a defense so stubborn, it lasts until Mackey returns from a neighboring ranch with a doctor and help. The rascals are foiled! Happily, the baby's life is saved and the mother so grateful, that a month later she becomes Mrs. Dick Mackey, and he takes up all the responsibilities of his late partner."

Selig release bulletin

1914 _____

BY UNSEEN HAND

Selig Polyscope Company. Released January 7, 1914 through General Film Company. *Length:* 1 reel

Director: William Duncan. *Scenario:* Hardee Kirkland.

Cast: William Duncan (Jimmy Norton), Lester Cuneo (Jack Warrington), Rex de Rosselli (Arthur Baxter), Marshall Stedman (John Masterson), Tom Mix (Chief Jackson), Myrtle Stedman (Margaret Warrington).

"Arthur Baxter comes to spend the week end with John Masterson, a wealthy merchant. With him are his nephew, Jack Warrington, and his niece, Margaret Warrington. Arthur is in love with Margaret; she repels his advances, but he persists. Her uncle, however, rather favors the match, as he thinks Baxter is wealthy. Jack Warrington, however, takes a different view of the matter and is badly worsted in a fist fight. He goes out hunting, and when he returns later, he finds Baxter asleep in the library; so he quietly slips in and lays his revolver and cartridge belt on the table. He leaves the room, and some time thereafter a shot is heard—Baxter is found dead in the chair; the police investigate and arrest Jack.

"Jimmy Norton, a keen police reporter, and friend of Margaret, refuses to believe that Jack is guilty. He discovers by accident, that the sun shining through a glass gold-fish bowl, has focused on a cartridge in the belt that Jack laid upon the table, exploded the shell and caused Baxter's death. The judge and jury immediately clear young Warrington, and Norton's interest in her brother's case inspires Margaret to give him the answer he has waited for so patiently and long."

Selig release bulletin

A FRIEND IN NEED

Selig Polyscope Company. Released January 22, 1914 through General Film Company. *Length:* 1 reel

Director: William Duncan. *Scenario:* William Duncan.

Cast: William Duncan (the chauffeur), Florence Dye (the girl), Eleanor Blevins (her sister), Lester Cuneo (her father), Tom Mix (the foreman), Charles Wheelock (the land shark).

"Jimmy Donovan gets a passenger for his automobile to make an all-day trip to the Stanley ranch. When they have almost reached their destination, the engine goes 'dead,' but the Stanley girls, riding bronchos, come to the rescue and drag the car on to the ranch at the end of their ropes. When they arrive at the place, it suddenly develops that Jim's passenger is a land-shark, who has come to force payment on the note of the ranchman. The latter is unable to pay and asks for time. This is refused and the shark decides to seize everything on the place by means of a hurried sale.

"This sets Jim's wits to work. He finds through a newspaper that the Northern Arizona Fair may be postponed by reason of lacking attractions. He gets a swift riding cowpuncher to take a note to the president of the Association, telling him that he can furnish an entire program. This information gets through by relays and word is quickly returned that a bonus of a thousand dollars will be paid and other prizes to aggregate five thousand, in case he keeps his promise. This gives opportunity to show all the broncho busters in wonderful feats of strength, nerve and agility, at the Fair. They capture every prize and the bonus. Then begins a wild ride across the plains to intercept the sheriff's sale at the Stanley ranch. The car reaches the ranch and the boys jump out with enough money to pay all the indebtedness, while the land shark is paid up and forced out on the toe of the boot.

"While Jimmy was busy thinking up plans to relieve the head of the ranch, he was not too busy to overlook one of the charming Stanley girls. He having rescued the father, the latter gives his consent to the wedding of the daughter."

Selig release bulletin

THE LITTLE SISTER

Selig Polyscope Company. Released February 5, 1914 through General Film Company. *Length:* 1 reel

Director: William Duncan. *Scenario:* Merla Marion Metcalf.

Cast: William Duncan, Tom Mix (two prospectors), Grace Tregarthen (Nell), Lester Cuneo, Charles Wheelock (two bad men)

Production number: 378

"The atmosphere in the picture is very good. During the absence of her brother's at their gold claim, two robbers visit the girl's home. The little sister sees them before they reach the log cabin and saves several bags of gold nuggets by placing them in the bottom of her baby brother's crib. Feigned illness of the babe prevents the robbers from searching the crib."

Motion Picture News, 2/21/14

"The one best thing about the play is its photography. This is of the sunny kind as concerns the exteriors, and brilliant and pleasing in the interiors. A continual use of the cut-back [intercutting from one location and set of characters to another], presumably to heighten the interest, affects the patience. The film does not possess the usual attraction that the child film has to offer, and lacks action. . . .The prospectors leave for their daily panning, and two renegades come to their cabin, but the little girl hides the gold and lies to the bad men until they go away. Then the prospectors come back from the hills and make a fuss over Nell."

New York Dramatic Mirror, 2/11/14

IN DEFIANCE OF THE LAW

Selig Polyscope Company. Released June 28, 1914 through General Film Company. *Length:* 3 reels

Director: Colin Campbell. *Story:* From the novel "Isobel" by James Oliver Curwood.

Cast: Wheeler Oakman (Billy McVeigh), Tom Mix (Corporal Nome), Joe King (Scottie Deane), Frank Clark (Jim Blake), Bessie Eyton (Isobel Deane), Baby Lillian Wade (Little Isobel), Lillian Hayward (Squaw).

Production Number: 930-32

"Billy McVeigh, a member of the Royal Northwest Mounted Police, runs amuck another person of this service undeserving of its uniform, named Nome. The latter becomes his sworn enemy and is alert for a chance to 'get even.' A mysterious murder is committed in the forest far to the north of the barracks , and Scottie Deane is reported to have committed same. Billy and Nome are selected to make the arrest, and the instructions are that Billy take the trail in one direction and Nome in another, the two converging later on. So they leave headquarters—the two enemies on their long, lonely and perilous mission.

"Some time later, as Billy battles his way through a snowstorm, he meets a young woman urging along a dog team almost exhausted. On the sled is a long box like a rude

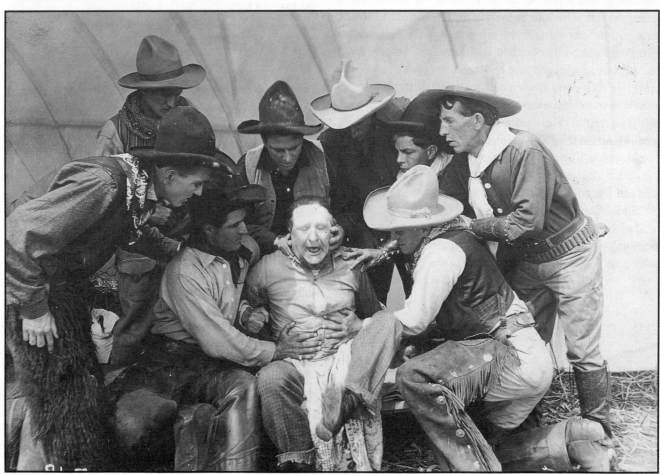

Above: Joan (Bessie Eyton) delivers her man to the Mountie lieutenant played by Selig contract player Charles Clary (at left). Eyton was a popular leading lady at Selig. A California girl, she came to the movies with no stage training. Her career faltered with the declining fortunes of the Selig company, and she disappeared without a trace after an argument with her family in the mid 1920's.

Above-opposite page: Tom and William Duncan are prospectors in *The Little Sister*, their final picture together. After its completion Selig called Tom to Chicago and later sent him to California to work with the studio's leading filmmaker, Colin Campbell. Selig was grooming Tom Mix to eventually become an actor/writer/director heading his own unit.

Below-opposite page: Tom Mix, as Chip of the Flying U Ranch, comforts Frank Clark as the ranch cook Patsy in *When the Cook Fell Ill*. 'Dopey' Dick Crawford stands at right, and Hoot Gibson stands second from right.

Right: Tom's first film for director Jim Campbell was *The Wilderness Mail*, although it was the second to be released. Based on a story by James Oliver Curwood, it was one of several Northwest pictures made by Tom in the early months of 1914. Tom played a villain, and here Joan (played by Bessie Eyton) forces the outlaw to Royal Mounted Police headquarters after she has discovered he murdered the mail carrier.

coffin. His inquiries elicit from her the story that she is taking her dead brother to the settlement. The warm-hearted Billy, deeply moved, decides to accompany her, and they camp for the night. He sets up a tent for her and one for himself. During the night, she slips into his tent, takes his rifle, goes to the apparent coffin, opens it, and liberates a live man, her husband, Scottie Deane—the man wanted. Scottie, however, is not a criminal, as he slew the other man in self-defense. Scottie's wife, Isobel, in extenuation, pins a note to Billy's tent explaining this, asking forgiveness for her seeming ingratitude , and asking him not to follow them for her sake.

Nome and another constable, Carter, happen across Billy's camp the next morning. Billy seeing his enemy, instinctively reaches for his gun, and then realizes that it is gone. Nome grows suspicious, and begins to question Billy concerning the two tents. Billy then tells the latter that a half-breed spent the night with him, but Nome, still suspicious, investigates the second tent and confronts Billy with some strands of golden hair from Isobel's head. Billy takes it from him, and makes as if to throw it in the fire, but really keeps it as a sacred souvenir. Nome and Carter laugh at his inability to explain away the hair, and tell Billy that after they have rested they intend to trail his 'half- breed.' They then retire to the second tent. Billy now realizes that the only way to save Isobel, with whom he is deeply smitten, is to rush on ahead and arrest Scottie himself. He appropriates the sleeping policeman's gun and sets out on his snowshoes to overtake the fugitives. He is a skilled trailer, and he soon overtakes Scottie and Isobel in their camp and overpowers the former. Isobel turns furiously on Billy. At this moment Nome and Carter appear. Nome denounces Billy, coarsley accuses the girl most unjustly, and a stand-off ensues, in which Carter and Nome are driven off. Billy then explains to Isobel why he arrested Scottie, liberates his prisoner and bids them good-bye. When Nome's report reaches headquarters, Billy is dismissed from service and he becomes a hunter in the solitudes.

"Scottie and his wife return to the wilds. He goes to a distant place to get their little daughter, who was placed in charge of a French family when they made their original flight. While he is there, the house is attacked by Indians, and all the whites are on the verge of being wiped out when Billy comes to the rescue. He finds Scottie dying, but Billy recognizes him as he enters the room, and he places his little girl (Isobel) into Billy's keeping, begging him to restore her to her mother (of that dear name) in the far forest home. Billy regards this trust as sacred, and they make the long trip to find the mother down with smallpox, and deserted even by her Indian servants. He gets help from a missionary, and Billy having obeyed the request of the dying man, resumes his wanderings. Some months later he receives a letter from the missionary, telling him that the mother and child were saved. Learning that Little Isobel is in Montreal, and seized with a longing to see her again, he goes to the big city, finds the little girl and meets the mother once again. Eventually, both the Isobels—mother and daughter—become the members of his own family."

Selig release bulletin

THE WILDERNESS MAIL

Selig Polyscope Company. Released July 13, 1914 through General Film Company. *Length:* 2 reels (1,663 feet)

Director: Colin Campbell. *Story:* James Oliver Curwood.

Cast: Wheeler Oakman (Jan, the trapper), Joe King (Otto, the mail driver), Bessie Eyton (Joan, a young French-Canadian), Lillian Hayward (Marie, her half-sister), Frank Clark (Joan's father), Tom Mix (the outlaw).

Production number: 926

"Jan, the hunter, strong and resourceful, and sufficient unto himself in almost every emergency, is in love with Marie, a French-Canadian girl, whose coquetery has not been subdued by a residence in the woods. The same charmer has captivated Otto, the driver of the Wilderness Mail, a vengeful and selfish individual, who has been spoiled by contact with civilization. Marie has a half-sister, Joan, a decided contrast to her—a sweet, lovable girl, not ordinarily bold or aggressive, but when aroused, firm to a finish. She resents the way her sister meets these two suitors, the one following the other, as quite unworthy of a modest woman, and hotly tells her so. First comes good-natured Jan, who presents Marie with the pelt of a beautiful red-fox. He is hardly out of sight in the woods when the mail driver comes, and she greets him even more effusively with kisses. He also gives her a present. Joan, outraged by her demonstration, speaks to Marie sharply, and Otto tries to conciliate her; but she in shame and mortification, runs to the woods.

"Otto soon drives his dog team down the snowy trail and meets Joan, roughly parleys with her and tries to kiss her. She struggles and screams. A little distance away in the woods, Jan is talking with some woodsmen. He hears Joan's cries, rushes valiantly to the rescue, leaps upon Otto, seizes him by the throat as a terrier catches a rat. Then follows a terrific hand-to-hand conflict—strong men half wild with rage. Eventually Otto is so sorely worsted, he can hardly stand alone, but is helped to his feet by the two woodsmen as Jan takes the girl away. The news of Jan's victory has reached the settlement, and the next morning when he arrives there, he is received as a man among men. He is given a commission to get a letter through to Fort Hope before the Wilderness Mail reaches there, carrying advices that would rob a good man of his fortune. With a fresh dog team, and a big reward in view, Jan forges ahead, and overtakes the phlegmatic Otto idly dull from his beating. In crossing a frozen lake, Jan falls through. Otto passes on with a deaf ear to all his calls for help, sure that his enemy will perish miserably. Happily, Jan's dogs are more humane, and tugging at their lines move him to safety on firm ice.

"An outlaw lies in wait to rob the Wilderness Mail. He is about to shoot the advancing man when he discovers his mistake, for Jan is again ahead. He lets Jan pass by, but when Otto comes upon the scenes, he kills him. Then he climbs a tree over the scene of the murder, and by dropping into the tracks of Jan, cunningly conceals his own trail. Soon two Northwest mounted police put in an appearance, find the body of Otto, and observing the trail of Jan, conclude he is the murderer.

"Jan, unconscious of the crime that has been committed, rushes on his way, delivers the packet entrusted to him, so that the good news gets there first, justice is done and the man's property is saved. He then recuperates after his long journey, takes the back trail home when he is met by the mounted police, who arrest him, accusing him of the murder of Otto. He denies the charge strenuously and, rankling under the injustice of it, makes a stout resistance, but is eventually overcome and carried back to Ft. Hope, bound as a prisoner. The news soon reaches the settlement and the lone cabin of the two sisters, Marie and Joan. The former immediately write a bitter note to Jan, upbraiding him wrathfully as the murderer of the only man she ever loved. Poor little Joan who is deeply distressed over the situation is so firmly convinced of the innocence of Jan that she concludes to go to him, making a long journey over the lonely trail to Ft. Hope. When she is admitted to the prisoner, he describes his trip in detail—how Otto left him to drown, and later tried to shoot him; but that he had gone ahead unmindful of it. This reassures Joan more than ever that Jan is innocent. Thereupon she determines an investigation upon her own account, returns to the scene of the crime and, by studying the situation carefully, observes how the murderer climbed the tree, traversed the long branch, and dropped into the trail of the man ahead. She then follows the side trail which leads to the lonely cabin of the outlaw.

"Joan draws her revolver, enters the cabin and finds the outlaw befuddled in liquor, mussing over the plundered mail. She tries to arrest him, but, drunk as he is, he makes resistance and endeavors to grapple with her. She shoots him in the arm, then binds his hands behind him and drives him

before her back to the headquarters of the police where she delivers him as the real murderer. Hers was the most unusual and daring deed, and was highly commended by the authorities. Jan is released upon the confession of the outlaw, and the last scene shows Jan and Joan entering their own cabin in the dimming light, presumably after the service in the little church in the clearing where their wedding had been celebrated.

Selig release bulletin

WHEN THE COOK FELL ILL

Selig Polyscope Company. Released July 31, 1914 through General Film Company. *Length:* 1 reel

Director: Colin Campbell. *Scenario:* B. M. Bower [Bertha Muzzy Sinclair]

Cast: Frank Clark (Patsy), Wheeler Oakman (Weary), Tom Mix (Chip), Frank Feehan (Doctor).

Production number: 967

"Patsy, the cook of the 'Flying U' ranch, is passionately fond of canned corn. Every time he goes to town to buy supplies for the camp, cases of canned corn head the list. Patsy may forget at time to order a special brand of tobacco for the boys, or some of the trimmings that go to make a camp dinner more acceptable, but he never fails to order the canned corn. Every day for breakfast, dinner and supper, the big kettle of canned corn forms the principal article of diet. The boys being 'good fellows' stand for this a long time until they feel that they cannot accept corn as the main article of diet any longer. Then they revolt and refuse to be served from Patsy's huge kettle any more. Patsy is sensitive, and his feelings are hurt, but his appetite for canned corn is still unimpaired. After the boys walk out on him and scorn the breakfast of canned corn, Patsy retires to the cook tent with the kettle and gorges himself to repletion from its contents.

"The boys are sore and hungry, but they leave the camp for the range to perform their regular day's work. As the boys disappear in the distance, Patsy is taken with terrific cramps. He has a horrible suspicion that he has been poisoned. His examination of the empty corn cans suggests ptomaine poison. The camp is deserted and the boys will not return until five o'clock in the evening. Patsy spends hours of agony and realizes that he has had too much of a good thing. After a day of suffering, the boys return to camp. No dinner in sight. Patsy is discovered groaning in pain. They realize his desperate condition. They are glad that Patsy has had a lesson, but do not want him to die. Weary, one of the boys, rides off to town to get a doctor, while the rest prepare supper. After many adventures with the doctor who is in no condition to travel, Weary brings him to camp. In the meantime, a good Samaritan, a stranger with a big whisky bottle, has doctored Patsy with liberal decoctions of liquor, so that the doctor's services are not required. All decide to climb on the 'water wagon.'"

Selig release bulletin

ETIENNE OF THE GLAD HEART

Selig Polyscope Company. Released August 3, 1914 through General Film Company. *Length:* 2 reels

Director: Colin Campbell. *Scenario:* Maibelle Heikes Justice

Cast: Wheeler Oakman (Etienne), Bessie Eyton (Marie), Joe King (Olaf), Tom Mix (Peter), Frank Clark (Old Man Paul), Lillian Hayward (Ritta, his wife).

Production Number: 937-38

"Etienne Cloquet, a young woodsman, is in love with Marie, the pretty daughter of Paul Le Groux, a salmon fisher. Etienne has such a sunny disposition that he has become generally known as 'Etienne of the Glad Heart.' Notwithstanding his sunny disposition, he has a fierce temper when aroused, so that those who know him realize that it will not do to press him too far. The plans for the marriage of the young couple have all been arranged and Etienne goes to the lumber camp to put in a final winter with the expectation that he will have enough money saved in the spring so that he and Marie can marry.

"Olaf, a young trapper, is a handsome fellow, but unscrupulous. He chances on the cabin of Paul, and becomes a boarder with the family. Naturally, he is attracted by Marie, and realizing her engagement to Etienne, plans to gain her affections. One of Etienne's accomplishments is the playing of the guitar, and it has been his custom to carry this instrument with him when he visited his sweetheart. They discover that Olaf is even a superior performer on the guitar, and Marie begins to show an interest in him as a result of his pleasant ways and musical skill. During Etienne's absence in the lumber camp, Olaf makes progress in the winning of Marie, her parents being unsuspicious of the change in her affections. While Etienne is in the lumber camp he rescues an Indian named Peter from a terrible death, and Peter has become his faithful friend. Peter accompanies Etienne on his return from the lumber camp. Just about the time of Etienne's return, old Paul becomes suspicious of Marie, and discovers her in the act of sewing a tiny garment, which

confirms his suspicions that there is something wrong. Paul demands the attendance of Etienne, believing him to be the culprit, and wishing to bring him face to face with the disgraced girl. At the cabin door, they meet Olaf returning from a trapping trip. They face Marie and Paul commands that his daughter shall name her betrayer. Marie is overwhelmed with shame, and does not speak. Etienne, to whom the information is wholly new, at once grasps the situation, and springing upon Olaf, endeavors to kill him with his bare hands. Marie's mother intervenes and saves Olaf's life. The disgraced girl is driven from home, accompanied by Olaf, her betrayer.

"The home-like cabin of Paul becomes a place of sorrow. Etienne has lost his spirit, and one night he takes his beloved guitar into the woods and hides it. Peter, believing that Etienne will once more be happy, rescues the guitar and takes it to the cabin, unknown to Etienne. The love of the mother impels her to urge Etienne to undertake a search for Marie. She misses her only child, and her heart yearns for her. She has not had word for months, and does not know whether Marie is alive or dead. Etienne consults with his friend Peter, and it is finally decided that a search shall be made for the outcast girl.

"Peter finally locates the cabin in which Olaf and Marie are living. He accompanies Etienne to the place, and they find the couple inside. Olaf's heartless and brutal treatment of Marie enrages Etienne, but Peter restrains him. They watch the cabin in secret until Olaf goes for an inspection of his traps. Then they hurriedly enter the cabin, urge the overjoyed girl to escape under their protection and the three hasten away to embark in Peter's canoe for the return trip. . . . Olaf returns unexpectedly to the cabin a short time after their departure. He notes the absence of Marie and cannot understand it. His skill in woodcraft discloses the tracks of Marie and her two companions, and he follows the trail to the river. There he notes the marks which show that another canoe has been hauled up at the landing. Furious with rage, he springs into his canoe, and follows with all the haste and speed that his skill can supply. Down the winding river he follows the heavily loaded canoe containing the girl and her two friends. Etienne and Peter are also experts at the battle, but the added weight in their canoe renders their progress slower than that of their frantic pursuer. Olaf finally gets within range, and pulling his six-shooter, he empties it at the occupants of the canoe. They proceed uninjured, and throwing the now useless weapon away, he continues to paddle after them. The leading canoe is propelled to the shore, and Marie and Etienne disembark in haste.

"Olaf drifts past undecided as to what his next step shall be, but Peter, what the friendship with Etienne means to him and what the despicable acts of Olaf in connection with Marie have meant to his friend, he dashes after Olaf, and upon arriving along side, he launches himself like a catapult on the shoulders of the doomed Olaf, upsetting the canoe, and both floundering into the ice cold stream. Peter returns alone. The anxious mother accepts the return of Marie with all of a mother's love. Gruff old Paul accepts the situation, while Etienne, with the sunshine once more in his heart, accepts his rescued guitar from the grinning Peter, and happy hearts beat once again."

Selig release bulletin

THE WHITE MOUSE

Selig Polyscope Company. Released August 24, 1914 through General Film Company. *Length:* 2 reels

Director: Colin Campbell. *Story:* James Oliver Curwood

Cast: Wheeler Oakman (Billy Silver), Bessie Eyton (Jean), Joe King (Lawler), Tom Mix (Sergeant Brokaw).

"Billy Silver, a clever young trapper, lives with his wife and little baby up in the region of the snows. Billy is energetic and finds trapping profitable. One morning while he is out examining his traps, the cabin catches fire. In the distance he hears the cries of his wife for help, and hastening to the scene as rapidly as he can make his way on snowshoes over the heaped up drifts, he arrives just in time to save the baby and a few necessities. Their little home is burned to the ground, leaving them wholly without shelter in the cold winter time. They have no materials with which to build another house. It is too cold to take any chance of exposing the wife and baby to the extreme cold, so Billy harnesses himself to the sledge upon which he loads his family, and in due time arrives without accident at the camp of a party of surveyors, fifty miles away.

"Jean, the young wife, is a beauty. Billy seeks work of Lawler, the boss of the camp, but is turned down until Lawler accidentally catches a glimpse of pretty Jean. His brutal mind at once schemes out a plan, and he hires Billy to accompany a party of men about to leave for a lengthy trip. . . . After Billy has gone, Lawler visits the pretty young wife in her cabin. Receiving no encouragement to pursue his attentions, he goes away, but with his brutal mind still fixed upon his devilish scheme, he returns. . . . Billy, after going a few miles with the surveying crew, is sent back to the camp for a map, which has been left behind. His unexpected return saves pretty Jean from the consequences of Lawler's brutal passion. Billy dashes into the cabin upon hearing her cries for help

and wrests Lawler from his victim. Billy does not desire to injure him, but his forebearance is a mistake. No sooner does Lawler find himself free, than he draws his revolver and tries to shoot Billy. There is a struggle for the possession of the weapon, and Lawler, in his attempt to kill Billy, pulls the trigger when the revolver is pointed at his own heart, with fatal consequences to himself. Others in the camp have heard the shot and rush into the cabin. They find Billy standing with the smoking revolver in his hand. He and Jean explain, but the men, who are creatures of Lawler, notify the Northwest Mounted Police representatives, an Billy is locked up on a charge of murder.

"Jean plans the escape of Billy from jail. The Northwest Mounted Policemen, who realize the true conditions because they are aware of the brutal character of Lawler, have an inkling of the plan of escape, but shut their eyes to it out of sympathy for Billy and his pretty wife, and believe that he is not guilty. The plan is successful, and Billy makes his headquarters in a deserted cabin several miles away from the camp, where he continues his work of trapping until the snows of winter shall go away, and he can leave the place to join his pretty wife among friends in another country.

"Billy has a pet and constant companion, a tiny white mouse, which has an inordinate and mischievous appetite for the moosehide thongs that form the net work on Billy's snowshoes. The little fellow is constantly trying the eat the snow shoe strings, and Billy has considerable mending to do as a consequence.

"The creatures of Lawler are angry at the escape of Bill, and they incite Sergeant Brokaw, known as the 'human blood hound,' to pick up Bill's trail and recapture him. The sergeant finds Billy in the lonely cabin, where his sole companion is the little white mouse. There is a surprise, and Billy finds himself a prisoner with hands and feet bound by moosehide thongs. The sergeant exalts in the capture and returns to where he has left his dog team for the purpose of bringing the sledge up to the cabin door, where he can load Billy upon it and take him back to jail. Billy is disconsolate. He fears the result of his trial on the charge of murder in view of the biased and false testimony which he believes will be given by the former employes of Lawler. He is despondent, but cannot do a thing with his hands and feet bound. The little white mouse, his pet and sole companion, comes to his aid. The little creature scents the moose hide thongs which bind the writs of his master, and finding itself unrebuked , begins to indulge its appetite with great gusto. Its needle-like teeth quickly separate the strands and Billy [finds] his hands free. It is but the work of a moment to cast the thongs from off his ankles. He hears the shouting of the sergeant outside, urging his dog team through the drifts up to the cabin, and by the time he throws the door open to carry out his prisoner, Billy springs upon him and quickly disarms the policeman. A short, quick struggle settles the affair. The police sergeant is locked within the cabin as a prisoner, and Billy escapes through the snowdrifts.

"Weeks of arduous adventure and hardship follow for Billy, but at last he makes his way to the distant locality, where pretty Jean and the baby are waiting for him. Yes, and the little white mouse also finds friends of its kind, and the last picture shows a happy family of mice in addition to Billy, Jean and the baby."

Selig release bulletin

CHIP OF THE FLYING U

Selig Polyscope Company. Released August 29, 1914 through General Film Company. *Length:* 3 reels

Director: Colin Campbell. *Story:* B. M. Bower [Bertha Muzzy Sinclair]

Cast: Tom Mix (Chip), Kathlyn Williams (Della, "the Little Doctor"), Wheeler Oakman (Weary), Frank Clark (Patsy), Fred Huntly ("Old Man").

Production number: 971-2

"Claude Bennett, a handsome young fellow, occupies a desk in his father's bank, but does not earn his salt. He has an artistic temperament, and has done some clever sketching, but he has never earned a dollar in his life. Idling one morning at his desk, he draws a ridiculous cartoon of his father, which comes to the attention of the bank president, who summarily tells Claude that the town is not big enough for him. After a moment's reflection, Claude replies with spirit: 'All right, Dad, I guess I'll go West.' Claude Bennett develops into 'Chip,' a lively young cowboy on the Flying 'U' Ranch down in Texas.

"Whitmore, the 'Old Man,' is a hard worker, and does not spare himself any more than he does the boys. Chip becomes an all-around man after a number of adventures in which the wildest bronchos test his staying powers as a rider, and one day the 'Old Man' tells him to hook up the team and drive to the station. Chip is told to meet the 'old man's' sister, who is a woman doctor. While putting on his other shirt to drive to town, Chip discusses the prospective arrival of the 'old maid doctor,' and they conjure up visions of an ancient she-dragon, with a face like a lemon. Chip waits around in a dejected manner until the train pulls in. He is delighted to discover that the 'old maid doctor' is nothing more or less

than a very pretty, charming, young girl (Kathlyn Williams). Chip improves the time during the ride to the ranch to get well acquainted with the 'little doctor,' as he already calls her in his own mind, whereas, she discovers in this tanned and sprightly young cowboy many of the elements which go to make up a hero, especially in the mind of a young girl. She demonstrates her skill with the ride by shooting a coyote, this feat of arms putting Chip absolutely at her mercy. He succumbs entirely to her natural fascination.

"Chip still does a little sketching now and then, some of which comes to the attention of the 'little doctor,' who encourages him to paint a really good picture. An accident occurs in which Chip is thrown from his horse and dragged at the end of a lasso over the plains at a gallop. His pert cayuse breaks a leg and Chip is about to end its misery with a bullet when the 'little doctor' announces that she can set the legs with splints. She does so, and another arrow from Cupid's bow goes to the heart of Chip. Then Chip is layed up with a sprained ankle and the 'little doctor' takes care of him. During his recovery he gets to work on the picture, which he paints with great natural skill, and the 'old man's' silent partner, Dunk, who comes to the ranch on a visit, sees the painting and promises to take it to the city and show it to someone with a knowledge of art. The picture sells for a good fat check.

"The 'little doctor' captivates everybody. Even Patsy, the cook, with his dirty apron, succumbs to her charms when she makes a professional visit to the kitchen and orders him to 'clean up," he obeys after much grumbling. The 'Old Man' hears the rattling of tins and kettles in the kitchen and makes an investigation. Patsy has the floor covered with soap suds, and is scrubbing away with great spirit. The "Old Man' dashes into the kitchen and sprawls all over the floor, sliding on the soap suds. He has it in his heart to murder Patsy and starts after him, but Patsy slides through the door on another installment of soap suds, and the 'Old Man' toboggans down the steps after him. The 'little doctor' is always up to something. She has all the cowboys her slaves, with Chip the worst of the lot. She gets a letter stating that Dr. Cecil Grantham, whose name Chip has heard her mention before and whom he looks upon as a formidable rival, is going to arrive on the next day's train, for a visit to the 'little doctor.' Chip feels very much disturbed in spirit. He imagines that Dr. Grantham is coming to claim his bride, and the 'little doctor' mischievously leads him to think so. So Chip is chosen as the instrument to bring his rival to the ranch, being ordered to accompany the 'little doctor' in the buckboard, and greet the expected visitor. They pull another one on Chip, for the formidable Dr. Cecil Grantham is a sweet and saucy Miss, a classmate of the 'little doctor.' Chip is so happy over the outcome that he visibly shows it and the girls have a great deal of fun at his expense, in consequence.

"The 'Old Man' becomes infatuated with the new arrival. Dunk, who has fallen in love with the 'little doctor,' finds himself outclassed by Chip, and that he hasn't a chance. He shows his jealousy, whereupon he is given to understand in unmistakable terms, that he is not in it. Dunk 'beats' it for the railroad station. Then follow gay days at the ranch. Chip saves the 'little doctor's' life when she is pursued by a locoed stallion, and there is no more coquetery on her part. The 'Old Man' wins the 'little doctor's' chum, and when the announcement is made and each loving couple confesses to the others, the 'Old Man' sends Patsy for a bottle of wine, so that they can all drink to each other's health. The path of love runs smooth for all—there is no serpent in their garden of Eden."

Selig release bulletin

WHEN THE WEST WAS YOUNG

Selig Polyscope Company. Released September 7, 1914 through General Film Company. *Length:* 2 reels

Director: Colin Campbell. *Story:* Cyrus Townsend Brady.

Cast: Bessie Eyton (Nellie Halton), Wheeler Oakman (Ned Halton), Jack McDonald (Settler), Gertrude Ryan (his wife), Frank Clark (bootlegger), Tom Mix (Indian Chief), Harry Lonsdale (The Saviour).

"Ned Halton and his attractive young bride, Nellie, depart from the east in a prairie schooner to seek a home in the western wilds. They traverse the plain until they arrive at a spot which seems to them suitable for the making of a permanent home. Ned builds a comfortable cabin, and in due time a crooning baby enlivens the monotony of their existence and fills a place in the mother's heart such as only a baby can. The silence and isolation which preyed upon the mind of the mother is forgotten, and the little family live happily. A neighboring tribe of Indians are most friendly to the young settler and his wife, and bring a host of barbaric gifts which to them represent the height of amity. The little baby is Christened by the frontier clergyman, and is looked upon by the settlers and red men as being a marvelous creation direct from the great Spirit.

"Then one day comes the shock. The doctor is called from the nearest village many miles away, but he is too late. The gentle little spirit fades away until the spark of life goes out. All of the happiness in that modest little western home is buried at the foot of the tree on the hill that overlooks the cabin, while the desolation of the silent world about penetrates into the cabin itself. Ned comforts his young wife as best he can, but the sorrow of a bereaved mother is not something to lightly pass away. Ned receives a summons to go to the settlement and complete the formalities in connection with the title to their home.

"In the absence of Ned, Nellie becomes disconsolate. She sits by the empty cradle and dreams of the little one gone beyond. In her spirit of disconsolation, she again visits the tiny grave where she has a vision of the Saviour holding her little babe in his arms and comforting her with assurance which rests in the words: 'Suffer little children to come unto me, for such is the Kingdom of Heaven.' Her faith in the spiritual life is reassured and her spirit of depression is dispelled in the belief that her baby is at rest and that she will see him in the next world. Her arms ache for something young and warm to hold and love, but the impression left upon her mind by the vision of the Saviour makes her life much more easy to live.

"On his return from the settlement, Ned Halton becomes a participant in one of those frightful tragedies, the unwritten records of which lie scattered over mountain, vale and plain, from the Mississippi River to the great Pacific. An itinerant bootlegger has supplied a band of Indians with whisky, which they drink with the usual consequence. A young immigrant and his wife and tiny baby riding in their prairie schooner through the hills are attacked in a drunken frenzy by the Indians. Despite the heroic defense on the part of both the man and woman, they are killed, while the baby lies quietly sleeping and unhurt beneath the overturned wagon. Ned Halton arrives in time to see the conclusion of the tragedy and to drive away the drunken redskins. He discovers the orphaned baby and carries it home.

"On the way, his horse, which has been wounded in the fight with the Indians, falls, and when Ned reaches the cabin door, he falls exhausted on the threshold. Nellie has been sitting by the empty cradle dreaming of the little one snatched from her arms by death. When she hears the stumbling footsteps of her husband, she springs to the door and finds him lying there almost unconscious from fatigue. She hastens to revive him, all eagerness and love and thoughtfulness for his comfort, and it is not until he has become refreshed that her attention is attracted to the tiny bundle, which he clasps tenderly in his arms. In all the struggles which he had undergone in his dazed condition, he had unconsciously kept the tiny baby from injury and harm. The joy of Nellie when she discovers what the bundle contains is unbounded, and she clasps the little one to her arms, and clutches it tenderly to her breast. To the two who stand there caressing the tiny baby, appears once more that vision of the gentle Saviour, together with the spirit of the murdered mother."

Selig release bulletin

THE GOING OF THE WHITE SWAN

Selig Polyscope Company. Released September 28, 1914 through General Film Company. *Length:* 2 reels

Director: Colin Campbell. *Story:* Gilbert Parker.

Cast: Bessie Eyton (Lucette), Wheeler Oakman (John Bagot), Roy Clark (Dominique), Frank Clark (Pere Corraine), Joe King (Indian Chief), Tom Mix

Note: Tom Mix is not credited in Selig release information, but his photo appears in the Selig bulletin announcement for this film. In the photos Tom Mix is dressed in costume as a young Indian.

Production Number: 933-36

"A two-part picture play, written by Gilbert Parker. with scenes laid in the Northwest snow country. Bessie Eyton and Wheeler Oakman, in the leading parts, who do excellent work, which requires much strenuousness and endurance. They are supported by an excellent cast, and the photography of the many forest snow scenes is excellently done. Much of heart interest is involved in the scenes. This release is worth the viewing."

The Moving Picture World, 10/10/14

THE REAL THING IN COWBOYS

Selig Polyscope Company. Released September 29, 1914 through General Film Company. *Length:* 1 reel

Director: Tom Mix. *Scenario:* Hettie Gray Baker

Cast: Tom Mix (Wallace Carey), Goldie Colwell (Elsie Mitchell), Miss Townsend (Mrs. Mitchell).

"Elsie's idea of a real man was a dummy dressed like a cowboy, reckless and wild and woolly. Wallace Carey, a gallant city business man, rich, attractive, and well dressed, was in love with her, but she wanted a real cowboy for a husband. Elsie departed for the West to visit relatives on a ranch, but Elsie's mother favored Carey, and planned to bring them together. Carey applied at the ranch where Elsie was staying, for a job, intimating that he had lost his fortune. He mixed with the cowboys, became a 'good fellow,' defeating them all at their sports and games, and cut a striking figure on horseback; so that Elsie finally began to believe that she had made a mistake. He rescued Elsie from a perilous situation, and proved himself to be a 'man' in every way. So Elsie was won after all by an Easterner, who admitted after their engagement that he had not lost his fortune, but was merely playing a part to win her love."

Selig release bulletin

THE MOVING PICTURE COWBOY

Selig Polyscope Company. Released October 5, 1914 through General Film Company. *Length:* 2 reels

Director: Tom Mix. *Scenario:* Tom Mix.

Cast: Tom Mix (Luke Barns), W. L. Lewis (Hawkins), Eleanor Blevins (Mary), Lester Cuneo (Director), Charles Wheelock (cameraman), Bobby Murdock (property man).

Still Code: 381-2

"A Western picture with plenty of good humor and comic situations. A motion picture actor departs for the West where he boasts of his feats of horsemanship. The way he actually did these stunts is laughable. Tom Mix plays the lead well."

Motion Picture News, 10/10/14

THE WAY OF THE RED MAN

Selig Polyscope Company. Released October 6, 1914 through General Film Company. *Length:* 1 reel

Director: Tom Mix. *Scenario:* Tom Mix.

Cast: Tom Mix (The Redman), Goldie Colwell (Bounding Fawn), Leo Maloney (The Gambler), Roy Watson (The Sheriff).

Production Number: C-451

"A very good Indian story with Tom Mix as the Indian. He befriends a gambler, who in turn steals his wife from him and mistreats her. The redman returns to his forefather's idea of punishment and ties the gambler to a stake and places food just out of reach. When, through the little girl, the gambler attempts to escape there is a death struggle between the Indian and the white man."

The Moving Picture World, 10/10/14

THE MEXICAN

Selig Polyscope Company. Released October 13, 1914 through General Film Company. *Length:* 1 reel

Director: Tom Mix. *Scenario:* Lynn F. Reynolds.

Above: Tom Mix (seated at left) plays a hand of poker with a bunkhouse pal in *Chip of the Flying U*, based on a story by Western novelist Bertha Muzzy Sinclair, who for commercial reasons used the more masculine pen name B. M. Bower. *Chip of the Flying U* was a three-reel production, more than a short subject but not quite a feature. This awkward length was common in the 1914-1915 period when producers wanted to respond to the demand for longer films without tying up the capital required for features.

Right: The poster for Tom Mix's first effort as a director/star, appropriately titled *The Real thing in Cowboys*. Leading lady Goldie Colwell stands beside Tom in the artist's rendering. Initially the Mix unit worked at the Bachmann Studio (a small rental lot owned by a dentist who liked to dabble in the picture business) located at 831 9th Street [now Windsor Road] in Glendale, California. The small studio was in the middle of a residential district and there were constant complaints from neighbors about the sound of gunshots and horses. For Tom Mix there were advantages and disadvantages to this out of the way studio. There was little interference from the front office, but Tom was removed from the company and advice of other filmmakers as he stepped into the director's chair.

In his second film as writer-director, Tom Mix starred as Luke Barns, an east coast actor who boasts of his prowess as a cowboy in order to land a movie job and is forced to put up or shut up. In the background are (l-r) Sid Jordan, ?, Charles Wheelock as the cameraman, Lester Cuneo as the director, and Bobby Murdock as the property man, watching *The Moving Picture Cowboy* as he attempts to lasso a docile dairy cow. Tom often poked fun at himself in his pictures, and audiences laughed harder knowing that their screen hero really could rope, ride, and shoot with the best of them. The ten-gallon Stetson hats favored by Tom and his cowboys presented a problem for early cameramen because they cast heavy shadows across the actors' faces. Later cameramen learned to use reflectors to bounce 'fill' light under the hat brims.

Cast: Tom Mix (The Mexican), Mrs. Walker (The Mexican's Wife), Leo D. Maloney (Sim Heflin), Goldie Colwell (Mrs. Heflin), "Baby" Lillian Wade (Baby Heflin).

"In order to keep his family from starving, a Mexican secures work on a ranch where his breed is not popular. He is persecuted until he tries to kill his foreman. He decides to burn the ranch, but instead hurries for a doctor for the rancher's daughter, who has been bitten by a snake. As he rides by in breakneck speed he is shot at by the foreman. He saves the baby and is rewarded. A good story well played."

The Moving Picture World, 10/10/14

JIMMY HAYES AND MURIEL

Selig Polyscope Company. Released October 20, 1914 through General Film Company. *Length:* 1 reel

Director: Tom Mix. *Story:* Sidney Porter

Cast: Tom Mix (Jimmy Hayes), Leo D. Maloney (Lieutenant Manning), Roy Watson (Sabastiano Saldar), Goldie Colwell (Emma Mason).

"A Western drama with a good story. Jimmy Hayes, who is supposed to have deserted under fire, really proves a hero. It is not, however, found out until a year after, when his bleaching bones are found in the shrubbery where he made his last stand. It is recognized as his skeleton because of a pet horned toad named Muriel, which is still faithful to him."

Motion Picture News, 10/24/14

WHY THE SHERIFF IS A BACHELOR

Selig Polyscope Company. Released October 27, 1914 through General Film Company. *Length:* 1 reel

Director: Tom Mix. *Scenario:* Tom Mix.

Cast: Tom Mix (The Sheriff), Goldie Colwell (Alice), Leo D. Maloney (her brother), Roy Watson (Roy Watson).

Production number: C-455

"This is a Tom Mix picture with plenty of riding and shooting and an interesting story. Tom in the discharge of his duties as sheriff, is compelled to arrest the brother of his sweetheart, whom he is soon to marry. She pleads with him to release her brother but duty compels him to take him to jail. The girl refuses to marry him because of this."

Motion Picture News, 10/31/14

THE TELL-TALE KNIFE

Selig Polyscope Company. Released November 3, 1914 through General Film Company. *Length:* 1 reel

Director: Tom Mix. *Scenario:* Tom Mix.

Cast: Tom Mix (Tom Mason), Goldie Colwell (Mabel Madden), Harry Loverin (Tip), Leo D. Maloney (the Sheriff), Hoot Gibson.

"An exceptionally interesting and well produced Western drama, by Tom Mix, in which the identity of the cattle rustler is disclosed through a knife given him by his sweetheart. A pistol fight in a saloon follows. The rustler gets away, only to be run down and killed after a most vivid and hair-raising chase. Contains lots of real fighting, and unusually good riding."

Motion Picture News, 10/31/14

THE RANGER'S ROMANCE

Selig Polyscope Company. Released November 10, 1914 through General Film Company. *Length:* 1 reel

Director: Tom Mix. *Scenario:* Tom Mix.

Cast: Tom Mix (Ranger), Goldie Colwell (Sally), Roy Watson (Settler), Inez Walker (Settler's wife).

Production number: C-456

"A Western drama by Tom Mix, featuring an exciting running fight between a prairie schooner and a band of drink-maddened Indians. Going at a terrific speed, one of the wheels of the prairie schooner comes off, hurling the heavy wagon and its occupants to the ground. After a brief defense, the Indians capture the girl, but she is later retaken by the ranger and his band."

Motion Picture News, 11/7/14

THE SHERIFF'S REWARD

Selig Polyscope Company. Released November 17, 1914 through General Film Company. *Length:* 1 reel

Director: Tom Mix. *Scenario:* Tom Mix.

Cast: Tom Mix (the Sheriff), Goldie Colwell (Rose Boland), Leo D. Maloney (the foreman), Roy Watson (rustler).

Production number: C-457

Note: This is a re-make of THE RANGE RIDERS made in 1910.

"Another of the Tom Mix very high grade cowboy dramas, in which he, as the sheriff, daringly rescues Rose, a pretty young ranch owner, from a band of cattle rustlers, by whom she had been kidnapped. They are married and their friends start them off on their honeymoon in typical cowboy fashion."

Motion Picture News, 11/14/14

THE SCAPEGOAT

Selig Polyscope Company. Released November 24, 1914 through General Film Company. *Length:* 1 reel

Director: Tom Mix. *Scenario:* Tom Mix.

Cast: Tom Mix (Tom Jackson, the scapegoat), Goldie Colwell (Nell, his sister), Leo D. Maloney (Jack Turner).

Production number: C-458

Note: Second use of title.

"A Tom Mix drama that contains some unusually exciting scenes. There is a real thrill when Tom Mix on horseback snatches Goldie Colwell from a buck board which is being drawn at terrific speed by a runaway horse. Tom Mix as sheriff captures a bank robber, and finds that he is a brother of the girl he loves. The robber is allowed to escape, and the sheriff himself leaves the country."

Motion Picture News, 11/28/14

IN THE DAYS OF THE THUNDERING HERD

Selig Polyscope Company. Released November 30, 1914 through General Film Company. *Length:* 5 reels

Director: Colin Campbell. *Scenario:* Gilson Willets.

Cast: Tom Mix (Tom Mingle), Bessie Eyton (Sally Madison), Red Wing (Starlight), Wheeler Oakman (Chief Swift Wing), John Bowers

Note: Reissued as a three-reeler in the early 1920's by Aywon Film Corporation as THE WAGON TRAIL.

Production Number: 950-55

"Colin Campbell has spared no pains nor expense in attempting to produce a wild west drama that will hold the audience's attention through five reels of film. Several quite remarkable features help to make this an interesting and truthful presentation of frontier life in '49.

"The largest of the few remaining wild buffalo herds is featured throughout the picture. You see them sleeping, grazing, stampeding, hunted, and killed by both rifle and bow and arrow. There is a regular Indian village with its hundreds of redskins in their original dress, and still maintaining their savage customs. They fight the plainsmen and hunt the buffalo with their bows and arrows, showing a skill with these instruments which has not been dulled by the years of civilization.

"Scores of prairie schooners of the kind used in old frontier days and an unlimited supply of horses are unstintingly used in this enormous production. The wild scenery of Pawnee Bill's ranch at Pawnee, Oklahoma, furnishes a particularly good setting for the drama.

". . . The story is simply a series of thrilling adventures of Tom Mingle and Sally Madison, who with a band of immigrants attempt a hazardous trip across the plains to the California gold fields where Sally's father is waiting for her. "The band is waylaid and wiped out by a strong tribe of Indians. Sally and Tom, the only survivors, are taken prisoner and their lives are spared, because the Indian chief and his sister take a fancy to them. After many adventures they finally manage to escape, and fall in with a band of buffalo hunters, who in turn are almost wiped out by Indians. Help arrives in the nick of time and Sally and Tom at last reach their destination safely."

T. S. Mead in *Motion Picture News,* 11/28/14

THE RIVAL STAGE LINES

Selig Polyscope Company. Released December 1, 1914 through General Film Company. *Length:* 1 reel

Director: Tom Mix. *Scenario:* Allen A. Martin.

Cast: Tom Mix (Harding Martin), Goldie Colwell (Elsie Johnson), Leo D. Maloney (David Patrick), Sid Jordan (Chalmers Brown), Inez Walker (Mrs. Katz), Lynn F. Reynolds (Reginald Smythe).

Production number: C-459

Note: This is a re-make of a 1911 Selig film, RIVAL STAGE LINES, which starred Sydney Ayres.

"A Western comedy with sufficient plot to enable Tom Mix to put across an exciting break-neck race between two coaches. The prize is an express contract and the heart of a girl both stage owners love. Each stage coach breaks down, and the two rivals lose the contract and the girl, but the

TOM MIX
in
"THE WAGON TRAIL"
Formerly
"THE DAYS OF THE THUNDERING HERD"

Above: Tom's first feature was a five-reel epic of wagon trains and Buffalo hunts called *In the Days of the Thundering Herd*. Directed by Colin Campbell, who was responsible for Selig's eight-reel version of *The Spoilers*, the film was a stodgy exercise that did not show Tom Mix to best advantage. As a result, it would be two years before the studio put the Western star in another feature. *In the Days of the Thundering Herd* was reissued in the '20s by Aywon Film Corporation as a three-reeler with the title *The Wagon Trail*.

Right: Two cowboys discover that Cactus Jim's girlfriend is a mannequin. Sid Jordan (left), the window dummy, and an unidentified cowboy (possibly Roy Watson) in *Cactus Jim's Shop Girl*. Most of the films Tom Mix wrote and directed for Selig were light situation comedies rather than action pictures.

misfortune turns them from bitter enemies into close friends."

Motion Picture News, 12/5/14

SAVED BY A WATCH

Selig Polyscope Company. Released December 8, 1914 through General Film Company. *Length:* 1 reel

Director: Tom Mix. *Scenario:* Tom Mix.

Cast: Tom Mix (Tom), Goldie Colwell (Alice), Leo D. Maloney (Heffron), Inez Walker (Alice's Mother).

"A Tom Mix picture which includes a stagecoach robbery and other diverting incidents. The hero is saved from death when a bullet strikes a watch in which he has a picture of the heroine. . ."

Motion Picture News, 12/12/14

THE MAN FROM THE EAST

Selig Polyscope Company. Released December 15, 1914 through General Film Company. *Length:* 1 reel

Director: Tom Mix. *Scenario:* Tom Mix.

Cast: Tom Mix (Tom Bates), Goldie Colwell (May), Leo D. Maloney (ranch foreman), Pat Chrisman (stage driver), Inez Walker (May's aunt), R. H. Kelly (tough), C. W. Bachman (valet), Ed "Hoot" Gibson (butler), Ed "Pardner" Jones (hotel keeper), Susie Morella (maid).

Production number: C-460

"As a result of a misunderstanding between Tom Mix and his fiance in the East, Tom returns to his former life of a Western cowboy. His sweetheart soon learns of her mistake. While she is on her way to visit an aunt on a Western ranch, Tom rescues her from a runaway stage coach, and they are happily reunited. The rescue is a remarkable piece of dare-devil riding."

Motion Picture News, 12/19/14

CACTUS JAKE, HEART-BREAKER

Selig Polyscope Company. Released December 29, 1914 through General Film Company. *Length:* 1 reel

Director: Tom Mix. *Scenario:* Edwin Ray Coffin.

Cast: Tom Mix (Bill), Goldie Colwell (Hazel Clark), Leo D. Maloney (Cactus Jake) , Josephine Miller (Mary Donelly).

"Hazel Clark, belle of the Diamond 'S' Ranch, is fascinated by Cactus Jake, a bold, dashing, reckless cowboy. Good-natured Bill, another cowpuncher, is really in love with Hazel. Mary Donelly, a very pretty and clever girl, who states that she comes from the East and is in search of health, becomes a guest at the ranch, whereupon Cactus Jake promptly forgets Hazel for the newcomer. Hazel is heartbroken and with the aid of her father, forms a plot for revenge. She announces that she is going away for a visit, but goes only to the next town where she obtains a false mustache and other disguises, and returns to the ranch where her father gives her employment as a gay and dashing young cowpuncher.

"She endeavors to win Mary away from Cactus Jake. One day her mustache falls off and her disguise is discovered. Bridget, a fearsome and red-headed, bony Irish woman, enters the camp at this time and corrals Cactus Jake, who is her recreant husband. Pretty Mary proves to be a female detective. Bill then wins the heart of Hazel."

Selig release bulletin

1915 _____

A MILITANT SCHOOLMA'AM

Selig Polyscope Company. Released January 5, 1915 through General Film Company. *Length:* 1 reel

Director: Tom Mix. *Scenario:* Edwin Ray Coffin

Cast: Leo Maloney (Jerald Bruce/the new schoolma'am), Goldie Colwell (Ruth Winter).

Note: Tom Mix directed this film but apparently did not appear in it.

"Jerald Bruce, a motion picture actor, has a dispute with his director, and as a result, Jerald joins the ranks of the unemployed. He learns that a school teacher is wanted in the range country and applies for the position to Ted Winter, a ranchman who is the school director. Jerald lands the job and also wins the admiration of Ruth Winter, the school director's daughter. Bill Benton, a neighboring rancher, is very much in love with Ruth and her father encourages him.

"Ruth falls head over ears in love with Jerald, and, as she is still attending school, they find many opportunities for courtship. Jerald compels her to stay after school. Old man Winter catches them love-making and promptly fires the schoolmaster. Jerald has his make-up box with him and, after dressing up as a girl, again applies for the position. This time as a schoolma'am, and gets the job. He has a great time spanking cowboy pupils. With the aid of Ruth, who does not suspect his disguise, he rounds up and captures a devastating cattle thief, who is none other than Bill Benton."

The Moving Picture World, 1/9/15

HAROLD'S BAD MAN

Selig Polyscope Company. Released January 12, 1915 through General Film Company. *Length:* 1 reel

Director: Tom Mix. *Scenario:* Edwin Ray Coffin

Cast: Tom Mix, Goldie Colwell, Sid Jordan, Ed Jones.

Production number: C-465

"This comedy picture contains some good points. A man who is elected sheriff has a daughter who has a lover, to whom the father objects. When it comes to a show down, the sheriff is lacking in nerve, although he is a great 'hornblower.' There is a bandit to be captured and the daughter and her sweetheart corral him, giving credit to the old man, winning his consent to their marriage. This is a satisfactory and well produced comedy."

The Moving Picture World, 1/30/15

CACTUS JIM'S SHOP GIRL

Selig Polyscope Company. Released January 19, 1915 through General Film Company. *Length:* 1 reel

Director: Tom Mix. *Scenario:* Edwin Ray Coffin.

Cast: Tom Mix (Cactus Jim), Goldie Colwell (Nell Morton), Sid Jordan (a ranch hand).

Production number: C-467

"Cactus Jim is tired of being a bachelor. He advertises in a newspaper for a wife and in response receives a telegram from Nell Morton, a shopgirl in the city, who bids him come at once, as she is willing to comply with the requirements of the advertisement. Jim shows this telegram to his fellow cowpunchers and excites their jealousy.

"When Jim appears in the store before Nell, all dolled up in his holiday attire, his appearance does not strike her favorably and she decides not to go further in the compact. While urging her to reconsider the matter, an angry customer intrudes and declares that Nell has short-changed her. She is fired.

"Cactus Jim considers this Rank injustice and he privately tells the floorwalker so, giving him the money to make up the shortage in Nell's wages.

"But Cactus Jim desires to avoid the laughter of his brother cowpunchers; so he buys a dummy figure, takes it home and pretends that it is his bride. However, the boys discover his ruse, but as Nell has a change of heart, she accepts Jim and makes him happy."

The Moving Picture World, 1/16/15

THE GRIZZLY GULCH CHARIOT RACE

Selig Polyscope Company. Released January 26, 1915 through General Film Company. *Length:* 1 reel

Director: Tom Mix. *Scenario:* O. A. Nelson.

Cast: Tom Mix, Inez Walker, Sid Jordan, Dick Crawford, Roy Watson.

Note: Elements of this story were re-worked in A ROMAN COWBOY (Fox, 1917).

"Pettie Lamm, a buxom maid of generous proportions and of uncertain age, is the belle of a western town where cowboys congregate. Tad and Joe are rivals for her hand, and their chances seem to be about equal, while Shrimp, another cowboy, is also a faithful suitor.

"However, because of Shrimp's lack of physical prowess, Tad and Joe inflict all sorts of ignominy upon Shrimp whenever they catch him in the vicinity of the fair Miss Lamm's domicile.

"She finally tells Tad and Joe that the one who shall win a chariot race may have her hand in marriage. With ingenuity, but without much skill, they construct two rather grotesque chariots with which to contest for her hand. The day for the race is set.

"The wily Shrimp inveigles the fair Pettie to the office of the Justice of the Peace, where they are quietly married. The chariot race ends in a smash for all concerned. Shrimp wins the bride."

The Moving Picture World, 1/23/15

Above: (l-r) Pat Chrisman at the Selig Polyscope camera, Sid Jordan, ?, Tom Mix, ?, William Fawcett, Louella Maxam, Dick Hunter, Ed 'Pardner' Jones, and 'Dopey Dick' Crawford in *Bill Haywood, Producer*. The word producer was used as the term director is used today.

Right: Tom Mix gets the drop on *Harold's Bad Man* (played by Sid Jordan) as a frightened Goldie Colwell looks on.

Above: Tom and Sid Jordan engage in a boot pulling contest for a scene missing from surviving prints of *Roping a Bride*. In the background (l-r): unidentified cowboy (possibly Roy Watson), C. W. Bachmann, 'Dopey' Dick Crawford, Ed 'Pardner' Jones, Pat Chrisman, and Dick Hunter.

Right: The course of true love never did run smooth. Sid Jordan (left) and Tom Mix are rivals for the rancher's daughter (Goldie Colwell) in *Roping a Bride*. With little variation, this simple situation served as the basis for most of Tom's Selig pictures. *Roping a Bride* was remade by Tom little more than a year later as *Roping a Sweetheart* with Victoria Forde in the Goldie Colwell role.

FORKED TRAILS

Selig Polyscope Company. Released February 2, 1915 through General Film Company. *Length:* 1 reel

Director: Tom Mix. *Story:* William MacLeod Raine.

Cast: Tom Mix

"There are some points of excellence in this picture, but there are also a number of weak points which might have been avoided. For instance, at the point where the Mexican enters the cabin where the girl has gone to hide and she lays the revolver on the table while she tries to tie his hands is rather a weak bit. At other points of the picture one is inclined to admire the quality of the work. Photographically speaking the production is good, and throughout many artistic scenes appear."

The Moving Picture World, 2/20/15

ROPING A BRIDE

Selig Polyscope Company. Released February 9, 1915 through General Film Company. *Length:* 1 reel

Director: Tom Mix. *Scenario:* E. Lynn Summers.

Cast: Tom Mix, Sid Jordan, Goldie Colwell, C. W. Bachman, Roy Watson, Inez Walker.

Production number: C-466

Note: Remade by Tom Mix in 1916 as ROPING A SWEETHEART

Tom and Sid are rivals for the hand of Goldie, and the poor girl cannot choose the one she likes best. The cowboys suggest a roping contest. Whoever ropes Goldie first will win her hand. The girl agrees, but when Tom wins she refuses his attentions, and when Sid tries to make time, she spurns him too.

BILL HAYWOOD, PRODUCER

Selig Polyscope Company. Released February 16, 1915 through General Film Company. *Length:* 1 reel

Director: Tom Mix. *Scenario:* Cecilie B. Peterson.

Cast: Tom Mix (Bill Haywood), Sid Jordan, George Fawcett, Pat Chrisman, Dick Hunter, Dick Crawford, Ed "Pardner" Jones.

Production number: C-469

Note: Reissued as MR. HAYWOOD, PRODUCER

"Bill Haywood is ambitious to become a motion picture producer. He writes a scenario, which, considering the results, must have been awful, and sends same to a motion picture concern for approval. The scenario is hurled back to him with unmitigated scorn, as there is nothing to commend it. Bill is stubborn as well as ambitious. He engages a company of stranded actors, buys a second-hand camera, and proceeds to produce his own picture.

"The scenario is highly melodramatic and is entitled to be called 'yellowdrama.' Bill falls in love with the leading lady and steps in all the pitfalls which surround him. He dresses his cowboy friends in evening clothes to do society 'stunts' and when the film is finished it is a 'bird.' The camera man films some of Bill's love scenes with the pretty leading lady, thinking them to be part of the picture. He also neglects certain scenes that he did not think belonged in the picture."

The Moving Picture World, 2/13/15

SLIM HIGGINS

Selig Polyscope Company. Released February 23, 1915 through General Film Company. *Length:* 1 reel

Director: Tom Mix. *Scenario:* Tom Mix.

Cast: Tom Mix ("Slim" Higgins).

Production number: C-470

Note: This story also served as the basis for the opening reel of A CORNER IN WATER, a Tom Mix two-reeler released September 23, 1916.

"Slim Higgins bears the reputation of a hard character out in the West. He is placarded as a desperate fighter, who is quick in drawing his six- shooter. The citizens are warned against him.

"An old settler and his pretty daughter are driving across the desert in their prairie schooner, exhausted and weary for lack of water and rest. They do not dare to stop because to stop would mean death among the sand hills; so they drive on in the hope of finding water.

"Pete Lawson, a disreputable semi-bandit, has discovered a pre-empted water hole. He will not permit anybody to take water unless they pay for it. He attacks the settler and his daughter. "Slim" witnesses the episode and rights the wrong by force of arms. He falls in love with the settler's daughter and decides to reform."

The Moving Picture World, 2/20/15

A CHILD OF THE PRAIRIE

Selig Polyscope Company. Released March 1, 1915 through General Film Company. *Length:* 2 reels

Director: Tom Mix. *Scenario:* Tom Mix.

Cast: Tom Mix (Tom Martin), Louella Maxam (his wife), Baby Norma Maxam (Ruth, their baby), Louella Maxam (Ruth, fifteen years later), E. J. Brady (the gambler).

Note: Second use of title. Different from 1913 film of the same name.

Production Number: C-473-4

"Tom Martin, a young rancher, has a wife and a small child. Unknown to Tom, his wife has become infatuated with a gambler, who, during Tom's absence from home, calls on the wife and tries to persuade her to leave with him. She refuses, and the gambler plots to get rid of Tom.

"He hires a team of horses and a buggy and goes to the gambling room of the saloon. Under a table he places a revolver with the barrel through a hole, ties a string to the trigger and when Tom enters later, he is invited to play cards. The gambler forces a quarrel, and Tom starts to pull his revolver when the gambler pulls the string and Tom is shot from under the table. The gambler then goes to Tom's home, tells Tom's wife her husband has been killed and takes her and the little one away.

"In packing her household goods, Tom's wife drops a baby dress, and the gambler tears up and leaves behind un-thinkingly, an old photograph of himself. In the hurried escape the baby wanders away and becomes lost, and as the gambler fears to remain and search for the child, he forces the woman into the buggy and drives away. Later, cowboys find the lost child. Tom recovers, goes to his home and finds the dress and torn photograph of the gambler. He makes up his mind that some day he will find the despoiler of his home.

"Fifteen years later Tom is sheriff of the county and he receives a letter telling him to arrest the man whose picture is enclosed. He recognizes the photograph as that of the gambler. He starts out to find the man when he sees a young girl in a runaway team. He rides to the side of the onrushing wagon and at his command the girl jumps to his arms. He sees in her a resemblance to his lost baby and tells her of it.

"Later, Tom encounters the gambler in town. There is an exchange of shots, and the bullet from the gambler's revolver shatters a lamp just above Tom's head, while the bullet Tom fires reaches the mark. The dying crook tells Tom of how the child was lost, and so father and daughter are finally reunited."

The Moving Picture World, 3/6/15

THE MAN FROM TEXAS

Selig Polyscope Company. Released March 2, 1915 through General Film Company. *Length:* 1 reel

Director: Tom Mix. *Scenario:* Tom Mix.

Cast: Tom Mix (The Man From Texas), Goldie Colwell (The Girl), Louella Maxam (The Sister), E. J. Brady (The Gambler).

Production Number: C-471

"The sister of 'The Man from Texas,' supposedly married to an unscrupulous gambler, is deserted, and before death relieves her, she writes a letter to her brother, who is a cowboy, enclosing a picture of the man who betrayed her. The brother leaves at once for the little frontier town, but arrives too late for death had won in the race.

"The gambler goes forth and arrives on a Montana ranch, where, in search of a new victim, he meets a beautiful girl. He makes love to her and they go horseback riding together. At an isolated spot he endeavors to force his attentions upon the girl and his action is seen by 'The Man from Texas.' He rushes to the girl's assistance, fells the brute and escorts her safely home. The gambler and the Texan later meet, and in self-preservation the gambler meets death from a bullet fired by "The Man from Texas.""

The Moving Picture World, 3/6/15

THE STAGE-COACH DRIVER AND THE GIRL

Selig Polyscope Company. Released March 9, 1915 through General Film Company. *Length:* 1 reel

Director: Tom Mix. *Scenario:* Tom Mix.

Cast: Louella Maxam (Edythe, the girl from the East), Tom Mix (Tom, the stage-coach driver), Goldie Colwell (Alice, his sister), E. J. Brady (the gambler), Ed Jones (sheriff).

Production number: C-472

"Edythe, an eastern girl, receives an invitation from Alice, her school days' chum, to visit her in the west. Alice sends a photograph of her brother Tom, who is a stage-coach driver.

"The gambler finds a letter lost by Tom, telling of the arrival of a shipment of money. With the aid of bandits he resolves to overtake the stage-coach on its return trip.

"Tom meets Edythe at the station, and gets the express box, and they start on their homeward journey. In the wilderness a wheel is broken. and as Tom is fixing it, he spies the bandits on a distant hill. There is a wild drive, and the pursuing bandits shoot down a horse. The horse is taken from the harness and the journey is continued with three horses until the front wheel comes off and the stage-coach upsets throwing Edythe and Tom to the ground. Bullets are flying around Tom and Edythe and one strikes Tom in the arm.

"However, the stage-coach guard gets the sheriff and posse in time capturing two of the bandits. The stage-coach driver is rewarded by the affections of his beautiful girl passenger."

The Moving Picture World, 3/13/15

SAGE-BRUSH TOM

Selig Polyscope Company. Released March 16, 1915 through General Film Company. *Length:* 1 reel

Director: Tom Mix. *Scenario:* Tom Mix.

Cast: Tom Mix (Sage-brush Tom), Goldie Colwell (moving picture actress), E. J. Brady (heavy man).

Note: Eugenie Forde was originally scheduled to play the part of the moving picture actress, but Goldie Colwell finally played the role.

Production number: C-480

"Sage-Brush Tom admires a moving picture actress. He buys a postal card photograph and worships it. Her company is engaged to take some motion pictures on the ranch where Sage-Brush works. He runs into the leading lady, and falls more in love with her, but the heavy-man objects, and they have a spirited fight.

"Tom wants to qualify as an actor, and is told that he must seize a bull by the horns and throw the animal like Ursus did in Quo Vadis. Tom ties a stuffed figure to the horns of a powerful young bull, and then practices trying to throw the bull, in which effort he is unsuccessful. His friends peer through the corral fence and joke him about his failure to throw the bull.

"Then Tom learns that the leading actress is already married; so he destroys her photograph and returns to cowpunching."

The Moving Picture World, 3/13/15

THE OUTLAW'S BRIDE

Selig Polyscope Company. Released March 23, 1915 through General Film Company. *Length:* 1 reel

Director: Tom Mix. *Scenario:* Cornelius Shea.

Cast: Tom Mix (Richard Sharpe), E. J. Brady (Dan Calvert), Pat Chrisman (Medford), Eugenie Forde (Jessie).

"Dan Calvert, an outlaw, comes with his plunder to the shack of old man Medford, who has a lovely daughter named Jessie. Calvert, in his plunder, finds money and a letter addressed to Richard Sharpe, who is on the outlaw's trail. Medford consents to the outlaw's marriage to his daughter in return for a sum of money. The outlaw gets the minister, and Sharpe, the sheriff, follows them. While the minister marries the outlaw and Jessie, the sheriff, who has climbed the shack roof, falls through and is taken prisoner. Calvert and his followers take the sheriff into the mountains and dispose of him, and Jessie and a guard are left to watch the camp.

"The outlaws ride along a ridge, the sheriff jumps bound from his horse, rolls down hill and escapes. Jessie has managed to escape and encounters the sheriff. There is a gun battle in which the sheriff kills the outlaw chief, and routs the others. Medford is remorseful and starts out to find Jessie. He meets her with the sheriff and begs her forgiveness. Reconciliation follows and Jessie and the sheriff plight their troth."

The Moving Picture World, 3/20/15

MA'S GIRLS

Selig Polyscope Company. Released March 29, 1915 through General Film Company. *Length:* 2 reels

Director: Tom Mix. *Scenario:* Tom Mix.

Cast: Tom Mix (The Gambler), Goldie Colwell (Madge), Louella Maxam (Rose), Eugenie Forde (Ma), Edward Brady (The Assayer).

Production number: C-475-6

"Ma and Dad, with their two daughters, live in a cottage in a small western town. The sheriff is a friend of the family and a frequent visitor. Tom, the gambler, has tried to force his attention on Madge and Rose. The gambler plays cards in a bar-room with an assayer, and breaks him. Thereupon the assayer decides to end his life, but the gambler advances him some money, and the assayer signs an I.O.U. for the amount. Dad owns a small mine in the hills, and the assayer, who is out walking, sees Dad working in the mine. The assayer approaches, finds a valuable piece of quartz, and hurries off to assay it. Soon afterward, Dad also finds that the ore is rich, and goes to town to have it assayed.

"Madge and Rose ride to town on horseback, and as they are about to enter a store, the gambler approaches and tries to force his attentions on Rose. The sheriff see the gambler's actions, and warns him about insulting the girls in the future. The assayer upon his return, finds a note from the gambler that if he can tip him to some rich mine and keep the owner in the dark, he will cancel the I.O.U. he holds against him. Dad enters with his sample of ore. He is told by the assayer that it is worthless. When Dad leaves, the assayer looks up the gambler, tips him off to Dad's rich mine, and both visit Dad's mine. In the meantime, Dad has assayed the sample of ore at home, and when the gambler calls and tries to buy the mine, Dad refuses to sell it.

"The gambler sees Madge and Rose riding home on horseback, and attacks Madge. Rose hears Madge's screams, rides back, throws her lariat over the gambler, and drags him by her horse across the ford. The following day the gambler visits a camp of renegades, and induces them to capture the two girls, and bring them to camp. Ma, becoming alarmed at their absence, mounts a horse and goes in search of them. She notifies the sheriff, who forms a posse, and led by Ma they start after the renegades. Ma kills the gambler in a running fight, after which Ma and the posse find the girls safe. The sheriff marries rose, while Ma keeps Madge for herself."

The Moving Picture World, 3/27/15

THE LEGAL LIGHT

Selig Polyscope Company. Released March 30, 1915 through General Film Company. *Length:* 1 reel

Director: Tom Mix. *Scenario:* Edwin Ray Coffin.

Cast: Tom Mix (Pete), Eugenie Forde (Carrie Simpkins), E. J. Brady (Smithers).

"Carrie Simpkins, a lady lawyer, arrives in a small western town and begins the practice of law. Pete, Jake, and Jerry, three cowboys, fall in love with her but do not progress. Smithers, the pioneer town lawyer happens by and sees the sign, 'Carrie Simpkins, Lawyer,' and decides to pay her a visit, which he does, and he also falls in love with her.

"Pete, Jake and Jerry all hit upon the same plan unbeknown to each other, which will help their chances with Carrie. They scheme to rob the town grocery store at night, and leave something behind that will convict them of the crime. That night two professional crooks, who have arrived in town that day, rob the grocery store. Pete arrives on the scene and discovers the robbery and leaves his spurs behind as evidence that he did it. Jerry arrives, sneaks into the store and leaves his six-shooter behind as evidence that he is the culprit. Then Jake makes his way into the store and leaves his revolver behind as evidence that he performed the deed.

"The storekeeper opens his establishment next morning and calls the sheriff. The officer places Pete, Jake and Jerry under arrest with their guns and spurs as evidence against them. In the meantime, Smithers, the town lawyer, has been ardently pressing his lovesuit with Carrie Simpkins with the result that they get married. The three cowpunchers in court ask for Carrie to defend them and the sheriff goes for her. He returns with Smithers, who smilingly tells the three boys that he has just married Carrie but would be pleased to defend them himself. This is too much for the boys to stand, and they fall back and collapse while Smithers looks on and laughs."

The Moving Picture World, 3/27/15

GETTING A START IN LIFE

Selig Polyscope Company. Released April 6, 1915 through General Film Company. *Length:* 1 reel

Director: Tom Mix. *Story:* James Oliver Curwood.

Cast: Tom Mix (Tom), Louella Maxam (Elizabeth Spunk), Sid Jordan (Jerry).

"A James Curwood comedy and an exceptionally breezy one. Expansive fun runs riot through the reel, the efforts of the Westerners to win the lady from the East, after stocking her home for her, is in the right comedy vein. . ."

The Moving Picture World, April 24, 1915

MRS. MURPHY'S COOKS

Selig Polyscope Company. Released April 13, 1915 through General Film Company. *Length:* 1 reel

Director: Tom Mix. *Scenario:* Tom Mix.

Cast: Tom Mix (Buck Martin), Louella Maxam (Louella Maxam), Anna Dodge (Mrs. Murphy).

Production number: C-485

Note: A remake of GO WEST, YOUNG WOMAN, GO WEST, made in 1910.

"Tom Mix, Louella Maxam and Anna Dodge have the leading roles in this one-reel farce, that raises a gale of laughter by its breezy humor. A real human touch, which underlies the extravagance of the situations, adds to the effectiveness of the fun."

The Moving Picture World, 5/1/15

THE CONVERSION OF SMILING TOM

Selig Polyscope Company. Released April 20, 1915 through General Film Company. *Length:* 1 reel

Director: Tom Mix. *Scenario:* Emma Bell.

Cast: Tom Mix (Smiling Tom), Eugenie Forde (Widow Wilson), Louella Maxam (Widow Wilson's daughter), William Brunton (Hiram Flint, lawyer), Sid Jordan.

Production number: C-484

"Hiram Flint is about to foreclose a mortgage on widow Wilson's ranch. Maude, the widow's daughter, pleads with Flint for further time. He says he might consider it and tries to make love to the girl, who spurns him. This enrages the lawyer, who says that if the mortgage is not paid by four o'clock that day he will take the place.

"The sheriff has received word to arrest "Smiling" Tom, who is wanted by the sheriff of another county. "Smiling" Tom and his partner are near the Wilson home and both are hungry. The widow Wilson receives them kindly, and gives them food. She later tells "Smiling" Tom of the lawyer's threat, whereupon Tom gives Mrs. Wilson the money to pay Flint, and then he and his partner depart.

"When Flint calls, the widow gives him five hundred dollar bills, and Flint leaves. "Smiling" Tom has decided to waylay Flint, and he and his partner rope the lawyer, drag him off his horse and take his money. A posse is formed, and Tom and his partner are cornered. Maude hears the shooting, and persuades the sheriff to let her speak to Tom. She induces "Smiling" Tom to surrender and promise to be a better man."

The Moving Picture World, April 24, 1915

AN ARIZONA WOOING

Selig Polyscope Company. Released May 4, 1915 through General Film Company. *Length:* 1 reel

Director: Tom Mix. *Scenario:* William MacLeod Raine.

Cast: Tom Mix (Tom Warner), Pat Chrisman (Manuel Paquito), Louella Maxam (Jean Dixon), Billy Brunton (Thomas Dixon)

"Manuel Paquito and Tom Warner are rivals for the love of Jean Dixon. Knowing that Paquito is an outlaw, Jean favors

Warner. In difficulties with the cattlemen, Tom Warner is captured by them one night; they peg him out on the desert to starve him to surrender. Paquito finds Warner and tortures him. Jean comes upon the scene and is forced by Paquito to promise to marry him, or see her lover killed. She reluctantly chooses the former.

"Dixon, Jean's father, returns to Warner, who tells him what has happened. Together, they summon the other cattlemen and start to run down the Mexican. Paquito and Jean reach the nearest village and ride to the house of a clergyman. However, Tom and Dixon ride up in time to prevent the marriage. After a revolver duel, the Mexican is captured and is forced to stand by and see the marriage of his rival to Jean."

Selig Monthly Herald, May, 1915

A MATRIMONIAL BOOMERANG

Selig Polyscope Company. Released May 14, 1915 through General Film Company. *Length:* 1 reel

Director: Tom Mix. *Scenario:* Edith Blumer.

Cast: Tom Mix (Tom Champion), Louella Maxam (Grace), Pat Chrisman (cowboy leader), Howard Farrell (Justice of the Peace)

"Grace, a school teacher, supports a delicate mother, and accepts a position to teach the Coyoteville school. When she arrives, she is driven to a boarding house by Tom Champion, the sheriff, who falls in love with her. Tom arrests Big Bill and other cowboys for gambling and they swear vengeance.

"Seeking refuge from a band of half drunken cowboys, Grace rushes into a notion store kept by Mrs. Leslie, a broken down actress. Mrs. Leslie tells her that she is too beautiful to be safe and disguises her as a hideous old hag, so that she may walk home unmolested. Tom Champion is taken prisoner by the cowboys. Big Bill sees Grace, disguised as a hideous old hag, coming along the road. He has an inspiration and gives Tom the choice of being hanged to a tree or married to the old hag. Tom, of course, chooses the latter. A marriage license is issued and the ceremony performed, and later it is found that the old hag is in reality the pretty schoolma'am. The cowboys are beaten at their own game."

Selig Monthly Herald, May, 1915

SAVED BY HER HORSE

Selig Polyscope Company. Released June 8, 1915 through General Film Company. *Length:* 1 reel

Above: Sid Jordan, Tom Mix and Louella Maxam in *The Conversion of Smiling Tom.*

Right: Tom was a sheepherder in *An Arizona Wooing.*

Below: Tom and his cowboys 'salt' some oil to stimulate the bidding on *The Auction Sale of Run-Down Ranch.*

Director: Tom Mix. *Scenario:* Cornelius Shea.

Cast: Tom Mix (Tom Golden), Louella Maxam (Nell Dodge), Sid Jordan (Captain of the Cavalry), Pat Chrisman (Indian Chief), Tony (a horse)

"A party of settlers emigrating westward with a wagon train to find new homes, go into camp for the night. Tom Golden bids his sweetheart, Nell, goodbye and rides off into the hills to look for hostile Indians.

"Savages are discovered. Nell offers to go for help, and is captured by Indians after her horse escapes. The horse, Tony, finds Nell's hat and carries it to the settler's camp, in his mouth. Tom Golden starts in search of Nell, with Nell's horse leading the way. Tom sees a cavalry camp in the hills and he rides thereto and tells the captain that an attack by Indians is feared.

"Nell's horse, Tony, runs to the Indian camp; Nell hears him neigh and she whistles. He runs to her, and she mounts him and starts to find help. The troop of cavalry arrive, with Tom in the lead, the Indians are routed, Tom and Nell have a happy reunion."

Selig Monthly Herald, June, 1915

PALS IN BLUE

Selig Polyscope Company. Released June 10, 1915 through General Film Company. *Length:* 3 reels

Director: Tom Mix. *Scenario:* Tom Mix.

Cast: Tom Mix (Tom), Sid Jordan (Lieutenant Manning), Eugenie Forde (Manning's wife), Howard Farrell (recruiting officer), Pat Chrisman (Indian Chief)

". . . Tom and Jerry, pals on a ranch in the West, go to the city where they fall easy victim to crooks, and, after getting into trouble, are sent to jail. Upon being freed they join the Army and are sent to Arizona. The commander of the post to which they belong forces his attentions on an inferior officer's wife. When exposed, he arranges a plan whereby the minor officer and a small company fall in the hands of raiding Indians. Tom and Jerry are in the party and ride to the fort for help. Jerry is killed but Tom reaches the fort in time to send re-enforcements and also to shoot the officer who has clasped the other man's wife in his embrace."

Selig Monthly Herald Clip Sheet, June, 1915

THE HEART OF THE SHERIFF

Selig Polyscope Company. Released June 15, 1915 through General Film Company. *Length:* 1 reel

Director: Tom Mix. *Scenario:* Tom Mix.

Cast: Tom Mix (Sheriff Martin), Sid Jordan (Buck Gibson), Louella Maxam (Grace Martin).

Production number: C-491

"Grace Martin, the adopted daughter of Sheriff Martin, was rescued by him from a band of Indians when she was an infant. She is in love with Buck Gibson. Grace asks the Sheriff's consent to marry Buck, and his thoughts revert back to the time when he saved Grace from Indians. He gives his consent to Grace's request to marry Gibson, and Grace runs away happy to tell her lover of the good news.

"That night Buck Gibson and some pals rob the town bank, and Buck is identified as one of the bandits. Sheriff Martin is notified and organizing a posse, gives chase, overtakes the robbers, and starts in pursuit of Buck who tries to escape alone after the others are captured. Sheriff Martin kills Buck Gibson. Grace, who has ridden away in hopes of finding her sweetheart comes upon her father standing over the dead body. She understands that Buck is guilty, and turns to the Sheriff, who takes the little girl home the second time."

Selig Monthly Herald, June, 1915

WITH THE AID OF THE LAW

Selig Polyscope Company. Released June 22, 1915 through General Film Company. *Length:* 1 reel

Director: Tom Mix. *Scenario:* Marshall E. Gamon.

Cast: Tom Mix (Lee Russell), Sid Jordan (Jeff Smith), Louella Maxam (Rose Butler), Pat Chrisman (Joe Butler).

"A moonshine-detective story varying little from the average production of this kind. There is much action and fitting acting throughout the reel. The mountain scenes are most pleasing. It is one of Tom Mix's dramas."

Motion Picture News, 6/26/15

THE FOREMAN OF THE BAR Z RANCH

Selig Polyscope Company. Released July 20, 1915 through General Film Company. *Length:* 1 reel

Director: Tom Mix. *Scenario:* Wallace C. Clifton.

Cast: Tom Mix (Tom Wallace), Louella Maxam (Fern Watkins), Bob Anderson (Sheriff Watkins), Pat Chrisman (Miguel Garcia).

Production number: C-523

"Tom Wallace lives with his uncle, John Higgins, and Tom is the sole heir to his uncle's wealth. Joe Watkins, the sheriff, and Higgins are life-long enemies, and when Higgins discovers that Tom is in love with Fern Watkins, he threatens to disinherit Tom.

"Marie and Miguel Garcia have purchased a farm from Higgins on the installment plan and Marie works hard to meet the payments, while Miguel spends his time in the town dance hall. Miguel wanting money for his revelries decides to rob Higgins. Higgins surprises Miguel in the act of robbing him, and Miguel shoots and kills Higgins and escapes.

"Cowboys find Higgins' dead body, and Tom is accused of murder. The party come upon the dead body of Miguel who had fallen off a cliff. The sheriff finds the money and tells Tom he is sorry he accused him. Fern pleads her love for Tom and her father relents."

Selig Monthly Herald, July 15, 1915

THE CHILD, THE DOG, AND THE VILLAIN

Selig Polyscope Company. Released July 27, 1915 through General Film Company. *Length:* 1 reel

Director: Tom Mix. *Scenario:* Campbell MacCulloch.

Cast: Sid Jordan (John Temple), Leo Maloney (Burnes), Pat Chrisman (Pedro Alvarez), Pearl Hoxie (The Little Girl)

Note: Tom Mix directed this film but did not appear in it.

"John Temple, owner of the Eagle Mining Company, decides to close down the mine and posts a notification to that effect. Pedro Alvarez, foreman of the mine, kicks a tramp named Burnes, out of the saloon. He has noticed the notification posted by Temple and incites the miners to riot. Temple refuses to negotiate with them.

"Burnes, the tramp, weak from hunger, falls exhausted in front of the Temples' home, and is cared for by Mrs. Temple. Alvarez and his gang overpower Temple in his office, and leave to blow up the mine. Burnes finds Temple bound and frees him.

"Temple's little girl has wandered away in search of her dog. Alvarez encounters the child and decides to kidnap her, but the dog saves the child. Temple telephones for the Sheriff, who arrives just in time to capture the outlaws. The tramp is given a good position in the mines by Temple."

Selig Monthly Herald, 7/15/15

THE TAKING OF MUSTANG PETE

Selig Polyscope Company. Released August 3, 1915 through General Film Company. *Length:* 1 reel

Director: Tom Mix. *Scenario:* Emma Bell.

Cast: Leo D. Maloney (Jim Bradley), Louella Maxam (Ruth Bradley), Henry Pagett (Tom Lacey), Pat Chrisman (Mustang Pete).

Production number: C-526

Note: Tom Mix directed this film but did not appear in it.

"Sheriff Jim Bradley is visited by his sister, Ruth, from the East, and all the cowboys are infatuated with the beautiful girl. A reward of $100.00 has been offered for the capture of Mustang Pete, a desperate train robber. Ruth tells her brother that she has not yet seen a real cowboy. To play a joke on his sister, the Sheriff has Bill Daily disguise himself like Mustang Pete and call on Ruth. Bill encounters the real Mustang Pete and is overcome.

"Mustang Pete visits the sheriff's house and orders food from Ruth. Her brother and the boys have witnessed the performance and thinking it is Bill, the cowboy, enjoy a laugh with a view of joshing Ruth about it the next day.

"Sheriff Tom Lacey of Tulare County is also on the lookout for Mustang Pete and captures him. Bill has recovered consciousness and goes back to tell the sheriff. He meets the boys and they start out after the real Mustang Pete. Then it is they discover that Sheriff Lacy has captured the bandit, who was once in their power."

Selig Monthly Herald, August 1, 1915

THE GOLD DUST AND THE SQUAW

Selig Polyscope Company. Released August 10, 1915 through General Film Company. *Length:* 1 reel

Director: Tom Mix. *Scenario:* Cornelius Shea.

Cast: Sid Jordan (Bob), Leo Maloney (Ned), Pat Chrisman (Lame Dog), Bob Anderson (Tall Elk), Bettie O'Neal (Hazel)

Note: Tom Mix directed this film but did not appear in it.

Production Number: C-529

"Ned and Bob strike it rich and hide the bags of gold dust under the floor in a shanty. When Ned leaves to tell Hazel of his good luck, Bob plots to take the gold. With the aid of Lame Dog, an Indian, he buries the gold in the woods. They are overseen by Little Fawn, a squaw. Bob has Lame Dog tie him fast to the floor in the shanty.

"Hazel and Ned arrive at the shack and find Bob helpless. Bob explains that he was overpowered by Indians and the gold was stolen. Little Fawn, captured by Lame Dog, escapes and falls over the edge of a cliff. Her dress catches on a tree. Ned, Hazel, and Bob discover her, and Ned lowers himself on a rope to rescue her. Bob decides to cut the rope and let his partner fall to his doom, when Tall Elk, an Indian who loves Little Fawn, sees the act and shoots Bob. Tall Elk pulls Ned and Little Fawn to safety, and Little Fawn shows Ned where the gold is hidden."

Selig Monthly Herald, August 1, 1915

A LUCKY DEAL

Selig Polyscope Company. Released August 21, 1915 through General Film Company. *Length:* 1 reel

Director: Tom Mix. *Scenario:* Tom Mix.

Cast: Leo Maloney (Joe), Sid Jordan (Doc), Pat Chrisman (Rustler Jack), Bettie O'Neal (Hazel).

Production number: 528

Note: Tom Mix directed this film but did not appear in it.

"Joe and Doc, partners in a mining town, are both in love with Hazel, daughter of the town storekeeper. Doc, believing he has no opportunity to win Hazel, sells his half of the claim to Joe for $200. Joe leaves town to work the claim further and rides a valuable horse he owns. Rustler Jack follows Joe to the claim with the object of stealing his horse. The horse paws over the ground and knocks over some rocks, revealing some rich ore. Joe discovers this, ties up his horse and starts to dig for the gold. Hazel appears and Joe tells her of his good luck.

"Rustler Jack approaches and steals Joe's horse. Doc, riding along, spies rustler Jack on Joe's horse, and finally captures the rustler. The rustler, however, overcomes Doc. In the meantime Hazel has notified the sheriff of the stealing of Joe's horse, and a posse is formed, but Joe appears in time to overcome the rustler. The rustler is then taken away by the sheriff, while Doc places Hazel's hand in Joe's and then slowly rides away."

The Moving Picture World, 8/21/15

NEVER AGAIN

Selig Polyscope Company. Released September 7, 1915 through General Film Company. *Length:* 1 reel

Director: Tom Mix. *Scenario:* Tom Mix.

Cast: Tom Mix, Victoria Forde, Leo Maloney, Sid Jordan.

Production number: 524

"Tom Mix has turned temperance advocate in this one-reel drama, written and produced and acted in by himself. The story is a natural bit of human experience. Mr. Mix is not the only good actor in the cast, his support including Victoria Forde, Sid Jordan and Leo Maloney."

The Moving Picture World, 9/25/15

WEARY GOES A-WOOING

Selig Polyscope Company. Released September 14, 1915 through General Film Company. *Length:* 1 reel

Director: Tom Mix. *Scenario:* B. M. Bower [Bertha Muzzy Sinclair].

Cast: Tom Mix (Weary), Victoria Forde (schoolmarm), Sid Jordan.

Note: Copyrighted as HOW WEARY WENT WOOING, the title was used for its reissue in the 1920's. Footage from this film was incorporated in the reissue version of AN ARIZONA WOOING. Filmed in Las Vegas, New Mexico.

Production Number: C-530

"This Western comedy release from Selig is full of laugh-provoking situations. The little schoolhouse in a cowboy community, and a new girl school teacher are used in a new and original setting that is a decided novelty. A welcome addition to any program."

Motion Picture News, 9/18/15

Weary Gus is infatuated with the new schoolmarm, and his cowboy friends play a practical joke by forging a love note to Weary in the young woman's handwriting. The joke is on them, however, when she actually shows up at the town dance on Weary's arm.

THE RANGE GIRL AND THE COWBOY

Selig Polyscope Company. Released September 21, 1915 through General Film Company. *Length:* 1 reel

Director: Tom Mix. *Scenario:* Tom Mix

Cast: Tom Mix (Tom), Victoria Forde (Vicky), Leo Maloney (Buck, the rustler), Sid Jordan (Sid, Vicky's father).

Production number: 531

"Tom is given the position of cowboy on Sid Jordan's ranch. Vicky, Sid's daughter, is annoyed by Buck, the ranch foreman, who is discharged and Tom is given the position. Buck decides to get even with Jordan, and with other cowboys, starts to rustle Jordan's cattle.

"Vicky sees Buck and the others change the brand on a calf. The outlaws shoot at her and her horse drops, pinning her to the ground. They take the girl a prisoner. Tom, in search of the rustlers follows Vicky's trail. He overcomes the cattle rustlers in an exciting revolver duel, and rescues Vicky, who can no longer withstand Tom's offer of marriage."

The Moving Picture World, 9/25/15

"'A slice of life' best describes this one-reel western drama . . . It is natural, dramatic and wholly entertaining. . ."

The Moving Picture World, 10/9/15

THE AUCTION SALE OF RUN-DOWN RANCH

Selig Polyscope Company. Released September 25, 1915 through General Film Company. *Length:* 1 reel

Director: Tom Mix. *Scenario:* Cornelius Shea.

Cast: Tom Mix (Tom Hickey), Victoria Forde (Vicky Herrick), Pat Chrisman (Bill Herrick), Leo Maloney (Reddy), Joe Simkins (Isaac Goldplate).

Production number: 532

"Bill Herrick, owner of "Run Down" ranch, finds the land is worthless and arranges to sell it at public auction. Tom Hickey, the foreman, and Vicky, the Rancher's daughter, who is Tom's sweetheart, assist.

"Isaac Goldplate prospects on the land for oil. A demijohn of oil has been broken, and Isaac Goldplate, arriving on the day of the ranch sale, spies the oil scattered on the ground and is convinced that oil is oozing from the earth. He offers $5,000.00 for the property. His offer is accepted, but Goldplate soon discovers that he has been duped out of $5,000. He starts for town to stop payment on the check, but is stopped by Tom Hickey, who gets the check cashed and returns with the money. Herrick gives Tom and Vicky a thousand dollars each with which to start housekeeping."

The Moving Picture World, 9/25/15

"There is more comedy than drama in this one-reel photoplay. . . The humor is of the true Western brand and makes merry at the expense of a certain Isaac Goldplate, who

is made to buy a "salted" oil well. . . A thoroughly amusing comedy reel."

The Moving Picture World, 10/9/15

HER SLIGHT MISTAKE

Selig Polyscope Company. Released September 28, 1915 through General Film Company. *Length:* 1 reel

Director: Tom Mix. *Scenario:* Epes Winthrop Sargent.

Cast: Tom Mix (Bill), Howard Farrell (Professor), Leo Maloney (Jack), Ethylyn Chrisman (Muriel).

"Epes Winthrop Sargent struck a happy idea in this one-reel comedy and sent it to the right shop when it was given to Tom Mix to produce. Tom plays the leading part and extracts the last drop of humor from the situations which are many and funny. . ."

The Moving Picture World, 10/16/15

THE GIRL AND THE MAIL BAG

Selig Polyscope Company. Released October 5, 1915 through General Film Company. *Length:* 1 reel

Director: Tom Mix. *Scenario:* Cornelius Shea.

Cast: Tom Mix (Tom Chester), Victoria Forde (Jessie Baird), Leo Maloney (Hankey), Sid Jordan (Big Pete).

"Jessie Baird, the postmaster's daughter, handles the registered mail. Hankey, a gambler, seeing the men sending money away from the mining town, decides to rob the stage coach of the mail bag. He orders Pete, a pal, to board the stage and throw the mail bag off at Deer Creek. Pete pushes the mail bag off the stage seat. Jessie takes a short cut and beats Hankey to the creek. She finds the mail bag, abstracts the money and puts rocks in its place. Tom Chester, owner of the stage, misses the mail bag. Going back to look for it, Tom is shot and wounded by Pete. Pete and Hankey accuse each other of treachery. Jessie, from her hiding place, gets the drop on both outlaws and brings them to justice."

The Moving Picture World, 10/9/15

"Victoria Forde gallops off with the most honors in this one-reel drama, written by Cornelius Shea. Tom Mix is as effective as ever while in action, but Tom gets shot rather early in the story, and Miss Victoria is forced to take matters into her own hands. She is equal to every emergency and, the situations being full of interest, wins her audience completely."

The Moving Picture World, 10/23/15

THE FOREMAN'S CHOICE

Selig Polyscope Company. Released October 12, 1915 through General Film Company. *Length:* 1 reel

Director: Tom Mix. *Scenario:* Cornelius Shea.

Cast: Tom Mix (Tom Hickson), Victoria Forde (Vicky), Sid Jordan (Bull Dexter), Pat Chrisman (Serrick), Howard Farrell (the Sheriff).

"Tom Mix introduces a new thrill into the one-reel drama and performs it with the neatness of execution with which he climbs into a saddle. The entire photoplay is decidedly worth watching."

The Moving Picture World, 10/30/15

THE BRAVE DESERVE THE FAIR

Selig Polyscope Company. Released October 18, 1915 through General Film Company. *Length:* 2 reels

Director: Tom Mix. *Scenario:* Tom Mix.

Cast: Tom Mix (Tom Martin), Victoria Forde (Vicky Johnson), Sid Jordan (Jim Brown).

Working Title: TWO MEN AND A GIRL

Production number: 536-7

"Tom Martin and Leo Binnis arrive in a small mining town. Andy Johnson, his wife, and daughter Vicky, are also seeking a Western home. Jim Brown, a cattleman, poisons the water holes to kill off the wild horses that are eating the range bare, and Johnson and his wife drink from the water hole and die. Vicky, upon returning from a hunt, finds her parents dead.

"Tom and Leo, wandering in the hills, become lost. They are almost exhausted when Tom sees Johnson's wagon in the distance. He also sees the poisonous water hole. He fills a tin cup, raises it to his lips, but Vicky , who has seen Tom and realizes his danger, grabs a rifle and shoots the cup from Tom's hand just as he is about to drink.

"Later, Tom, Leo and Vicky arrive at the small mining town. Tom and Leo assist Vicky to engage in the restaurant business. The boys pan out a snug sum from the creek. Vicky by this time discovers that she loves both the boys, and after much thought decides to try them out to see which one she likes best. Vicky sees a physician and tells him to explain to the boys that she has been injured in a stage coach wreck; that she was thrown out and was disfigured for life.

"The doctor tells Tom and Leo the story. Both are horror-stricken. Tom is sorry and starts off to see Vicky, while Leo shows that he could not love her now. Vicky, from a window, sees Tom approaching, and when he walks into the room Vicky greets him in good health. She then tells him of the method she employed to find out which of the boys loved her best. Leo, in the meantime, leaves town to seek his fortune elsewhere, while Tom is happy planning with Vicky for their future."

The Moving Picture World, 10/23/15

"Tom Mix comes near being the entire outfit in this two-reel drama, and shines brilliantly as author, actor and producer. As he keeps the location in the West, retains his "chaps" and shares the acting with a well chosen company, his success will occasion no surprise."

The Moving Picture World, 10/30a/15

THE STAGE COACH GUARD

Selig Polyscope Company. Released October 19, 1915 through General Film Company. *Length:* 1 reel

Director: Tom Mix. *Scenario:* Tom Mix.

Cast: Tom Mix

Production number: 534

"When the stagecoach is about to pull out on its daily trip, Jack, the driver, finally locates Tom, the coach guard, in a saloon where a fight is in progress and Jack helps Tom whip several of the cowboys. One of the cowboys vows revenge and plots to hold up the stagecoach.

"Four passengers are in the coach on its return, including a good looking young lady named Vicky, with whom Tom immediately falls in love. When half way on their journey, Tom spies the outlaw cowboys in the distance. The stage gets by the outlaws, but one of the wheel horses is killed. The stage goes on with the three horses. After a desperate fight, Tom shoots and kills two of the outlaws while the rest disperse.

"Tom and Jack, the coach driver, meet Vicky and her aunt and the four take a stroll. While Jack and the aunt are engaged in conversation, Tom makes love to Vicky. Despite the objections of the aunt, Vicky shows that she admires the dashing coach guard, who had saved her from the outlaws."

The Moving Picture World, 10/23/15

Above: Sid Jordan sported a full crepe beard in *The Brave Deserve the Fair*, as he and cowboy Dick Parker prepare to poison the water holes on his ranch to control wild horses that are destroying the range grass.

Below: Tommy the tenderfoot arrives from the east and introduces himself to rancher Joe Simkins (left), foreman Sid Jordan (2nd from left), and the rancher's daughter, played by Hazel Daly (at right) in *The Tenderfoot's Triumph*.

THE RACE FOR A GOLD MINE

Selig Polyscope Company. Released October 26, 1915 through General Film Company. *Length:* 1 reel

Director: Tom Mix. *Scenario:* Cornelius Shea.

Cast: Tom Mix (Tom Cummins), Victoria Forde (Nell Meade), Sid Jordan (John Meade), Pat Chrisman (Griner)

"John Meade is discouraged at not finding paydirt on his claim and he puts up a sign offering it for sale. Griner, a Mexican, thinks the claim might be valuable [and] decides to do some secret prospecting on it. He has an eye on Nell, Meade's daughter. Tom Cummins, Nell's sweetheart, thinks the claim a good buy; gets a three day option on it from Meade and goes off to raise the money. Griner discovers the claim is valuable and makes Meade an offer on it just as Tom's option has expired. Nell endeavors to prevent her father from accepting Griner's offer, but her objections are overruled.

"While the Mexican is arranging with a notary for the purchase of the claim, Tom rides in with enough money to buy it. He meets Nell and shows her the money. They ride off to her father's home. Griner overhears them talking and endeavors to get there first. There is an exciting chase between Tom and Nell and the Mexicans, in which the Mexicans are outdistanced. When Tom and Nell reach Meade's home they find Meade with several large nuggets in his hand, and he tells them of his rich find. Meade takes Tom into partnership and Tom takes Nell in his arms."

The Moving Picture World, 10/30/15

ATHLETIC AMBITIONS

Selig Polyscope Company. Released November 2, 1915 through General Film Company. *Length:* 1 reel

Director: Tom Mix. *Scenario:* Tom Mix.

Cast: Tom Mix (The Wild Man), Victoria Forde (Vicky), Sid Jordan (ranch owner), Howard Farrell (hunter), Pat Chrisman.

Working Title: THE WILD MAN OF THE DIAMOND S RANCH

Production number: C-541

"Vicky pays a visit to her uncle's ranch in the West, and tells the cowboys that she could not love a man who is not an athlete. Tom and Sid, two of the cowboys, thereupon practice physical culture. Tom, while practicing, throws a sheep hide over his shoulders. A party of picnickers see him, think he is a

wild man, give chase and are joined by the cowboys. Vicky sees Tom running, notices his wonderful speed and decides he is the man for her."

The Moving Picture World, 11/6/15

THE CHEF AT CIRCLE G

Selig Polyscope Company. Released November 9, 1915 through General Film Company. *Length:* 1 reel

Director: Tom Mix. *Scenario:* Edwin Ray Coffin.

Cast: Tom Mix (the ranch cook), Hazel Page (Rose Blake), Sid Jordan, Pat Chrisman.

"This Western comedy is not revolutionary, but the action never lags, and Tom Mix is his usual amusing self. Rose Blake, the daughter of a ranch foreman, is in love with Tom, the cook, but her father frowns at the affair. Tom is discharged, and the cowboys have to prepare their own meals. The ensuing dissatisfaction, and Tom's exploits in capturing a bandit convince Rose's father that he might do worse than have a culinary son-in-law."

Motion Picture News, 11/13/15

THE TENDERFOOT'S TRIUMPH

Selig Polyscope Company. Released November 16, 1915 through General Film Company. *Length:* 1 reel

Director: Tom Mix. *Scenario:* Cornelius Shea.

Cast: Tom Mix, Hazel Daly, Joe Simkins, Sid Jordan, Pat Chrisman.

"When Tommy, an Eastern young man, arrives in a Western town, the cowboys see that he is a tenderfoot and make him dance to the tune of a gun. Beecher, a ranchman, Hazel, his daughter, and Sid, the foreman, who is in love with Hazel, rescue Tommy.

"Tommy and Hazel start out to look for Pete Boak, an outlaw. They chase a negro, mistaking him for Boak. The Ethiopian jumps from the top of a cliff and falls on Boak in camp below, knocking Boak unconscious. Tommy and Hazel find the unconscious Boak, make him a prisoner and win a $500 reward."

The Moving Picture World, 11/13/15

In late 1915, the Commercial Club of Las Vegas, New Mexico, persuaded the Selig Polyscope Company to send the Tom Mix unit to make pictures in the town. Tom used studio facilities built in 1913 by Romaine Fielding for the Lubin Mfg. Co. Southwest unit. Las Vegas was located in the last area of open range in the West.

Above: Tom is convinced that John Meade (Sid Jordan) and his daughter Nell (Victoria Forde) have discovered pay dirt in *The Race For a Gold Mine*.

Right: Grace Williams (Victoria Forde) tries to get reluctant rivals Buck Miller (Sid Jordan) and Tom Martin (Tom Mix) to shake hands *Along the Border*.

THE IMPERSONATION OF TOM

Selig Polyscope Company. Released November 23, 1915 through General Film Company. *Length:* 1 reel

Director: Tom Mix. *Scenario:* Cornelius Shea.

Cast: Tom Mix, Hazel Daly, Sid Jordan, Pat Chrisman, Babe Chrisman

"This Western comedy featuring Tom Mix is typical of the Mix school of productions. The atmosphere is that of the plains, the situations are mainly conventional, and the acting has more vitality than subtlety.

"Tom's father wants him to marry the daughter of his old chum. Tom is already in love with another girl, so this proposed alliance does not meet with his approval. Tom discovers that the daughter of his father's friend is also engaged, and so all four of the young people conspire to thwart the parental wishes.

"Tom's girl poses as the daughter of the chum, while the fiance of the real daughter impersonates Tom. When the parents discover the fraud they agree to forgive the ruse."

Motion Picture News, 11/27/15

BAD MAN BOBBS

Selig Polyscope Company. Released November 30, 1915 through General Film Company. *Length:* 1 reel

Director: Tom Mix. *Scenario:* Edwin Ray Coffin.

Cast: Pat Chrisman, Ethylyn Chrisman, Sid Jordan

Note: Tom Mix directed this film but did not appear in it.

"Not shown for review; the story follows: Bobbs, a hen-pecked husband, leaves his militant wife and goes to a small western town. There he sees a bad man shoot up a saloon and gather up a bag of gold. He resolves to do likewise and gains a reputation as a bandit.

"The overbearing wife, unknown to him, buys a nearby ranch and when Bobbs is confronted by the wife, she takes away his gun and makes him foreman of the ranch."

Motion Picture News, 12/4/15

ON THE EAGLE TRAIL

Selig Polyscope Company. Released December 14, 1915 through General Film Company. *Length:* 1 reel

Director: Tom Mix. *Scenario:* Cornelius Shea.

Cast: Tom Mix (Tom Merry), Victoria Forde (Vicky), Joe Simkins (Henderson), Sid Jordan (Jordan)

"Not shown for review; the story follows: Tom Merry, a stagecoach driver, is in love with Vicky, daughter of the superintendent of a mining company. She returns his love, thereby causing the enmity of another suitor named Jordan. This unsuccessful lover plans to rob the stagecoach when Tom is bringing money for the payroll.

"Vicky discovers this plot, and rides to warn her fiance. He gives her the money, and drives on. When he reaches the mining buildings, he finds that Jordan has incited the men to riot. He settles the dispute, and the father blesses the lovers."

Motion Picture News, 12/18/15

1916 _____

THE DESERT CALLS ITS OWN

Selig Polyscope Company. Released February 5, 1916 through General Film Company. *Length:* 1 reel

Director: Tom Mix. *Scenario:* W. E. Wing.

Cast: Victoria Forde (Vicky), Pat Chrisman (Desert Joe), Sid Jordan (Sheriff Billy), Ethylyn Chrisman (Old Mary).

Note: Tom Mix directed this film but did not appear in it.

"Sheriff Billy goes on the trail of Desert Joe, an outlaw. Desert Joe lives in a shack with Old Mary and Vicky, her adopted daughter, who thinks Old Mary is her mother. Billy falls in love with Vicky, although he has suspicions regarding the character of Desert Joe. Desert Joe also loves Vicky.

"The sheriff and Joe meet on the desert, and Joe believes that after a struggle he has killed Sheriff Billy. The sheriff recovers and finds Old Mary wandering—lost in the desert.

"Desert Joe, while trying to cross the desert, finds a note in his canteen saying that the water is poisoned, and he finally dies of thirst. Vicky finds Sheriff Billy and Old Mary in the desert. She revives them and Old Mary places Vicky in the arms of the sheriff."

The Moving Picture World, 2/5/16

A MIX-UP IN MOVIES

Selig Polyscope Company. Released February 12, 1916 through General Film Company. *Length:* 1 reel

Director: Tom Mix. *Scenario:* Tom Mix.

Cast: Tom Mix (Tom), Sid Jordan (Sid), Joe Simkins (Banker), Pat Chrisman (Pat), Babe Chrisman (Leading Lady).

Production Number: 546

"Tom, Pat and Sid, three cowpunchers, arrive in a small Western town, and seeing a motion picture company at work taking scenes in front of the bank gives Tom an idea. That night Tom and his two companions steal the movie camera, and the next day they start a fake scene in front of the bank. While Tom grinds the camera, Pat and Sid enter the bank, get a bundle of money and the onlookers think it is a scene. The three cowpunchers then escape into the hills with the money.

"The real movie company form a posse after the sheriff refuses to interfere, thinking the whole thing a joke. The company follow the boys into the hills, accompanied by the leading lady. She discovers the boys, tells them they are real good actors, and can make more money in the movie business, and so the boys follow the leading lady's advice and return the money to the bank."

The Moving Picture World, 2/12/16

MAKING GOOD

Selig Polyscope Company. Released February 19, 1916 through General Film Company. *Length:* 1 reel

Director: Tom Mix. *Scenario:* Tom Mix.

Cast: Tom Mix (Tom), Victoria Forde (Vicky), Pat Chrisman (Ginto), Joe Ryan (Wilson).

"Tom, a cowpuncher, is in love with Vicky, Wilson's only daughter, but Wilson objects. Ginto, a Mexican, is secretly in love with Vicky. Ginto discovering that Wilson is to receive a large amount of cash for cattle plans with other Mexicans to hold up the stage and get the money. Vicky overhears the plot and tells Tom.

"The outlaws hold up the stage and get the money. Just as they blow up the strong box Tom and Vicky surprise them. Vicky rides back to town to tell her father and the two ride back to meet Tom with the prisoners. They come upon Tom with the three outlaws secured to a rope and Tom holding them in line with a six-shooter. When Wilson sees that the money is safe and that Vicky really loves Tom, he gives his consent to their marriage."

The Moving Picture World, 2/19/16

THE PASSING OF PETE

Selig Polyscope Company. Released March 11, 1916 through General Film Company. *Length:* 1 reel

Director: Tom Mix. *Scenario:* Tom Mix.

Cast: Tom Mix (Pete), Victoria Forde (Loresta) (The Prospector), Betty Keller (his wife), Ethylyn Chrisman (Mona).

Production Number: 556

"Pete lives with his Indian wife, Mona, but has fallen in love with Loresta of the dance hall. Bob, a young prospector, and his wife, Betty, live near Pete. Pete oversees Bob find a pocket of gold. Bob takes the gold home, but after he leaves Pete enters. Pete's wife follows and sees her husband steal the gold.

"After Pete obtains the gold he goes to Loresta and hands her the bag. Pete's wife tells the sheriff of her husband's theft, and the posse follows the desperado. After a desperate battle Pete is shot. His wife, Mona, finds a new home in Bob's family."

The Moving Picture World, 3/11/16

TRILBY'S LOVE DISASTER

Selig Polyscope Company. Released February 25, 1916 through General Film Company. *Length:* 1 reel

Director: Tom Mix. *Scenario:* Tom Mix.

Cast: Victoria Forde (Vicky), Joe Ryan (Trilby), Ethylyn Chrisman (Mathilda), Betty Keller (Betty).

Note: Tom Mix directed but did not appear in this film.

Production Number: 557

"Trilby, a ranch hand, is in love with Mathilda, cook for the Big 'G' Ranch. Vicky, the ranchman's daughter, and her chum Betty, plan with the cowboys to have fun at Trilby's expense. While Trilby is courting Mathilda, Vicky, Betty and the boys perform all manner of practical jokes upon them.

"Trilby calls at the ranch in his buggy, to take Mathilda for a ride. Vicky and Betty, by poking the horse with sticks, get him fractious, and when Trilby and Mathilda arrive and try to get into the buggy, the horse kicks, breaks free from the buggy and runs off. This is the last straw for Mathilda, who is tired of Trilby's manner of making love. Trilby also is disgusted, and shaking his fist at the girls who are laughing at him, leaves the ranch and his love affair."

The Moving Picture World, 3/25/16

Above:Sid Jordan (left), Ed Jones (2nd from right), Dick Parker (right) and the rest of the posse wait in ambush for Tom Mix who played a womanizing outlaw in *The Passing of Pete*.

Below: Ruth Whitmore (Victoria Forde) tries to change the bad habits of her father's ranch hands, but Tom and the boys don't take kindly to her suggestions in *Too Many Chefs!*. Note the poor lighting with unfiltered sunlight from overhead and harsh reflectors supplying the fill light. Reviewers often commented on the poor photography of the Mix Selig pictures.

ALONG THE BORDER

Selig Polyscope Company. Released April 8, 1916 through General Film Company. *Length:* 1 reel

Director: Tom Mix. *Scenario:* Tom Mix.

Cast: Tom Mix (Tom Martin), Victoria Forde (Grace), Sid Jordan (Buck Miller), Joe Ryan (Delgado), Joe Simkins (Jim Williams).

Production Number: 558

"Grace, daughter of Jim Williams, a ranch owner, and Tom Martin, a Texas ranger, love one another. Buck Miller is the disappointed rival in love. Buck swears vengeance and plans with Delgado, a Mexican outlaw, to capture Grace and her father and hold them for ransom.

"Grace makes her escape and tells Tom and his pals of the outlaws' action. Tom, Grace and the boys then go to the rescue of Jim Williams. Delgado, the outlaws and their prisoner take refuge on an abandoned ranch. In the fight that ensues between the cowboys and the outlaws, all the outlaws but Delgado are killed. Delgado attempts to escape on a horse, but grace sees him and kills him with a shot from her revolver. Tom finds Jim Williams safe in a cellar of the ranch to the joy of Grace. Tom then takes Grace in his arms."

The Moving Picture World, 4/8/16

TOO MANY CHEFS!

Selig Polyscope Company. Released April 22, 1916 through General Film Company. *Length:* 1 reel

Director: Tom Mix. *Scenario:* Tom Mix.

Cast: Tom Mix (Tom Forde), Victoria Forde (Ruth Whitmore), Joe Ryan (John Whitmore).

Working Title: FRENCH COOKING ON THE BAR "G" RANCH

Production Number: 547

"When Ruth returns to the Bar 'G' ranch after acquiring eastern polish she chides the cowboys for chewing tobacco, cussing and smoking cigarets. When Tom, the foreman, orders the boys out on the range to round up cattle they are pleased, for they are anxious to be away from Ruth's constant admonitions.

"Out on the range the cook becomes warmed with wine, is discharged, and in revenge puts his pipe and tobacco in the coffee pot. Tom sends a cowboy to the ranch and asks Ruth to find another cook for them. Ruth resolves to impersonate a French cook. She calls on Tom at the range in male attire. Starting in on her new duties, she makes a pan of fudge instead of cooking dinner. The boys are infuriated and are about to drive the French cook from the camp when she makes her identity known to Tom. Ruth is so attractive that Tom proposes on the spot and is accepted."

The Moving Picture World, 4/22/16

THE MAN WITHIN

Selig Polyscope Company. Released May 1, 1916 through General Film Company. *Length:* 3 reels

Director: Tom Mix. *Scenario:* E. Lynn Summers.

Cast: Tom Mix (Tom Melford), Victoria Forde (Vi Gatlin), Sid Jordan (Gafney), Pat Chrisman (John Gatlin), Joe Ryan (Gunner).

"Tom Melford, foreman of the Double O ranch, has one weakness—that of strong drink. John Gatlin and his daughter, Vi, arrive at the Redwood Hotel, where it is a case of love at first sight between Tom and Gatlin's daughter.

"Gatlin purchases the Double O ranch, and Tom continues as his ranch foreman. He also discovers Tom's secret fondness for whiskey. Tom and Vi marry and announce the news to Vi's father, who, infuriated, denounces Tom as a drunkard and drives them both away from the ranch.

"The home of Tom and Vi is blessed with a little daughter. Tom, one day, is summoned to Sonora to break wild horses, just as Lorraine, the little one, becomes ill. After his work, Tom is tempted to drink, visits the Golden Nugget saloon and indulges in a spree. Vi sends word to Tom that their little daughter is dying.

"The Baby dies and Vi leaves her home. She returns to her father, but again he refuses her a home. Vi, now homeless, accepts the position of cook at the Golden Nugget saloon. There, the photo of her dead child is taken from her and made sport of by the habitues of the place.

"Tom sobers up, returns home and finds a note from Vi telling him of the death of their child. He then and there vows never again to touch strong drink and goes forth in search of gold and becomes a better man.

"A renegade discovers Tom's gold mine, ties Tom to a tree, and flees to the claim agent's office. Tom shoots the rope tying him to the tree into two parts, makes his escape, overtakes the renegade and after a sensational battle, overpowers the man and registers his claim.

"In the meantime, Vi makes her escape from the place and is pursued by two ruffians. Tom sees the picture of his dead baby behind the bar, recovers it, mounts a horse and goes in search of his wife. He rescues her just in time."

The Moving Picture World, 5/13/16

THE SHERIFF'S DUTY

Selig Polyscope Company. Released May 13, 1916 through General Film Company. *Length:* 1 reel

Director: Tom Mix. *Scenario:* Tom Mix.

Cast: Joe Ryan (Sheriff Gibbons), Pat Chrisman (Dan Nelson), Betty Keller (Betty Nelson), Sid Jordan (Ed Jones).

Note: Tom Mix wrote and directed, but did not appear in this film.

Production Number: 560

"Sheriff Gibbons is in love with Betty Nelson, daughter of Dan Nelson, an old miner. Ed Jones, infuriated because he has lost in the game of love, threatens Nelson and is reprimanded by the sheriff.

"Ed Jones discovers that Betty's father has found pay dirt. He overpowers Nelson in his home and escapes with the gold. The sheriff and Betty, returning from a ride, find the old man in a weakened condition. Sheriff Gibbons and a posse go in pursuit of Jones, locate him, and by strategy the sheriff captures the cowpuncher without a shot. The sheriff returns with the stolen gold to Dan Nelson. The boys take Jones to the lock-up, but the sheriff remains behind and takes Betty into his arms."

The Moving Picture World, 5/13/16

THE FIVE THOUSAND DOLLAR ELOPEMENT

Selig Polyscope Company. Released May 27, 1916 through General Film Company. *Length:* 1 reel

Director: Tom Mix. *Scenario:* Cornelius Shea.

Cast: Tom Mix, Victoria Forde, Sid Jordan, Joe Ryan, Chet Ryan.

Production Number: 561

"Two crooks attempt to steal five thousand dollars from the father of Tom's sweetheart, and find that they have carried off the young lady as well. Tom is mixed up in the affair, but manages to win the girl. An interesting one-reel western drama. . ."

The Moving Picture World, 6/17/16

CROOKED TRAILS

Selig Polyscope Company. Released June 3, 1916 through General Film Company. *Length:* 1 reel

Director: Tom Mix. *Scenario:* Tom Mix.

Cast: Tom Mix (Dick Taylor), Victoria Forde (Irene Norris), Sid Jordan (John Robertson), Pat Chrisman (William Norris), Joe Ryan (Poncho).

"Irene Norris returns to the ranch from boarding school. She sees Dick Taylor, ranch foreman, win over Poncho, a half-breed, in a bucking broncho contest. She admires Dick's ability as a rider, and a friendship springs up between them much to the rage of Poncho, who loves the girl.

"Robertson, a cattle buyer, visits the ranch with a large sum of money. Poncho resolves to get this money, and with confederates, captures Robertson, but not before Irene, who is with him, makes a sensational escape. Dick and the cowboys seeing Poncho in pursuit of Irene, capture him. They then go in pursuit of the other outlaws, surround them and after a battle in which Dick is wounded, the desperadoes are overcome."

The Moving Picture World, 6/3/16

GOING WEST TO MAKE GOOD

Selig Polyscope Company. Released June 10, 1916 through General Film Company. *Length:* 1 reel

Director: Tom Mix. *Scenario:* Tom Mix.

Cast: Tom Mix (Tom Gilmore), Victoria Forde (Vicky Denton), Joe Ryan (Jim Whitmore).

Production Number: 555

"Tom Gilmore, a wealthy young easterner, loves Vicky, but she refuses to marry him because of her thoughts of the great free west. Vicky visits her uncle, a western ranch owner.

"Tom decides to follow Vicky westward, and try the life of a cowboy. However, he reaches the west before Vicky, and soon learns the ways of the cowpunchers.

"Vicky is soon to arrive, but in the meantime, three outlaws plan to hold up the stage. The bandits kill the driver and the stage team runs off with Vicky inside. Tom sees the driverless stage going at break-neck speed. He overtakes it in a desperate ride, rescues Vicky, who finds that the easterner has become a westerner."

The Moving Picture World, 6/10/16

Right: Lovesick Dad Miller (Joe Ryan, right) takes a shine to visiting artist Grace Williams (Victoria Forde) and interferes with son Tom's love-making as Sid Jordan observes the generational rivalry in *An Angelic Attitude*. Ryan was a chameleon-like actor who could age years with a little hair whitener and change his looks completely with the addition of a lip brush or beard stubble.

Left: Bad men Chet Ryan (left) and Sid Jordan are held at bay by Joe Ryan as Tom comforts Vicky, who clutches the cash that will allow the lovers to enjoy *The Five Thousand Dollar Elopement*.

Left: Tom and Vicky share a clinch after the rescue in *Going West to Make Good* as Sid Jordan takes the reins of the stagecoach.

Below: The Sheriff (George Panky) is about to haul city-bred con-man Henry Weir (Joe Ryan) to the hoosegow after his capture by Tom Manton (Mix) after a thrilling horse and auto chase in *Taking a Chance*. Sid Jordan and Vicky Forde look on at left. A print of this film is held by the Danish Film Archive.

THE COWPUNCHER'S PERIL

Selig Polyscope Company. Released June 17, 1916 through General Film Company. *Length:* 1 reel

Director: Tom Mix. *Scenario:* Tom Mix.

Cast: Tom Mix (Tom Meyers), Victoria Forde (Betty), Pat Chrisman, Joe Ryan.

Working Title: A COWPUNCHER'S BEST FRIEND

Production Number: 576

"This Tom Mix Western is in every respect similar to the scores he has already produced. The simple plot is merely a vehicle to carry the numerous riding and shooting feats. These, as usual, are of a spectacular kind. Audiences that appreciate conventional Westerns will like this release. . .

"Tom Meyers, having found a rich gold mine, starts out to register it at the Claim Office. Padgett, a man who envies Tom, wounds him, steals the description of the mine, and rides off to register the claim. Betty, a ranch owner's daughter, sees the episode and by furious riding beats Padgett to the office and saves Tom's property. This act impresses Tom so much that he asks her to be his wife."

Motion Picture News, 6/17/16

TAKING A CHANCE

Selig Polyscope Company. Released June 24, 1916 through General Film Company. *Length:* 1 reel

Director: Tom Mix. *Scenario:* Tom Mix.

Cast: Tom Mix (Tom Manton), Victoria Forde (Flo Saunders), Pat Chrisman (William Saunders), Joe Ryan (Henry Weir).

"Tom Manton, a cowboy on the ranch of William Saunders, is in love with Flo, Saunders' daughter. The ranchman is not in favor of the match.

"Henry Weir, a crook, tries to sell Saunders an automobile, and Weir takes Flo out for a ride. Tom learns the Weir is wanted by the authorities. Meantime, Weir endeavors to make love to Flo, who escapes, meets Tom and tells him of Weir's actions. Tom chases Weir in his auto, rides alongside and jumps to the top of the automobile, where he is taken into town by Weir. When at the railroad station Weir jumps from the car and tries to escape, he is confronted by the cowboy.

"Saunders has so much admiration for Tom that he gives his consent to the marriage of Tom and Flo."

The Moving Picture World, 6/24/16

THE GIRL OF GOLD GULCH

Selig Polyscope Company. Released July 1, 1916 through General Film Company. *Length:* 1 reel

Director: Tom Mix. *Scenario:* Cornelius Shea.

Cast: Tom Mix, Victoria Forde, Joe Ryan, Ed "Pardner" Jones.

"The plot of this picture is not clear to the casual observer, but nevertheless it furnishes the foundation for the unusual horseback and stage-coach riding of the Tom Mix Western dramas. A stage-coach driver and his sweetheart outwit a schemer who attempts to secure the claim to a mine by tampering with the stage-coach so that it breaks down en route. The girl leaves the stage-coach and by hard riding on horseback arrives at the destination before the schemer, with the money necessary to buy the claim. . ."

Motion Picture News, 7/1/16

SOME DUEL

Selig Polyscope Company. Released July 8, 1916 through General Film Company. *Length:* 1 reel

Director: Tom Mix. *Scenario:* Tom Mix

Cast: Tom Mix (Tom), Victoria Forde (Grace), Sid Jordan (Jordan), Joe Ryan (Centiped Pete), Pat Chrisman.

"Grace, daughter of Jim Jordan, a ranch owner, has just returned from school, and Tom, leader of the Lazy S cowboy outfit, and Centiped Pete, leader of a rival cowboy outfit, fall in love with the girl. They both attire themselves in their best bib and tucker, and head for Grace's home.

"Enroute, they stop to settle a strenuous argument, and before the argument is ended, the cowboys of the rival ranches become involved in a free-for-all. Centiped Pete, subdued by Tom, challenges him to fight a duel. Before the duel the rivals practice plain and fancy shooting.

"Grace plots with Tom to fool and frighten Pete, which they do by trick marksmanship. On the day of the duel blank cartridges are placed in the guns unknown to the principals. When the undertaker arrives, it is too much for Pete, who takes to his heels. Grace then tells Tom how brave he was to stick to his ground, and he appreciates that he has won her love."

The Moving Picture World, 7/8/16

LEGAL ADVICE

Selig Polyscope Company. Released July 15, 1916 through General Film Company. *Length:* 1 reel

Director: Tom Mix. *Scenario:* Tom Mix.

Cast: Tom Mix, Pat Chrisman, George Panky, Joe Ryan, Victoria Forde.

Production Number: 575

"This is a burlesque comedy, written and produced by Tom Mix. It gives a comic view of the havoc created among a crowd of cowboys by the arrival of a lady lawyer. They are all ready and willing to break any or all the laws, in order to hire the new attorney. . ."

The Moving Picture World, 7/29/92

SHOOTING UP THE MOVIES

Selig Polyscope Company. Released July 22, 1916 through General Film Company. *Length:* 2 reels.

Director: Tom Mix. *Scenario:* Tom Mix.

Cast: Tom Mix (Tom Travis), Victoria Forde (Vicky Wilson), Sid Jordan (Sheriff Wilson), Howard Farrell (Murry), Hazel Daly (Hazel), Joe Ryan (Bad Man of Hell's Half Acre).

Production Number: 550-551

"Tom Travis, a bad man, comes to New Mexico. He sees Vicky, the sheriff's daughter, playing a part for a motion picture company. The action calls for Vicky to be overcome by the villain and thrown on a horse. Tom, not understanding the action, blazes away at the villain, and the bullet passes through the actor's hat, chasing the horse upon which Vicky is riding. Tom, coming up with Vicky, believes he has saved her.

"The director and Vicky's father think Tom a great actor. The sheriff, however, discovers that Tom has the reputation of a 'bad' man, and orders him to stay away. Tom, of course, ignores the admonition, and spends his time making love to Vicky. The sheriff again orders Tom away, and in a rage, Tom proceeds to shoot up part of the town known as Hell's Half Acre.

"A posse and the sheriff pursue Tom, but on second thought the sheriff decides to make Tom a deputy, because of his good work in cleaning up the neighborhood.

"Tom and Vicky again meet and refuse to renounce their love for one another. Then it is that father decides that he must make the best of the love match, and permits the couple to plight their troth."

The Moving Picture World, 7/22/16

LOCAL COLOR ON THE A-1 RANCH

Selig Polyscope Company. Released July 29, 1916 through General Film Company. *Length:* 1 reel

Director: Tom Mix. *Scenario:* Tom Mix.

Cast: Tom Mix (Tom), Victoria Forde (Vicky Hoskins), Joe Simkins (John Hoskins, Vicky's father), Joe Ryan (John Hicks, the ranch owner), Sid Jordan, Dick Parker.

Note: Also known as LOCAL COLOR.

Production Number: 552

"Vicky Hoskins, an Eastern girl with story writing ambitions, goes West to get local color for a story. Tom, foreman of John Hicks' ranch, plans to joke the Eastern girl. With cowboys, Tom rigs up a dummy, proceeds to hang it to a tree and tells Vicky that they were merely hanging a story writer who happened to come to the ranch, and Vicky nearly collapses with fright.

"Vicky decides to make love to Tom just to see how he acts, and so that she can tell what to do with her hero in her Western story. John Hicks, the ranch owner, discovers Vicky's plot and tells Tom. Then Hicks and the boys accuse Vicky of trifling with Tom's affections. A stranger, who looks exceedingly seedy, approaches and he is asked to perform a supposed marriage ceremony between Tom and Vicky. Too late the boys discover that the stranger is a real clergyman, and the matrimonial ties are binding. Later, however, Tom finds a means to cause Vicky to become content with her lot."

The Moving Picture World, 8/5/16

AN ANGELIC ATTITUDE

Selig Polyscope Company. Released August 5, 1916 through General Film Company. *Length:* 1 reel

Director: Tom Mix. *Scenario:* Edwin Ray Coffin.

Cast: Tom Mix (Tom Miller), Victoria Forde (Grace Williams), Joe Ryan (Daniel Miller), Sid Jordan.

"Al Matthews writes to his old friend, Daniel Miller, that a young lady wishes to come west to sketch some real Western scenery, and will arrive at Miller's ranch within a few days. Daniel Miller is well along in years, but when Grace, the

Above: In the cold light of dawn the romantic concept of taking the field of honor lost its appeal in *Some Duel*. Vicky eggs on the love sick rivals, Joe Ryan and Tom Mix, but they don't realize she's substituted blanks for lead.

Below: Two flabbergasted cowboys fall in exhausted disbelief when they find that Vicky doesn't want the pet bear they worked so hard to capture in *A Bear of a Story*.

Left: "Never again!" Tom and Sid Jordan swear off women in *Roping a Sweetheart*. This 1916 film was a remake of *Roping a Bride* made by Tom the year before. While Tom wears a colorful striped shirt that is a prototype of his later Western costumes, Sid Jordan wears more authentic range garb with white flannel shirt, vest, and a necktie as well as a neckerchief.

Below: Joe Ryan faces off with Tom Mix in a tense moment from *The Cowpuncher's Peril*. The members of the Mix stock company in this no-nonsense outdoor saloon set at Newhall, California, include Sid Jordan as the sheriff; George Panky, Vic Frith, and Boss Glenn seated at the table; and Banty Caldwell behind the bar. Chet Ryan and Pres Frith stand at the roulette table on the right.

artist, appears at the ranch, visions of matrimony again come to the old gentleman.

"Tom, Daniel Miller's son, also admires the pretty girl. It does not take long for Tom and Grace to fall in love, but their love-making is constantly interrupted by the interference of father. Grace wishes to paint a picture, and she induces Tom's father to pose as an angel hanging from a rope which is tied to the limb of a tree. When father is thus made secure, Tom and Grace escape to plight their troth uninteruptedly."

The Moving Picture World, 8/5/16

A WESTERN MASQUERADE

Selig Polyscope Company. Released August 12, 1916 through General Film Company. *Length:* 1 reel

Director: Tom Mix. *Scenario:* Tom Mix.

Cast: Tom Mix, Victoria Forde, Joe Ryan, Sid Jordan.

"Another one-reel comedy with Tom Mix in the three-ply role of author, star and producer. The erstwhile cowboy forsakes his old calling, however, and makes his first appearance as a stranded actor. He secures the position of school teacher and proceeds to make love to the best looking and wealthiest of his pupils. Jim Withers, the girl's father, finds it out, fires Tom, and advertises for a lady school teacher. Tom makes up as one of the fair sex, gets the job, and is slightly embarrassed when the school trustee falls in love with him. Withers discovers his mistake when he sees Tom pull off his wig and thrash the bully of the neighborhood for getting too familiar with Miss Vicky. Pa Withers says yes, after that . . . The picture grades up to the usual Tom Mix comedy."

The Moving Picture News, 8/26/16

A BEAR OF A STORY

Selig Polyscope Company. Released August 19, 1916 through General Film Company. *Length:* 1 reel

Director: Tom Mix. *Scenario:* Tom Mix.

Cast: Tom Mix, Victoria Forde, Sid Jordan, Betty Keller.

Production Number: 579

"This Tom Mix picture has more of a story and more genuinely humorous incidents than most of his Western comedy releases. The trained bear that cavorts through most of the reel will send the average audience into gales of laughter, and supplemented by the well known Mix kind of

riding, roping and shooting, ought to go well in most houses. . .

"Tom, a cowpuncher, is engaged to Vicky, a ranch girl. Her chum has a tame bear, and Vicky insists that Tom must get her one too. After risking his life a hundred times, and after a terrific battle with a ferocious bear, Tom finally captures the much desired Bruin. He takes the bear to Vicky, but she has decided that she does not want such an animal, because her chum's pet has scratched her finger. Tom falls in a faint."

Motion Picture News, 8/19/16

ROPING A SWEETHEART

Selig Polyscope Company. Released August 26, 1916 through General Film Company. *Length:* 1 reel

Director: Tom Mix. *Scenario:* Tom Mix.

Cast: Tom Mix (Tom Walker, a cowpuncher), Sid Jordan (Sid Taylor, a cowpuncher), Victoria Forde (Vicky Miller, the girl), Pat Chrisman (James Weathers [sic], Vicky's father).

Note: This film is a re-make of ROPING A BRIDE (Selig, 1915).

Working Title: TRYING TO ROPE A SWEETHEART

Production Number: 580

"This Tom Mix Western comedy is more exaggerated and more given over to slap-stick than are his average offerings. There is plenty of good stuff in it, however, and it will be appreciated by audiences that like the ordinary Western. . .

"Vicky, a ranchman's daughter, returns West after a long sojourn in the East. Tom and Sid, two cowboys, fall in love with her and become bitter rivals. Sid practices the gentle art of proposing on a calf and Tom rehearses his sweet nothings in the ear of a goat. Then they decide to hold a roping contest, the winner to marry Vicky. Tom is the victor, but when he tries to kiss Vicky, she kicks him in the face. Sid also gets a facial massage at the end of her shoe. The two cowpunchers decide that women are fickle."

Motion Picture News, 8/26/16

TOM'S STRATEGY

Selig Polyscope Company. Released September 2, 1916 through General Film Company. *Length:* 1 reel

Director: Tom Mix. *Scenario:* Tom Mix.

Cast: Tom Mix, Victoria Forde, Howard Farrell, Betty Keller.

Working Title: TOM'S BEAR STRATEGY

Production Number: 583

"This is an excellent Western comedy, full of action from start to finish, and punctuated with several novel and effective thrills. Occasional blurred photography is the only fault. . .Tom Miller, a cowboy, is engaged to the ranch manager's daughter, Florence. Tom snatches a girl from in front of a runaway horse, and when she faints in his arms, Florence sees the embrace and misunderstands it. Florence breaks the engagement, and Tom schemes to reinstate himself in her favor. He shoots a bear, and after tearing his shirt and covering himself with mud, lies down beside the bear and pretends to be dead. Florence sees him and her hauteur is changed to love. Her forgiveness is complete when the husband of the girl Tom rescued thanks him for his bravery."

Motion Picture News, 9/2/16

TAMING GROUCHY BILL

Selig Polyscope Company. Released September 9, 1916 through General Film Company. *Length:* 1 reel

Director: Tom Mix. *Scenario:* Tom Mix.

Cast: Tom Mix (Tom), Victoria Forde (Vicky), Joe Ryan (Grouchy Bill), Pat Chrisman.

Working Title: THE TAMING OF GROUCHY BILL. The film was copyrighted under this title.

Production Number: 582

"Admirers of Tom Mix will doubtless enjoy this Western comedy, although it contains little of the Mix riding, shooting and lariat stunts. There is a large amount of slap-stick work, much of it being entertaining. . . Grouchy Bill mistreats his wife Vicky so much that it is a county scandal. Tom, a cowboy, plans to teach Bill a lesson. He disguises himself as Vicky's mother-in-law [sic] and pays the couple a visit. Every time Bill opens his mouth, Tom either kicks him or knocks him down with his fist. After several days of this treatment Bill is thoroughly subdued, and when Tom reveals his identity Bill swears that he will be a model husband."

Motion Picture News, 9/9/16

THE PONY EXPRESS RIDER

Selig Polyscope Company. Released September 11, 1916 through General Film Company. *Length:* 3 reels

Director: Tom Mix. *Scenario:* Tom Mix.

Cast: Tom Mix (Tom Orbig), Victoria Forde (Grace Miller), Sid Jordan (Ed Wilson), Joe Ryan (Jim Blake), Pat Chrisman (Happy Jack).

Note: Copyright records state this was a 2 reel film, but trade reviews indicate it was a 3 reeler. A remake of the 1911 film SAVED BY THE PONY EXPRESS.

Production Number: 562-3-4

"Tom Orbig, a cowpuncher who has escaped from jail, and for whom reward notices have been posted, gets the position of pony express rider when Jim Blake is discharged. A strong friendship between Ed Wilson, foreman of the Diamond Circle Ranch, and Tom Orbig develops after Blake tries to shoot Tom.

"Ed Wilson is in love with Grace Miller. Tom and the cowboys attend a dance given in her honor, and that evening Jim Blake, the discharged rider, forces his attentions on her. Grace tells Ed Wilson and Tom of this incident, and the two men make Blake apologize to the girl, Happy Jack, a cowpuncher, presents Grace a bouquet of flowers. Wilson becomes angry and the two come to blows.

"The next day Happy Jack's revolver is accidentally discharged and he is killed. Wilson, arriving at Happy Jack's cabin to apologize, finds the man dead. Jim Blake appears, charges Wilson with killing Happy Jack, and Wilson is turned over to the sheriff as a murderer. A week later Happy Jack's pal finds a note in the corner of the cabin which Jack had written before dying, saying that the gun had gone off accidentally. The pal starts out to clear Wilson of the crime.

"Jim Blake and his confederates plot to get Wilson, break into jail, overpower him and take him to the hills to hang him. Grace Miller, who has overheard the plotting, finds Tom Orbig, and Tom, in a desperate ride, arrives at the scene of hanging just in time to save Wilson's life. Blake, proven guilty of falsifying, is placed in jail."

The Moving Picture World, 9/23/16

". . .The effect of the picture could have been greatly improved by more frequent and more specific subtitles. Some of these would have made the finale less ambiguous. The photography is not consistently good. The locations were well chosen."

Motion Picture News, 9/16/16

A CORNER IN WATER

Selig Polyscope Company. Released September 23, 1916 through General Film Company. *Length:* 1 reel

Right: Tom Mix, in dress and wig, poses as the bride's mother to teach a wife-beating cowboy to mind his manners in *Taming Grouchy Bill*. Vic Frith (left), Sid Jordan (right), and an unknown player share in the laughter.

Both of these films were among the films Tom produced in Newhall, California, after leaving Las Vegas, New Mexico.

Below: Vicky overhears a plot by crooked sheriff Sid Jordan and bad men Dick Parker (center) and Dick Hunter, two of *The Canby Hill Outlaws*.

Director: Tom Mix. *Scenario:* Tom Mix.

Cast: Tom Mix, Victoria Forde, Pat Chrisman, Joe Ryan, Chet Ryan.

"This is a crackerjack Western that will be sure-fire in audiences that like the cowboy flavor. There is action from start to finish, and excellent comedy relief. . . Joe Simpson and his daughter Vicky stop their prairie schooner at a well to get some water. A man arrives on the scene who says he owns the well, and that they must pay him for the water they take. Tom, a cowboy, overhears the argument, and, lassoeing the stingy man, drags him away. Later some drunken Indians attack Simpson's wagon, but Tom melodramatically saves them. Vicky is so grateful that she promises to wed the gallant plainsman."

Motion Picture News, 9/23/16

THE RAIDERS

Selig Polyscope Company. Released September 30, 1916 through General Film Company. *Length:* 1 reel

Director: Tom Mix. *Scenario:* Tom Mix.

Cast: Tom Mix (Tom Gardner), Victoria Forde (Vicky Nelson), Sid Jordan (Jim Nelson), Pat Chrisman (Ramero).

"Tom Gardner, a Texas ranger, while riding the border looking for raiders, visits his sweetheart, Vicky, who is just leaving with her father, Jim Nelson, for town. Ramero, leader of Mexican outlaws, sees Tom, and vows to 'get' him if possible.

"Later, Ramero and his band give chase to Nelson and his daughter, who are returning home with their supplies. Nelson is killed during an exchange of shots. Tom hears the shots and goes to the rescue, arriving just in time to save Vicky. Ramero escapes. Tom and Vicky pursue him, and later he falls dead before Tom's well directed shot. Then it is that Vicky consents to become Tom's new deputy for life."

The Moving Picture World, 9/30/16

THE CANBY HILL OUTLAWS

Selig Polyscope Company. Released October 7, 1916 through General Film Company. *Length:* 1 reel

Director: Tom Mix. *Scenario:* Tom Mix.

Cast: Tom Mix (Tom Gordon), Victoria Forde (Vicky Miller), Sid Jordan (Jim Grant), Pat Chrisman (Bill Tracy).

Working Title: THE SHERIFF'S DOUBLE-CROSS

Production Number: 578

"The Canbyhill outlaws terrorize the country for a long time, owing to the sheriff of the county being lax in his duty. Tom Gordon, the deputy, decides to capture Bill Tracy and his gang.

"Tom is in love with Vicky Miller, and tells her that he will bring back the gang. The sheriff, Jim Grant, is also in love with Vicky. He plans to get word to Tracy and his outlaws that Tom is after them. Vicky becomes suspicious and overhears the plot. She follows the messenger into the hills and is captured by the gang. Tom finds her hat, follows the trail and rescues the girl.

"Tom then overcomes the outlaws and finds a note on the leader from the sheriff, warning the outlaws of Tom's plan to capture them. Tom, after jailing the outlaws, goes to the sheriff. That officer sees him coming, and shoots at Tom and misses, Tom locates the shot and drops the sheriff. He then goes to Vicky's home and tells her of the sheriff's double-cross."

The Moving Picture World, 10/7/16

A MISTAKE IN RUSTLERS

Selig Polyscope Company. Released October 14, 1916 through General Film Company. *Length:* 1 reel

Director: Tom Mix. *Scenario:* Tom Mix.

Cast: Tom Mix (Tom), Victoria Forde (Vicky), Sid Jordan (Buck), Leo Maloney (Sheriff).

"Tom and Vicky are sweethearts and plan to marry soon. There has been rustling of cattle on the range, and the sheriff offers a reward for the capture of the rustlers. Tom prizes a silk handkerchief presented to him by Vicky, and hides it in the bunkhouse. Buck, a cowboy, guilty of rustling, steals the kerchief, ropes a calf and ties the animal with the kerchief that Vicky gave Tom.

"The cowboys find the calf tied on the ground, take the kerchief, show it to the sheriff, who at once recognizes it as belonging to Tom. Tom, after a battle, escapes the sheriff, for he does not know what the officer has against him. Buck believes he is safe and resumes his rustling. However, Vicky detects him in the act of branding a calf belonging to her father. She captures Buck, brings him back to the ranch and Tom is exonerated."

The Moving Picture World, 10/21/16

AN EVENTFUL EVENING

Selig Polyscope Company. Released October 21, 1916 through General Film Company. *Length:* 1 reel

Director: Tom Mix. *Scenario:* Victoria Forde.

Cast: Tom Mix (Jack Winton), Victoria Forde (Marion Mathews), Betty Keller (Betty Mathews), Pat Chrisman (Jim Mathews).

"Jack Winton arrives at Jim Mathews' ranch to carry out a schedule by which he is to fall in love with Betty Mathews. Instead, he is attracted to Betty's sister, Marion, who does all the work, while Betty plays the lady in the parlor.

"Later, Betty overhears Jack and Marion planning to elope at midnight. Betty takes the place of Marion, much to the disgust of Jack when he discovers that he has a different girl. Jim Mathews, the father, discovers that Jack and Betty are missing. He goes in pursuit, and finds Betty crying at the locality where Jack had deserted her in his return to the ranch for Marion. Mathews and Betty then go in search of Jack and Marion, but the two elopers are already married when they are overtaken."

The Moving Picture World, 10/21/16

A CLOSE CALL

Selig Polyscope Company. Released October 28, 1916 through General Film Company. *Length:* 1 reel

Director: Tom Mix. *Scenario:* Tom Mix.

Cast: Tom Mix (Dick Masters), Victoria Forde (Rose Brown), Joe Ryan (Jim Brown), Pat Chrisman (Jones), Sid Jordan (Sam Gillison).

Production Number: 577

"Jim Brown and his daughter, Rose, arrive in the town of Dry Lake to buy Jones' ranch. There Rose sees Dick Masters, the ranch foreman. Jones refuses to accept a check in payment of the ranch, and Dick is deputized to go to town and get the check cashed. Sam Gillison, a crooked ranchman, overhears the conversation, and with pals plans to rob Dick on his return.

"An hour later, Rose through field glasses, sees the crooks ride over the hill. She suspects that something is wrong, informs her father and rides after them. Dick is roped an pulled from his horse by the desperadoes, but the horse runs off with the money which had been placed under the saddle by Dick. Dick finally escapes, finds his horse, and after a

running fight, overcomes the outlaws. He delivers the money and wins Rose's love."

The Moving Picture World, 10/28/16

TOM'S SACRIFICE

Selig Polyscope Company. Released November 4, 1916 through General Film Company. *Length:* 1 reel

Director: Tom Mix. *Scenario:* Tom Mix.

Cast: Tom Mix (Tom Miller), Victoria Forde (Maude Warner), Howard Farrell (Dan Miller), Joe Simkins (William Miller), Sid Jordan (Sid Jackson), Joe Ryan (Joe Warner).

Production Number: 554

"Rather than tell on his brother, Dan Miller, who is discovered to be a thief, Tom shoulders the blame and leaves for the West to try and make good as a cowboy once more. On the ranch Tom is heartily greeted by his old pals.

"Joe Warner, the ranch owner, has two daughters, and one of them, Maude, falls in love with Tom, much to the resentment of Sid Jackson, a cowboy. Intense rivalry ensues between the two for the hand of the girl, but finally Jackson is cleverly outwitted and Tom and Maude decide on their wedding day."

The Moving Picture World, 11/4/16

WHEN CUPID SLIPPED

Selig Polyscope Company. Released November 11, 1916 through General Film Company. *Length:* 1 reel

Director: Victoria Forde. *Scenario:* Victoria Forde.

Cast: Victoria Forde (Lizzie), Pat Chrisman (her father), Sid Jordan (Hiram)

Note: Tom Mix did not appear in this film. It was produced by the Mix unit under his supervision.

"Lizzie and Hiram, in love with one another, decide to elope. Lizzie's pa does not favor the union. The sheriff of the county receives word that a couple of 'nuts' have escaped from an asylum.

"Lizzie and Hiram steal downstairs, clamber into a buggy and drive away, seeking a minister. Pa discovers their escape and starts in pursuit. He, unfortunately, spies the 'nutty' couple, who are driving along, and follows them, but too late discovers that they are strangers to him. However, he places them in jail.

"The sheriff has gone forth in search of the two lunatics and mistakes Lizzie and Hiram for them. He arrests the elopers, and places them in jail as the supposed lunatics. There Lizzie and Hiram meet Lizzie's Pa. He escorts Lizzie home and sets her to peeling potatoes."

The Moving Picture World, 11/11/16

THE SHERIFF'S BLUNDER

Selig Polyscope Company. Released November 20, 1916 through General Film Company. *Length:* 2 reels

Director: Tom Mix. *Scenario:* Tom Mix.

Cast: Tom Mix, Victoria Forde, Sid Jordan.

"This Tom Mix Western starts out with the customary rapid fire action and good riding stunts usually found in these releases. The action later becomes involved and hard to understand. A good comedy finish helps to counteract the dragged effect of the foregoing footage. This number will moderately please the uncritical audience.

"Hal Whitcomb, a bank messenger, steals a large sum of money entrusted to him for delivery. He is later caught by the sheriff's posse, and about to be hung when he tells a story. He tells of a twin brother named Steve, who was the one who took the money. He says that he himself is on his way to see his sweetheart who is dying. The sheriff's heart is touched. He believes the man's story and releases him. When the sheriff arrives at his office, he finds letters from officers in another county, telling him to beware of a notorious outlaw who tells a story of a dying sweetheart and a twin brother."

Motion Picture News, 11/25/16

MISTAKES WILL HAPPEN

Selig Polyscope Company. Released December 2, 1916 through General Film Company. *Length:* 1 reel

Director: Tom Mix. *Scenario:* Tom Mix.

Cast: Tom Mix, Victoria Forde, Sid Jordan, Pat Chrisman.

"This Tom Mix release falls far short of the average Mix picture. The aim was to produce comedy, but only the very unsophisticated people will be amused by the action. This comedy ineffectiveness is mainly due to the poor work of Victoria Forde, who is neither physically nor histrionically fitted for her part.

"Tom Warner and Vicky Mason are about to be married when Tom discovers he has forgotten the marriage license. He rides to town for it, but is forced to change horses with a fleeing horse thief. Tom is arrested by a sheriff's posse and the waiting bride gnashes her teeth until the real thief is caught and Tom is released."

Motion Picture News, 12/2/16

TWISTED TRAILS

Selig Polyscope Company. Released December 11, 1916 through General Film Company. *Length:* 3 reels

Director: Tom Mix. *Scenario:* Edwin Ray Coffin.

Cast: Tom Mix (Tom Snow), Bessie Eyton (Sunshine), Eugenie Besserer (Martha), Al W. Filson (Old Doc Snow), Will Machin (Craig Keyes), Pat Chrisman (Luke Fisher), Sid Jordan (Brad Foster).

Production Number: C-581

"Luke Fisher, a rascally sheriff, and Brad Foster, his deputy, are in reality cattle rustlers. To protect themselves, they endeavor to fasten the guilt on Tom Snow, foreman of the Three 'A' Ranch. When they come to arrest Tom, he drives them off at the muzzle of a gun and makes his escape. After a daring ride, horse and rider dash across a narrow foot-log which bridges a chasm. Should the horse make a mis-step, the rider would have been plunged to a horrible death on the rocks hundreds of feet below.

"West, proprietor of the 'Haven Delight' saloon, has adopted a pretty girl, whom he calls Sunshine. Craig Keyes, a gambler at the Haven Delight saloon, resolves to marry the girl, but when she refuses him, he endeavors to overpower her. Finally, after a sensational struggle, she escapes into a driving storm. As Sunshine wanders in the rain, she encounters Tom Snow. He cares for her, and thus it is that the two come to love each other.

"The sheriff and his deputy, fearful of detection, leave the country, and Tom is again free. Then it is that he marries Sunshine. After the wedding, by means of old tin-types, the two are led to believe that they are brother and sister. As they sit horror-stricken, Martha, the housekeeper, who has seen the tin-types, tells them that their belief is a wrong one.

"Martha tells them that twenty years ago while she was a nurse in a hospital, she changed the real infant brother and sister, and that Sunshine is in reality the sister of Craig Keyes and that she, Martha, is Tom's mother. In the meantime, Craig Keyes, the gambler, has followed Sunshine to her home,

Above: Tom Mix, with script, goes over the days' work with his company at the Selig East Lake Park Studio in 1916.

Below left: Boss Glenn, one of Tom's cowboy troupe. Below right: A dramatic study of Sid Jordan in one of Tom's last Selig films, *The Golden Thought*.

and outside he overhears Martha's story. Conscience-stricken, he resolves to renounce all relationship and to leave the country."

The Moving Picture World, 12/16/16

". . .Bessie Eyton gives [Tom Mix] the best support he has had in years. It is to be hoped that Miss Eyton will continue to play opposite him."

Motion Picture News, 12/16/16

THE GOLDEN THOUGHT

Selig Polyscope Company. Released December 25, 1916 through General Film Company. *Length:* 3 reels

Director: Tom Mix. *Scenario:* J. A. Lacey.

Cast: Tom Mix (Tom Daton), Victoria Forde (Bess Jackson), Barney Furey (Gene Hammond), Lily Clark (Estella Hammond), Sid Jordan (Doc Breede), Pat Chrisman (Bill Blevins).

"Tom Daton, deputy marshal, is ordered to Chico County to keep an eye upon a number of desperate characters reported to have been terrorizing the vicinity. Bess Jackson, a beautiful young woman, acts as faro bank dealer in an adjacent county, and when Tom arrives there he is much attracted by her beauty.

"Gene Hammond, a wealthy mining man, bids his wife farewell and goes to Chico County to develop a claim. There Doc Breede, leader of a gang of desperadoes, resents the appearance of the deputy marshal on the scene, and plans with his gang to make away with Tom. He plots with confederates that they shoot through a window and kill the deputy marshal making it appear that Hammond did the shooting.

"The shots are fired but just at that instant, Tom unconsciously withdraws from range, and it is one of Doc Breede's pals who is stuck by the bullet. Hammond is arrested by the sheriff charged with doing the shooting. His revolver, which had been tampered with, is placed in evidence. Hammond's wife hearing of his incarceration, rushes to his aid.

"Tom, the deputy marshal, believing in Hammond's innocence resolves to force a confession from Doc Breede. He does so, and after an exciting battle with the desperadoes, members of the gang are rounded up. As a reward for breaking up the plot, Tom claims Bess Jackson as his bride."

The Moving Picture World, 1/6/17

1917

STARRING IN WESTERN STUFF

Selig Polyscope Company. Released January 8, 1917 through General Film Company. *Length:* 2 reels

Director: Tom Mix. *Scenario:* Tom Mix.

Cast: Tom Mix (Tom Sage), Victoria Forde (Vivian Larkin), Sid Jordan (Bill Spruce), Pat Chrisman (Harry McNutt), Ethylyn Chrisman (Jane Hope), Pete Bender (Percy Brown).

Note: This film is largely a re-make of SAGE-BRUSH TOM (1915), except Tom wins the movie star in this version of the story. A fragment of this film survives in the UCLA Film and Television Archive.

"STARRING IN WESTERN STUFF concerns a motion picture company which goes west to produce a film play. The drama being produced is mistaken by Tom Sage, a cow-puncher, as the real thing. He rescues the leading lady. This action leads to a number of unusual climaxes, the final climax being the manner in which the cowpuncher wins the heart and hand of the movie star."

The Moving Picture World, 1/13/17

THE LUCK THAT JEALOUSY BROUGHT

Selig Polyscope Company. Released February 10, 1917 through General Film Company. *Length:* 1 reel

Director: Tom Mix. *Scenario:* Cornelius Shea.

Cast: Tom Mix (Joe Barr), Louella Maxam (Rose Dent), Sid Jordan (Carey), Pat Chrisman (John Dent).

Note: This picture was produced in early 1915, but was not released until 1917.

Production Number: C-489

"John Dent has worked hard at mining with poor results. A mining company has learned there is a rich lode on Dent's claim. Carey, a dudish bookkeeper, employed by the mining company, flirts with Rose, daughter of Dent, in an endeavor to have Rose induce her father to sell his claim to the mining company. Carey offers Dent a thousand dollars for the claim.

"Carey's attentiveness to the girl arouses the jealousy of Joe Barr, a young miner, who long has loved Rose. Joe Barr, consumed with jealousy, has followed Carey and Rose, and in so doing discovers a pocket of gold on Dent's claim, and in his honest way, tells Dent of the good fortune. Rose then appreciates that Carey has been attentive to her only from ulterior motives, while Joe Barr has proven his honesty and love. The girl refuses Carey's further advances, and tells Joe that she never loved anyone else but him."

The Moving Picture World, 2/10/17

THE SADDLE GIRTH

Selig Polyscope Company. Released February 17, 1917 through General Film Company. *Length:* 1 reel

Director: Tom Mix. *Scenario:* Tom Mix.

Cast: Tom Mix (Tom, a cowpuncher), Sid Jordan (Jim, his rival in love), Louella Maxam (Mary).

Note: This film may have been produced in 1915 and withheld from distribution until 1917.

"In Arizona when the rodeo is held, the boys on the Diamond S Ranch capture the majority of awards in almost all feats of skill peculiar to the Western plains. Particularly does Tom . . . prove his skill in riding and roping, an added incentive, perhaps, being the fact that Mary Johnson is an eye-witness.

"Jim Owens is a rival for the love of Mary, and is also a cowpuncher without principle. He is consumed with jealousy when he sees Tom capture prize after prize, and he resolves that any means are worthy to put an end to Tom's triumphs. He secretly severs the girth of Tom's saddle, and when the cowpuncher is performing a daredevil feat of horsemanship, the saddle breaks and he is flung to earth and rendered unconscious.

"The cause of the accident is discovered and a search is made for the guilty one. Mary suspicions Jim, and Tom's accident finally causes her to make up her mind between the two men, and she promises Tom to be his wife."

The Moving Picture World, 2/17/17

THE HEART OF TEXAS RYAN

Selig Polyscope Company. A Red Seal Play. Released February 12, 1917 through K-E-S-E Service [Kleine-Edison-Selig-Essanay]. *Length:* 5 reels

Director: E. A. Martin. *Scenario:* Gilson Willets

Cast: Tom Mix (Jack Parker), Bessie Eyton (Texas Ryan), George Fawcett (Colonel William Ryan), Frank Campeau ("Dice" Mc Allister), William Ryno (Moreno), Charles Gerrard (Senator Allison), Goldie Colwell (Marion Smith).

Note: Because it was a feature, *The Heart of Texas Ryan* received more advertising attention than any of the Mix shorts over the previous year, however George Fawcett, Bessie Eyton, and Frank Campeau all received billing over Mix in the trade ads. *The Heart of Texas Ryan* was Reissued in 1923 by Exclusive Features, Inc. under the title *Single Shot Parker*.

Original Selig studio records indicate the following credits for *THE LIGHT OF WESTERN STARS* before the picture was alterred and re-titled *The Heart of Texas Ryan*.

Director: E. A. Martin from book by Zane Grey

Cast: Tom Mix (Gene Stewart), Bessie Eyton (Majesty Hammond), Sid Jordan (Alfred Hammond), Coldie Colwell (Florence Kingsley), George Fawcett (Bill Stillwell), W. H. Ryno (Don Carlos), Frank Campeau (Sheriff Hawes), Victoria Forde (Bonita), William Hutchison (Danny Mains), Mr. Jones (Speed, Hawes's deputy), Dick Crawford (Monty), Chet Ryan (Nels), Vic Frith (Nick Steel), George Panky (Ed Linton), Vivian Reed (Helen Hammond), Lord Casstleton (Charles Gerrard), Pat Chrisman (Colonel Montes), A. von Harder (Padre Marcos), Charles Le Moyne (Pedro).

"If you want a film antidote for sex, morbidity, and problems, here it is. 'The Heart of Texas Ryan' has more variety than a vaudeville bill and more action than a pack of firecrackers. It is a Western of the very best type and it is well calculated to entertain everybody from little Johnny to his venerable grand-dad "

. . . the only point that invites criticism is the photography, which is fair, but not equal to the other factors of the picture.

THE STORY

"Colonel William Ryan, a Lone Star State ranch owner, names his daughter Texas Ryan. She is the idol of the cowboys, and is especially worshiped by Jack Parker, the head cowpuncher. Texas is also courted by Moreno, the Mexican head of a gang of bandits.

"Parker goes on a spree and incurs the enmity of McAllister, the town marshal and secret ally of Moreno. Parker saves Texas from Moreno's unwelcome attentions and so wins the hatred of the Mexican. McAllister and Moreno combine to kidnap Texas and steal her father's cattle. Their plots are all thwarted by Parker's ingenuity and daring. (These various plots and counter- plots create a lot of excitement and make possible a series of excellent riding, roping and shooting stunts.)

"Parker is finally captured by Moreno and is about to be shot, when Texas saves him after a wild ride across the desert.

Sid Jordan and Tom Mix in *The Heart of Texas Ryan*. The feature was started as a screen version of Zane Grey's *The Light of Western Stars*, but a dispute over the rights forced the Selig Company to change the title and the character names.

She offers Parker her life and her heart, both of which are gratefully accepted by the cowboy."

Motion Picture News, 3/3/17

MOVIE STUNTS BY TOM MIX

Selig Polyscope Company. Released July, 1917 through General Film Company. *Length:* 2 reels

"All of the thrilling stunts that Tom Mix, the Cowboy Actor, performed while making Western pictures have been arranged into a two reel release that is a genuine thriller. They have been so well selected and are so full of genuine daredevil, limb and death defying stunts that we are loth [sic] to see the two reels come to an end."

Moving Picture News, quoted in a Selig trade ad in *The Moving Picture World,* 7/7/17

WIZEL
HOLLYWOOD

FAME AND FORTUNE

In 1916 the Fox Film Corporation was on the move. After nearly two years of producing feature films in New Jersey, William Fox decided to transfer most of his production activities to Los Angeles. In an effort to compete with Paramount, which offered exhibitors a complete service of feature films and short subjects, Fox began producing his own series of two-reel Foxfilm Comedies, and hired Tom Mix with these short comedies in mind. The cowboy star had an established following and brought with him a unit that could turn out films with little or no supervision. His contract called for a salary of $350 a week, the same as he had been making at Selig.

Tom set up shop in Silver Lake at the Winna Brown ranch, not far from the Edendale studio. The ranch property had been used by other companies for several years but it became so closely associated with Fox's new star that it was dubbed Mixville. Only minutes from downtown Los Angeles, it offered a fair approximation of the wide open spaces, as well as a barn and corrals for the horses, a false-front Western town set and a small wooden bungalow that served as Mix's office.

When Fox moved into a new studio in the heart of Hollywood at the corner of Sunset Boulevard and Western Avenue, Tom transferred his offices to the new lot, but he continued to shoot at Mixville until about 1925 when he consolidated his operation at the Mix Rancho in West Los Angles. In 1928, Fox renamed the rancho Movietone City, and it became the company's primary studio facility with the coming of sound.

Mixville. Only minutes from downtown Los Angeles on Glendale Boulevard, the former Winna Brown ranch was turned into a studio for making Western pictures. A shopping center now occupies the site where Tom Mix once found wide open spaces.

Hearts and Saddles (1917), the first Foxfilm comedy, is the only Tom Mix Fox short known to survive, and it exists only in fragmentary form. Still, enough remains to suggest that the Fox shorts had somewhat better production values and were more fluid in execution than the Seligs. Some of this may be attributed to Robert Eddy, a comedy specialist who was assigned to co-direct with Mix; however, Tom was left on his own for the remaining two-reelers, and it must be presumed the studio felt that the extra man behind the megaphone was an unnecessary extravagance.

While Mix was an audience favorite during his tenure at Selig, his popularity soared with the increased distribution offered by the Fox organization. After completing five two-reelers, he was given a supporting role in the Dustin Farnum feature *Durand of the Badlands*. Realizing that Mix could handle himself in a more dramatic role, Fox gave him a contract to star in feature Westerns along with a $50 raise. Mix made only one other starring short, *Who's Your Father?*, released in 1918 as part of the Fox Sunshine Comedy series.

The Fox Film Corporation struck gold with the Tom Mix features, and this was reflected in Tom's salary. In early 1919 he was earning $600 a week, but later in the year he signed a new contract calling for $1,500 a week. By 1920, Tom Mix seemed destined to topple William S. Hart as the screen's top Western star.

While Victoria Forde continued in her role as Tom's leading lady in the Fox shorts, she made only one co-starring feature with Tom, *Western Blood*. Tom finally divorced Olive Stokes in 1917, and married Victoria early in 1918. As Mrs. Mix, Vicky gave up her acting career to take an active interest in promoting Tom's career behind the scenes. She treated visiting Fox exhibitors like royalty to encourage their continued booking of Tom's films, and she also made sure the front office paid proper attention to their leading cowboy star. "My father was energetic but not ambitious," recalls their daughter Thomasina, "my mother helped push him to the top."

Like other Hollywood stars, Tom was active in selling Liberty Bonds during World War I. At a 1918 Liberty Loan testimonial dinner at the Alexandria Hotel in downtown Los Angeles Mix and his company staged a comic square dance as part of the entertainment. After the dance, the cowboys left the dance floor with their ladies and a planted villain came out of the crowd and stole Vicky from Tom. Mix saw the benefit of fudging the line between image and reality. Even

When Old Blue stumbled in his corral and broke a leg, he was put to sleep and buried at Mixville. A wooden marker was placed on Old Blue's grave, and Tom laid a wreath on the marker each Decoration Day.

In memory of 'Old Blue' the best horse I ever rode, born July 1st 1897 killed Jan 29– 1919 We grew old together
Tom Mix,
Witzel L.A.

in a tuxedo he wore cowboy boots and a Stetson, and though he drove a Stutz touring car, he liked to leave audiences with the impression that his primary transportation sported four legs rather than four wheels. After the Liberty Loan banquet, Tom was asked to say a few words, and he spoke of the first testimonial dinner he had attended some years before.

"I'd never had so much good food at one time in my life," Tom remembered, "but when I rode down the trail to home I was talking to my horse, Old Blue, and I said: 'Ya know Blue, I can't remember anything I ate tonight except a radish.'"

Tom rode several different horses in his early Fox films, but Old Blue was his favorite. In January, 1919, Blue took a tumble in his corral and broke a leg. Reluctantly, Tom put the twenty-one year old horse to sleep and buried him beneath a wooden marker at Mixville. Every Decoration Day he laid a wreath on Old Blue's grave. Although he had ridden Tony for Selig's *The Heart of Texas Ryan,* and bought the horse from Pat Chrisman in 1917 for $600, it was not until the death of Old Blue that Tom took Tony "The Wonder Horse" as his full-time movie mount.

In many ways Mixville was like a working ranch. Most of Tom's cowboys lived in apartments or cottages in nearby Silver Lake, and "stabled around" the lot

The Tom Mix company on the steps of Tom's office at Mixville about 1919. Front row, l-r: ?, assistant cameraman Chuck Welty, Tom, asistant director Walter de Courcey, ?, ?, George Panky, Pat Chrisman. Second row, seated, l-r: Jack Frith, Goober Glenn, Floyd "Kildee" Alderson [Wally Wales], ?, "Dopey" Dick Crawford. Third row, seated, l-r: ?, ?, Dick Hunter, ?, Chad Powers. Last row, l-r: Vic Frith, Sid Jordan, ?, Boss Glenn, Craig Whitespeare, Bill Ward, chuck wagon cook Banty Caldwell, ?.

when they weren't working in front of the camera. The company ate meals prepared by Tom's chuck wagon cook, "Banty" Caldwell, a former sheepherder who was a deadly accurate shot with a sling fashioned from his neckerchief. To put it simply, you didn't argue with the chef.

Mix had virtual autonomy at Selig. He also enjoyed great freedom at Fox, but the new studio did exert more control on his unit. William Fox spent most of his time at the corporate office in New York, while West Coast studio operations were supervised by his former secretary, Sol Wurtzel. This is not to say that Fox did not take an active interest in day-to-day operations. He often sent lengthy "Dear Sol" letters commenting on scripts, actors, and directors. For example, William Fox became disenchanted with the work of Edward J. Le Saint (who directed six of Mix's early features) and wrote Wurtzel not to renew the director's contract. Several times a year Fox sent Winfield Sheehan, his second in command, to the West Coast to stir up the troops. The former secretary of New York Police Commissioner Rhinelander Waldo, Sheehan was a tough, two-faced Irishman, who could glad-hand with the best of them and be utterly cold-blooded if the occasion demanded. On his jaunts to Los Angeles, Sheehan was noted for handing out jobs like Rockefeller handed out dimes, in a calculated campaign to be well liked by the Hollywood community. When he returned east, he would get off the train in New Mexico and wire Wurtzel to fire all his new employees, making Wurtzel take the rap for his own ruthlessness.

Despite Sheehan's tactics, however, the Fox company didn't put up much of a fight when Tom added cowboys to the payroll. New members of the Mix stock company included Herman Nowlin, an old friend from Oklahoma, and Buck Gebhardt, who would soon become better known as Buck Jones. Earl Simpson, Pee Wee Holmes, Clyde "Kid Kinney" Ruffner, and Yakima Canutt were others who signed on with the TM-Bar brand. The poet of the group was a range hand named Raymond Smith, who called himself Colorado Cotton. He offered this assessment of working with Tom: "When you start a Mix picture, you'd best leave your right mind hanging on the gate post."

Just as Vicky gave up acting, Tom gave up the megaphone. He directed only one of his Fox features, *The Daredevil* (1920); however, he wrote or co-wrote several early feature scenarios and continued to contribute script ideas throughout the rest of his film career. While he did not receive screen credit as director, he was still largely responsible for staging the films. According to Roscoe "Rocky" Cline, a member of the Mix unit from 1921 to 1928, "The directors really didn't do much. Tom would say: 'This is what I'm going to do,' and then he did it. The director's main job was to do the scenes Tom wasn't in."

This may account for the fact that the generally undistinguished Lynn

A power lunch, circa 1919. Director Edward J. Le Saint stands talking with Tom and Fox studio executives Sol Wurtzel (in glasses) and Winfield Sheehan during production of *Hell Roarin' Reform*. Sid Jordan and B. J. "Smoke" Turner are standing behind Tom looking on.

Reynolds was Tom's favored director through most of his years at Fox, while stronger filmmakers like Emmett Flynn, Lambert Hillyer, or John Ford each made only a few Mix pictures. Mix had few illusions about his abilities as an actor. According to Cline, when visitors were on the set Tom would often ask his director: "Do you want expression number one, two, or three?"

George Marshall, who directed several Mix pictures, offered some insight into the star's disposition. "Tom was temperamental," he wrote in 1967, "but it ran in streaks. Every once in awhile this would come to the surface, particularly if he was drinking. One picture would sail along with not a problem; the next would be full of them and he would be sullen and unapproachable. As a whole, though, his better nature prevailed, as he loved his work.

"Oddly enough, the horse, Tony, was very much like his owner. Pat Chrisman would rehearse him in some tricks for a picture and he would perform beautifully, but when it came time to shoot—nothing! He could be whipped, pulled, jerked, have the bits changed, but still no performance. Come out the next morning and he would run through the whole scene with barely a rehearsal. Then he'd look at you as much as to say: 'How do you like that? Yesterday I didn't feel like working.' This was Tom, too.

"Another item which I think few people know," continued Marshall, " was that Tom was responsible for the present-day cowboy clothes. I have been in his dressing room when he was working with his tailor designing the tight-fitting

High above the Royal Gorge in Colorado, hanging from a rope, Tom slides for his life in a daring moment from *The Great K & A Train Robbery* (1926).

pants, the angled pockets, and the shirts with the many buttons—and always very vivid colors. No question, he was a real showman."

Part of the Mix legend is that he did all his own stunts, and cowboy Ted French said flat out that "Tom Mix wouldn't let nobody double him." The surviving Mix films add credence to French's contention. Many of the stunts are shot close on, and it is clear that Tom Mix is doing the hazardous work himself.

"It was the action things that attracted Mr. Fox," added George Marshall. "At that time Tom was doing all his own stunts—the horse falls, crashing through glass windows on horseback, and so on. There was no imitation glass during this period either and they didn't dig up the ground to spot a fall. Wherever they were shooting that's where you fell."

Director Lambert Hillyer offered a more realistic view. "Tom carried a complete stock company of cowboys—from cook to wranglers, and they all doubled him at times," Hillyer wrote in 1954. "However, this fact was considered top-secret and not one of them would have admitted the fact to a stranger. Mix had guts and to spare. Sometimes if he didn't like the way a stunt looked, he'd get sore and do it himself. Better not try to stop him either. Pat Chrisman and I spread lead around him in picture after picture with him always yelling: 'Come closer!' . . . Mix was himself a good man with a rifle, rope or six-gun. Very fast on the draw and as a stage coach driver, one of the best."

"The stunts were all worked out in advance," recalled "Rocky" Cline. "Tom would supervise the rigging of the stunts, and most always did the stunts himself."

In 1968, Cline did break silence and admit that he doubled for Mix in some swimming stunts. "I did some underwater work on a picture at Catalina Island, also some underwater work for him on *The Best Bad Man* (1925) with Clara Bow as the leading lady. I also doubled Wallace MacDonald, who played the heavy in *Tumbling River* (1927) on the Merced River. We had an accident and lost Ethel Hall, who doubled for leading lady Dorothy Dwan."

One of the most spectacular feats in a Mix picture was the jump across the Fremont (now Beale's) Cut in *Three Jumps Ahead* (1923). "Tom Mix did not make this jump . . .," writes Judy Ishkanian, "but my great uncle, Earl Simpson, did, on his specially trained horse. Earl Simpson was a horse trainer, stunt man and stand-in for Tom Mix. He had a ranch in Searchlight, Nevada where he trained horses for movie stunts. That famous photo of Earl making the leap hung for many years on my great aunt's wall."

These exceptions, should not take away any of Tom's reputation as a screen daredevil. In *The Last Trail* (1927) Mix clearly did all of his own wagon stunts. With the camera on a rig above the stage coach tongue, Tom is seen clinging to the tongue and wrestling with the broken reins only inches from the ground as the wagon races along. When the coach topples over, Mix mounts the front wheels and rides them like a chariot. Again the camera does not play tricks. There is no question that Tom Mix is performing the action himself. *The Great K & A Train Robbery* (1926) offers additional evidence of Tom's willingness and ability to perform his own stunts. No other Western star ever risked his own life so often in pursuit of a screen thrill.

In *Eyes of the Forest* (1923) Tom's character rode through a canyon which was set to be dynamited by the villains. The scene was played in long shot to take in the full force of the explosion and to keep the crew from danger. Any other star would have used a double because there was no chance the substitution could be detected by even the keenest eye—but Tom insisted on doing the scene himself. The blast was scheduled to go off after he passed the buried charge, but the powder man misjudged the distance and pushed the plunger just as Tom and Tony were directly over the explosives. According to H. M. and F. M. Christeson in their book *Tony and His Pals,* "The force of the blast threw them more than fifty feet away and knocked them both unconscious." Tony received a large cut, and Tom's back looked as if he had taken a hit from a barrage of shotgun pellets.

All of the bruises and injuries and broken bones were not without their reward, however. Tom's popularity and salary continued to grow, especially after he adopted a tongue-in-cheek approach to his screen heroics. The picture that solidified the Tom Mix screen image was *Sky High* (Fox, 1922). Up to this time, most of the Mix features were straight forward Western dramas with just a touch of comedy. But in *Sky High* Tom took a page from Douglas Fairbanks and *The Mark of Zorro* and began to blur the line between realism and fantasy.

Sky High is a tale of a government agent sent to to stem the tide of alien Chinese being smuggled into the country by an unscrupulous gang. However, the plot serves only as a device to motivate the stunts. When Tom's undercover work is discovered by the outlaws, he fights off twenty men, hops on Tony and rides full-tilt up the switchbacks of a steep Grand Canyon trail. To rescue the heroine, he commandeers an airplane, flies into the canyon and jumps into the Colorado River from the air, only to find the outlaws have fled with the girl. He climbs the canyon wall on foot and effortlessly rounds up the bad guys at the canyon rim. Some reviewers complained that the action was unrealistic, but others saw the picture for what it was—a light-hearted romp, not to be taken too seriously. Audiences didn't care—they just went along for the ride. There was action for the kids, romance for the ladies, and a sly wink for the hard-nosed cynics. Mix repeated the formula often, although he continued to make occasional "straight" Westerns like *The Last of the Duanes* (1924) or *Riders of the Purple Sage* (1925) to keep the recipe from getting stale.

Tom signed a new two-and-a-half-year contract with Fox in May, 1923; but eighteen months later the deal was renegotiated. Under the new agreement, which took effect after the completion of *The Rainbow Trail* and extended to December, 1926, Tom's salary was raised to $6,500 a week through the end of 1925, and $7,500 a week thereafter. It is no surprise that others tried to imitate the Mix formula.

In 1920, the Fox Film Corporation plucked Buck Gebhardt from the ranks of the Mix cowboys and turned him into Buck Jones, a move Victoria Mix felt was intended to keep Tom in line. At first, Mix resented Buck's success, but friendship overcame jealousy, and the two stars remained close over the years. Even though

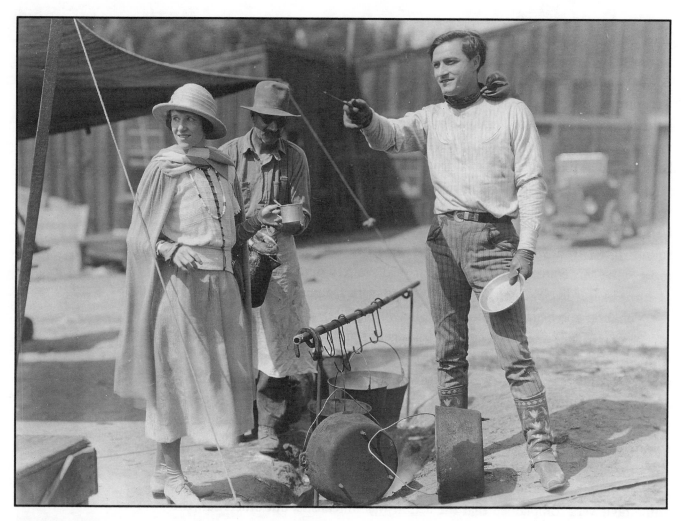

Another lunch at Mixville, this time about 1921. Banty Caldwell dishes up the grub for Tom and his secretary Theresa "Teddy" Eason. Teddy was shy and hard of hearing and many believed, quietly in love with the cowboy star. She committed suicide shortly after Tom's death.

Buck Jones became a popular Western star, he never seriously threatened Mix at the box-office.

In 1924, producer Andrew J. Callaghan joined with Charles R. Rogers, Harry Joe Brown, and director Albert Rogell to develop a Western series around Fred Thomson, a former star athlete and Army chaplain. Thomson quickly developed a following in Mix-styled romps like *Thundering Hoofs* (FBO, 1924), but in terms of box-office returns he only rivaled Buck Jones for second place.

By the mid-'20s Fox spent about $175,000 on each Tom Mix picture, and the world-wide film rentals ranged between $300,000 and $375,000. The Buck Jones pictures were budgeted between $50,000 and $75,000 and returned an average of $125,000 to the studio. The films Thomson made for FBO cost $85,000, but grossed no more than the Jones films. When Thomson went to Paramount for a series of four big-budget Western spectaculars, he was paid $100,000 for each film and an additional $150,000 each was spent on production. All four were box-office flops.

Several fly-by-night producers tried to cash in on the Mix name, even though they couldn't hope to compete with the Mix production values. Victor Adamson, who called himself Denver Dixon, hired George "Whitey" Kesterson, one of the cowboys in the Mix unit, to star in a series of low-budget Westerns. Adamson then signed an agreement with one Arthur J. Mix (no relation) for the use of his name and turned out a series of "Art Mix" pictures. One had to read the titles carefully to realize that Kesterson and not "Art Mix" was the star of these poverty row sagebrush sagas. Tom Mix and Fox sued. The lawsuit was settled in September, 1924, when Dixon agreed to call the films "Arthur J. Mix Productions" and display the story titles in type at least three times as large as the Arthur J. Mix name, and Kesterson's name in type at least twice as large as the Mix name. For a brief time there was another player who called himself Bill Mix, but neither of these pretenders created much of a stir. In the early '30s Kesterson adopted the Art Mix moniker as his screen name, but by that time Tom didn't seem to care.

By the late '20s there were dozens of new Western stars cast more or less in the Mix mold, but none offered the spectacular action and production values of the Mix pictures. Fox gave Tom 30-day shooting schedules, and the company often went on distant locations to seek out spectacular backgrounds—Zion Canyon for *The Deadwood Coach* (Fox, 1925), Yellowstone for *The Yankee Senor* (Fox, 1926), Lone Pine, California for *Riders of the Purple Sage* (Fox, 1925), and Royal Gorge, Colorado for *The Great K & A Train Robbery* (Fox, 1925). While on

On location during production of *The Texan* in 1920. Director Lynn Reynolds holds his script (center) while Tom talks with another member of the crew.

Opposite page: Tom Mix looks over several different insurance policies in preparation for a new season of even more daring stunts in William Fox photoplays.

location, Tom and company would sing around the campfire after the day's work, and often they put on amateur shows or rodeos for local residents, usually with cameraman Dan Clark acting as master of ceremonies.

One of the distinctive features of the Mix films was their outstanding photography. Dev Jennings, Fred Le Roy Granville and Friend F. Baker were Tom's first Fox cameramen, followed by Benjamin Kline. Daniel B. Clark moved to the first camera position on *The Fighting Streak* (Fox, 1922), and photographed all of Tom's Fox films thereafter. Clark had a fine eye for composition, and was a master of outdoor photography. Norman De Vol was second cameraman, working alongside Clark and shooting the foreign negative. Jodee Novak, Clay Crapnell, Curtis Fetters, Griff Thomas, and Roscoe Cline were among the assistants and special cameramen that worked with the Mix unit.

As far as the public could tell, Tom Mix and Victoria Forde lived a storybook life off screen. On February 12, 1922 their daughter, Thomasina, was born; and the following year they moved from a relatively modest home in Hollywood to a mansion in Beverly Hills. According to all who knew them, Vicky

Below: The Mix camera crew in Yellowstone, Wyoming in late 1925 on location for *The Yankee Senor*, l-r: Dan Clark, Jodee Novak (behind car), Curtis Fetters, ?, Clay Crapnell, Griff Thomas, and Norman De Vol.

was the love of Tom's life. He worshiped her, but their relationship became strained as Vicky took to social climbing and Tom remained intractably "democratic." There were often bitter arguments, and during one of these battles Vicky grabbed a pistol and shot her husband. Tom told the police he shot himself while twirling the gun, and the studio managed to cover up the scandal. The true story did not come out until a 1933 property settlement trial.

"It was in March, 1924," Tom testified. "Mrs. Mix had been down with some friends looking at a boat. I came on home and there were some people there.

"Shortly before this I had been doing some stunts—jumping out of a window to a girder. I had a picture of myself doing it. There was a friend—one of those gigolos—there.

"He picked up the picture and said, 'Mrs. Mix, If I were you I'd have my husband's head examined.' I didn't like the remark and I threw him out. The argument started over that.

"I called Mrs. Mix's brother, Gene Forde, to arbitrate. Mrs. Mix went upstairs. Then she came down while her brother was there and she had her hand behind her back with a gun in her hand. Her brother took the gun away from her and said, 'No, nothing like that, Victoria,' and laid it on the table.

"Her brother went out and the argument started all over again. Mrs. Mix began to throw things at me, but I turned them aside. She threw a silver ash tray or something at me and the first thing I knew she had the gun.

"She shot and hit me in the arm. She shot five times. One bullet lodged in the chair and I don't know where the others went. I leaped up and took the gun away from her."

Tom was hit through the left arm, and the bullet lodged near his spine. Dr. Nichol Smith operated to remove the slug.

Vicky's version of the incident was even more lurid than Tom's. "Mr. Mix had been drinking very heavily," she told the court. "I had been trying to get him to go to a hospital to get straightened out. We quarreled about one thing and another. He wanted to go out to the [car] and I wanted him to go to bed. One word led to another and there was quite a discussion.

"Mr. Mix started to hit me and beat me," she continued. "I was knocked to the ground and after I was down, he kicked me. I don't know what came over me. I grabbed the gun and shot him."

Victoria claimed she had been cut above the eye and severely bruised in the beating. She told the court that her injuries were attended by a Dr. Maurice Kahn, but Kahn was reportedly in Europe during the 1933 trial, and was not available to corroborate her testimony.

Despite the gunplay, Mix remained devoted to Vicky. She developed a

RESIDENCE OF TOM MIX, BEVERLY HILLS, CALIFORNIA

Right: The exterior of Tom Mix's Beverly Hills mansion at 1010 Summit Drive.

Below: Tom's den filled with guns, saddles, hats, and souvenirs in his earlier Hollywood home at 5845 Carlton Way.

Right: Victoria, Tom, Eugenie Forde and little Thomasina Mix set off by train from Los Angeles on the first leg of their 1925 European tour.

Below: In London, the reception for Tom Mix was amazing. Everywhere he went in Europe he was greeted by a sea of fans all anxious to catch a glimpse of their idol. Tom was amazed at the reception, but upset that he was unable to visit all the points of interest without creating a near riot.

distaste for his cowboy roles and successfully campaigned the studio to give Tom a chance to branch out and show what he could do without his chaps and Stetson. *Dick Turpin* (Fox, 1925), based on the exploits of a legendary English highwayman was the result. It proved to be little more than a standard horse opera in frock coat and lace. Audience reaction was negative, and Tom never repeated the experiment.

The Dick Turpin character was a reflection of Vicky's own longing for a real taste of European culture, so Tom took her and Thomasina, as well as Tony, on a two-month sojourn that combined vacation with publicity tour. Tom was mobbed by fans throughout the Continent and came to realize just how popular he was throughout the world. However, while the trip was a personal triumph, it proved to be a disappointment as well.

"... I went to Europe to see something of those far-away countries," Tom wrote readers of *Movie Monthly* on his return. "Because of crowds and receptions I failed to see the things I wanted to see. I was unable to ascertain many things I had hoped to learn about. My impression of France, Germany, England and Belgium remains a great sea of faces and shouting throngs. Tony was patted by so many people its a wonder he has any hair left. I shook hands so often it is a miracle how my arm held out. Riding over cliffs, jumping over bridgeless streams, swinging over hazardous precipices, is surely a restful occupation for Tony and me after Europe. We enjoyed a real vacation making *The Lucky Horseshoe*—just completed..."

Despite the fact that Tom had only completed the fifth grade, he had great respect for education. Adela Rogers St. Johns, who wrote stories for Mix, remembered the cowboy star sitting down to read all the plays of Shakespeare just because he thought he should. He would come to her office and discuss the plays with her, and his analysis of the Bard's work was enthusiastic and well reasoned.

Thomasina remembers that when dignitaries came to their Beverly Hills home, Tom would prepare by going to the encyclopedia. "He had a photographic memory and he would read up on all his guests' interests and accomplishments. He'd be able to talk with them about what they were interested in and put them immediately at ease.

"I've had people tell me they knew my father very well," continues Thomasina, "and later it turns out that they'd only talked with him for maybe a couple of hours. But, I don't think they're lying to me, they really feel as if they knew him. He had that effect on people."

By 1927, Tom's career at Fox was nearing its end. There were a number of factors that contributed to his leaving the studio. Problems with Victoria led to more frequent bouts with alcohol, and as a result the studio exercised more supervisory control. Tom lamented the simpler days when he could just go off and

Tom's sparring ring at the Fox Western Avenue Studio. A rare shot of the cowboy star dressed in civvies. Longtime Mix associate Howard Farrell (in cap with glasses) and boxer Frankie Dolan (right) joined Mix for this 1925 training session.

make a picture on the fly, and made no secret of his dislike for the new Hollywood. In addition, His hefty salary and the high rentals charged for his films were less realistic with all the low-budget imitations flooding the market. And finally, the Fox Film Corporation was heavily committed to the development of talking pictures, and sound presented technical problems that made shooting outdoors difficult. All of these factors contributed to the studio's decision not to renew Tom's contract in 1928. As it was, he spent nearly eleven years at a company that had a policy of terminating star contracts after five years, and his personal popularity was undiminished.

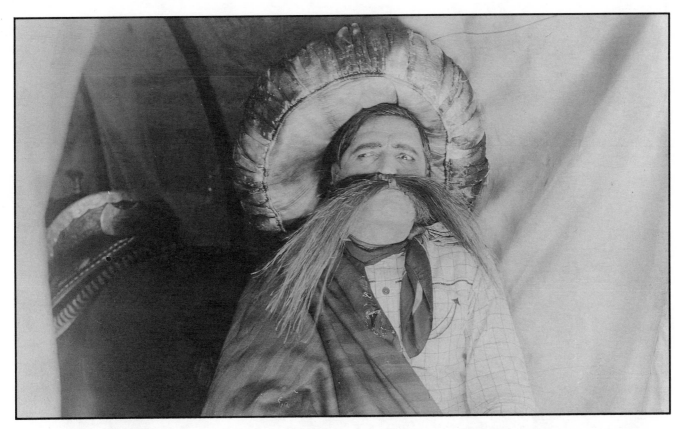

A hasty disguise as a Mexican homesteader with Tony the Wonder Horse hidden in the wagon behind Tom in *The Heart Buster (1924)*. Tom's object is to get past the villain's guards. The tongue-in-cheek approach Mix took in his Westerns found great favor in the 1920's.

In 1937, 20th Century-Fox suffered a major vault fire at its east coast storage facility, and the original negatives for virtually all of the Fox Film Corporation's silents and early talkies were lost. For years it was thought that only two of Tom's eighty-five Fox pictures survived, *Sky High* (1922) and *Riders of the Purple Sage* (1925). However, in the late '60s, 20th Century-Fox embarked on a search for its early film heritage and a few more Mix titles turned up, including *The Untamed* (1920), *The Night Horsemen* (1921), *Trailin'* and *Just Tony* (both 1922), *Soft Boiled* (1923), *The Rainbow Trail* and *Dick Turpin* (both 1925), *The Great K & A Train Robbery* (1926), and *The Last Trail* (1927). Another dozen or so titles turned up in Czechoslovakia, including *The Road Demon* (1921), *Teeth* (1924), *North of Hudson Bay* (1924), *The Best Bad Man* (1925), and *Oh, You Tony!* (1924). Unfortunately the Czech versions generally survive in beat up exchange prints, with missing footage, and four-frame Czech flash titles, making them virtually incomprehensible. A print of *The Texan* (1920) is known to survive at the Danish Film Archive, and others may yet surface—although time is running out for any fragile nitrate prints that might rest in a forgotten vault, attic or garage as tantalizing fragments of *Hearts and Saddles* (1917) and *Fighting For Gold* (1919) attest.

Tom Mix and Victoria Forde pose for a portrait at Mixville during production of their first Foxfilm comedy, *Hearts and Saddles*.

FOX FILM CORPORATION 1917-1928

1917 ─────────────────────────────

HEARTS AND SADDLES

Fox Film Corporation. Foxfilm Comedy. Released March 19, 1917. *Length:* 2 reels
Directors: Tom Mix and Robert Eddy. *Scenario:* Tom Mix.

Cast: Tom Mix (a sagebrush lover), Sid Jordan (his rival), Victoria Forde (the girl), Pat Chrisman (her father), George Panky (Sheriff), Victor Potel (express agent).

Still code: 1-

"Out in the land where the cactus flourishes there dwelt a sweet young girl whose father owned a ranch. Two of father's cowboys fell in love with her.

"One of the cowboys brought her a box of flowers and the other substituted a pair of corsets for the boquet, so that when the presentation was made, the presenter was forthwith out of the running. The fight that followed resulted in the discharge of the rivals.

"One got a job as bartender and bouncer in a saloon. He was unsuccessful as a bartender for his first ambition seemed to be to decorate the bar and those who had been admitted thereto with a fresco of 'Tom and Jerry.' Then a keg of beer got beyond his control and nearly drowned fourteen regular saloon attendants. So he was discharged. He entered a stage driving contest in which his competitor was his rival for the hand of the ranch owner's daughter. At the same time the two

leading burglars of the town stole $10,000 from the express office and secreted themselves in the stage coach.

"The race started, the Sagebrush lover inadvertently driving off with his sweetheart's father tied by the feet to the rear axle. After both coaches have been wrecked, the Sagebrush lover was declared the winner. The bandits were captured and the express agent was foiled.'

The Moving Picture World, 3/31/17

A ROMAN COWBOY

Fox Film Corporation. Foxfilm Comedy. Released May 13, 1917. *Length:* 2 reels
Director: Tom Mix. *Scenario:* Tom Mix.

Cast: Tom Mix ('Bud" Ballard), Sid Jordan ('Coyote" Tim), Victoria Forde (The Girl), Vic Frith (General Cactus Frijole).

Still code: 2-

"In the frontier settlement of 'Red Dog,' a keen rivalry existed among the cowboys for the hand and heart of the Colonel's daughter. She, beautiful and spirited, assisted her father, who ran the village store and who sold commodities of every description, from strong drink to stronger cheese. Principal among the broncho busters who longed to lead the maid to the shrine where knots are tied were 'Bud' Ballard and 'Coyote' Tim. 'Bud' had been gifted with an appearance above the ordinary while Tim's looks would cause even the

Hearts and Saddles, Tom's first Foxfilm comedy, followed the "two-rivals-and-a-girl" formula that served as the basis for so many of his Selig films.

Left: Pat Chrisman does not approve of either of Vicky's sagebrush suitors, Tom Mix and Sid Jordan. Chrisman began his film career with the American branch of the French company, Lux Films. He joined Mix at Selig in 1914 and served as Tom's horse trainer. It was Chrisman who trained Tony the Wonder Horse. He remained with Mix through the cowboy star's film career, and also worked with the Tom Mix Circus.

Below: Victor "Slippery Slim" Potel ties a rope attached to Tom Mix's stagecoach around Pat Chrisman's ankle as the big race is about to begin. Victoria Forde plugs her ears in anticipation of the starter's gunshot while Sid Jordan drives the stage at left. One thing that set the Foxfilm comedies apart from the Selig pictures was an increase in budget as evidenced by the army of extras on hand for this scene.

stage mules to smile. As time passed, the rivalry became bitter and finally narrowed to 'Bud' and Tim.

"Things were in this state, when The Girl suddenly discovered Ben-Hur. He arrived by the afternoon mail from a city book-store and from that moment 'Bud' and Tim were forgotten. The girl read the chariot race and its great finish and how she admired the manly form of Ben-Hur in his charioteer's costume. How handsome, how wonderful the men in those days must have been she thought, as she sat in front of the store oblivious to the desperate flirtations of 'Bud' and Tim some distance away.

"Seated upon a rail, 'Bud' exerted his every fascination to attract her attention and receive some little recognition for his ardent passion, but without avail. Her thoughts and her heart were in the long ago, in the great Circus at Antioch and she heard thousands cheering Ben-Hur as he won over the Roman champion, Messala. Tim was seated upon a can of glue enjoying his rival's discomfiture. If he himself could not win her, he was glad to see her falling in love with the hero of a book and not a real man, after all. Perhaps he might do something heroic, something greater even than Ben-Hur had done to win her love. He might shave regularly, might even wear a tunic and win her. There was yet a chance for him.

"And as 'Bud' looked with all his eyes, the rail suddenly swung and he went with it. Round and round he whirled and the faster he went, the harder Tim laughed. This was his hour of triumph. 'Bud' was humbled before the very girl he longed for and she in love with the hero of a book, something very seldom seen in Red Dog. The Girl, her attention momentarily attracted by 'Bud's' predicament, laughed also and thus was Tim's triumph doubled. But 'Bud' suddenly recovered himself and realized that he was the butt of ridicule. He determined to 'get even' with his hated rival. Without hesitation he drew his six shooter and fired into the pot of glue upon which Tim sat. The can collapsed and Tim was suddenly and unexpectedly immersed in an ocean of glue. He strove to rise but could not move. His triumph turned to chagrin. Then 'Bud,' to make his ridiculous position more so, mounted his broncho, the rope fell over Tim's neck and he was precipitately dragged from the porch. But the plank came with him and across the prairie and wild country they went. 'Bud' on his broncho dragging the discomfited Tim after him.

"They fetched up against a board fence. The back of Tim's pants has been completely ripped out, the board had left him and taken with it a very important portion of his attire. To complete his embarrassment, the Girl was coming, so Tim hurriedly made his vest serve as a pair of trousers and thus concealed his semi-nudity. The Girl arrived as the animosity between 'Bud' and Tim had grown to the point of fistic encounter. She it was who settled the question definitely. She told the belligerents that she would give her heart and hand to him who should win in a chariot race. If she could not have Ben-Hur in the flesh, she would have him in the spirit. The match was decided upon and the contestants looked about for means of making the chariots which must be had ere the race could be contested.

"However, when love calls there is always a way. The Doctor came to town and his buggy invited 'Bud,' who surreptitiously took the two back wheels. With the body of an old trunk, he proceeded to manufacture the chariot necessary. Tim, however, was on the job also and he took the other two wheels, leaving the Doctor's rig propped up on axles. The Doctor, a near-sighted, rheumatic individual, never suspected the fraud. He got into his rig, the cowboys were familiar with the deception. As he drove away, the axles went from under the buggy and there was great rejoicing in Red Dog at the Doctor's plight, as his horse kicked and balked amidst the gun fire from the cowboys.

"While this was progressing, the chariots were being hurriedly constructed. Tim had utilized an old barrel set between the wheels of the buggy and thus the contestants were prepared. And the great day rapidly arrived. The Colonel donned his old uniform and sword, and while he was engaged in this pleasant and time- honored occupation, 'Red Eye' Pete arrived. 'Red Eye' howled once a year, wolf like, and that day was the Fourth of July. To ease his stomach a bit, for he had been drinking, he took a light lunch consisting of dynamite and also a box for his claim high up in the hills.

"With his faithful donkey, he jogged along, 'liquoring up' at various points on the crossroads, much to the displeasure of the donkey—a drinking animal himself—who looked back and observing his master taking all the liquid refreshment himself, determined to be even. If he could not have a drink, he would not pull the equipage in which 'Red Eye' rode.

"At the fair ground, 'Bud' and Tim, dressed in Roman regalia of more or less accuracy, were prepared to contest the race. 'Bud' was undoubtedly handsomer than Tim and the ladies gathered around him to admire his manly beauty, among whom was the Colonel's daughter. A friend of Tim's slipped him a large hook with a rope attached as, if Tim failed to win the contest one way, he could win it another. And so they started, amid the shouts and plaudits of the multitude.

"Far out in the surrounding country was General Cactus Frijole, the exiled President of a carbon copy republic. That day it was he determined to drill his cohorts, consisting of five men and a base drummer, to prepare them to successfully install him upon the presidential chair of his republic. The drill being finished, General Cactus Frijole and his men proceeded upon the march.

Left: Sid Jordan and Tom Mix are all set to make like Ben-Hur in their home-made chariots. *A Roman Cowboy* was Tom's second Foxfilm comedy, and his first solo effort as a director for his new studio. Mix learned to drive a chariot during his days with the Miller Brothers' 101 Ranch show, and over the years several of his films featured chariot sequences, including *The Grizzly Gulch Chariot Race* (1916), *The Last Trail* (1927), and *A Horseman of the Plains.* (1928).

Right: Vic Frith (center) played the caricatured Mexican bandit General Cactus Frijole in *A Roman Cowboy*. The long-running Mexican revolution and several raids into United States territory by Mexican bandits like Pancho Villa in the early Teens inspired American filmmakers to turn Mexican characters into dastardly villains and comic buffoons.

"To the accompaniment of band and shout the charioteers tore around the course. The fact that a girl above the base drummer unconsciously kicked over a big pail of water and that it was running into the business end of the bass horn, did not disturb the enthusiasm, save that, as he blew, great jets of water came up and the multitude began to put up umbrellas as it appeared to be raining. Out on the course, 'Bud' was slowly winning. Tim tried to restrain him and there was a hand to hand fight between the chariots. But 'Bud' forged steadily ahead and then Tim determined to play his final card. He unloosed the hook and the rope and boldly cast it into the atmosphere. It landed upon the body of 'Bud's' chariot and separated it from the wheels and 'Bud' himself was left floundering on the road. The hook caught him in the seat of the tunic and 'Bud' floundered miserably along, through streams, along roads, and Tim triumphantly whipped his horses over the course, presumably victorious.

"Meanwhile, 'Red Eye' Pete was in a precarious position. The hill which he ascended with his donkey appeared to be perpendicular. He had difficulty in restraining himself from falling over the face of the cliff. Each moment, the dynamite he carried threatened to become dislodged from the cart and roll down the hill, for the donkey absolutely refused to stir further. The grass upon the hill top interesting him strangely.

"Meanwhile, 'Bud' and Tim had been having difficulties. As Tim was fast approaching the goal of victory, the barrel, which constituted the body of his chariot, slipped precipitating him violently upon 'Bud' who was being dragged behind and both men proceeded to adjust their long-standing grievance by a spirited fistic encounter. As this progressed, they were surprised by General Cactus Frijole and his marching band of patriots. But no Mexicans could settle this mooted question between 'Bud' and Tim and an effort to do so was an insult and both men turned their batteries upon the Mexican patriots and a 'free for all' ensued, with the Mexicans decidedly getting the worst of it.

"But far above, the donkey of 'Red Eye' Pete settled the question in a better way. With a sudden movement, he dislodged the dynamite. Down hill and into dale it rolled, fetching up the contestants below. There was a mighty explosion and chaos ensued.

"Then it was that the Colonel's daughter regretted her harshness towards 'Bud,' whom she really loved. The only relic of him they could discover in the debris was a boot. But as she sobbed, 'Bud' himself rolled down the side of the steep embankment, saved from death by a mysterious intervention of Providence. There was a moment of surprise, then joy, and then came the loving reunion of 'Bud' and his girl, whom the machinations of a cowboy villain had nearly separated, and she realized that 'Bud' was better than Ben-Hur, for he was a man and the hero who won the chariot race in the olden days was only a spirit."

Synopsis for Copyright

SIX-CYLINDER LOVE

Fox Film Corporation. Foxfilm Comedy. Released June 11, 1917. *Length:* 2 reels

Director: Tom Mix. *Scenario:* Tom Mix.

Cast: Tom Mix ('Buck" Saunders), Victoria Forde (Violet Ray), Sid Jordan (Steve Jordan).

"'Buck' Saunders is the pride of Cactusburg, an outlying settlement not yet graduated from the 'wild and woolly' stage. 'Buck's' principal ambition is to forcibly subdue bronchos and handle his 'six shooter' with a dexterity which will surpass all other inhabitants of Cactusburg, and he has realized his ambition fairly well. 'Buck' has become acquainted with Mr. and Mrs. Colonel Bean. Mrs. Bean has inherited a yard full of chickens and a six foot husband, and in these possessions she rejoices.

"While 'Buck' is engaged in subduing a cantankerous broncho, his favorite pastime, Colonel Bean arrives at his home with a telegram announcing the arrival of his Niece, Violet Ray, from school and Buck is summoned. Colonel Bean commissions him to proceed immediately to the station, meet and welcome Violet, and escort the stage to the Bean home. 'Buck' is only too delighted to do this as a prior and warm friendship exists between himself and Violet, who is a handsome, lively girl.

"At the station, the train arrives and Violet is seen by 'Steve' Jordan, a villainous 'road-agent' or 'hold-up' man, and he—attracted by her beauty—accosts her, to her displeasure. 'Buck' arrives and is warmly welcomed by Violet and he assists her to mount the stage. On the same train is a 'cullud' lady, whose color resembles in inkiness the Ace of Spades, and who has the beliggerency of her class generally. Upon mounting the stage, her hosiery is revealed, striped like the zebra, and excites the laughter of an individual with 'buck' teeth lingering nearby, on the lookout for sights of this kind. Steve approaches the stage and attempts to make himself gallant by handing Violet her satchel. 'Buck' resents this and a tussle ensues for the satchel, during which it is split open and Violet's underwear is disclosed to her chagrin and mortification—also the embarrassment of 'Buck,' who conceals a pair of unmentionables under his shirt. 'Steve' leaves vowing vengeance, after carefully brushing off a 'combination suit' of Violet's. At the last moment, Violet remembers that her trunk must be taken care of and commissions 'Buck' to look out for it. He goes to investigate and the stage leaves. Buck secures a trunk—the wrong one—lassoes it, and proceeds wildly down the road on horseback, with the truck banging after him.

"Meanwhile, Steve—on vengeance bent—has interviewed his band of desperadoes and told them that there is 'gold' upon the stage for them and a 'gal' for him. They set off wildly to intercept the stage. 'Buck' is coming with the trunk, having difficulties of his own. The bandits intercept the stage and are engaged in terrifying the occupants, when two of the men rush away and the stage leaves suddenly. The bandits are nonplused, and in the midst of their confusion 'Buck'—who has seen the occurrence—rides through them with the trunk, knocking the bandits down and proceeding on in his pursuit of the stage, which is 'running amuck,' the occupants and Violet—in particular— terrified and in imminent danger. Meanwhile, the station master, a rheumatic character with elongated whiskers—a 'mop'—discovers that the wrong trunk has been taken by 'Buck.' He mounts his trusty steed—a mule of stubbornness and character—and proceeds on his way in pursuit of the stage.

"'Buck' comes upon the stage and—in a spectacular manner—mounts the top of it and drives furiously off. In the distance, the bandits are coming in furious and vengeful pursuit. So furious is the pace at which the stage is being driven by 'Buck,' that it becomes separated from the horses and 'Buck' drives on while the stage 'runs amuck' down hill and dale with no one to guide it, and terrified females inside. The Negro lady jumps, and 'Buck' discovering her—her back being turned—imagines it is the girl of his heart, Violet. Upon getting a near view of her black physiognomy, he discovers his mistake and the 'cullud' lady is a bit 'peeved' at his attitude. She produces her trusty blade and informs 'Buck' that if there is any rabbit in him, he'd better flap his ears now.

"'Buck' unaccustomed to this sort of warfare, backs near the cliff upon which they are standing, and, grasping a windlass, lowers himself over the cliff to escape her threatening movements. Far below is a bull, a fine specimen of the class. 'Buck' is lowered nearly to him when he discovers the animal and makes frantic efforts to evade him. On the cliff, the 'cullud' lady sees 'Buck's' danger and is engaged in drawing up the windlass when the Station Master arrives on his mule and both proceed to draw 'Buck' up. When nearly to the top of the cliff, the rope slips and again 'Buck' is lowered precipitately to the near vicinity of the bull below. The bull tries but cannot quite get at 'Buck,' tho' he is in a tempting position for this operation on the part of the bull.

"Meanwhile, the stage has been careening up hill and down dale at a terrible pace when the bandits come upon it

and, stretching a rope, they intercept the stage and stop its mad career. The girl, Violet, is threatened by the revolver of Steve, the villainous leader of the band. But the sheriff, having gotten wind of the affair, is also on the trail and, coming upon the bandits in their villainous activities, 'rounds them up' and ties them to a tree. Their career of villainy is ended for the time being.

'Meanwhile, on the cliff, the Station Master has hitched his rope to his mule and he and the 'cullud' lady are engaged in pulling 'Buck' up. Prior to this, the trunk is opened and the 'cullud' lady discloses her black pickaninny, whom she was hiding in the trunk, presumably to avoid paying a fare on the railroad.

"And 'Percy,' the bull dog of Mrs. Bean, gets loose and arrives in the vicinity of the bull at the bottom of the cliff. He succeeds in chasing the bull away, but when 'Buck' is lowered into the scene from above, he sees a good opportunity and attaches himself to 'Buck's' coat tails. 'Buck is thus menaced by a greater danger.

"On the top of the cliff, Violet has arrived and is terrified at the danger of 'Buck' below. She engages in pulling up 'Buck.' Below, Mrs. Bean has arrived, accompanied by Colonel Bean, and both become attached to 'Buck's' legs and the trio are shot up and down the cliff at an alarming rate.

"Violet's interference above excites the animosity of the 'cullud' lady, and she severs the rope with an axe, thus precipitating Violet, Mrs. Bean, Colonel Bean, and 'Buck' to the bottom of the cliff. All are uninjured, happily, and as 'Percy' the dog comes in, he forms one of a happy family party where all is content and thankfulness at their recent escape from danger."

Synopsis for Copyright

A SOFT TENDERFOOT

Fox Film Corporation. Foxfilm Comedy. Released July 23, 1917. *Length:* 2 reels

Director: Tom Mix. *Scenario:* Tom Mix.

Cast: Tom Mix (The Tenderfoot), Pat Chrisman (His Uncle), Victoria Forde (The Ward), Sid Jordan (The Villian), Billy Mason (Negro Valet).

"Tom Mix has the role of an eastern college youth who knows nothing about the wild life of a ranch, and very little of anything else. After he is graduated—the university tires of the sight of him—he gets word from his uncle that the thing he, Tom, has long feared has come to pass: his uncle has found work for him.

"This solicitous relative informs his nephew that if he manages his ranch for a stated time, and the ranch is still there at the end of the period set, the uncle will make him a present of the land. Tom determines to go West in real style, so he engages a valet and starts out.

"Meantime, the superintendent of the ranch is atempting to gain possession of the property and also of the owner's ward. When Tom arrives in town and sees the ranch he decides that it is too good to lose. One look at the ward makes him reach the same conclusion in regard to her.

"The superintendent believes that a speedy revelation of Tom's tenderfoot tendencies will soon cause him to take a dislike to the village. At his instigation the cowboys put Tom through a series of wild experiences, accompanied by a vast amount of gun-play, but the youth never hesitates—in his fight to get away from 'those rough men.' The uncle is disgusted with his nephew and drives him from him, but the pretty ward's pleas eventually make him relent.

"The girl rides to tell Tom that all has been smoothed over. On her return journey with him the two are held up by Mexican bandits. Tom uses his fists to such good advantage that he routs the attacking band and redeeems himself in the eyes of the girl and the uncle."

The Moving Picture World, 8/18/17

DURAND OF THE BADLANDS

Fox Film Corporation. Released August 12, 1917. *Length:* 5 reels

Director: Richard Stanton. *Scenario:* Maibelle Heikes Justice. *Photography:* J. D. Jennings

Cast: Dustin Farnum (Dick Durand), Winifred Kingston (Molly Gore), Tom Mix (Clem Alison), Babe Chrisman (May Bond), Lee Morris ('Kingdom Come" Knapp), Amy Jerome (Inez), Frankie Lee (Jimmy)

Note: Reissued in 1920. Remade in 1925 with Buck Jones.

"Dick Durand, an engaging young outlaw, has robbed so many stage coaches that his name has come to be associated, however unjustly, with every misdeed in the zone in which he operates. . . .

"While out on a plundering expedition one day, Dick happens upon a band of marauding Indians attacking a group of settlers. Dick opens fire on the Redskins, but before he forces them to flee they kill all except three children and Durand himself.

"Dick places the kiddies in the care of Molly Gore, to whom he has lost his heart. Molly does not suspect that the kindly horseman is the outlaw on whose head a price has been put; and whom sheriff and posse are seeking because he is blamed for the massacre.

"Although he knows the sheriff is in hot pursuit, Dick stops in his ride for the border to rescue a girl who has been kidnapped by Indians. After he returns her to her father, the sheriff takes Durand prisoner, and Dick is found guilty of murdering the settlers. It then transpires that the girl Dick has saved is the Governor's daughter. The executive pardons Durand because he believes in him—and because Molly Gore does—an instant before conclusive evidence is brought in that Dick was innocent of any guilt in the massacre."

The Moving Picture World, 8/25/17

TOM AND JERRY MIX

Fox Film Corporation. Foxfilm Comedy. Released September 3, 1917. *Length:* 2 reels

Director: Tom Mix. *Scenario:* Tom Mix.

Cast: Tom Mix (The Foreman), Victoria Forde (Daisy Fields), Sid Jordan (The Sheriff), Pat Chrisman (Colonel Fields), Floyd Alderson.

Still code: 4-

"Daisy Fields, daughter of Colonel Fields, is the Queen-Bee attraction of the Bar-M Ranch, in the cactus country where things happen and happen rapidly. Principal among her admirers are the Ranch Foreman and the Sheriff of the cactus community. A pleasant rivalry exists between these Western gentlemen, sometimes interspersed with promiscuous gun-play of a dangerous nature. Colonel Fields is hand in glove with the Sheriff and distinctly antagonistic to the suit of the Ranch Foreman. As is usual in such cases, the girl inclines to the man whom her father is antagonistic to, which further complicates the situation. Colonel Fields discovers a little amorous passage between his daughter and the Ranch Foreman and disrupts the meeting, commanding the foreman to attend to the horses and other cattle about the place, while he and his daughter set out for the Cactus community some miles away. The never ending pastime of the natives of this far away and arid spot is to watch the daily trains come through. Accordingly the Colonel and daughter set out with a somewhat unquiet steed attached to the family equipage. While this is transpiring, the Sheriff sees the Foreman lamenting in a windy sigh over the temporary disruption of his love affair and laughs heartily. The Foreman, without a great deal of hesitation, unlimbers his side artillery and 'gets the drop' on the Sheriff; afterwards, depositing a shot in his neighborhood which grazes the posterior of his legal anatomy, causing him to become unbalanced and fall into the water trough behind him. After extricating himself and gathering up his belongings, he departs vowing vengeance on the Foreman, but leaving him temporarily the victor. The Foreman visits the corral and attends to the horses and communicates his victory over the Sheriff to the 'boys' who laugh heartily over the incident.

"Meanwhile, some United States Army officers arrive for the purpose of purchasing some Army horses and the Foreman closes the deal. Immediately, he conceives the idea of visiting the Beach and having a time of it. Manning the stage coach, they leave for the beach. Colonel Fields and his daughter, while en route in the family equipage formerly alluded to, sustain an accident. The vehicle becomes cantankerous and deposits the Colonel and his dutiful child in the sand while the horses make a hurried departure for the place from whence they came—that is, home. The Colonel hurriedly leaves for a more stable animal and, while the girl stands waiting, she sees the wild ride of the cowboys on top of the stage coach for the Beach. The Foreman also sees her and she is promptly taken aboard. All start. The father from a distance, having dickered with a nearby farmer for a burro, sees the departing retinue and starts in pursuit. The Sheriff also, very disgruntled, also sees the stage coach and joins issues with the father in the pursuit and rounding up of the culprits. A very enjoyable incident disturbs the even tenor of the stage coach. A Dachshund is howling in a yard and the Foreman dislikes his nationality. He is so distinctively German that he is a living affront to our flag and to our patriotism likewise. So the Foreman hurriedly dismounts and chastises the Dachshund. The owner, a German individual with wooden shoes, emerges with a shot gun and fires a load of something into the Foreman's anatomy which temporarily impedes his progress. But finally he reaches the stage coach and the party merrily depart; with the German, the shot gun, and his family of female Gretchens in pursuit of the stage. He creates somewhat of a diversion, but is finally 'roped' from a distance and dragged along after the stage coach. His daugh-

ters adhere to the German's coat tails, and the Teutonic family form quite a pleasant little enforced procession at the back of the stage coach, being taken, much against their will, through several streams and over several rocky places which had a tendency to remove certain portions of their attire besides making vary painful lacerations upon divers portions of their persons. Affairs continued merrily thus for a time, with the cowboys in huge merriment.

"The 'boys' arrive at Venice, the great California resort, and the girl goes into some stores to make a few purchases, while the 'boys' go into a cafe to 'liquor up' and accumulate an 'edge' generally. They emerge primed with red-eye and fun and while conferring as to their future movements they are seen by the Sheriff, who playfully levels a .45 Colt in their direction and fires a broadside. The chase begins. The boys betake themselves of the Scenic Railway with the Sheriff in pursuit. The chase is dangerous, zig-zagging around curves with the Sheriff's trusty Howitzer constantly in action. All leave the Scenic Railway and repair to a cafe to get something to eat. The Sheriff for the moment is temporarily lost. In the cafe, there is a dear chap there, a "Willie" who excites the wonderment of the boys. They are unacquainted with his brand of 'steer,' but the Foreman takes a bead on him with a small sized hand battery [a pistol] and uproots the ornamental lamp from the table. This precipitates the melee. The Proprietor objects somewhat to having his cabaret demolished, but the boys, after almost demolishing the place, proceed outside.

"But the Cook also is a desperate individual and he has appeared on the scene armed with an instrument that appears to be a cross between a Turkish scimitar and the French guillotine. He holds the Foreman up when another man enters and lassoes him from behind. He is dragged ignominiously to his downfall. Outside, the Sheriff is waiting. The chase again commences. They proceed along the beach and the Sheriff meets with a great many accidents and the 'boys' in returning practically enter the same restaurant. The cabaret girls are singing on the mat when one of the cowboys attaches an ice hook to the mat and the entire cabaret are dragged [sic] to the beach on the mat and into the water. One of the girls has fallen off, however, into the arms of Colonel Fields and he, compromised at the discovery of his apparent perfidy, makes a mad dash for the waves to commit suicide. The Foreman, who has been rejoined by the girl, sees him and lassoes him from the shore, dragging the old man to safety through the waves. In the ocean, the engagement of the girl and the cowboy is pledged by the old man, who finally comes to recognize the Foreman's heroism and is desirous of rewarding it."

Synopsis for Copyright

A rare action sequence captured by the still cameraman during production of *Ace High.* Shots like these are rare because the bulky 8"x10" still cameras used at the time did not lend themselves to clicking off pictures in rapid succession.

Right: Tom makes a transfer from his horse, Tony, to a runaway stagecoach. The bearskin rug draped over the driver's box hides the driver who guided the wagon during the stunt.

Left: Seconds later--one of the mules pulling the coach takes an unplanned tumble. Tom stands on the brake and hauls in the reins in a desperate effort to keep from running over the animal.

1918

CUPID'S ROUNDUP

Fox Film Corporation. Fox Special Feature. Released January 13, 1918. *Length:* 5 reels

Director: Edward J. Le Saint. *Scenario:* Charles Kenyon, based on an unpublished story by George Scarborough titled "Cupid's Checker Board."

Cast: Tom Mix (Larry Kelly), Wanda Petit [Hawley] (Helen Baldwin), E. B. Tilton (James Kelly), Roy Watson (Buckland), Verne Mesereau (Peggy Blair), Alfred Padgett (Jim Cocksey), Fred Clark (McGinnis), Eugenie Forde (The Red Bird).

"The old Western melodrama plays a return engagement in 'Cupid's Round Up,' a new five-reel Fox picture with Tom Mix. The plot could have been improved by leaving out one or two of the old-fashioned expedients; but the value of the picture is high in spite of its story. It is a welcome revival of something that always had a warm place in the hearts of audiences and was unmercifully overdone until it became like a pie to a sick man. The chase and the running fight are and always will be high cards in the pictures, and so are bronchos and rustlers driving off herds of cattle against Western backgrounds. There are plenty of these things in this picture. What is lacking is a strong, concrete story that would have given the director a chance to show his imagination. He proves he has it even here. The picture depends almost wholly on Tom Mix's ability to ride and shoot and handle a red-blood situation. Tom Mix makes it a good picture for the average audience.

"Two Western fathers have agreed to have their children, a boy and a girl, marry. When the story opens the time has come. Two young people have reluctantly agreed to take their medicine in a month's time. The young man is going to 'have a fling' and hopes to get to the wedding a wreck. The girl (Wanda Petit) goes to her ranch. The man sees her on the train, and not knowing her, is interested. He manages to get off at her station. 'The' hotel is kept by a woman (Eugenie Forde) and is a nest of cattle thieves. Tom astonishes the natives and the woman falls in love with him. The foreman of the ranch next to the girl's gives him a job. The girl has made her maid say she is the lady, and Tom makes love to his heart's content, remembering that the month must close only when he sees the 'mistress.' He is accused by the villain of murder and has to make a gallop for it. He catches a train and jumps in through an open window just where the girl is seated."

Hanford C. Judson
The Moving Picture World, 2/2/18

SIX-SHOOTER ANDY

Fox Film Corporation. Released February 24, 1918. *Length:* 5 reels

Director: Sidney A. Franklin. *Scenario:* Bernard McConville, based on his unpublished story titled "The Temple of Justice." *Photography:* J. D. Jennings.

Working title: VIGILANTE DAYS

Still code: 8-

Cast: Tom Mix (Andy Crawford), Enid Markey (Susan Allenby), Bert Woodruff (William Crawford), Sam De Grasse (Tom Slade), Charles Stevens (Mexican John), Pat Chrisman (Ned Skinner), Bob Fleming (Whiskey Bill), Jack Plank (Cy Gallagher), Ben Hammer (Allenby), Georgie Stone (Susan's brother), Lewis Sargent, Buddy Messenger, Virginia Lee Corbin, Violet Radcliffe, Beulah Burns, Raymond Lee, Vivian Plank, Dick Hunter.

"Bannack was the wickedest mining camp in all the West, and the marshal, instead of preventing crime, was at the head of the outlaws himself. Andy Crawford expected a few killings, but when his father was murdered he 'got' the man who did it, even if he was a sheriff's deputy, and then he went after the man higher up and added him to the little list, to say nothing of winning the girl and cleaning up the camp."

The Moving Picture World, 3/2/18

WESTERN BLOOD

Fox Film Corporation. Released April 14, 1918. *Length:* 5 reels

Director: Lynn F. Reynolds. *Scenario:* Tom Mix, from an unpublished story by Mix titled "Ranching De Luxe."

Cast: Tom Mix (Tex Wilson), Victoria Forde (Roberta Stephens), Frank Clark (Col. Stephens), Barney Furey (Wallace Payton), Pat Chrisman (Juan), Buck Gebhardt [Jones].

Still code: 1-

"Tex Wilson, owner of a ranch in New Mexico, is supplying the government with horses. On his way to Los Angeles he sees a runaway horse. He gallops after it and lifts the girl from the saddle of the frightened animal. However, she shows she likes the spirit of Tex. She invites him to a party at her home, where Tex finds he is the only man without a dress suit. He overcomes this difficulty by forcing a guest who had laughed at him to change clothes with him.

"Tex back on the ranch gives a party himself and has all the cowboys in dress suits, despite their objections. Enemies of U.

Right: *Six Shooter Andy* was one of director Sidney A. Franklin's first solo efforts after years of co-directing several series of kiddie films at Majestic, Triangle and Fox with his brother, Chester M. Franklin. Sidney Franklin's success was commemorated by the in-joke name on the saloon front. Here Tom Mix confronts veteran film heavy Sam De Grasse on the streets of Mixville.

Left: *Mr. Logan, U. S. A.* combined Western elements with World War I espionage. In this dramatic moment Suzanne Morton (Kathleen Connors) goes motoring with Gage (Val Paul). She sees her sweetheart, Logan (Mix), with Dolly Dugan (Maud Emery) and guesses the worst. Little does she know that Gage is really a German spy and Dolly is a Secret Service operative working with Tom to thwart his attempts at sabotage.

S. cause the ranch to be raided. Roberta is carried off. Tex follows her across the border and finally effects her rescue."

The Moving Picture World, 4/20/18

". . . It is not an absolutely sure picture for the highbrows or particular audiences, as it is not critic proof. The players 'play up to their parts' in the accepted way in many places and the scenes with running horses are really fine. The lesser characters are likable. The photography is good."

The Moving Picture World, 5/4/18

ACE HIGH

Fox Film Corporation. Released June 9, 1918. *Length:* 5 reels

Director: Lynn F. Reynolds. *Scenario:* Lynn F. Reynolds, based on his unpublished story "Jean of Smoky River." *Photography:* J, D. Jennings, George Richter, William A. Reinhart.

Cast: Tom Mix (Jean Rivard), Lloyd Perl (Jean Rivard, age 10), Lewis Sargent (Jean Rivard, age 15), Kathleen Connors (Annette Dupre), Virginia Lee Corbin (Annette Dupre as a child), Lawrence Peyton (Jack Keefe), Colin Chase (Baptiste Dupre), Jay Morley (Harvey Wright), Pat Chrisman (Louis Cartier).

Still code: 2-

"Such good work is done in the recent Fox picture, 'Ace High,' by everybody concerned, even the Indian players, that it might be called an all-star production without stretching the truth. Tom Mix himself makes a splendid hero for this kind of story, in which he takes the role of a Northwest mounted officer and, as champion of an unprotected girl (Kathleen Connors), saves her from the villainous sheriff from over the border (Lawrence Peyton).

"The Ace High is the name of a rough saloon where the bar can be moved at a signal across a room from the United States into Canada, or the other way, as the coming of authority makes necessary. It is kept by a venal character, perfectly played by Colin Chase, whose wife, now dead, had adopted a baby girl found in the woods and, unknown to him, daughter of an American engineer. She is now grown up and away at a convent, but is coming back. The mounted officer and the sheriff both drop in at the saloon now and again. The officer had been the girl's playmate a few years before and the sheriff, seeing her picture, takes a fancy to her and the plot is on.

"The officer is out on the mountain—the best kind of backgrounds distinguish the whole picture—the girl is coming on the stage. The sheriff has set his gang on to rob the stage of a package of money and the officer sees it held up. There's a dash to the rescue and a runaway, with the girl the

only occupant of the rocking vehicle; then more wild galloping and a few well-handled scenes in which the girl and the man recognize each other. The officer knows that he is taking the girl back to danger, but doesn't know that her foster father has decided to sell her to the sheriff.

"There is no lack of fresh interest in the story that follows a path often taken by other pictures of this kind, and it comes largely from the new and apparently extemporaneous way the players go about the business. The flight of the man with the girl down a dangerous looking rapid to escape the gang of the sheriff seems a bit too perilous to be at all trite. It isn't likely to be repeated often and carries through some beautiful scenery.

"Director Lynn Reynolds has scored another triumph in outdoor directing."

The Moving Picture World, 6/15/18

WHO'S YOUR FATHER?

Fox Film Corporation. Henry Lehrman Production. A Fox Sunshine Comedy. Released June 30, 1918. *Length:* 2 reels.

Producer: Henry Lehrman. *Director:* Tom Mix.

Cast: Tom Mix (Tom Hartrigger)

Note: Tom Mix directed and starred in this two-reel Sunshine comedy, but additional cast members and synopsis have not been found. The copyright deposit material on the picture consists of a seven page continuity, which outlines the shots in a general way (for example: "13 Ext. yard-Mix enters by gate") and gives the first few words of the subtitles (for example: "S.T. And if Gumboot lives till"). From this continuity it is possible to determine that Tom and Sheriff Oscar Gumboot are rivals for the hand of Olive Raspberry. Other characters included: Bud Ranson, the outlaw; The Mayor; a white baby; a black couple and their baby; a lion; and a mule. The plot is set in motion when a prairie schooner rolls into a body of water and overturns. A baby cradle in the wagon floats away, and Tom rescues the baby. The balance of the plot deals with a series of mistaken identity gags revolving around the white baby, and the black baby. From the brief descriptions, the action seems to have been rude and raucous in the manner of TOM AND JERRY MIX.

MR. LOGAN, U. S. A.

Fox Film Corporation. Fox Victory Pictures. Released September 8, 1918. *Length:* 4,135 feet [5 reels]

Director: Lynn F. Reynolds. *Scenario:* Lynn F. Reynolds, based on "Mysterious Logan" by Jay Coffin. *Photography:* J. D. Jennings.

Still code: #4-

Cast: Tom Mix (Jim Logan), Kathleen Connors (Suzanne Morton), Dick La Reno (Uncle Billy Morton), Charles Le Moyne (Jim Crosby), Jack W. Dill (Olsen), Val Paul (J. Alexander Gage, also known as Meier), Maude Emery (Dolly Dugan).

"In New Mexico one of the large tungsten mines is owned and operated by William Morton, affectionately known by his associates and employees as Uncle Billy Morton. At the outbreak of the war he increases his activities as this metal is of great value to the Government for war purposes. Uncle Billy lives near the shaft of the mine with his niece, Suzanne. When things at the mine are humming a man giving his name as Gage arrives in the town. He is in reality an agent of the German government, come with the purpose of instigating a strike among the miners. His accomplice turns out to be the superintendent of the mine.

"About the same time Jim Logan comes to town. He shortly wins Suzanne's gratitude and admiration by shooting a gila monster as it is about to strike at her and then rescuing her from a perilous position on the side of a cliff, where in her nervous fright she fell.

"Gage is successful in persuading the miners to call a strike, but Logan succeeds in frustrating his plot for the present by breaking up the meeting. To discredit him with Suzanne, Gage circulates stories about his relations with a chorus girl in the public place by the name of Dolly Dugan. Uncle Billy is beset by four of the plotters and is rescued by Logan. But Gage again plays against him. On a trumped up charge Logan is arrested by the sheriff. Dolly aids in his escape.

"Gage kidnaps Suzanne and lays plans to blow up the mine. But Logan at last gains the upper hand. He routs the strikers with the assistance of some mule skinners and their animals and captures Gage and Suzanne after a long pursuit. Not until then does he disclose the fact that he and Dolly are Secret Service operatives and so, of course, all ends happily."

Motion Picture News, 9/28/18

FAME AND FORTUNE

Fox Film Corporation. Fox Victory Pictures. Released October 20, 1918. *Length:* 5 reels

Director: Lynn F. Reynolds. *Scenario:* Bennett R. Cohen, based on the story "Slow Burgess" by Charles Alden Seltzer. *Photography:* J. D. Jennings.

Still code: #3-

Cast: Tom Mix (Clay Burgess), Kathleen Connors (Della Bowen), George Nicholls ("Big" Dave Dawley), Charles McHugh (Judge Quinn), Annette DeFoe (Mattie Carson), Val Paul (Flash Denby), Jack Dill (Ben Davis), E. N. Wallock (Kuneen), Clarence Burton (Sheriff of Palo).

"When William Burgess, president and owner of the only bank in the little Western town of Palo, died, 'Big' Dave Dawley (George Nicholls) hit upon a clever plan, as he thought, of getting possession of the bank. Clay Burgess (Tom Mix), the son, was a wanderer and had been absent from his home several years and it was not until his father had been buried that he received news of his death.

"'Big' Dave enlists the aid of Judge Quinn (Charles McHugh), who was the only source of law Palo had. The judge did not favor 'Big' Dave's plan but he was bullied into assisting in it. Dawley succeeds in bullying the judge but he is not so successful in getting Ben Davis (Jack Dill) in affixing his signature as a notary public. For refusing, Ben is driven from town by a threat of mal-treatment from Dawley's henchmen. Dawley gets information that Clay Burgess is due to arrive in Palo to take over his late father's bank, and he sends his henchmen to prevent his coming. They meet Clay just outside of the town but Clay bests the lot of them and rides to the nearest ranch house, where lives Della Bowen (Kathleen Connors) and Ben Davis, who works the ranch for her since his expulsion from Palo by Dawley's men. Davis had in his possession, the will of the late William Burgess, which provided that his son, Clay, should get all of his possessions, including the bank. After Clay's wounds have been nursed by Della, he departs for the lawless town in which lives William Cache and his band. He enlists their aid to assist him in wiping out Dawley and his gang. From this time on there is enacted a series of adventures in which Clay Burgess is the hero. He eventually exterminates the Dawley gang, wins Kathleen [sic] and takes the office of president and owner of the Palo bank.

Motion Picture News, 9/7/18

1919

TREAT 'EM ROUGH

Fox Film Corporation. Released January 5, 1919. *Length:* 5 reels

Left: Tom gets the drop on his pursuers in *Fame and Fortune*. Although many of his early Fox features were relatively serious in theme, Tom Mix brought a light-hearted spirit to the proceedings that set him apart from more somber screen cowboys of the Teens. Here Tom rides Tony, the future Wonder Horse, but he had not yet settled on his permanent movie mount, and rode several different animals in his early Fox features.

Below: Nearly five years after he worked at the Diamond S Ranch studio, Tom returned to Prescott, Arizona in 1918 for *Treat 'em Rough*. The picture was notable as the last film in which Tom rode his favorite horse, Old Blue. On the trail of rustlers, two-gun man Ned Ferguson (Mix), seeks information from some hands around the chuck wagon. Howard Farrell (in apron) is the cook, Boss Glenn shoulders an axe, and heavyset Jack Curtis helps himself to a meal.

Director: Lynn F. Reynolds. *Scenario:* Lynn F. Reynolds, based on the novel "Two Gun Man" by Charles Alden Seltzer.

Cast: Tom Mix (Ned Ferguson), Jane Novak (Mary Radford), Val Paul (Ben Radford), Charles Le Moyne (Dave Leviatt), Jack Curtis (John Stafford), Smoke Turner.

Working title: THE TWO-GUN MAN

Note: Filmed on location at Prescott, Arizona.

"In certain important respects this five-reel subject, 'Treat 'Em Rough,' sets a new high water mark for Western dramas. It is built from the ground up, as the saying goes, and contains much that will amuse and astonish observers. It conveys a sense of authority in every scene.

"Tom Mix, whose previous good work in 'Ace High,' 'Cupid's Round Up,' and other numbers has the leading role, that of a two-gun man named Ned Ferguson. Ned has a breezy way with 'wimen and hosses,' and some of the stunts he accomplishes are truly unusual. In one instance he performs the extremely hazardous job of bulldogging a steer for the purpose of splitting a stampede of cattle, incidentally saving his own life and that of the heroine. The stampede and accompanying prairie fire are brilliantly staged, and reflect great credit on all concerned.

"Subtitles, of which there are many, play an important part in this frontier yarn. They are true to plot and characterization, and contain many an additional gleam of good humor. They read as though they might have been judiciously selected from the original novel by Charles Alden Seltzer. If so, the practice should be followed more frequently, for these subtitles have a freshness of their own, and are not mere explanatory lines thrown in for the sake of continuity.

"Jane Novak plays the part of the heroine in good style; Charles LeMoyne makes an interesting villain, and Val Paul plays the heroine's brother.

"This successful subject, which is 'big' and reflects the West in every department in what may be called a grand scale, was adapted and directed by Lynn Reynolds, with photography by Dev. Jennings."

Robert C. McElvray
The Moving Picture World, 12/21/18

HELL ROARIN' REFORM

Fox Film Corporation. Fox Victory Pictures. Released February 16, 1919. *Length:* 5 reels

Director: Edward J. Le Saint. *Scenario:* Charles Kenyon, based on an unpublished story by Joseph Anthony Roach titled "Fakin' for God." *Photography:* Friend F. Baker.

Cast: Tom Mix (Tim), Kathleen Connors (Doris Jenkins), George Barell (Jenkins, her father), B. M. "Smoke" Turner (Minister), Jack Curtis (Baxter), Cupie Morgan (Bartender).

Still code: 10-

"Tarantula had driven one preacher out of town and didn't want another one so soon. So when one came riding in shortly after his brother's enforced departure there was much disgust among the Tarantula townsfolk. Unlucky for them, they didn't know the identity of this preacher. For preacher he was not and never thought to be, really. It so happened that while Tim, cowboy, good-fellow, was riding along the road with money of a Belgian Babies' Milk Fund, he had been set upon by bandits and robbed. Shortly after, he had met the preacher who had been run out of Tarantula. Then and there he decided to aproach the wicked town and teach its inhabitants a whole bunch of lessons.

"So Tim arrives and opens church. Not for long, however. The bandits lock him in and then by skillfully employing their lariats they pull the house of worship down over his ears. He escapes and determining upon revenge, rides to Baxter's saloon. Baxter just about owns Tarantula. At least he operates it according to his own way of thinking. Baxter had locked the doors, anticipating the coming of Tim but, nothing daunted, the pseudo minister rides his horse up on a balcony, leaps him to the roof of the saloon and crashes through to the floor. Baxter escapes him and—stealing Tim's girl—dashes off to force her to marry him. Tim gives pursuit and overtakes the villain just in time. At the point of a gun he forces Baxter to be a witness to his marriage while, still at the point of a gun, he forces him to make out a check to go toward building a new church."

Motion Picture News, 3/1/19

FIGHTING FOR GOLD

Fox Film Corporation. Fox Victory Pictures. Released March 30, 1919. *Length:* 5 reels

Director: Edward J. Le Saint. *Scenario:* Charles Kenyon, based on the novel "Highgrader" by William MacLeod Raine.

Cast: Tom Mix (Jack Kilmeny), Teddy Sampson (Moya), Sid Jordan (Jim Bleyer), Jack Nelson (Curly Brandon), Harry Lounsdale (Bobyan Verinder), Robert Dunbar (Lord Farquar), Hattie Buskirk (Lady Farquar), Frank Clark (Sheriff), Lucille Young (Pansy)

Note: Approximately two reels of FIGHTING FOR GOLD are known to survive.

'Left: Tom applies a little *Hell Roarin' Reform* to the town bad man played by Jack Curtis. The picture was the first of six Tom Mix films directed by Edward J. Le Saint. In the early 1930's, when Le Saint was no longer directing and somewhat down on his luck, Mix gave him work as a character actor in *Destry Rides Again* and *The Texas Bad Man*.

Right: Jack Kilmeny (Tom Mix) sits down for some libation with Lord and Lady Farquar (Robert Dunbar and Hattie Buskirk) in *Fighting For Gold*. Approximately two of the five reels of *Fighting For Gold* still exist, and show it to have been a well-produced entertainment. It is the earliest example of Tom's Fox feature work to survive.

Right: Kent Hollis (Mix) insists that he can clean up the town without resorting to firearms in *The Coming of the Law*. The identity of the incredulous bad man is unknown. The curved pockets with arrow tip points on Tom's slacks are among the many style innovations developed by Mix that have become standard in Western clothes over the years.

Left: Donald McTavish (Tom Mix) tries to free himself before frost bite sets in on *The Wilderness Trail*. Critics complained that there were fewer stunts in this than in previous Mix features.

Still code: 11-

"... Mix again demonstrates that he can ride up and down at any angle, that he can rope four men at one time and break up a plot against him, and that he is a wonderful marksman. He proves, too, that his leading lady, Teddy Sampson, is much safer in his arms than she is riding alone in a runaway wagon. In this scene Mix, riding at breakneck speed, calls to the girl to jump from the wagon and he catches her in his arms as easily as a professional catches a baseball.

"... It tells the story of an English miner working a claim in the United States. His troubles are looking after his wayward partner and keeping the British firm operating on the land next to him from jumping his claim. Even when romance enters the routine of this by no means dull existence, the fellow's troubles increase instead of disappearing. There is much villainy afoot and the hero has a hard time of it keeping himself out of jail for a crime he did not commit, keeping his mine and keeping his girl. However, he comes through with flying colors after the thrills are over."

Pressbook copy

THE COMING OF THE LAW

Fox Film Corporation. Fox Victory Pictures. Released May 11, 1919. *Length:* 5 reels

Director: Arthur Rosson and Lynn F. Reynolds [see note]. *Scenario:* Dennison Clift and Arthur Rosson, based on the novel by Charles Alden Seltzer. *Photography:* Fred Le Roy Granville. Assistant Cameraman: Dan Clark. *Assistant Director:* Richard Rosson.

Cast: Tom Mix (Kent Hollis), Brownie Vernon (Nellie Hazelton), George Nicholls (Big Bill Dunleavy), Jack Curtis (Judge Graney), Sid Jordan (Neal Norton), B. M. "Smoke" Turner (Potter), Charles Le Moyne ("Ten Spot"), Pat Chrisman ("Yuma Ed"), Lewis Sargent (Jiggs), Jack Dill (Ace), Harry Dunkinson (Sheriff), Banty Caldwell, Earl Simpson, Dick Hunter, Buck Gebhardt [Jones], Pedro Leone, Pres Frith.

Note: Lynn F. Reynolds was announced as director, and receives credit on studio release still photos. A surviving daily cast report and production still show Arthur Rosson as director. The still code is consistent with Lynn Reynolds's numerical sequence.

Still code: 6-

"In the story, Mix, in the character of Kent Hollis, enters Dry Bottom, New Mexico, like any other tenderfoot, without guns; but he has brought with him two powerful fists and a clear and cool brain. There is no law in Dry Bottom when he arrives. The cattle rustlers, headed by big Bill Dunlavey, are running the town. The sheriff does their will, and the only honest official is Judge Graney, whose attempts to keep things straight are continually thwarted. But when the Judge and Hollis get going they soon rout the bad men and bring the law into Dry Bottom to stay.

"Hollis is aided in his fight by Nellie Hazelton, a charming and fearless girl of the plains. Nellie gets her reward by marrying Kent."

Pressbook copy

THE WILDERNESS TRAIL

Fox Film Corporation. Released July 6, 1919. *Length:* 5 reels

Director: Edward J. Le Saint. *Scenario:* Charles Kenyon, based on an unpublished story by Frank Williams. *Photography:* Friend F. Baker. *Assistant Director:* Walter de Courcey.

Cast: Tom Mix (Donald MacTavish), Colleen Moore (Jeanne Fitzpatrick), Sid Jordan (Sergius), Frank M. Clark (Angus Fitzpatrick), Lulu Warrenton (Old Mary), Pat Chrisman (Indian), Jack Nelson (Half-breed).

Still code: L-12

"It is good to see Tom Mix out of his chaps and sombrero and bedecked for a change in the outfit of a Hudson Bay trapper. The only thing amiss as far as the star is concerned is the fact that he is not so well supplied with stunts as heretofore. In 'The Wilderness Trail' he emerges from his familiar role of performing hazardous feats in order to take up the story's burden.

"It presents as vividly as ever the primitive account of the Hudson Bay colonists. The Factor is the same stern, relentless ruler and the hero is painted in tremendous conflict with him. And the latter has to fight his way through a horde of enemies before he marries the Factor's daughter. A few inconsistencies creep out which are almost negligible when the fine points of the picture are appreciated.

"There is an unlimited quota of action unfolded and every scene is charged with suspense. And embellishing it all is a picturesque background of northern scenery with the elements of nature in ceaseless conflict. Director Le Saint has not missed a single opportunity to give a colorful star a colorful picture. Every detail of plot, characterization, and setting is in its proper place."

Laurence Reid *Motion Picture News, 7/19/19*

ROUGH RIDING ROMANCE

Fox Film Corporation. Tom Mix Series. Released August 24, 1919. *Length:* 5 reels

Director: Arthur Rosson. *Scenario:* Charles Kenyon, based on his unpublished story "The Romance of Cow Hollow." *Photography:* Fred Le Roy Granville.

Cast: Tom Mix (Phineas Dobbs), Juanita Hansen (The Princess), Pat Chrisman (Curley), Spotiswoode Aitken (The King), Jack Nelson (Pietro, the spy), Sid Jordan (Pat Leary), Frankie Lee.

Note: Some scenes for this film were shot in San Franciso. ROUGH RIDING ROMANCE was reissued in 1929.

Working title: THE ROMANCE OF COW HOLLOW

Still code: R-2

"Phineas Dobbs (Tom Mix), day dreamer, owns a small ranch in Cow Hollow. Petroleum is found and Phineas is made rich.

"Then comes a girl—held up at the town by brief railroad trouble. Mix rescues her from the Cow Hollow bad man, and because of his bravery she begs him to follow her to San Francisco, where she'll need him.

"He follows the girl. The girl's father turns out to be a Balkan king and she a real princess, both in distress and held by conspirators hoping to obtain ransom. But Phineas and his wonderful horse, in a series of the most hazardous stunts ever screened, liberates both princess and king.

"For the fair lady's sake, Mix does a wonderful lassoing of a flying train, pulling himself up by his lariat to the roof of a car.

"For her sake, Mix and his famous horse, Tony, tear like mad up six flights of fire-escape.

"Then, bold in rescue but shy in love, Phineas returns sadly to the modest hamlet he calls home, believing that the 'love stuff' in fairy stories does not come true and striving to console himself in lovelorn fashion.

"But the princess knew the woman's way of making fairy tales come all true, and so she follows Phineas to little Cow Hollow and—no, she doesn't actually propose to him, but the fade out of the picture makes the fairy tale complete."

Pressbook copy

THE SPEED MANIAC

Fox Film Corporation. Tom Mix Series. Released October 19, 1919. *Length:* 5 reels

Director: Edward J. Le Saint. *Scenario:* Dennison Clift, based on the story "High Speed" by H. H. Van Loan. *Photography:* Fred Le Roy Granville.

Cast: Tom Mix (Billy Porter), Eva Novak (Pearl Matthews), Charles K. French (John B. Prescott), Hayward Mack (Philip Malcolm), L. C. Shumway (Knockout McClusky), Helen Wright (Mary), Jack Curtis (Red Meegan), Georgie Stone (Jim McClusky), George H. Hackathorn (Tom Matthews), Charles Hill Mailes (John Matthews), Ernest Shields (Cigarette Keefe), Buck Gebhardt [Jones].

Working title: HIGH SPEED

"From the introductory scene until the final close- up the action mingles thrills and laughs in such generous proportions that the interest is never allowed to drop . . . Mr. Mix assumes the role of Billy Porter, a ranch owner, who gives up country life for the more strenuous one of the city [to try to sell his new car invention]. No sooner does he step off the Frisco ferryboat than he is fleeced out of his money. A little newsboy expends him so much sympathy that Billy takes him in charge, and also his father, a pugilist. And trains the latter for the bout with Tiger Doran. But Knockout's good right arm is feared, and when the moment of the fight arrives the enemy camp ses to it that he is drugged.

"With a sum of $5,000 on the fight Billy is forced to enter the ring himself or forfeit the money. And he wins via the knockout route. [With the winnings from the fight, Billy perfects his car and wins the big race].

Pressbook copy

THE FEUD

Fox Film Corporation. Tom Mix Series. Released December 7, 1919. *Length:* 5 reels

Director: Edward J. Le Saint. *Scenario:* Charles Kenyon, based on his unpublished story. *Photography:* J. Dev Jennings, John Leezer, Irving Rosenberg.

Cast: Tom Mix (Jere Lynch/John Smith), Eva Novak (Betty Summers/Betty Brown), Claire McDowell (Mary Lynch), J. Arthur Mackley (William Lynch), John Cosar (Horace Summers), Mollie McConnell (Mrs. Summers), Lloyd Bacon (Ben Summers), Joseph Bennett (Cal Brown), Jean Calhoun (Ray Saunders), Frank Thorne (Bob Lynch), Guy Eakins (Dan Lynch), Sid Jordan (Bill Brady), Nelson McDowell (McFadden), Lucretia Harris (Nancy, the negro mammy).

Still code: L 15

Left: Tom Mix strikes a menacing pose while Tony the wonder horse plays dead in *Rough Riding Romance*. While the company was on location in San Francisco on this picture, Mix met young George O'Brien and offered him a job if he ever came to Hollywood. O'Brien came and worked for a time as an assistant cameraman with both the Mix and the Buck Jones units before the heavy economic recession of 1921 caused cut-backs in the studios.

Right: The young inventor poses for a snapshot in his new racing car in *The Speed Maniac*. Off screen, Tom Mix was a fair race car driver in his own right. On July 20, 1919 he won the Moving Picture Stars-Producers-Directors Race at Ascot Speedway. The trophy he received is now on display at the Tom Mix Museum in Dewey, Oklahoma.

"Memories of the days of crinolines and hoopskirts, of men who wore their hair long and were quick on the trigger—of pioneer days and romance are conjured up by 'The Feud' . . . This new production is rich in interest, for its action is laid in the most stirring days of American history. Tom Mix appears quite at home in the 1860 costume which he wears during the episode when he is drawn into the feud as the son of one of the warring families. Later the star is seen as a pioneer in the early days of the West. He fits the role of frontiersman perfectly, and his expert horsemanship enables him to perform several unique feats. . .

"The famous Santa Fe trail, which was blazed westward by the blood of pioneers, is seen. . . . Some of the exciting incidents of this thrilling photoplay show Tom Mix as Jere Lynch, at the head of a caravan which is proceeding along the Santa Fe trail when it is attacked by Indians. The stubborn defense by the pioneers and a daring dash through the Indians are shown."

Pressbook copy

1920 ——————————————

THE CYCLONE

Fox Film Corporation. Released January 24, 1920. *Length:* 5 reels.

Director: Cliff Smith. *Scenario:* J. Anthony Roach. Based on "Sergeant Jim" by Col. Todhunter Marigold. *Photography:* Frank Good.

Cast: Tom Mix (Sergeant Tim Ryerson), Colleen Moore (Sylvia Sturgis), Henry Hebert (Ferdinand Baird), William Ellingford (Silas Sturgis).

Working title: CHINATOWN

Still code: S-1

"The plot casts Mr. Mix as Sergt. Tim Ryerson, champion rider and crack shot of the Northwest Mounted Police, who is assigned to detect an unknown murderer of another Northwest Mounted officer, who had previously been put on the trail of a band of smugglers. Ryerson gets evidence convicting Ferdinand Baird, range boss on the ranch of Silas Sturgis, father of Ryerson's sweetheart, Sylvia. He postpones the arrest, however, until he also uncovers the fact that Baird is the head of a gang of smugglers who are taking Chinese and valuable goods of the race into Vancouver.

"Baird escapes at the border and hurries back to the Sturgis ranch to kidnap Sylvia. Ryerson follows and arrests him, but in backing off the porch, Ryerson stumbles, falls, and Baird fells him. Every time Ryerson tries to rise, Baird brutally kicks him. Only a superman could recover so quickly as does Ryerson.

" . . . Baird gets away with Sylvia, taking her to Vancouver's Chinatown. Ryerson follows a little later and with his clever horse rides to the top of the ramshackled building which houses the dive, plunges through three floors to the cellar, rescues Sylvia and with the aid of a band of policemen who appear on signal, arrest Baird and the other inmates of the place."

Pressbook copy

THE DAREDEVIL

Fox Film Corporation. Released March 20, 1920. *Length:* 5 reels.

Director: Tom Mix. *Scenario:* J. Anthony Roach, from the story "A Hard-Boiled Tenderfoot" by Tom Mix. *Photography:* Dev Jennings.

Cast: Tom Mix (Timothy Atkinson), Eva Novak (Alice Spencer), Charles K. French (Ralph Spencer), L. C. Shumway (Gilroy Blake), Sid Jordan (Black Donlin), Lucille Young (Mazie), L. S. McKee (Sheriff), Pat Chrisman (Mexican outlaw), George Hernandez (Buchanan Atkinson), Harry Dunkinson (ranch owner).

" . . . Knowing best what he can do, Mr. Mix has fashioned a story which outdoes all his previous offerings in the unadulterated play of action. He provides himself opportunities to execute haxardous feats which are positively amazing. Playing the part of a tenderfoot he arrives in the West to make good. And his entrance is made via the roof of a Pullman train. He gets a position as operator at the telegraph station and his chance to save the heroine arives when in pursuit of the bandit.

"Riding his horse alongside of a moving freight train he shoots the padlock off the door of a car, rescues the imprisoned girl and places her in the saddle. Then he jumps into the car and eventually captures the highwaymen. The picture is punctuated with thrill after thrill and all of them are executed with the utmost skill and dash. Let it be said that never has Tom Mix appeared in such a fast-moving picture as 'The Daredevil.' The backgrounds are pictorially perfect and harmonize with the plethora of dramatic scenes. . . ."

Motion Picture News 3/20/20

Left: *The Cyclone* was the second of two pictures young Colleen Moore made with Tom Mix. The films helped bring Moore to the attention of Hollywood producers and gave her career a boost. She went on to become one of the brightest stars of the silent screen.

Below: Black Donlin (Sid Jordan) sizes up his opponent Timothy Atkinson (Tom Mix), as *The Daredevil* takes target practice in an underground speakeasy. *The Daredevil* was the only Fox feature film directed by Mix, although he took an active interest in the production of his films throughout his screen career.

DESERT LOVE

Fox Film Corporation. Released April 24, 1920. *Length:* 5 reels.

Director: Jacques Jaccard. *Scenario:* Jacques Jaccard, based on "One-Quarter Apache," an unpublished story by Tom Mix. *Photography:* Frank Good. *Film Editor:* Lloyd L. Nosler.

Cast: Tom Mix (Buck Marston, Jr.), Francilia Billington (Barbara Remington), Eva Novak (Dolly Remington), Lester Cuneo (The Whelp), Charles K. French (Jack Remington), Jack Curtis (The Wolf).

Still code: J-1

"Mix plays the the part of 'Buck' Marston, sheriff of an Arizona county. Twenty-five years before his father, also a sheriff, had been killed by a band of outlaws, whose names have come into the possession of the son. With endless vigor and energy he runs them down one by one, and finally captures their chief after a thrilling chase. Only one is left, The Whelp, who steals away with the girl loved by Mix. In a scene that is fraught with dangerous stunts the young sheriff rescues the girl and revenges his murdered father."

Presbook copy

THE TERROR

Fox Film Corporation. Released May 29, 1920. *Length:* 5 reels.

Director: Jacques Jaccard. *Scenario:* Jacques Jaccard, based on "No Limit Carson," an unpublished story by Tom Mix. *Photography:* Frank Good.

Cast: Tom Mix (Bat Carson), Francelia Billington (Phyllis Harland), Lester Cuneo ("Con" Norton), Charles K. French (Sheriff Jim Canby), Lucille Younge (Fay LaCrosse), Joseph Bennett (Phil Harland), Wilber Higby (John D. Sutherland).

Still code: J-2

"THE TERROR is a story of the rush for gold in the Sierra Nevada Mountains, and the picture, without question, is the most thrilling Mix has done this season. He is seen as Bat Carson, a deputy United States Marshal who goes to the town of Sonora to investigate mysterious leakages of gold while on its way from mine to town.

"Carson runs down the thieves, one of whom is the Sheriff of Sonora and the other the owner of the dance hall. He also wins a beautiful bride as a reward. The manner in which the intrepid Carson traps the thieves in the mountains when they attempt to hold up a gold shipment furnishes one of the biggest thrills of the picture. . ."

Pressbook copy

THREE GOLD COINS

Fox Film Corporation. Released July 4, 1920. *Length:* 5 reels.

Director: Cliff Smith. *Scenario:* Alvin J. Neitz, based on a story by H. H. Van Loan. *Photography:* Frank Good.

Cast: Tom Mix (Bob Fleming/Bad Pat Duncan), Margaret Loomis (Betty Reed), Frank Whitson (Luther M. Reed), Bert Hadley (J. M. Ballinger), Dick Rush (Rufus Berry), Margaret Cullington (Maria Bimble), Sylvia Jocelyn (Peggy Benson), Bonnie Hill (Katherine Briggs), Sid Jordan (Boots), Walt Robins (Spike), Frank Weed (one- legged townsman).

Still code: S-2

"Mix plays a double role in this new picture. He is first seen as Bob Fleming, a happy-go-lucky cowpuncher, and then as 'Bad Pat' Duncan, a highwayman, wanted for murder. As Bob Fleming, Mix shows such prowess with his pistol that he wins three gold coins offered by a millionaire who seeks to test Bob's marksmanship. Bob also makes a hit with the millionaire's daughter. Two crooks have sold thousands of dollars worth of stock on the representation that Bob's 640 acres of land contain oil—they having 'planted a little oil— try to make away with the stockholder's money. Bob, who has innocently been drawn into the scheme, takes the money and turns it over to the millionaire for safekeeping. Then he is arrested and found guilty of defrauding the stockholders, but escapes. Later he succeeds in capturing 'Bad Pat' Duncan, the outlaw. He is subsequently cleared of the stock swindling charge, and then wins the millionaire's daughter as his bride."

Pressbook copy

THE UNTAMED

Fox Film Corporation. Released August 29, 1920. *Length:* 5 reels.

Director: Emmett J. Flynn. *Scenario:* H. P. Keeler, based on the novel "Untamed" by Max Brand [Frederick Faust]. *Photography:* Frank Good and Irving Rosenberg.

Cast: Tom Mix (Whistling Dan), Pauline Starke (Kate Cumberland), George Siegmann (Jim Silent), Philo McCullough (Lee Haines), James O. Barrows (Joe Cumberland), Charles K. French (Tex Calder), Pat Chrisman (Kilduff), Sid Jordan (Hal Purvis), Major J. A. McGuire (Morgan), Frank M. Clark (Sheriff Morris), Joe Connelly (Buck Daniels).

Still code: F-6

Right: Dolly Remington (Eva Novak) lifts Tom's keys while he breaks a wishbone with older sister Barbara (Francelia Billington) in *Desert Love*. On stage and screen from a tender age, Billington was an accomplished actress, although she was unable to read with any great proficiency. She married long-time Mix co-worker, Lester Cuneo. Novak became Tom's favorite leading lady, appearing in ten of his Fox features.

Left: An exchange of icy stares between Tom Mix and Sid Jordan (at right) signals the beginning of conflict in *The Terror*. Director Jacques (pronounced Jack) Jaccard kept things moving on the set by yelling at his actors and crew whether they deserved it or not. Cowboy Ted French called Jaccard "The screamenist damn man I ever saw." *The Terror* was filmed on location in Sonora, California.

Right: Tom, Sid Jordan, and Walt Robins find themselves intruding at a ladies' tea in *Three Gold Coins*. Leading lady Margaret Loomis is in the white dress with dark jacket. Tom played a double role in this one as the good Bob Fleming and "Bad" Pat Duncan.

Below: Based on a novel by Max Brand, *The Untamed* tells the story of "Whistlin'" Dan Barry, a free soul who follows the migration of the birds. The popularity of the Mix film led to a sequel, and led Brand to change the title of the novel from *Wild Geese* to *The Untamed* when it was reprinted. This is the earliest Mix Fox feature to survive in complete form.

Note: Production started April 20, 1920, and finished June 29, 1920. Filmed on location in Victorville, California

"As a rough and ready cowboy hero and doer of perilous stunts, Tom Mix has for some time been gaining favor with picture goers. In this new Fox subject, very appropriately called 'The Untamed,' he is provided with a finer grade of production than usual, still a western, but one that carries with it a touch of the psychological. He approaches, the character of 'Whistling Dan,' nearer to the outstanding type of screen performers who compel admiration by force of controlled personality rather than by a succession of reckless deeds. . . . Tom Mix has perhaps never before reached the melodramatic heights he attains in the last scenes of this subject, when he has his final accounting with Jim Silent.

"The production shows capable direction throughout. . . . Pauline Starke plays with fine restraint the role of Kate Cumberland, and George Seigmann is forceful as Jim Silent. The picture as a whole is strong in characters, atmosphere, and plot development."

Robert C. McElravy *The Moving Picture World,* 9/4/20

THE TEXAN

Fox Film Corporation. Released October, 1920. *Length:* 6 reels.

Director: Lynn F. Reynolds. *Scenario:* Lynn F. Reynolds and Jules G. Furthman, based on a novel by James B. Hendryx. *Photography:* Frank Good. *Assistant Director:* George H. Webster.

Cast: Tom Mix (Tex Benton), Gloria Hope (Alice Marcum), Robert Walker (Winthrop Endicott), Charles K. French (Wolf River Mayor), Sid Jordan (Jack Purdy), Pat Chrisman ("Bat," a half-breed).

Note: A print of THE TEXAN is said to exist at the Danish Film Museum.

Still code: R-10

". . . Like many of its forerunners it offers the star a full measure of incidents—incidents which he has made peculiarly his own. He is a hard riding, fearless, dextrous, six-shooting cowboy from the plains of Texas who rides over into New Mexico and proceeds to show the natives how 'they do it in the Lone Star state!' A train is stalled in the town and among the travelers are Alice Marcum and Winthrop Endicott, Easterners.

"Of course Mix as Tex Benton makes a decided hit with the girl much to the discomfiture of the young man. Jack Purdy,

who is quite unscrupulous, plans to belittle Tex in the coming rodeo show. But Tex turns up and wins all the laurels. Purdy meanwhile has lured the girl away but she is rescued by Endicott. Believing that he has killed the wretch, he is locked up in jail but is eventually rescued by Tex. So Purdy and his gang start in pursuit but Benton attends to them single-handed. But the girl belongs to the East and the conclusion shows her ready to accept Endicott who has proven himself a man of courage. The picture carries any quantity of stunts and thrills and the humor is quite infectious. Lynn Reynolds' direction is first-rate in every particular."

Motion Picture News, 11/27/20

PRAIRIE TRAILS

Fox Film Corporation. Released December, 1920. *Length:* 6 reels.

Director: George Marshall. *Scenario:* Frank Howard Clark, based on the novel "Prairie Flowers" by James B. Hendryx. *Photography:* Frank B. Good.

Cast: Tom Mix (Tex Benton), Charles K. French (Stephen McWhorter), Kathleen O'Connor (Janet McWhorter), Robert Walker (Witnthrop Adams Endicott), Gloria Hope (Alice Endicott), Sid Jordan (Jack Purdy), Harry Dunkinson (Ike Stork), Billy Elmer (Rod Blake).

Note: A sequel to THE TEXAN.

Still code: MAR-1

"It is very probable that you could run this at matinees for several weeks. The youngsters would storm the box office for it has Tom Mix as its star and enough action to satisfy them— which is going some. But to an evening audience it will appear to be a jumble of unending riding, shooting and diving over cliffs with a story that would hardly be strong enough for a two reeler.

"Its titles are written in farce comedy style, and with their puns and foolishnes, are out of place. But the result is probably no worse than if the title writer had endeavored to make an audience take it seriously. With so much absurd 'wild and woolly' action, it has just about as much convincing drama in it as a serial. It is only in comedy that we expect to see a man jump from a precipice through the wooden roof of a shack, pick himself up and knock out two heavies without a moment's hesitation or without even a scratch as a result.

"The excuse for all this action is very slight. The star, disappointed in love, goes to a small Montana town, gets into an argument, and shoots up the whole town. The sheriff and his posse pursue him and there is considerable riding and

Right: *Prairie Trails* was a follow-up to *The Texan*, proving that sequels are not new to the movies. Today it would be called *The Texan II*, but movie makers in 1920 showed a bit more imagination. In this comic moment from *Prairie Trails* Tom loses his boot, hat and horse after being forced to tend sheep. Although *The Texan* was somewhat serious in tone, under the direction of George Marshall *Prairie Trails* was played largely for laughs.

Below: Tom falls victim to foul play. The villainous Sid Jordan takes Tom by the arms as former boxer Billy Elmer relieves the cowboy of his gun belt and Tom's off-screen valet, known as "Stumpy," takes the feet in a perilous moment from *The Texan*. The Danish Film Museum is said to hold a print of *The Texan*.

chasing. The bandit captures a girl who is rescued after a lot of more riding and shooting, and the star marries the lady of his heart, whose father finally gives his consent. There are in this picture some of the best daredevil stunts which Mix has ever done. But when he shoots the buttons off the sheriff's vest at twenty yards, disguises himself by sticking some straw on his face for a mustache, hangs from a limb of a tree as his enemies ride beneath, knocking one after another off their horses with a swipe of his boot, it is more than any audience can stand. "The production is almost entirely exteriors and the film is colored sepia. Playing opposite the star is Kathleen O'Connor, who has not much to do, and does not look very attractive doing it. As a piece of dramatic construction it is hopeless."

Matthew A. Taylor
Motion Picture News, 1/1/21

1921

THE ROAD DEMON

Fox Film Corporation. Released February, 1921. *Length:* 5 reels.

Director: Lynn F. Reynolds. *Scenario:* Lynn F. Reynolds, based on his unpublished story "Happy-Go-Lucky." *Photography:* Frank B. Good and Benjamin Kline.

Cast: Tom Mix (Hap Higgins), Claire Anderson (Patricia O'Malley), Charles K. French (Dad Higgins), George Hernandez (John O'Malley), Lloyd Bacon (Luther McCabe), Sid Jordan (Lone Weatherby), Charles Arling (Wade Waters), Harold Goodwin (Johnny Brooks), Billy Elmer (Wilson), Frank Tokawaja (Japanese businessman), Lee Phelps (Ryan).

Still code: R-11

Note: Production started September 27, 1920, and completed on November 17, 1920. Filmed on location in Victorville, California.

"Los Angeles-Phoenix road race forms the bulk of this picture. Cross country, up hill and down race over rough country roads and perfect highways. Depends upon thrills, suspense and excitement. Deals mostly with corrupt racing drivers and a struggle between two rival auto manufacturers for a foreign contract. Star acquires his car first place by swapping it for his horse."

Motion Picture News Booking Guide, 12/20-9/21

HANDS OFF!

Fox Film Corporation. Released April, 1921. *Length:* 5 reels (4,158 feet).

Director: George Marshall. *Scenario:* Frank Howard Clark, based on the novel "Oh You Tex" by William MacLeod Raine. *Photography:* Benjamin Kline.

Cast: Tom Mix (Tex Roberts), Pauline Curley (Ramona Wadley), Charles K. French (Clint Wadley), Lloyd Bacon (Ford Wadley), Frank Clark (Captain Jim Ellison), Sid Jordan (Pete Dinsmore), William McCormick (Tony Alviro), Virginia Warwick (Bonita), J. Webster Dill (The Terrible Swede), Marvin Loback (Jumbo).

Still code: MAR-3

". . . Needless to state, this picture is replete with action of the most virile sort. Probably one of the biggest productions Mix has offered to the public. It contains among its thrilling sequences a realistic stampede of horses which has seldom if ever been equalled in picture history. In the path of the maddened animals is a four-year-old youngster, whom Mix reaches just in time. Escape on either side is impossible, so the star simply rushes ahead and jumps into the town pump, stands in the center of the road until the stampede is over.

"There are many other unusually thrilling scenes in this picture which is well up to the standard which this star established for himself when he first started making Western productions."

Motion Picture News, 4/16/21

THE QUEEN OF SHEBA

Fox Film Corporation. Released April, 1921. *Length:* 9 reels (8,279 feet).

Director: J. Gordon Edwards. Supervisor of chariot race sequence: Tom Mix. *Scenario:* Virginia Tracy. *Photography:* John W. Boyle.

Cast: Betty Blythe (The Queen of Sheba), Fritz Leiber (King Solomon), Claire De Lorez (Queen Amrath, wife of Solomon), George Seigmann (King Armud of Sheba), Herbert Heyes (Tamaran, courtier of Sheba), Herschel Mayall (Menton, Sheba's Minister of State), G. Raymond Nye (Adonijah, brother of Solomon), George Nicholls (King David), Genevieve Blinn (Beth-Sheba), Pat Moore (Sheba's son, age 4), Joan Gordon (Nomis, Sheba's sister), William Hardy (Olos, Sheba's giant slave), Paul Cazeneuve (envoy of the Pharaoh), John Cosgrove (King of Tyre), Nell Craig (Princess

Above: Tom and co-driver Harold Goodwin take an unorthodox route in their effort to win the L. A. - Phoenix auto race and secure a big foreign contract for their employer in *The Road Demon*. This is one of a number of films said to be held by the Czech Film Archive in Prague.

Right: Mix makes a flying leap to capture future film director Lloyd Bacon in a tense moment from *Hands Off!* "At that time, Tom was doing all his own stunts," director George Marshall remembered. "There wasn't nothin' he wouldn't do," added cowboy Ted French.

Left: Billy Elmer, who played the role of Cash Hawkins in Cecil B. DeMille's 1914 version of *The Squaw Man*, tries to seduce a young Laura La Plante, but Tom Mix will protect the girl's virtue in *Big Town Round Up*. La Plante is one of several leading ladies who gained attention in Tom Mix pictures. She later became a major star at Universal and is best remembered for her work in *The Cat and the Canary* (1927).

Above-opposite: Tom Mix and Tony in *After Your Own Heart* in which daring and love conquer hate and six-shooters. . .

Below-opposite: Charles K. French and Tom Mix in *The Night Horseman*, sequel to *The Untamed*.

Below: *The Queen of Sheba* was a 1921 Fox super production directed by J. Gordon Edwards and starring Betty Blythe. With his skill as a charioteer and his proven ability with action scenes, Tom Mix was given the responsibility of staging the chariot race sequence. It would be interesting to compare Mix's chariot race with 'Breezy' Eason's and Yakima Canutt's in the 1926 and 1959 versions of *Ben-Hur* but alas, *The Queen of Sheba* is thought to be a lost film.

Vashti), Al Fremont (Captain of Adonijah's army), Earl Crain (Joab).

Still code: E-44

"A historical romance of the Queen of Sheba and King Solomon. The queen saves her people from destruction and proffers her love to Solomon through gratitude for his aid in distress. Spectacular picture of ancient Judea."

Motion Picture News Booking Guide, 9/1/'21–3/1/22

". . . [The chariot race] is punctuated by one long extended thrill with first one rival in the lead and then the other. The director has staged the scene with startling effects. His close-ups and long shots are well timed and placed. One instinctively grasps the arms of the seat as the chariots come tearing straight toward the camera. And Sheba wins. The director made an error of omission in failing to catch the enthusiasm of the stadium throng. Tom Mix is credited with being responsible for the hippodrome events, and he deserves unbounded praise for the manner in which he has enlivened the scene and made it throb with vigorous action. It is our impression that the chariot race should have been placed at the finish. Coming as it does before intermission one anticipates something even more overwhelming in thrill. The concluding reels given up to ancient battle falter—not so much because they are inadequate, but because one expected more from them. . . ."

Laurence Reid *Motion Picture News*, 4/23/21

A RIDIN' ROMEO

Fox Film Corporation. Released June, 1921. *Length:* 5 reels (4,700 feet).

Director: George Marshall. *Scenario:* George Marshall, based on "All Pep," an unpublished story by Tom Mix. *Photography:* Benjamin Kline. *Titles:* Ralph Spence.

Cast: Tom Mix (Jim Rose), Rhea Mitchell (Mabel Brentwood), Pat Chrisman (Highlow, the Indian), Sid Jordan (Jack Walters), Harry Dunkinson (King Brentwood), Eugenie Forde (Queenie Farell), Minnie (squaw).

Working title: THE HORNET'S NEST

Still code: MAR-4

"Western farce, with a few quiet moments. Inventive cowboy has devised all sorts of labor saving devices which he uses in his home. Machinery cooks his breakfast and washes his dishes. Unwelcome suitor gets himself in further touble with prospective father-in-law, chased over countryside by

'gang.' Story ends with star breaking out of jail and winning girl of his choice."

Motion Picture News Booking Guide, 12/20–9/21

BIG TOWN ROUND-UP

Fox Film Corporation. Released July, 1921. *Length:* 5 reels (4,249 feet).

Director: Lynn F. Reynolds. *Scenario:* Lynn F. Reynolds, based on a novel by William MacLeod Raine. *Photography:* Benjamin Kline.

Cast: Tom Mix (Larry McBride), Gilbert "Pee Wee" Holmes (Pee Wee, the runt), Ora Carew (Alice Beaumont), Harry Dunkinson (Luther Beaumont), Laura La Plante (Mildred Hart), William Buckley (Rodney Curtis), Billy Elmer (Jerry Casey), William Crinley (Tim Johnson).

Still code: Rey-14

Note: Production started March 31, 1921, and completed May 11, 1921. Filmed on location in San Francisco, Burbank, and Los Angeles, California.

"Western cowboy goes to city, dresses up to date and gets into thrilling and humorous adventures, after having saved a girl back west from a rattlesnake and from a wild steer. On his way east throws villain off train and is no more than arrived until the protection of a very little girl falls to his lot. Sweetheart becomes jealous of child."

Motion Picture News Booking Guide, 12/20–9/21

AFTER YOUR OWN HEART

Fox Film Corporation. Released August, 1921. *Length:* 5 reels (4,244 feet).

Director: George Marshall. *Scenario:* John Montague. Adaptation: Tom Mix. Based on the short story "After His Own Heart" by William Wallace Cook. *Photography:* Benjamin Kline.

Cast: Tom Mix (Herbert Parker), Ora Carew (Loretta Bramley), George Hernandez (Luke Bramley), William Buckley (Peter Ruddock), Sid Jordan (Tex Marole), E. C. Robinson (aviator), Bill Ward (Fighting Kid).

Still code: Mar-5

"Romance of an up-to-date rachman, woven from dispute over an old waterhole, in which daring and love conquer hate and six-shooters. Wins daughter of enemy ranchman, whom he saves from injury by superb presence of mind and good horsemanship.

Motion Picture News Booking Guide, 12/20-9/21

THE NIGHT HORSEMEN

Fox Film Corporation. Released September, 1921. *Length:* 5 reels (4,970 feet).

Director: Lynn F. Reynolds. *Scenario:* Lynn F. Reynolds, based on the novel WILD GEESE [a.k.a. THE NIGHT HORSE-MAN] by Max Brand (Frederick Faust). *Photography:* Benjamin Kline.

Cast: Tom Mix (Whistling Dan), May Hopkins (Kate Cumberland), Harry Lonsdale (Old Joe Cumberland), Joseph Bennett (Dr. Byrne), Sid Jordan(Buck Daniels), Bert Sprotte (Mac Strann), Cap Anderson (Jerry Strann), Lon Poff (Haw Haw), Charles K. French (Marshal).

"To see Tom Mix as an eccentric, not to say dreamy, knight of the saddle, who wanders off north the night before the date set for his wedding because the wild geese are flying in the same direction, comes somewhat in the nature of a shock. Tom has been enacting such a long line of straight-thinking, no-nonsense-about-'em chaps, that he just doesn't seem the same old daredevil. However, before 'The Night Horseman' is finished the star shows that there is still plenty of fight left in him; also, hard riding; and there is every indication that he will marry and settle down into a properly subdued head of a family. Much is made of the flight of the wild geese, and the director has captured several fine shots of these scenes. The sentiment is frankly theatric and there is a deal more of hate and vengeance than there is of love and tender embraces, but the thrills have not been forgotten and Tom's mount and his dog play important parts in the unfolding of the story. The support is adequate."

Moving Picture World, 9/17/21

THE ROUGH DIAMOND

Fox Film Corporation. Released October, 1921. *Length:* 5 reels (4,458 feet).

Director: Edward Sedgwick. *Scenario:* Edward Sedgwick, based on an unpublished story titled "lay It Out" by Tom Mix and Edward Sedgwick. *Photography:* Benjamin Kline. *Film Editor:* Ralph Spence.

Cast: Tom Mix (Hank Sherman), Eva Novak (Gloria Gomez), Hector Sarno (Emeliano Gomez), Edwin J. Brady (Pedro Sachet), Sid Jordan (Manuel Garcia).

Still code: S-1, or Sedg-1

"Melo-comedy treating of a good-natured adventurer who is responsive to any and every kind of action. Owns a trick horse and joins a circus only to be discharged. Next bobs up as the saviour of a South American republic through his reckless courage."

Motion Picture News Booking Guide, 9/1/21-3/1/22

TRAILIN'

Fox Film Corporation. Released December 11, 1921. *Length:* 5 reels (4,355 feet).

Director: Lynn F. Reynolds. *Scenario:* Lynn F. Reynolds, based on a novel by Max Brand (Frederick Faust). *Photography:* Benjamin Kline.
Cast-Prologue: Jay Morley (William Drew), Cecil Van Auker (John Bard), J. Farrell MacDonald (Piotto), Carol Halloway (Joan).
Cast-*Story:* Tom Mix (Anthony Woodbury), Eva Novak (Sally Fortune), Bert Sprotte (John Woodbury/John Bard), James Gordon (William Drew), Sid Jordan (Steve Nash), William Duvall (Deputy Glendon), Duke Lee (Butch Conklin), Harry Dunkinson (Sandy Ferguson), Al Fremont (Lawlor), Bert Handley (Dr. Young), Carol Halloway (Joan).

Still code: Rey-15

"Mystery melodrama concerning the identity of a youth. He does not know his parentage and complications develop which find him escaping from desperate villains. He eventually confronts the man who is believed to be responsible for his father's death, but finds that this man is his father. Explanations clear the situation."

Motion Picture News Booking Guide, 9/1/21-3/1/22

1922 _____

SKY HIGH

Fox Film Corporation. Released January 15, 1922. *Length:* 5 reels (4,456 feet).

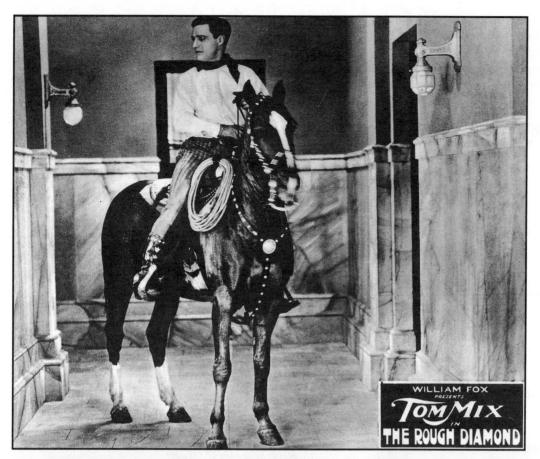

The plots for most Tom Mix westerns were strictly standard issue dime-novel hokum. *The Rough Diamond* (left) told of a circus cowboy who becomes embroiled in a South American revolution, while *Trailin'* (below) used the time-worn "son in search of his father's killer" motif, although novelist Max Brand provided the tale with a novel twist.

Director: Lynn F. Reynolds. *Scenario:* Lynn F. Reynolds, from his unpublished story titled "The Go Getter." *Assistant Director:* George Webster. *Photography:* Benjamin Kline.

Cast: Tom Mix (Grant Newburg), J. Farrell MacDonald (Jim Halloway), Eva Novak (Estelle, his daughter), Sid Jordan (Bates), William Buckley (Victor Castle), Adele Warner (Marguerite), Wynn Mace (Patterson), Pat Chrisman (Pasquale).

Note: Filmed on location at Grand Canyon, Arizona. Reissued in 1929.

Still Code: Rey-16

"The Grand Canyon of Arizona serves as a background for picture's enactment. Concerns efforts of young immigration officer to squelch a gang which is smuggling Chinese into U. S. from Mexico. He falls in love with ward of the gang leader. Brings about culprit's imprisonment and wins the girl."

Motion Picture News Booking Guide, 4/22

"There is probably no doubt that every exhibitor and patron thought that Tom Mix had reached the peak of his pictures—that having conquered the West from many variations the star was up against it for novel ideas. But Mix has shown in his latest release that he is a figure to be reckoned with—one reason being that he is ever in search for novel adventure. 'Sky High' is well named. The Fox cowboy star is certainly up in the clouds here, for the backgrounds have been caught against the Grand Canyon. Mix has taken the entire company to the wonder spot of America and placed them on locations that are not only appealing to the eye, but magnificent places in which to enact a truly vivid Western.

"If Fox has linked up any newsreels with this feature they have done it in such a skillful manner that the scenes coordinate perfectly with the vital action. The star plays a government agent whose duty is to capture the smugglers of Chinese coolies and prevent the Orientals from crossing the border. Word reaches him that they are quartered in the Grand Canyon. And before you know it you are in for a pictorial treat which is positively amazing in scenic scope. There is Mix cutting up some new stunts. You've never seen him scaling the cliffs of the canyon before. He has placed his horse out in pasture at times and trusts his own steady feet here. The marvelous long shots—the collection of close-ups showing the immense rock formations or the deep cliffs and the other beautiful vistas—these are all in the picture. It is the most satisfying pictorial treat that has been offered in a photoplay in many moons.

"It doesn't matter if the plot is rather conventional—that it is a variation on an old theme. Your eyes are feasting on other things. You see Mix capture the ringleaders and effect rescues of the girl whose father is the real culprit. You see him scale these cliffs in dexterous fashion. You see the heroine perched in a rocky cove far up the perpendicular wall. The Colorado River is far beneath and the eye drinks in the landscape and you admit to yourself—'that's fine!' A finale introduces some aeroplane views which present the bird's eye shots. The machine figures in the story to some extent. But the plot is mainly a capture and rescue formula. Your crowd is going to like this one. They are going to sit on the edge of their seats and grip the arms of the chairs. For it carries one big thrill from beginning to end. Eva Novak as the heroine shows plenty of courage which enhances her vivid personality. Sid Jordan is a dependable bad man. Hats off to Lynn Reynolds and Ben Kline, the director and cameraman."

Laurence Reid *Motion Picture News,* 12/31/21

CHASING THE MOON

Fox Film Corporation. Released February 26, 1922. *Length:* 5 reels (5,092 feet).

Director: Edward Sedgwick. *Scenario:* Tom Mix and Edward Sedgwick, from an unpublished story titled "'Round the World in Nothing Flat." *Photography:* Benjamin Kline. *Film Editor:* Ralph Spence.

Cast: Tom Mix (Dwight Locke), Eva Novak (Jane Norworth), William Buckley (Milton Norworth), Sid Jordan (Velvet Joe), Elsie Danbric (Princess Sonia), Wynn Mace (Prince Albert).

Still Code: Sedg-4

"Tom Mix, who has been hitting the bull's eye in his previous efforts, especially in his last release, 'Sky High,' has missed the mark in his new offering, 'Chasing the Moon.' This story lacks a plot and the sponsors must have gauged it correctly for they have attempted to dress it up with snappy titles. It is a good deal like a comic opera story, the little thread of plot intruding here and there but making no impression.

". . . Mix becomes inoculated with some deadly germ, the cure of which is owned by a professor in a foreign country. So the offering becomes a mad race to reach the learned scientist.. One cannot become critical because the action is so absurd. There is [sic] some good thrills displayed on a train and the star has moments when he shows his daring in the saddle. An ultimate rescue brings the story to an end. The titles are snappy enough but often miss their mark through repetition. If one character talked in witty fashion the action would ring more genuine, but the other figures retort with crisp dialogue. And a play or picture which reveals the characters hurling snappy sayings at each other is always

Left: Tom rears up on Tony at the rim of the Grand Canyon while on location for *Sky High*. The plot about smuggling Chinese immigrants into the U. S. was only an excuse for the action. For the first time he played the heroic exploits not just with humor but with a sly tongue in cheek approach that delighted audiences of the 1920's, *Sky High* brought Tom Mix his best critical notices to date and set the pattern for much of his best-loved screen work.

Right: Jane Novak shows concern over a poison infested cut on Tom's hand as William Buckley calls to find an antidote in *Chasing The Moon*. After the critical success of *Sky High*, this film, which found Tom racing 'round the world in search of the scientist who holds the secret cure, was considered something of a disappointment. Director Edward Sedgwick was responsible for some of Hoot Gibson's best Universal Westerns in the 1920's.

WILLIAM FOX
Presents
TOM MIX
in
CHASING THE MOON

Right: A light dusting of snow in Victorville, California brought a halt to filming one morning on *The Fighting Streak*, so Tom took time out for this gag shot creating a monument to himself using a local World War I monument as the base. Sid Jordan stands guard at right.

Below: Only in Hollywood! A wonderfully incongruous shot of Tom Mix in his Canadian Royal Mounted Police costume driving to location in his Stutz touring car in the shadow of California palm trees during production of *Up and Going*.

overdrawn, for the simple reason that you couldn't find such a gifted crowd. . ."

Laurence Reid Motion Picture News, 2/18/22

UP AND GOING

Fox Film Corporation. Released April 2, 1922. *Length:* 5 reels (4,350 feet).

Director: Lynn F. Reynolds. *Scenario:* Lynn F. Reynolds, from an unpublished story titled "Arctic Trails" by Tom Mix and Lynn F. Reynolds. *Photography:* Benjamin Kline and Dan Clark.

Cast: Tom Mix (David Brandon), Eva Novak (Jackie McNabb), William Conklin (Basil Du Bois), Sid Jordan (Louis Patie), Tom O'Brien (Sergeant Langley), Pat Chrisman (Sandy McNabb), Paul Weigel (Father Le Claire).

Still Code: Rey-17

"Treats of English youth whose father in falling heir to a title is ashamed of his wife. He divorces her and informs the boy that she is dead. The mother returns to her native Canada and marries her ex-husband's old partner. Later the youth comes to Canada and joins the Northwest Mounted where he is instrumental in rescuing his mother and childhood sweetheart from two lawbreakers."

Motion Picture News Booking Guide

"With 'Up and Going' coming right on top of 'Sky High' it looks as if Tom Mix is out for a record. The newest release contains all the fine qualities of the last-mentioned with the possible exception of the pictorial values. The Grand Canyon carried 'Sky High' to the heights of photographic appeal. However the latest offering releases some remarkable shots which are fully taken advantage of by an appreciative director. And Lynn Reynolds has long been noted for his ability to collect picturesque locations. He also collaborated with the star in fashioning the story.

"They have chosen a plot a trifle out of the ordinary. Mix appears as a polo player at his introduction and he shows his versatility in other directions besides his horsemanship and his skill with the trigger finger. He can paddle a birch canoe like a son of Deerfoot. The idea behind the story centers upon an old favorite formula—the Northwest Mounted. There is a sort of prologue to this tale which shows the son of an Englishman arriving in Canada in search of adventure. He joins the Mounted and is assigned to the task of bringing in a couple of whisky smugglers—one of whom is married to his mother. And she is forced to flee with him taking with her the hero's childhood swetheart because she knows too much about the crime of the smugglers.

"The picture offers several thrills which take up man-to-man fights. The battle in the canoes and the struggle in the water is sufficiently picturesque to score anywhere. Of course the offering carries its padded scenes. In reality the climax is a long time coming, but the intervening moments are packed with enough punch to carry over the lapses. The hero eventually meets his mother and falls in love with the girl. The star executes some new stunts and his supporting cast is entirely competent consisting as it does of Carol Halloway, trained in the William Duncan school, William Conklin, and Sidney Jordan, who is rapidly becomming 'wallybeery' like in his villainy."

Laurence Reid Motion Picture News, 4/8/22

THE FIGHTING STREAK

Fox Film Corporation. Released May 14, 1922. *Length:* 5 reels (4,888 feet).

Director: Arthur Rosson. *Scenario:* Arthur Rosson, based on the novel "Free Range Lanning" by George Owen Baxter [Frederick Faust]. *Photography:* Dan Clark.

Cast: Tom Mix (Andrew Lanning), Patsy Ruth Miller (Ann Withero), Gerald Pring (Charles Merchant), Al Fremont (Jasper Lanning), Sid Jordan (Bill Dozier), Bert Sprotte (Hal Dozier), Robert Fleming (Chick Heath).

Still Code: Ross-4

"Village blacksmith of meek character rescues girl from runaway. Rival, piqued at the fact that girl is interested in her rescuer, provokes a quarrel with him. The easy going 'smithy' surprises himself by giving his enemy a thorough thrashing. After knocking him unconscious he rides away believing him dead. The man recovers, but hero later kills unscrupulous sheriff in self-defense. Girl aids him and justice and love finally triumph."

Motion Picture News Booking Guide

FOR BIG STAKES

Fox Film Corporation. Released June 18, 1922. *Length:* 5 reels (4,378 feet).

Director: Lynn F. Reynolds. *Scenario:* Lynn F. Reynolds, from his original unpublished story. *Photography:* Dan Clark. *Film Editor:* Ralph Spence.

Right: Tony the Wonder Horse gives Tom a loving nod on location for *Just Tony*. Pat Chrisman made good money when he sold the horse to Tom in 1917 for $600 (on a $14 investment), but Tom got the better of the deal. Tony proved to be a box-office drawing card in his own right.

Left: Inspired by his grandfather's tales of his adventures in the old West, young Henry Boone (Tom Mix) sets out for South America and finds himself smack dab in the middle of yet another Hollywood-style South American revolution in *Do And Dare*. Claire Adams played the role of Juanita Sanchez. Cinematographer Dan Clark's dramatic night-for-night location photography added to the film's appeal. After years of indifferent camera work at Selig, the Mix Fox films were noted for their outstanding photography.

Cast: Tom Mix ("Clean Up" Sudden), Patsy Ruth Miller (Dorothy Clark), Sid Jordan (Scott Mason), Bert Sprotte (Rowell Clark), Joe Harris (Ramon Valdez), Al Fremont (Sheriff Blaisdell), Earl Simpson (Tin Horn Johnnie), Tony (a horse).

Still Code: Rey-18

". . . The hero rides into the picture keeping his identity more or less hidden from the ranch owner and the boys. They never suspect that he is the real owner. And he starts things a-humming by cleaning out the place, capturing the crooked sheriff, aiding a young boy and the latter's father, and riding to the rescue of the girl who has been tied to a tree by the arch-villain. The latter, through revenge for being discarded, returns to burn the ranch house and barn. This scene provides the thrilling climax—and it is exciting to say the least. The fire soon spreads to the adjoining alfalfa and creeps toward the girl. Be it said that the villain perishes in the flames—after which the hero discloses the information that he is the real owner. . . ."

Laurence Reid *Motion Picture News,* 7/1/22

JUST TONY

Fox Film Corporation. Released August 20, 1922. *Length:* 5 reels (5,233 feet).

Director: Lynn F. Reynolds. *Scenario:* Lynn F. Reynolds, based on the short story "Alcatraz" by Max Brand [Frederick Faust]. *Photography:* Dan Clark.

Cast: Tom Mix ("Red" Ferris), Tony (a horse), Claire Adams (Marianne Jordan), J. P. Lockney (Oliver Jordan), Duke Lee (Manuel Cordova), Frank Campeau (Lew Hervey), Walt Robbins (Shorty).
Note: Reissued in 1929.

Still Code: Rey-19

"Novelty Western melodrama. Traces the methods of revenge employed by a wild mustang on the men who mistreated him. He is finally brought to an understanding of the human race when a cowboy and his sweetheart save him from a beating. Later, he saves the cowboy and his sweetheart from the villains and refuses his proffered freedom, preferring to remain with them. The star's trained horse, Tony, plays a principal role and most of the action centers around him."

Motion Picture News Booking Guide

DO AND DARE

Fox Film Corporation. Released October 1, 1922. *Length:* 5 reels (4,744 feet).

Director: Edward Sedgwick. *Scenario:* Edward Sedgwick, from an unpublished story titled "A Kiss In The Dark" by Marion Brooks [Mrs. Oscar C. Apfel]. *Photography:* Dan Clark. *Film Editor:* Ralph Spence.

Cast: Tom Mix (Kit Carson Boone/Henry Boone), Dulcie Cooper (Mary Lee), Claire Adams (Juanita Sanchez), Claude Peyton (Cordoba), Jack Rollins (Jose Sanchez), Hector Sarno (General Sanchez), Wilbur Higby (Col. "Handy" Lee), Bob Klein (Yellow Crow), Gretchen Hartman (Zita).

Working Title: A KISS IN THE DARK

Note: Production started June 28, 1922, completed July 29, 1922. Filmed on location in Chatsworth and Los Angeles, California.

Still Code: Sedg-7

"Like the well advertised shoe polish, Tom Mix has Two in One here. And for two or three reels he is in there fighting and executing thrills in dare-devilish fashion. Then the picture sags while he turns his attention to the comedy. And as a comedian Tom Mix is a good tragedian. The forepart of 'Do and Dare' starts out like an old fashioned western, with the Indians on the rampage, and you begin to sit up and take notice. After a while you discover that it is a narrative within a narrative, told by an old man to his grandson, the former being Kit Carson Boone, an Indian fighter.

"The aged veteran relates how he rescued the boy's grandmother from the redskins and married her. This is told in the flash back style and the action punctuated with plenty of punch and excitement. Particularly well done is the Indian sequence at the time of the attack on the fort. Again the raid on the Wells-Fargo coach stands out as extremely vivid. But the moment that the old man is finished with his story and the grandson resolves to hunt adventure, the picture loses its punch and develops into pretty weak comedy.

"In the first place the comic-opera revolution has long since outlived its usefulness. Only the slapstick can make use of it now. Yet it is employed here for some reason, probably to give Mix a chance to show his versatility. We have seen him in the mythical kingdom plot before, but not without plenty of melodrama. In this secondary plot one sees some helter-skelter action which reveals aimless fighting and considerable chasing. And to give it breath, there are the usual assortment of bloodthirsty revolutionists and facetious sub-titles. Yes, he

Above: In *Catch My Smoke* Tom played a "ghost" returning from World War I to find his ranch in other hands after he is presumed killed in action.

Left: Cashing in on the popularity of Rudolph Valentino, Tom landed in *Arabia* to save the throne of a desert prince. L-R: Edward Piel, Ed Hendershot, [?] MacDonald, Robert 'Clyde Kinney' Ruffner, Tom Mix, Shiney Smith, J. Gamble, and Earl Simpson.

saves the ruler's daughter. And her name is Juanita. That's all there is; there isn't any more."

Laurence Reid Motion Picture News, 10/7/22

ARABIA

Fox Film Corporation. Released November 5, 1922. *Length:* 5 reels (4,448 feet).

Director: Lynn F. Reynolds. *Scenario:* Lynn F. Reynolds, from an unpublished story titled "An Arabian Knight" by Tom Mix and Lynn F. Reynolds. *Photography:* Dan Clark. *Titles:* Hettie Grey Baker.

Cast: Tom Mix (Billy Evans), Barbara Bedford (Janice Terhune), George Hernandez (Arthur Edward Terhune), Norman "Kid McCoy" Selby (Pussy Foot Boggs), Edward Piel (Ibrahim Bulamar), Ralph Yearsley (Waldemar Terhune), Hector Sarno (Ali Hasson).

Note: Production started August 6, 1922, completed September 14, 1922. Also known as TOM MIX IN ARABIA.

Still Code: Rey-20

"A comedy romance. Cowboy meets pretty girl who specializes in dead language. She travels on to Arabia. The hero then tastes adventure when he is tossed out of his hammock by a speeding roadster which is driven by an Arabian prince, heir to the throne. The latter employs the cowboy to double for him in order to evade pursuing Arabs. He goes to Arabia and incurs the enmity of another aspirant to the throne. This man has him kidnapped. He learns that the American girl is also held captive. Overpowering the outlaw band, he rescues the girl. The real prince returns and the lovers prepare to leave for America."

Motion Picture News Booking Guide, #4

"With Douglas Fairbanks using his name for the title of a picture [note: the official title of Fairbanks's 1922 release was *Douglas Fairbanks in Robin Hood*], and Tom Mix coming along with the same idea, we may expect that selling one's self through the title will get some attention from the passing throng. [Comedian] Bull Montana will hear of the stunt soon and will probably exploit himself as 'Bull Montana in Evening Clothes.' Tom Mix, as the title indicates, does a 'Valentino' here to the tune of snappy action, adequate love interest and comedy. It's a rattling good attraction—with the star putting on several new gags to make his Westerns enjoyable. Leave it to this star—he usually gets off the beaten track. . . ."

Laurence Reid Motion Picture News, 11/11/22

CATCH MY SMOKE

Fox Film Corporation. Released December 3, 1922. *Length:* 5 reels (4,070 feet).

Director: William Beaudine. *Scenario:* Jack Strumwasser, based on the novel "Shoe-Bar Stratton" by Joseph B. Ames. *Photography:* Dan Clark.

Cast: Tom Mix (Bob Stratton), Lillian Rich (Mary Thorne), Claude Peyton (Tex Lynch), Gordon Griffith (Bub Jessup), Harry Griffith (Al Draper), Robert Milash (Frank Hurd), Pat Chrisman (Joe Bloss), Cap Anderson (Sheriff), Ruby Lafayette (Mrs. Archer).

Still Code: B-1 or Bea-1

"Cowboy soldier returns from war to find his horse mistreated and his ranch in possession of a pretty girl. He suspects something is wrong. The foreman is responsible for the villainy and is determined to get rid of the girl because the ranch has proven valuable through the discovery of oil. The hero masquerades under an assumed name and restores order. He is compelled to rescue the kidnapped girl and beat the enemies single-handed."

Motion Picture News, 1/13/23

1923

ROMANCE LAND

Fox Film Corporation. Released February 11, 1923. *Length:* 5 reels (4,500 feet).

Director: Edward Sedgwick. *Scenario:* Joseph Franklin Poland, based on "The Gun Fanner" by Kenneth Perkins. *Photography:* Dan Clark.

Cast: Tom Mix ("Pep" Hawkins), Barbara Bedford (Nan Harvess), Frank Brownlee ("Scrub" Hazem), George Webb (Counterfeit Bill), Pat Chrisman (White Eagle), Wynn Mace (Sheriff).

Still Code: Sed-6 or Sedg-6

"Features a romantic cowboy who dreams of rescuing damsels in distress. He finally rescues one from a runaway—the girl being the daughter of the wealthy rancher who is trying to force her into marriage with the foreman. He agrees however, to give his consent to the winner of the rodeo. The cowboy wins and rescues the girl again after she has been kidnapped."

Motion Picture News, 2/24/23

Right: In *Romance Land* Tom played a cowboy dreamer who filled his head with visions of days when knights were bold. Barbara Bedford was the object of his affections.

Left: After being Shanghaied aboard a steamer bound for China, Tom gets the best of his tormentor, played by veteran screen villain George Seigmann, in *Stepping Fast*. Herman Nowlin is in the white shirt and cap at left.

Two jumps from *Three Jumps Ahead*.

Left: Although this still photo is a "doctored" composite, the jump of Fremont Cut (now Beale's Cut) was actually performed for the film by Earl Simpson, who doubled for Mix. In proper perspective, horse and rider were twice the size pictured here. The ramp that gave Simpson the lift to get across the narrow wagon cut is partially visible at left. Although *Three Jumps Ahead* is thought to be a lost film, footage of the jump survives in a trailer prepared by Tom in the 1930's to announce his personal appearances.

Below: Tom Mix and Tony jump a fence, while Dan Clark (right) and the second cameraman stand in a dugout to capture an interesting angle. The second camera was used to make a negative for foreign territories.

THREE JUMPS AHEAD

Fox Film Corporation. Released March 25, 1923. *Length:* 5 reels (4,854 feet).

Director: Jack Ford. *Scenario:* Jack Ford, based on his unpublished story "The Hostage." *Photography:* Dan Clark.

Cast: Tom Mix (Steve Clancy), Alma Bennett (Ann Darrell), Edward Piel (Buck Taggitt), Joseph Girard (John Darrell), Virginia True Boardman (Mrs. Darrell), Margaret Joslin (Alicia), Frank Forde (Ben McLean), Harry Todd (Lige McLean), Earl Simpson.

Still Code: Ford-7

". . . The hero and his uncle are captured by a desperate band of bandits and secreted in a cave where they are flogged by an unwilling prisoner. The later escapes and the westerner is ordered to re-capture him or suffer the death of his uncle. This is the point to introduce some humor. Knowing that the escaped man is hard up for money he plans a ruse whereby his cousins, masquerading as wealthy men, get him interested in a tract of land. They drop a fake telegram on the floor which contains the information that a large sum of money is being sent to them by stagecoach. The old fellow holds up the coach but it carries the leader of the gang. Here he is captured. Then it is up to Mix to effect his rescue because he has fallen in love with his daughter. And so we have the star executing various stunts and putting pep into the picture at the same time.

"It's a complicated story yet one can follow it without losing touch with a single episode. The star's horsemanship is superb. Put this number down as among Mix's best. It is filled with action and suspense and competently played by a well selected cast."

Motion Picture News, 4/14/23

STEPPING FAST

Fox Film Corporation. Released May 13, 1923. *Length:* 5 reels (4,608 feet).

Director: Joseph J. Franz. *Scenario:* Bernard McConville, from his story titled "A Modern Monte Cristo." *Photography:* Dan Clark.

Cast: Tom Mix (Grant Malvern), Claire Adams (Helen Durant), Donald MacDonald (Fabian), Hector Sarno (Martinez), Edward Piel (Sun Yat), George Seigmann ("Red" Pollock), Tom S. Guise (Quentin Durant), Edward Jobson (Commodore Simpson), Ethel Wales (Miss Higgins), Minna Redman (Mrs. Malvern), Tony (a horse).

Note: Production started December 12, 1922, completed January 25, 1923. Locations in Victorville, California.

Still Code: Franz-4

"A young ranchman is captured by criminals because he possesses the secret of the location of a gold mine in the Arizona desert. After being thrown into San Francisco Bay, he is picked up by a tramp steamer and forced to work his way to China, where he again meets the gang. With the aid of some American sailors, Mix and the daughter of the scientist who discovered the mine fight their way out of a Chinese den and start back to the States, where they succeed in getting the treasure."

The Moving Picture World, 5/26/23

SOFT BOILED

Fox Film Corporation. Released August 26, 1923. *Length:* 8 reels (7,054 feet).

Director: John G. Blystone. *Scenario:* John G. Blystone, from an unpublished story by John G. Blystone and Edward Moran titled "Tempered Steel." *Photography:* Dan Clark.

Cast: Tom Mix (Tom Steele), Joseph Girard (the ranch owner), Billie Dove (the girl), L. C. Shumway (road house manager), Tom Wilson (the colored butler), Frank Beal (John Steele), Jack Curtis (ranch foreman), Charles Hill Mailes (the lawyer), Harry Dunkinson (storekeeper), Wilson Hummell (the reformer), Tony (a horse).

Note: Production started March 23, 1923, completed May 14, 1923. Locations in Los Angeles, California. Reissued in 1929.

Still Code: Bly-27

"Romantic comedy-drama. Ill-tempered youth is put on probation to control himself. His wealthy uncle threatens to disinherit him should he fight within thirty days. He avoids temptation and devotes most of his time in training to beat up the villain. He wins the fortune and a wife."

Motion Picture News Booking Guide, #5

"This is the best picture Tom Mix has ever made. . . . As for the star he shows that he is a real comedian in addition to being a stunt actor par excellence. His admirers will be delightfully surprised to see him in 'civvies,' instead of his usual cowboy outfit which he wears for only a few hundred feet. Tom is just as good without his Western accoutrements—in fact, we like him better this way if he can always get such good stories as 'Soft Boiled.' . . . "

Frank Shelton *Motion Picture News*, 8/4/23

THE LONE STAR RANGER

Fox Film Corporation. Released September 9, 1923. *Length:* 6 reels (5,259 feet).

Director: Lambert Hillyer. *Scenario:* Lambert Hillyer, based on the novel by Zane Grey. *Photography:* Dan Clark.

Cast: Tom Mix (Buck Duane), Billie Dove (Helen Longstreth), L. C. Shumway (Lawson), Stanton Heck (Poggin), Edward Peil (Kane), Frank Clark (Laramie), Minna Redman (Mrs. Laramie), Francis Carpenter (Laramie's son), William Conklin (Major Longstreth/Cheseldine), Tom Lingham (Captain McNally), Tony (a horse).

Note: Production started May 25, 1923, completed July 15, 1923. Locations in Los Angeles, California. Reissued in 1928.

Still Code: Hil-1

"Texas Ranger is assigned the task of capturing band of desperate cattle rustlers. He learns, however, that the leader of the gang is the father of his sweetheart—which complicates matters considerably. The Ranger captures the bandits and effects a pardon for the leader for the sake of the girl."

". . . Zane Grey establishes a clientele right off the first reel—to say nothing of Mix's following which is said to be of good sized portions in the towns some distance from the key centers. We would like to see the star, however, in those bright semi-burlesques which featured him the past two seasons."

Laurence Reid *Motion Picture News*, 9/22/23

MILE-A-MINUTE ROMEO

Fox Film Corporation. Released October 28, 1923. *Length:* 6 reels (5,306 feet).

Director: Lambert Hillyer. *Scenario:* Robert N. Lee, based on "The Gun Gentleman" by Max Brand [Frederick Faust].

Cast: Tom Mix (Lucky Bill), Betty Jewel (Molly), J. Gordon Russell (Landry), James Mason (Morgan), Duke Lee (Sheriff), James Quinn (coronor), Tony (a horse).

Note: Production started July 24, 1923, completed September 1, 1923. Locations in Los Angeles, California.

Still Code: Hil-2

"Western melodrama presenting the usual assignment of gun fights and thrills in which Tom Mix specializes. Lucky Bill falls in love with a girl betrothed to another. He takes matters into his own hands and the girl in his arms and rides away with her. She is finally won by his heroism and becomes a willing bride."

Motion Picture News Booking Guide, #6

NORTH OF HUDSON BAY

Fox Film Corporation. Released November 18, 1923. *Length:* 5 reels (4,973 feet).

Director: John Ford. *Scenario:* Jules Furthman, from his unpublished story "Journey of Death." *Photography:* Dan Clark.

Cast: Tom Mix (Michael Dane), Kathleen Key (Estelle McDonald), Jennie Lee (Dane's mother), Frank Campeau (Cameron McDonald), Eugene Pallette (Peter Dane), Will Walling (Angus McKenzie), Frank Leigh (Jeffrey Clough), Fred Kohler (Armand LeMoir).

Note: This film survives in the Czech Film Archive. A 16mm print with Czech flash titles is held by the UCLA Film and Television Archives.

Still Code: Ford-8

"Rancher leaves his mother in States to join his brother and the latter's partner in the Northland where they have made a gold strike. Meets girl on boat and develops a romantic interest in her. Arriving at trading post the hero discovers his brother has been killed and the partner sentenced to death as his supposed murderer. Later he discovers that the girl's uncle, the factor, is guilty. The assassin is accidentally killed and the love interest is renewed."

Motion Picture News, 2/23/24

EYES OF THE FOREST

Fox Film Corporation. Released December 30, 1923. *Length:* 5 reels (4,408 feet).

Director: Lambert Hillyer. *Scenario:* LeRoy Stone, based on a story by Shannon Fife. *Photography:* Daniel Clark.

Cast: Tom Mix (Bruce Thornton), Pauline Starke (Ruth Miller), Sid Jordan (Horgan), Buster Gardner (Sheriff), J. P. Lockney (Jaol Fierro), Tom Lingham (Dr. Jerry MacGinnity), Edwin Wallock (Julius Duval), Tony (a horse).

Above-left: Tom is a bespectacled shoe salesman in *Soft Boiled*. Of course, before the eight reels are finished he dons his Stetson and saves the day. *Soft Boiled* survives in the archive of the George Eastman House in Rochester, New York.

Above-right: The "powder man" detonated the explosion a fraction of a second too early and nearly killed Tom and Tony during this stunt for *Eyes of the Forest*.

Right: Tom performed most of his stunts with cameras close-on so audiences could see that he was doing them himself. This photo from *Mile-a-Minute Romeo* has been retouched to remove some of the blur, but it is still possible to see the support rigging between the stirrups under the saddle. The lack of white socks on the horse's rear legs reveals that although Tom performed this stunt himself, Tony used a double.

Left: Billie Dove, Tom, and William Conklin in *The Lone Star Ranger*, the first of several Zane Grey novels adapted for Mix. Fox recycled their Zane Grey properties every few years making versions with William Farnum in the Teens, Mix in the '20s, George O'Brien in the '30s, and George Montgomery in the '40s.

Below: *North of Hudson Bay* was the first film on which the name John Ford appeared as director. Up to this time he had always been credited as "Jack" Ford. *North of Hudson Bay* survives at the Czech Film Archive. The UCLA Film and Television Archive holds a 16mm copy with Czech flash titles.

Note: Production started September 26, 1923, completed November 5, 1923. Shot on location in Santa Cruz, California.

Still Code: Hil-3

"Not Tom Mix's best picture, but a good one, nevertheless. It is characterized by a good quantity of fast action, the usual heroics, as well as some heart interest and suspense. There are the usual exhibitions of Mix horsemanship, which means, of course, that Tony is one of the picture's assets. Mr. Mix performs some daring aerial acrobatics, such as swinging from horseback onto the dangling rope ladder of a maneuvering airplane and later dropping from it to the ground without the customary aid of a parachute. These feats should prove popular to a majority of picture-goers:—

"An aviation ranger (hero) is successful in apprehending and arresting a man who had committed murder, but for the commission of which the victim's step-daughter (heroine) had been detained. A romance results between the girl and the ranger.

"Tom Mix's legion of followers should be well pleased with 'Eyes of the Forest'; others should find it worthwhile."

Harrison's Reports, 3/29/24

1924 _____

LADIES TO BOARD

Fox Film Corporation. Released February 3, 1924. *Length:* 6 reels.

Director: John G. Blystone. *Scenario:* Donald W. Lee, from on a story by William Dudley Pelley. *Photography:* Daniel Clark.

Cast: Tom Mix (Tom Faxton), Gertrude Olmstead (Edith Oliver), Philo McCullough (Evan Carmichael), Pee Wee Holmes (Bunk McGinnis), Gertrude Claire (Mrs. Carmichael), Dolores Rousse (model).

Note: Production started November 8, 1923, completed December 14, 1923. Shot on locations in Los Angeles, California.

Still Code: Bly-28

"Elderly lady of cantankerous disposition is rescued by westerner when she loses control of her car while touring the open spaces. At her death she remembers his kindness and leaves him her estate, consisting of an Old Ladies Home in East. He induces his cowboy friend to accompany him—and both fall in love—the hero with a pretty nurse, the friend with a housekeeper. The westerner forces a lonely mother's son to return to her—and happines is supreme all around."

Motion PIcture News, 3/1/24

THE TROUBLE SHOOTER

Fox Film Corporation. Released May 4, 1924. *Length:* 6 reels (5,702 feet).

Director: Jack Conway. *Scenario:* Frederic and Fanny Hatton, from their own unpublished story. *Photography:* Daniel Clark.

Cast: Tom Mix (Tom Steele), Kathleen Key (Nancy Brewster), Frank Currier (Benjamin Brewster), J. Gunnis Davis (Pete Highley/Francis Earle), Mike Donlin (Chet Connors), Dolores Rousse (Chiquita), Charles McHugh (Scotty McTavish), Al Fremont (Stephen Kirby).

Still Code: Con-1

"Lineman for power company meets daughter of capitalist, the head of rival company. Both companies want rights to strip of intervening land. The government rules that first company staking claim will be entitled to ownership. The lineman succeeds in getting the rights for his company against tremendous odds—and also gains rival capitalist's consent in winning his daughter.

"... In his job as lineman he puts over a number of hazardous feats. And when mounted on his spirited horse, Tony, he dashes across a trestle spanning a yawning chasm pursued by an express train ... Another scene shows him and his horse narrowly escaping from drowning while stemming the current of a turbulent stream. And to furnish a real novel incident Mix puts his horse on snow shoes and mushes through the white spaces. ..."

Laurence Reid *Motion Picture News, 5/24/24*

THE HEART BUSTER

Fox Film Corporation. Released July 6, 1924. *Length:* 5 reels (4,500 feet).

Director: Jack Conway. *Scenario:* John Stone, based on an unpublished story titled "The Love Bandit" by George Scarborough. *Photography:* Daniel Clark.

Right: Tom Paxton (Tom Mix), becomes the reluctant owner of an old ladies home in the oddball comedy-drama *Ladies to Board*. Here he rescues nurse Edith Oliver (Gertrude Olmstead) from the clutches of Evan Carmichael (Philo McCullough).

Left: Dinner on location during production of *The Trouble Shooter*. Seated at the table (l-r): leading lady Kathleen Key, director Jack Conway, cinematographer Daniel Clark, Dolores Rousse, Tom Mix, assistant director Eugene J. Forde. Seated on the ground tending the campfire is Jim Rush who replaced Banty Caldwell as Tom's chuck wagon cook in the mid-1920's.

Right: Tom is comforted by Lucy Beaumont as Harry Lonsdale looks on in a well-lit and nicely staged moment from *The Last of the Duanes*. This and several other Mix films were reissued by Fox in the 1928-1929 season to supply the demand from exhibitors after Tom left the studio.

Below: The title lobby card for *The Heart Buster*. Tom interrupts a wedding to tell Esther Ralston that her fiance, Cyril Chadwick, is already married. Interestingly, the Tom Mix film was similar in theme to Harold Lloyd's *Girl Shy* made the same year.

William Fox presents

Tom Mix

IN

The Heart Buster

Story by GEORGE SCARBOROUGH
Scenario by JOHN STONE
Directed by
JACK CONWAY

Left: Tom cautions his cowboys on their table manners in *Oh, You Tony!* Among the people at the table: Herman Nowlin (left foreground), Dolores Rousse (at head of table, left, next to Tom), Pat Chrisman (as Indian in Derby), Pee Wee Holmes (near head of table, right, with face just above table), Dick Hunter (third from right), "Bear Valley" Charley Miller (second from right). *Oh You, Tony!* survives at the Library of Congress in materials copied from the Czech Film Archive.

Right: One of the best shots of Tom and Tony is this scene from *Teeth*. Like Tom, Tony had several doubles who were painted up to resemble his distinctive markings. One horse was used for jumps, another for more dangerous stunts. Black Bess was often used for long shots because she was bigger, but Tony was always on hand for the closer angles because he was more compact and looked good with Tom. *Teeth* survives at the Library of Congress in materials copied from elements in the Czech Film Archive.

Cast: Tom Mix (Tod Walton), Esther Ralston (Rose Hillyer), Cyril Chadwick (Edward Gordon), William Courtwright (Justice of the Peace), Frank Currier (John Hillyer), Tom Wilson (George).

Note: Production started May 13, 1924, completed June 14, 1924. Filmed on locations in Los Angeles, California.

Still Code: Con-2

"Cowboy loves a girl who is about to be married to a scoundrel. His attempts to persuade her not to enter the matrimonial yoke are fruitless. The girl continues with her wedding preparations. The cowboy, remembering that villain is already married, tries to establish this evidence—and succeeds. He kidnaps several ministers and finally wins the girl.

"It's a good guess that the principal reason for Tom Mix's popularity is based upon the idea of providing novelty in his pictures. Not a single one of the star's features is a duplicate of another—and while he has been putting over thrills and stunts for several seasons he never follows the beaten path— for each successive picture carries either a new treatment of old tricks or a fulsome quota that must be catalogued as new and up-to-date. Mix in his efforts to surprise filmgoers indicates that he is something of a showman. . ."

Laurence Reid *Motion Picture News,* 7/19/24

THE LAST OF THE DUANES

Fox Film Corporation. Released August 24, 1924. *Length:* 7 reels (6,942 feet).

Director: Lynn F. Reynolds. *Scenario:* Edward J. Montague, from a short story by Zane Grey. *Photography:* Daniel Clark.

Cast: Tom Mix (Buck Duane), Marian Nixon (Jenny), Brinsley Shaw (Cal Bain), Frank Nelson (Euchre), Lucy Beaumont (Mother), Harry Lonsdale (Father).

Note: Reissued in 1929.

Still Code: Rey-23

"Buck Duane is compelled by continuous insults to fight and kill Cal Bain. He makes his getaway and after many adventures joins an outlaw band. He learns that Sheriff Hawkins, bully and cattle rustler, has imprisoned a girl through David Bland, leader of Buck's gang. Buck eventually rescues the girl, makes prisoners of the gang, turns them over to the rangers, of which he becomes one, and marries the girl."

Motion Picture News, 8/30/24

OH, YOU TONY!

Fox Film Corporation. Released September 21, 1924. *Length:* 7 reels (6,302 feet).

Director: John G. Blystone. *Scenario:* Donald W. Lee, from his unpublished story titled "Mixed Manners." *Photography:* Daniel Clark.

Cast: Tom Mix (Tom Masters), Claire Adams (Bety Faine), Dick La Reno (Mark Langdon), Earle Foxe (Jim Overton), Dolores Rousse (The Countess), Charles K. French (Blakely), Pat Chrisman (The Chief), Miles McCarthy (Senator from Arizona), Mathilda Brundage (Senator's wife), May Wallace (etiquette instructor).

Still Code: Bly-29

"Rancher is ignorant that his property is rich in oil. Goes to Washington to have legislation effected toward benefiting ranchers. Gets in power of scheming lobbyists who would mulct him of his money. Squanders money in taking up ettiquette, but saves property by staking it all on horse, Tony, who wins the race. Complications are cleared away and romance triumphs."

"Tom Mix is up to his old tricks of burlesquing conventional western plots. Appreciating the fact that his popularity has increased through furnishing novelty in his patterns, he sees to it that his newest story is fully incorporated with novel high jinks. This one releases more broad comedy than some of his recent efforts. And most of it is highly enjoyable. . . ."

Laurence Reid *Motion Picture News,* 9/27/24

TEETH

Fox Film Corporation. Released November 2, 1924. *Length:* 7 reels (6,190 feet).

Director: John G. Blystone. *Scenario:* Donald W. Lee, from a short story by Clinton H. Stagg and Virginia Hudson Brightman. *Photography:* Daniel Clark.

Cast: Tom Mix (Dave Deering), Lucy Fox (Paula Grayson), George Bancroft (Dan Angus), Edward Piel (Sheriff), Lucien Littlefield (under sheriff), Tony (a horse), Duke (a dog).

Still Code: Bly-31

"Young prospector finds dog sorely wounded. Adopts him. The dog has been thrown off train by villainous baggageman. Hero is sought as murderer but eludes capture for a while—and dog saves him. He is captured eventually but dog enables him to make a getaway. The dog is claimed by his owner, the heroine. Hero wins her love after rescuing her from forest fire."

"The 'toot-ensemble' of the Mix organization has been augmented by Duke, the dog. With Tony, the cowboy star's horse, the animals carry the burden of the story—which is of a familiar western design. But Mix sees to it that like most of his pictures there must be an element of novelty, and the dog does so much in providing excitement and thrills that the gaps in the plot are easily covered by the action and incident. . . . "

Laurence Reid *Motion Picture News, 11/15/24*

THE DEADWOOD COACH

Fox Film Corporation. Released December 7, 1924. *Length:* 7 reels (6,346 feet).

Director: Lynn F. Reynolds. *Scenario:* Lynn F. Reynolds, based on the novel "The Orphan" by Clarence E. Mulford. *Photography:* Daniel Clark.
Cast - Prologue: Frank Coffyn (Walter Gordon), Jane Keckley (Mrs. Gordon), Ernest Butterworth (Jimmie Gordon).
Cast - The Story: Tom Mix (The Orphan), George Bancroft (Tex Wilson), De Witt Jennings (Jim Shields), Buster Gardner (Bill Howland), Lucien Littlefield (Charlie Winter), Doris May (Helen Shields), Norma Wills (Mrs. Shields), Sid Jordan (Need), Nora Cecil (Matilda Shields).

Note: Production started July 28, 1924, completed August, 1924. Filmed on location at Cedar City, Utah and Zion National Park.

Still Code: Rey-24

"Boy living in vicinity of Dakota Bad Lands vows vengeance against man who killed his father. Grows to maturity and earns a notorious reputation as a bandit, though he always escapes the law. Becomes a deadly sharpshooter and succeds in capturing bandits. Falls in love with sheriff's daughter, whom he protects from outlaws. Finally identifies his father's assassin and executes his vengeance."

". . . Any picture dealing with the old stage-coach days when outlaws ruled the road has vital elements provided it is done with a degree of fidelity. Here Lynn Reynolds has captured the spirit of the story and has made a film that should make box-office history. Certainly it is Mix's most elaborate feature and should be his most successful in a long list of winners. The photography is awe-inspiring. It offers rich coloring and is finely tinted."

Laurence Reid *Motion Picture News, 1/10/25*

1925

DICK TURPIN

Fox Film Corporation. Released February 1, 1925. *Length:* 7 reels (6,716 feet).

Director: John G. Blystone. *Scenario:* Charles Kenyon, from a story by Charles Danton and Charles Kenyon. *Photography:* Daniel Clark.

Cast: Tom Mix (Dick Turpin), Kathleen Myers (Alice Brookfield), Philo McCullough (Lord Churlton), James Marcus (Squire Crabstone), Lucille Hutton (Sally, the maid), Alan Hale (Tom King), Bull Montana (Bully Boy), Fay Holderness (barmaid), Jack Herrick (Bristol Bully), Fred Kohler (Taylor).

Still Code: Bly-32

"Notorious highwayman of England steals from rich to give to poor. Runs afoul of aristocrat whose daughter has fallen in love with him. In his attempt to rescue her from being married to cad he places his life in jeopardy. But he outwits his enemies through his timely escapes and finally eludes his pursuers."

"Back to the trimmings and trappings of England's romantic age goes Tom Mix for his latest role—and it is just about the most elaborate picture in which he has ever appeared. You might label it 'costume'—but after watching its lively incident, its compact action—its atmosphere—and the exploits of the central figure . . . you never think of it in the light of costume drama. True the star puts aside his chaps and adorns himself with laces and plumes, but the idea is comparable to the westerns in which he has made himself such a popular figure. He rescues the girl after a dashing exhibition of heroics. The sense of humor which he has flashed in his westerns is in evidence here. . . ."

Laurence Reid
Motion Picture News, 2/7/25

RIDERS OF THE PURPLE SAGE

Fox Film Corporation. Released March 15, 1925. *Length:* 6 reels (5,578 feet).

Director: Lynn F. Reynolds. *Scenario:* Edfrid Bingham, based on the novel by Zane Grey. *Photography:* Daniel Clark.

Cast: Tom Mix (Jim Lassiter), Beatrice Burnham (Millie Erne), Arthur Morrison (Frank Erne), Seesel Ann Johnson (Bess Erne, as a child), Warner Oland (Lew Walters/Judge Dyer), Fred Kohler (Metzger), Charles Newton (Herd), Joe

Right: Doris May and Tom Mix at the rim of Zion Canyon in Utah for *The Deadwood Coach*, based on a novel by Clarence E. Mulford. With thirty day shooting schedules and ample budgets, Mix often made his films in the most spectacular Western locations.

Left: Vicky Mix felt her husband should aspire to more artistic screen efforts, and to please his wife Tom made *Dick Turpin*, a tale of the legendary British highwayman. Despite the frock coats and lace, it resembles a Mix picture in all the other essentials. Here Tom tries to slice an apple off the head of James Marcus with only limited success while Kathleen Myers and Alan Hale look on.

Left: Tom Mix played Lassiter, the man in black, in Zane Grey's *Riders of the Purple Sage*. He kneels over character actor Fred Kohler. Grey's novel has been brought to the screen many times, and the title is the most famous in Western literature, but the story about "sealed wives" and bigamy in hidden Mormon communities has always been sanitized for the movies.

Below: Anne Cornwall restrains Thomas Delmar while Tom is lashed to a chair in a tense moment from *The Rainbow Trail*, sequel to *Riders of the Purple Sage*. While *Riders* was shot in Lone Pine, California, the Mix company went to the Painted Desert in Arizona to shoot *The Rainbow Trail*.

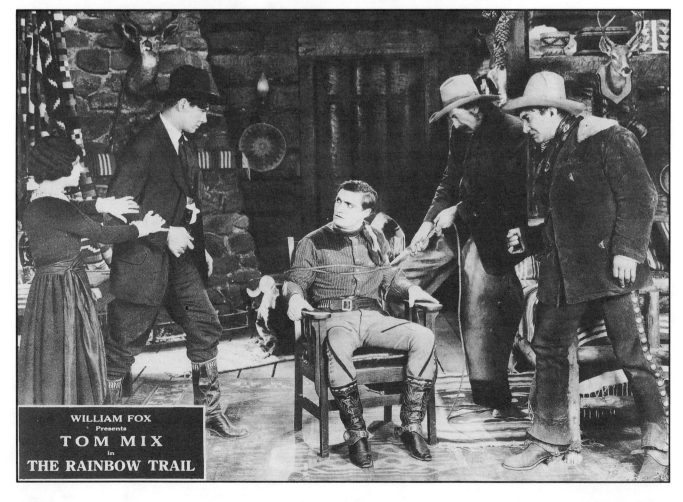

WILLIAM FOX
Presents
TOM MIX
in
THE RAINBOW TRAIL

Rickson (Slack), Mabel Ballin (Jane Withersteen), Charles Le Moyne (Richard Tull), Harold Goodwin (Bern Venters), Marion Nixon (Bess Erne), Dawn O'Day [Anne Shirley] (Fay Larkin), Wilfred Lucas (Oldring).

Note: Production started November 7, 1924, completed December 13, 1924. Filmed on location at Lone Pine, California.

Still Code: Rey-25

"Texas ranger pursues kidnappers of his sister. Encounters youth about to be whipped by rustlers and rescues him. He becomes manager of girl's ranch and a romance develops between them. The ranger discovers the lair of the bandits and the youth captures and falls in love with their apparent leader, a young woman. The bandits outnumbering the ranger pursue him and the ranch owner and chase them into a valley where they become hemmed in from all sides. They prepare to spend their days there."

Motion Picture News, 3/28/25

THE RAINBOW TRAIL

Fox Film Corporation. Released May 24, 1925. *Length:* 6 reels (5,251 feet).

Director: Lynn F. Reynolds. Adaptation: Lynn F. Reynolds, based on the novel by Zane Grey. *Photography:* Daniel Clark.

Cast: Tom Mix (John Shefford), Anne Cornwall (Fay Larkin), George Bancroft (Jake Willets), Lucien Littlefield (Joe Lake), Mark Hamilton (Beasley Willets), Vivian Oakland (Bessie Erne), Thomas Delmar (Venters), Fred De Silva (Shadd), Steve Clements (Nas Ta Bega), Doc Roberts (Lassiter), Carol Halloway (Jane), Diana Miller (Anne).

Note: Filmed on location in Arizona. A sequel to Riders of the Purple Sage.

Still Code: Rey-26

"Western roamer goes in search of his uncle and companions who are imprisoned in valley. To reach them hero has to enter lawless settlement. Protects girl and saves her from forced marriage—but in effecting her rescue he is forced to fight against tremendous odds. Reaches the valley and rescues the victims after encountering danger at every turn."

Motion Picture News, 4/25/25

THE LUCKY HORSESHOE

Fox Film Corporation. Released August 29, 1925. *Length:* 5 reels.

Director: John G. Blystone. *Scenario:* John Stone, based on an unpublished story by Robert Lord. *Assistant Director:* Jasper Blystone. *Photography:* Daniel Clark.

Cast: Tom Mix (Tom Foster), Billie Dove (Eleanor Hunt), Malcolm Waite (Denman), J. Farrell MacDonald (Mack), Clarissa Selwynne (Aunt Ruth), Ann Pennington (dancer), J. Gunnis Davis (valet to Denman), Gary Cooper.

Still Code: Blys-34

"Despite her protestations based on love for Rand Foster, foreman of the ranch left her at the death of her father, Elvira Hunt is hustled off by Aunt Ruth on a tour of European capitals. Her absence is over a period of two years during which she is wooed by a foreigner of alleged distinction, Denman by name. At home Rand patiently awaits her return and has in the meantime placed the ranch on a paying basis. Much to his surprise he finds Denman accompanying Elvira on her return and the wedding announced for the following week. Rand is despondent but is urged by Mack, his chief assistant, to take the lady by force. Mack tells him the story of Don Juan and how that romantic lover took the woman he loved regardless of circumstance and conditions. Denman then orders his servants to kidnap Rand and hold him until the wedding ceremony is over. Accordingly the cowboy is clubbed and bound and during his unconscious moments dreams that he is Don Juan in the court days of Barcelona. The dream sequence is highly interesting, but soon he awakes to the realization he must act quickly or he will have lost Elvira. Freeing himself with a knife he rides to the ranch house in time to expose Denman and claim the bride for his own."

Motion Picture News, 8/29/25

THE EVERLASTING WHISPER

Fox Film Corporation. Released October 11, 1925. *Length:* 6 reels (5,611 feet).

Director: John G. Blystone. *Scenario:* Wyndham Gittens, based on the novel by Jackson Gregory. *Photography:* Daniel Clark.

Left: Playing leading lady to Tom Mix in *The Everlasting Whisper* was a bit of a comedown for Alice Calhoun who had recently been a star with her name above the title at Vitagraph. The film was based on a novel by Jackson Gregory

Below: An offstage shot made during production of *The Lucky Horseshoe*. It should come as no surprise that the story was about a cowhand who loves a rancher's daughter.

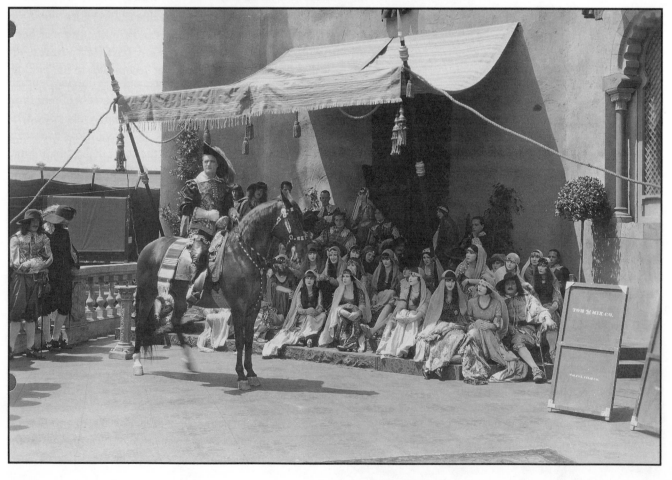

Cast: Tom Mix (Mark King), Alice Calhoun (Gloria Gaynor), Robert Cain (Gratton), George Berrell (Old Honeycutt), Walter James (Aswin Brody), Virginia Madison (Mrs. Gaynor), Karl Dane (Jarrold).

Still Code: Blys-33

"Mark King saves Gloria Gaynor from faling over a cliff when her horse stumbles. He rides with her to her mother's lodge. In the early morning they go together to the cabin of old Honeycutt, who holds the secret of a gold mine. In gratitude for King's kindness Honeycutt reveals the location of the mine. King prevents the marriage of Gloria to Gratton, a swindler and weds her himself. The gold is finally found and Gloria and her lover, in the everlasting whisper of the pines, start their pursuit of happiness."

". . . it would not be fair to class 'The Everlasting Whisper' as just a Westerner, and let it go at that. The picture is distinctly high-grade in point of direction, acting and photography and should be listed as a super-product of the open-air, romance, adventure sort."

George T. Pardy *Motion Picture News,* 10/24/25

THE BEST BAD MAN

Fox Film Corporation. Released December 12, 1925. *Length:* 5 reels (4,983 feet).

Director: John G. Blystone. *Scenario:* Lillie Hayward, based on the novel "Senor Jingle Bells" by Max Brand [Frederick Faust]. *Assistant Director:* Jasper Blystone. *Photography:* Daniel Clark.

Cast: Tom Mix (Hugh Nichols), Clara Bow (Peggy Swain), Buster Gardner (Hank Smith), Cyril Chadwick (Frank Dunlap), Tom Kennedy (Dan Ellis), Frank Beal (Mr. Swain), Judy King (Molly Jones), Tom Wilson (Sam, the butler), Paul Panzer (Sheriff), Tony (a horse).

Still Code: Bly-35

"Jim Nichols visits his Colorado properties in disguise. He finds his agent Dunlap cheating the homesteaders and trying to ruin old Swain, whose daughter Peggy he covets. Dunlap, supposed to be building a great dam, does his best to obstruct the work. When, after many adventures, Jim spoils his schemes, Dunlap blows up the dam. Jim saves Peggy's life in the flood and his horse Tony draws them both to safety. Peggy and Jim are united."

Motion Picture News, 12/12/25

1926

THE YANKEE SEÑOR

Fox Film Corporation. Released January 10, 1926. *Length:* 5 reels (4,902 feet).

Director: Emmett J. Flynn. *Scenario:* Eve Unsell, based on the novel "Conqistador" by Katherine Fullerton Gerould. *Assistant Director:* Ray Flynn. *Photography:* Daniel Clark.

Cast: Tom Mix (Paul Wharton), Olive Borden (Manuelita), Tom Kennedy (Luke Martin), Francis McDonald (Juan Gutierrez), Margaret Livingston (Flora), Alec B. Francis (Don Fernando), Kathryn Hill (Doris Mayne), Martha Mattox (Aunt Abigail), Raymond Wells (ranch foreman), Tony (a horse).

Note: Production started July 12, 1925, completed August 31, 1925.

Still Code: Flynn-19

"A Tom Mix starring picture that has been lifted above the average story and production Fox has given this star heretofore in the regular run of westerns. It is a class picture made that way by just a little touch of Technicolor in the production. It is a shot showing a Mexican fiesta and in natural colors reveals the vari-colored garments of the players in amazing fashion.

"Story is corking with sufficient suspense to make one wonder which girl the hero is finally going to grab off in the finish. From a box office angle the Tom Mix name is enough, but coupled with the snappy production this should be a top money getter.

"With it all it is an action picture with the punch present right from the start. Emmett Flynn, who directed, and the star saw to that.

"The action opens with Mix acting as the general manager and paymaster of a railroad construction gang. He is a soldier of fortune, his natural inclination being the Latin countries, because of his parentage. His mother was a high caste Mexican and his father a New Englander. Both are dead.

"A letter from his mother's father has followed him across the world. When it reaches him he is at the head of the railroad gang.

"About this time a bunch of bandits arrive on the scene intent on copping the pay roll. Mix fools them as far as the money is concerned, but they wreck the camp.

Above: Jacqueline Logan restrains a rifleman as Tom pummels the dress heavy in *Tony Runs Wild*. In the movie world of Tom Mix it was common for the hero to best twenty men single-handed, and audiences came to expect such scenes in Mix pictures.

Below: Clara Bow's career got a boost from her work with Tom Mix in *The Best Bad Man*, which included a daring water rescue. Mix and Bow are seen here, but Roscoe Cline doubled for Mix in some of the more hazardous scenes. *The Best Bad Man* is yet another Mix film that survives with Czech flash titles.

"He then seeks out his grandfather who has adopted a foster child, and when the Yankee-Mex makes himself known he is taken to the old man's heart. He tells his story of the bandit raid and how he fooled the gang. When he returns to get the money his foster uncle goes with him. The uncle is in reality the head of the bandit gang, and he plans to kill two birds with one stone. Mix is bound to a wild horse and is doing a male Mazeppa when Tony comes to his rescue and saves his life.

"From then on it is nip and tuck between Mix and Unk. Money and women play the principal pawns between the two. Finally winding up with a corking rough and tumble fight, with Mix the victor.

"Olive Bordon is opposite Mix. At first she is the betrothed of the Unk, but falls in love with the newcomer, and when he brings a girl from Boston on the scene, there is the deuce to pay. The Unk, foxy greaser, brings in a dancing dame to vamp the ridin' kid. She does her best to put over the little job for him and evidently because she would like to do it, but when turned down she gives a corking imitation of the well known 'hell hath no fury, etc.' Margaret Livingston handles this role nicely.

"Kathryn Hill, as the Back Bay lady, leaves much to be desired, although in the color stuff she looked fairly good. Tom Kennedy and Francis McDonald handle the heavy work, the latter getting his role over with atmospheric clarity.

"A touch of comedy is added through the dragging in of a dirty story that is cleaned up and suggested. It's the old gag of 'boys will do anything for a jack-knife,' so they have the aunt of the Back Bay lady, an evident spinster, carrying a load of pocket knives into Mexico with her. Martha Mattox, in this role, gets a couple of touches over that implant the jack-knife gag.

"In all, this is one of the best Mix westerns that has come along in some time."

Fred. *Variety,* 1/27/26

MY OWN PAL

Fox Film Corporation. Released February 28, 1926. *Length:* 6 reels.

Director: John G. Blystone. *Scenario:* Lillie Hayward, based on a story titled "My Little Pal" by Gerald Beaumont. *Assistant Director:* Jasper Blystone. *Photography:* Daniel Clark.

Cast: Tom Mix (Tom O'Hara), Olive Borden (Alice Deering), Tom Santschi (August Deering), Virginia Marshall (Jill), Bardson Bard [Ben Bard] (Baxter Barton), William Colvin (Jud McIntire), Virginia Warwick (Molly), Jay Hunt (clown),

Hedda Nova (Mrs. Jud McIntire), Tom McGuire (Pat McQuire), Helen Lynch (Trixie Tremaine), Jacques Rollens (Slippery Sam).

Still Code: Bly-36

"Cowboy turns policeman, is successful in running down and eliminating crook gang, also saves girl he loves from kidnappers."

Motion Picture News Booking Guide

"Tom Mix's admiring cohorts will like this one, and so, for the matter of that will every fan who rejoices in fast-moving melodrama, spiced with timely comedy and the usual romantic seasoning. It gets away from the beaten Western trail too, for the hero cowboy turns cop and proves himself a most valuable member of the force when it comes to running down desperadoes. Of course, the never-to-be-forgotten Tony the horse figures in his master's feats of daring, although there is a stage where Tom does some natty riding stunts on a motorcycle, not dispensing with his trusty lariat, however, which is coiled over the handlebars, and is used triumphantly for the roping in of a thug who tried a flivver getaway. There's a little terrier dog which makes a big hit in surprising comedy stunts, and all-in-all the picture provides entertainment that is bound to have a universal audience appeal. Mix at his best, support fine!"

George T. Pardy *Motion Picture News,* 3/27/26

TONY RUNS WILD

Fox Film Corporation. Released April 18, 1926. *Length:* 6 reels (5,477 feet).

Director: Thomas Buckingham. *Scenario:* Edfrid Bingham and Robert Lord, based on an unpublished story by Henry Herbert Knibbs. *Assistant Director:* Wynn Mace. *Photography:* Daniel Clark.

Cast: Tom Mix (Tom Trent), Tony (himself, a horse), Jacqueline Logan (Grace Percival), Lawford Davidson (Slade), Duke Lee (Bender), Vivian Oakland (Mrs. Johnson), Marion Harlan (Ethel Johnson), Raymond Wells (Sheriff), Richard Carter (ranch foreman), Arthur Morrison (auto stage driver), Lucien Littlefield (Red), Jack Padjeon (Deputy Sheriff).

Still Code: Bu-14, or Buck-14

"Rancher saves girl from wild horses which renegades are chasing in order to capture Tony, wild stallion. Rancher

Right: *The Yankee Senor* boasted a two-color Technicolor fiesta sequence which showed leading lady Olive Borden to good advantage. Borden was being groomed for stardom by Fox in the late '20s before alcoholism caused her career to falter.

Opposite: Tom prepares to rescue Eva Novak in *No Man's Gold*, the last of her ten films with Mix. Elements of this story were reworked for Mix's best sound film, *The Rider of Death Valley*.

Below: *My Own Pal* was an early-day version of *Coogan's Bluff*, a cowboy comes to the city and becomes a cop. Here Mix uses his ranch skills to capture and deliver a crook to the police commissioner played by Tom Santschi (at left).

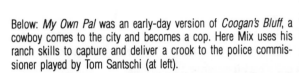

WILLIAM FOX
PRESENTS
Tom Mix
IN
MY OWN PAL

captures horse for girl. Tony runs down renegades who abduct her. They agree to share Tony for life."

Motion Picture News Booking Guide

HARD BOILED

Fox Film Corporation. Released June 6, 1926. *Length:* 6 reels (5,679 feet).

Director: John G. Blystone. *Scenario:* Charles Darnton and John Stone, based on a story titled "Ridin' With Youth" by Shannon Fife. *Titles:* Ralph Spence. *Assistant Director:* Jasper Blystone. *Photography:* Daniel Clark.

Cast: Tom Mix (Tom Bouden), Helene Chadwick (Marjorie Gregg), William Lawrence (Gordon Andrews), Charles Conklin (Bill Grimes), Emily Fitzroy (Abigail Gregg), Phyllis Haver (Justine Morton), Dan Mason (Abrue Bouden), Walter "Spec" O'Donnell (Eddie Blix), Ethel Grey Terry (Mrs. Sarah Morton), Edward Sturgis (first crook), Eddie Boland (second crook), Emmett Wagner (third crook), Tony (a horse).

Still Code: Bly-37

"Sent West by irate uncle, Jeff Boyden is thrown in contact with Marjorie Gregg, whose anger he incurred by some derogatory remark. Jeff poses as doctor but is driven from ranch through conspiracy. He vanquishes the conspirators in hand-to-hand tussle, and wins Marjorie for his bride."

Motion Picture News Booking guide

NO MAN'S GOLD

Fox Film Corporation. Released August 29, 1926. *Length:* 6 reels (5,745 feet).

Director: Lewis Seiler. Adaptation and *Scenario:* John Stone, based on a short story titled "Dead Man's Gold" by J. Allan Dunn. *Assistant Director:* Wynn Mace. *Photography:* Daniel Clark.

Cast: Tom Mix (Tom Stone), Eva Novak (Jane Rogers), Frank Campeau (Frank Healy), Forrest Taylor (Wat Lyman), Harry Grippe (Lefty Logan), Malcolm Waite (Pete Krell), Mickey Moore (Jimmy), Tony (a horse), Tom Santschi.

Note: Director Thomas Buckingham started this film, but was replaced mid-production by Lewis Seiler. Elements of the plot were re-worked into *The Rider of Death Valley*, a Tom Mix Universal picture released in 1932.

Still Code: Bu-15, Bu-15-S-22, or Sei-22

"A first-class cowboy melodrama, with all the merits that usually go into that class of picture, including scenic beauties and hard riding, and in addition a particularly interesting and tricky plot built up with much ingenuity.

"The picture has a wealth of stunts which grow naturally out of the story instead of being dragged in, working up to a smashing climax when Mix the dare devil cow puncher, makes a dizzy ride across a valley on the slender thread of a mine carrier in a suspended bucket that crashes through and demolishes the house where 'bad men' are besieging the hero and heroine. "The locale of the action is in the high mountains, and the hero and his followers are beleaguered on a lofty peak, with the outlaws holding them at bay from a deep canyon. This situation provides a stunning pictorial background with camera shots of giddy altitudes and striking vistas. Also it makes possible the hero's feat of descending the sheer cliff by a rope, apparently lowered by Mix's horse, Tony, in an effective bit of tense melodrama.

"The story gets under way promptly. At the very outset an outlaw shoots a miner from ambush in a plot to jump his rich gold claim. Dying, the miner gives up the map showing the location of his bonanza, but tears it into three parts, giving one part to the murderous outlaw, one part to a comedy character and the third and vital part to the hero. All three start for the mine, accompanied by the dead miner's orphaned son, Jimmy.

"The outlaw's confederates scheme to follow at a distance and seize the mine when at length it has been found. The three have to keep together to that point, because none knows the other's section of the mapped route. They stop en route at a rodeo, which furnishes the excuse for some fine riding displays. It is here that Tom, the hero, meets and falls in love with the heroine before they go on their quest.

"The girl learns of the plot to seize the mine after the trio have departed, and, following to warn Tom, she is captured by the skulking outlaws. Thus is furnished the romantic interest of the siege, when Tom and his little band are held at bay defending their narrow mountain pass.

The accumulated melodrama from here to the end when the hero wins out is a never-ending series of thrills. The use of dynamite to block the attack, the scaling of towering cliffs and finally the hero's wild ride through the air on an inclined cable, all make for smashing melodrama that keeps suspense a tip-toe to the final moment.

"Mr. Mix plays in his familiar vein of casual comedy while his support is always convincing in situations that make up in 'punch' what they lack in plausibility, which is all that one can say for stories of this type."

Rush. Variety, 9/15/26

Right: Tom posed as a doctor in order to get close to leading lady Helene Chadwick in *Hard Boiled*. Mix always stressed the romance angle in his pictures, which boosted his popularity with female audiences.

Left: Tom lands in the Pullman bed of a distraught female passenger as he escapes from pursuers in *The Great K & A Train Robbery*, one of Mix's best and most action-packed films.

THE GREAT K & A TRAIN ROBBERY

Fox Film Corporation. Released October 17, 1926. *Length:* 5 reels (4,800 feet).

Director: Lewis R. Seiler. *Scenario:* John Stone, based on the novel by Paul Leicester Ford. *Assistant Director:* Wynn Mace. *Photography:* Daniel Clark.

Cast: Tom Mix (Tom Gordon), Dorothy Dwan (Madge Cullen), William Walling (Eugene Cullen), Harry Grippe (De Luxe Harry), Carl Miller (Burton), Edward Piel (bandit leader), Curtis McHenry (Cullen's butler), Tony (a horse).

Note: Filmed on location at Royal Gorge, Colorado.

Still Code: Sei-23

"Probably the fastest picture in action ever filmed. This Tom Mix latest starts in action and never stops. It's through before you know it, leaving the impression the picture has not run over 30 minutes, whereas it goes 55.

"Within the first thousand feet a witness will say, 'That's a lot of action to start with,' and wonder when it's going to slow down. It never does.

"Action alone here would have placed this Mix in a Broadway first-run if one had been available. For intermingled with the melodramatics is plenty of comedy, much to real laughs.

"There are thrills with the opening scenes, finding Mix sitting in a basket on a very long rope reaching up to the top of the Royal Gorge in Colorado, where the picture was mostly taken. Discovered by train robbers, Tom slides down the rope to land right in 'Tony's' saddle.

"From that moment the agile Mix starts to do things and never stops, winding up by swimming across a stream to capture a band of about 15 bandits, single handed. If you believe that you can believe some of the other things, but they happen, nevertheless, and through the way they are done, one can overlook plausibility.

"Otherwise and in continuity this picture is perfect as a western. Mix doing new stunts and adding a love interest besides. In character he is a detective from Texas, sent for by the K. &. A. Railroad to hunt down the train robbers. A secretary of the president of the road is in cahoots with the robbers, tipping them off on coin deliveries by express. Mix appears first in the picture as an apparent bandit himself, masked, and rescues the president's daughter, 'the girl,' who believes he is a highwayman.

"Besides a western and a bandit story, this is almost a railroad tale in addition.

"Tom Mix, always the great looking guy in a picture, has set a high mark for the 'western boys' in this one. They will have to go a lot to approach it in action; and, in fact, Tom will have to do the same to keep up with his record here.

"The Great K. & A. Train Robbery could safely be billed as the fastest-moving picture ever put on the screen."

Sime. *Variety,* 10/27/26

THE CANYON OF LIGHT

Fox Film Corporation. Released December 5, 1926. *Length:* 6 reels (5,399 feet).

Director: Benjamin Stoloff. *Scenario:* John Stone, based on a novel by Kenneth Perkins. *Titles:* William Conselman. *Assistant Director:* Wynn Mace. *Photography:* Dan Clark.

Cast: Tom Mix (Tom Mills), Dorothy Dwan (Concha Deane), Carl Miller (Ed Bardin), Ralph Sipperly (Jerry Shanks), Barry Norton (Ricardo Deane), Carmelita Geraghty (Ellen Bardin), William Walling (Cyrus Deane), Duke Lee (Joe Novardo), Tony (a horse).

Still Code: Sto-20

"In this, the object of every producer and star, 'something different,' is achieved. Tom Mix mounts a motorcycle while serving as a dispatch rider in France during the World War. This is a short episode in his newest picture, 'The Canyon of Light,' and serves the additional plot-purpose of his returning to find that the villain has done wrong by his wife, and has masqueraded as Mix himself. This is hardly a fair return when Tom has saved the villain from hanging that he may see his dying wife, but that is merely another instance of the ingratitude of villains, screen or otherwise. The World War episode (Tom Mix's personal popularity resulted in innumerable cowboys enlisting)—the thwarted hanging and the villain's duplicity are only part of the tale.

"Packed with thrills and unusual situations, which are always two characteristics of Mix pictures, this one is bound to please. A good company, including Dorothy Dwan, Barry Norton, Ralph Sipperly and William Walling, good direction and effective backgrounds help, too. There is an infinite variety, a stage hold-up, a run-away rescue, a near hanging, a rodeo, cliff and river riding by the star, of course, on Tony, and any number of other exciting and thrilling shots for full measure."

Paul Thompson *Motion Picture News,* 12/25/26

Above: Taking advantage of sets built for the Fox special *What Price Glory?*, a World War I prologue in which Tom played an Army dispatcher was added to *The Canyon of Light*. Barry Norton is on the motorcycle at right.

Right: Mix seemed to like "back stories" that established his character in a prologue to the main action. *The Last Trail* featured such a prologue in which Tom rescues a woman from an Indian attack. Zane Grey's novel was largely ignored in this screen version.

Left: Orville O. "Bunny" Dull (with megaphone), a director with a most unfortunate name, during production of *The Broncho Twister*. Dull eventually gave up directing to become a production executive at M-G-M in the 1930's. Assistant cameraman Curtis Fetters stands behind Dull, and cinematographer Dan Clark stands behind the Mitchell camera. The child is unidentified.

Below: A scene from *The Broncho Twister*. Trapped in a tower filled with gunpowder, Mix drops cans of powder on his assailants and sets them off with shots from his pistols. Helene Costello, sister of Dolores Costello and daughter of early-day matinee idol Maurice Costello, is the heroine. Starting as a youngster in her father's Vitagraph productions in the early Teens, Helene's career lasted nearly 25 years, but her sister proved to be the bigger box-office star. A young laborer and extra named Lou Cristillo had a crush on Helene, and borrowed her surname to become Lou Costello. Snaggle-toothed Jack Pennick, in one of his first screen appearances, provides the comic relief.

1927

THE LAST TRAIL

Fox Film Corporation. Released January 23, 1927. *Length:* (5,190 feet).

Director: Lewis R. Seiler. *Scenario:* John Stone, based on a novel by Zane Grey. *Film Editor:* Robert W. Bischoff. *Titles:* Garrett Graham. *Photography:* Daniel Clark.

Cast: Tom Mix (Tom Dane), Carmelita Geraghty (Nita Carrol), William Davidson (Morley), Frank Hagney (Ben Ligget), Lee Shumway (Joe Pascal), Robert Brower (Pete), Oliver Eckhardt (Carrol), Tony (a horse).

Still Code: Sei-24

"In 'The Last Trail' Tom Mix has turned out one of the fastest action pictures that he has had in a long while. It starts with a zip and bang and never leaves the pace for a minute, right up to the finish. Both Tom and Tony get a lot of action in this one and there are more thrills in it in a minute than there usually is in a whole five reels of the average western.

"In this one there is a free-for-all stage coach race that comes near rivaling the famous chariot race in 'Ben-Hur.' It is replete with thrills and spills. From a box office angle this one is sure to do better than the average Mix and that is saying a lot, for his average is always high.

"Also, in this picture there is something of an added attraction in the fact that Mix has Jerry, the Giant, a cute youngster with him almost throughout the picture. Carmelita Geraghty, who played a small role in Mix's last picture, 'The Canyon of Light,' is his leading woman and she more than makes good. That girl is going to go to bigger things on the screen before she is through.

"The picturization of the Zane Grey story opens with an Indian fight. Mix saves the life of the wife of Joe Pascal and Joe, in return, promises to name his first born in his honor. Ten years later Mix, as Tom Dane, is still riding the west when he gets a note from his old friend to come and see the youngster that bears his name. Pascal in the meantime is the sheriff at Carson City and the stage line, which is carrying the gold, has been repeatedly robbed until the sheriff decides to drive the stage through to the railroad with a guard. Soon after leaving Carson he is attacked by bandits, and they are chasing the stage across the country when Tom rides into the picture to help give battle. The robbers are driven off, but the sheriff is mortally wounded. As he is dying, he places his son in care of the man that the youngster is named after.

"The contractor of the stage line is afraid that he is going to lose out because of his inability to protect his freight. A representative of the U. S. Express arrives and suggests a free-for-all stage coach race to decide who shall get the contract, the leader of the bandits, who, under cover, is one of the big shippers in town, lines up his hold-up men as the contestants.

"But the old contractor has a daughter that Tom Dane has fallen for and he decides to help the old man out in the race. It is one of those last-minute starts, and Mix and a half-dozen others start the race, driving four-in-hand lumbering stage coaches with the others all banded against him. He finally comes through to victory, even though he has but a team and the two front wheels of his coach left at the finish, arriving just in time to jump on Tony's back and start off on another race to catch the leader of the bandits, who is trying to escape with the girl and the loot taken from the stage coach office. That makes for the hurrah finish for the final fade-out.

"Interspersed in all this melodrama is sufficient comedy to slip the audience a couple of hearty laughs, especially the work done by Robert Brower and a blood-hound with a pair of trick ears that are worked on wires from the looks of things. William Davidson slips over a good performance as the heavy without overacting.

"An extra good Mix western."

Fred. *Variety,* 1/26/27

THE BRONCHO TWISTER

Fox Film Corporation. Released March 13, 1927. *Length:* 6 reels (5,435 feet).

Director: Orville O. Dull. *Scenario:* John Stone, based on an unpublished story titled "The Great Feud" by Adela Rogers St. Johns. *Assistant Director:* Wynn Mace. *Photography:* Daniel Clark.

Cast: Tom Mix (Tom Mason), Helene Costello (Paulita Brady), George Irving (Ned Mason), Dorothy Kitchen (Daisy Mason), Paul Nicholson (Black Jack Brady), Doris Lloyd (Teresa Brady), Malcolm Waite (Dan Bell), Jack Pennick (Jinx Johnson), Otto Fries (Sheriff), Tony (a horse).

Still Code: Dull-6

"A typical melo of the plains with this riding star at his best. Scene is picturesquely set in the plains and hills of Arizona, where some tricky scenic work has been done by an expert cameraman who repeats the Fox trick of getting remarkable sky and cloud effects into the action backgrounds.

"This picture will get to the Mix admirers, for it is one revel of riding and fighting action, culminating in a whale of a screen situation. The hero is in a Spanish mission ranch house tower used for the storage of dynamite by the rancher. Thither he has brought the heroine to save her from an unwelcome marriage dictated by her evil stepfather. A third member of the beleaguered party is a comedy buddy of the hero and his pal during service with the Marines during the war.

"The trio are surrounded by shooting enemies and protect themselves by dropping cans of dynamite upon them from the tower balcony. This situation is worked up with variations as the climax of the single-handed hero prevailing, of course, against a score or so of enemies and making his getaway by a trick and his good right arm.

"This episode is the culmination of abundant action in the earlier footage. Two neighboring ranchers, the Mortons and the Bradys, are at feud when Tom comes home from the World War. His father has been wounded in an ambush and Tom goes out after the murderous clan. His meeting with the beautiful heroine, stepdaughter of the enemy feud leader, complicates his task, but his difficulties are made into the materials for a first-class western thriller, with Tony playing an important part. Miss Costello making a highly satisfactory Spanish heroine and Jack Pennick, an unknown, contributing first-rate comedy values as the ex-marine who wanted to be a cow puncher but had no talent for sitting in the saddle. A shrewd touch given to this character was his sudden switch from low comedy tumbler to the heroic role of the girl's rescuer in the hero's momentary absence.

"A good action picture, done in the best Tom Mix manner, and warranted to bring out in full force the Mix fans."

Rush. *Variety*, 3/30/27

OUTLAWS OF RED RIVER

Fox Film Corporation. Released May 8, 1927. *Length:* 6 reels (5,327 feet).

Director: Lewis R. Seiler. *Acenario:* Harold Shumate, based on an unpublished story by Gerald Beaumont titled "The Fighting Falcon." *Titles:* Malcolm Stuart Boylan. *Assistant Director:* Wynn Mace. *Photography:* Daniel Clark.
Cast-Prologue: Lee Shumway (Mr. Torrence), Ellen Woonston (Mrs. Torrence), Jimmy Downs (Tom Morley), Virgina Marshall (Mary as a child).
Cast-*Story:* Tom Mix (Tom Morley), Marjorie Daw (Mary Torrence), Arthur Clayton (Sam Hardwick), William Con-

klin (Captain Dunning), Duke Lee (Dick Williams), Francis McDonald (Ben Tanner).

Still Code: Sei-25

". . . It was while fighting with [Francis] McDonald during the making of this picture that Mix was accidentally burned by gun powder from which it is understood he is still laid up. . . . "

Variety, 5/11/27

"So much has been written in the past of the exploits of Tom Mix and his wonder horse 'Tony' that there isn't much more to write about unless it is to let you know that Tom rides and fights as well as ever; that Tony is not in immediate danger of being uncrowned as the king of all motion picture horses, or that Tom has uncovered a brand new gag for use in this particular picture. Now, you know what to expect—plenty of action and an entirely new method of exterminating a crew of desperadoes.

"As Fighting Ace of the Texas Rangers, Tom is engaged in the interesting task of breaking up a band of outlaws whose weekly diversion is the robbing of the stage coach. As a special incentive for this work, he nurses the pet grievance of having lost his parents at the hands of the bandit leader. The latest robbery is foiled by Tom holding up the stage himself, during which he meets one of the occupants—a girl who later is identified as the bandit's daughter. Of course, this serves to complicate matters. But anyway, Tom gains access to the bandit's lair where their chief lies dying and eventually finds that the girl is an orphan by the same circumstances that deprived him of his parents. A successful raid by Tom, in conjunction with other Rangers, is made. It is here that the new gag is used. See it yourself, it's a good one."

E. G. Johnston *Motion Picture News,* 5/6/27

THE CIRCUS ACE

Fox Film Corporation. Released June 26, 1927. *Length:* 5 reels (4,810 feet).

Director: Benjamin Stoloff. *Scenario:* Jack Jungmeyer, based on an unpublished story by Harold Shumate. *Assistant Director:* Wynn Mace. *Photography:* Daniel Clark.

Cast: Tom Mix (Tom Terry), Natalie Joyce (Millie Jane Raleigh), Jack Baston (Kirk Mallory), Duke Lee (Job Jasper), James Bradbury (Gus Peabody), Stanley Blystone (boss canvas man), Dudley Smith (Durgan, the miller), Buster Gardner (Sheriff), Clarence (a kangaroo), Tony (a horse).

Still Code: Sto-23

Right: Tom gives Natalie Joyce a shooting lesson in *The Circus Ace*. Joyce was greeted with enthusiasm by reviewers for her work in this film, and she later appeared with Mix in *Daredevil's Reward* in 1928. She once told Sid Jordan's wife Alice, "I'll never get anywhere in this business, because I won't put out."

Below: In a spectacular conclusion, Tom and his fellow Texas Rangers shoot it out with the *Outlaws of Red River* after crashing their stagecoach through the wall of the outlaws' fortified stronghold. The set looks substantial, but the painted backdrop of the log wall outside the opening gives away the fact that it was built on a stage in the Fox studio.

Left: Tom threatens to throw his boot at comic Monte Collins, Jr. in *The Arizona Wildcat*. The star's contract called for him to supply his own wardrobe, so he often included scenes that showed off his costumes in order to write them off. In 1925, Mix claimed tax deductions of $9,766.07 for wardrobe and another $1,540.05 for cleaning and repair.

Below: In *Tumbling River* Tom lowered himself over the river so he could lasso the heroine who was about to be swept over the falls. Tragedy struck when Ethel Hall, who was doubling for leading lady Dorothy Dwan, drowned while shooting the scene.

"Tom Mix in a good story is a double pleasure.

"'The Circus Ace' as a story probably ranks any regular program release a western star has had in years. It's consistent with proper continuity, and while the basic ingredients are of the formula, they are secreted here as far as the picture going public is concerned.

"For the western fans, this picture is there a mile; for the Mix fans its perfect and at the Keith-Albee Woolworth stand for a week, all of the fans besides those who grow stubbed-nosed looking at westerns will take to the film.

"It's a nice evenly balanced picture, and that it has a new leading woman or at least one who sounds new, Natalie Joyce, a girl who can do something else besides wearing make-up, may be adding an extra charm. Miss Joyce is an athlete or gymnast. Despite any doubling or camera faking, the girl handles herself like an aerialist. This is made evident when she goes into the cradle to take off on the trapeze. Even though that cradle were on the ground a girl couldn't do it the way she does without experience. And Miss Joyce can smile without her mouth looking like a purple chasm.

"Background is a small town tent outfit, one ring, one lion and one elephant. Also a boxing kangaroo that lands some of the several laughs in the running. Mix does stunts in and about the circus, acrobatics, climbing, jumping, riding, shooting, lassoing—in fact he works in almost all of his tricks.

"At one time it seemed as though Tom was about to set a new world's record by lassoing an elephant, but instead he roped the girl on the animal.

"The picture starts at a fast pace with a balloon ascension with Miss Joyce as the parachute jumper. Imagine a balloon ascension with a two-car show! Nellie Revell will die over that one.

"Mix is a careless cowboy, always whittling wood. His whittling grows into a steady laugh as the picture progresses, also giving a pretty little fadeout, as, after the customary marriage, the 'little chip off the old block' is seen to have picked up his pop's best habit. Tom hauls the girl off the parachute, crabbing her act and she bawls him for it.

"But Tom likes the girl and wants another lamp. So he watches the circus parade the following morning. Seeing some toy baloons escaping he stops the calamity by shooting them while in the air. The shots frighten the elephant his lady friend is gracing and the big beast starts off on a swift gallop, with Tom racing after to lasso the jane.

"Then comes the villain, the political boss of Sage, Ariz. If there is a tank in Arizona by the name of Sage, its political leader had better take the air or else. The boss wants the gal, holds a mortgage on the show but is willing to forego

payment if, etc. And then Tom with 'Tony' and the kid whittler.

"An excellent Mix picture, so much so it may be said that 'The Circus Ace' is the best picture the Hippodrome thus far has played, although to give the Hip due consideration, it had to play the P.D.C.'s [the films produced and released by Producers Distributing Corporation].

"The Roxy could have used this Mix film. It would have been a good change for the Roxy picture end and a great chance to send Mix away over on Broadway, for 'The Circus Ace' is more interesting as a program release than 70 percent of the stuff the Broadway houses have been using in recent months."

Sime. *Variety*, 7/6/27

TUMBLING RIVER

Fox Film Corporation. Released August 21, 1927. *Length:* 5 reels (4,675 feet).

Director: Lewis R. Seiler. *Scenario:* Jack Jungmeyer, based on the novel "The Scourge of the Little C" by Jesse Edward Grinstead. *Assistant Director:* Wynn Mace. *Photography:* Daniel Clark.

Cast: Tom Mix (Tom Gier), Dorothy Dwan (Edna Barton), William Conklin (Jim Barton), Stella Essex (Eileen Barton), Elmo Billings (Kit Mason), Edward Piel, Sr. (Roan Tibbets), Wallace MacDonald (Keechie), Buster Gardner (Cory), Harry Grippe (Titus), Tony (a horse), Buster (another horse).

Still Code: Sei-26

"There is something about Tom Mix pictures that seems to differ just a trifle from those of other Western stars. While the stories are usually about the same, with the trusted ranch foreman the villainous cattle rustler, at the same time when a thrill is called for Tom puts it on pretty. And there are thrills galore in this one.

"It seems just a matter of course for Tom and Tony to plunge over a deep embankment and both to come up uninjured. It is a trivial matter for Tom to lower himself over the river and lasso the girl as she is about to be plunged to death with the villain, who is abducting her as they descend the rapids and near the falls. It is just an incident when the herd of horses being taken across the river by the rustlers become stampeded and each of the head plunges into the river and swims to safety.

"The story is the usual one of the type. Dorothy Dwan, young and winning daughter of the rich rancher is a romantic miss with a penchant for getting into and being saved from serious situation. But she hadn't seen anything till Tom came into her life; then she was saved so often that it must have become monotonous to her. At any rate she liked it well enough to marry the hero, which made the story perfect."

Chester J. Smith *Motion Picture News, 8/26/27*

SILVER VALLEY

Fox Film Corporation. Released October 2, 1927. *Length:* 5 reels (5,011 feet).

Director: Benjamin Stoloff. *Scenario:* Harold B. Lipsitz, from an unpublished story by Harry Sinclair Drago. *Titles:* Malcolm Stuart Boylan. *Photography:* Daniel Clark. Assistant Cameraman: Clay Crapnell.

Cast: Tom Mix (Tom Tracey), Dorothy Dwan (Sheila Blaine), Philo McCullough (Black Jack Lundy), Jocky Hoefli (Silent Kid), Tom Kennedy (Hayfever Hawkins), Lon Poff (Slim Snitzer), Harry Dunkinson (Mike McCool), Clark Comstock (Wash Taylor).

Still Code: Sto-22

"'Silver Valley' is both a good western and a good Tom Mix western. It has a plurality of action, an assortment of laughs and the sure touch that a well-seasoned organization gets into a picture.

"Tom, fired for wrecking his boss' ranch with a bum invention, becomes the sheriff of a town with a high mortality rate among sheriffs. He shows up the master mind of the gang and wins the gal, the appealing Dorothy Dwan.

"For a different touch the rendezvous of the gang is the crater of a defunct volcano. The volcano comes to life and spurts lava all over the villain.

"Photography excellent. Dan Clark, Mix's regular cameraman, is ace high for fast-action stuff, always keeping the galloping smooth and the horse in the middle of the focus.

"Should be a characteristic Mix bull's-eye for the box offices that front on Main Street."

Variety, 11/2/27

THE ARIZONA WILDCAT

Fox Film Corporation. Released November 20, 1927. *Length:* 5 reels (4,665 feet).

Director: R. William Neill. *Scenario:* John Stone, based on an unpublished story titled "High Society" by Adela Rogers St. Johns. *Assistant Director:* Wynn Mace. *Photography:* Daniel Clark.

Cast: Tom Mix (Tom Phelan), Dorothy Sebastian (Regina Schyler), Ben Bard (Wallace Van Acker), Gordon Elliott [Wild Bill Elliott] (Roy Schyler), Monte Collins, Jr. (Low Jack Wilkins), Cissy Fitzgerald (Mother Schyler), Doris Dawson (Marie), Marcella Daly (Helen Van Acker), Tony (a horse).

Still Code: R.N.-8

"A western to be sure, but somehow one that nobody needs to apologize for. The story is full of capital angles. It has an amusing comedy start with the hero as a kid (Mickey Moore), organizing an amateur rodeo which leads up to some interesting horse tricks by youngsters, ending in a runaway team with rescue by the boy hero on horseback.

"A twist to the western motif is the idea of hooking it up with a high society atmosphere. This is contrived by having the cowboy hero go in for breeding and training polo ponies, which he supplies to the society polo fans. Heroine is the childhood sweetheart, now grown up and moving in the haute monde of the Pacific coast. Her brother is a polo player, and buys his mounts from Tom.

"Thus, when one of brother's teammates is knocked out on the eve of an important polo match, he sends for Tom to take his place. Here we turn to the polite atmosphere for the dramatic finale, which is a polo game for a scoiety crowd, building up to an excellent effect with fast play and good shots at the flying horses.

"The heavy is the polo leader on the opposing team, a blackguard, who, of course, is only after the heroine's money. When his side is defeated and the government secret service is closing in on him for mail frauds, he abducts the girl, and it is here that Tom dashes off the polo field for the usual pursuit.

"The climax is worked up with stunt riding effect rivalling the stuff that made Fairbanks famous. The kidnapper takes the girl to one of those Spanish mission palaces familiar to followers of the California made movies, and riding his mount up outside staircases, the hero gallops into the room where the villain is struggling with the girl. The stunt of riding back and forth about the house is elaborated while Tom puts the heavy's retainers to flight, finally throwing the girl across his saddle and dashing off down the steep steps and away.

"It's all veritable movie hokum, exaggerated and flamboyant, but it does give a certain dime novel dramatic kick, in the way that is familiar to Mix fans. The point is that it gets away from the stereotyped westerns, goes into a fresh locale and takes interest from its society atmosphere of luxury instead of everlasting dreary ranch house and corral.

"Nicely played, with good comedy values in a hard-boiled and serious minded cowboy who falls hard for heroine's short skirted French maid. Will please the Mix fans. Picture has

Tom Mix played a would-be inventor in *Silver Valley*, but when his invention fails to get off the ground, he turns in his drawing board for a sheriff's badge.

Below: the camera crew catches Tom's invention in action.

Right: Tom's final Fox film, *Painted Post* was considered slower and less exciting than his earlier work for the studio.

Top left-opposite: *Hello, Cheyenne!* was a tale about stringing telephone wires to Cheyenne, Wyoming.

Top right-opposite: Tom's dressing room at Fox pulling on his boots for *A Horseman of the Plains.*

Below-opposite: On location in Arizona for *Hello, Cheyenne!.* At the table (l-r): Director Eugene Forde, Tom, The Governor of Arizona, Al St. John, Caryl Lincoln, ?, the governor's wife, and Dan Clark. Jim Rush stands to the right of the chuck wagon.

Below: Production economies showed as Tom neared the end of his Fox contract as evidenced by the unconvincing cyclorama used for this fight scene in *Daredevil's Reward.*

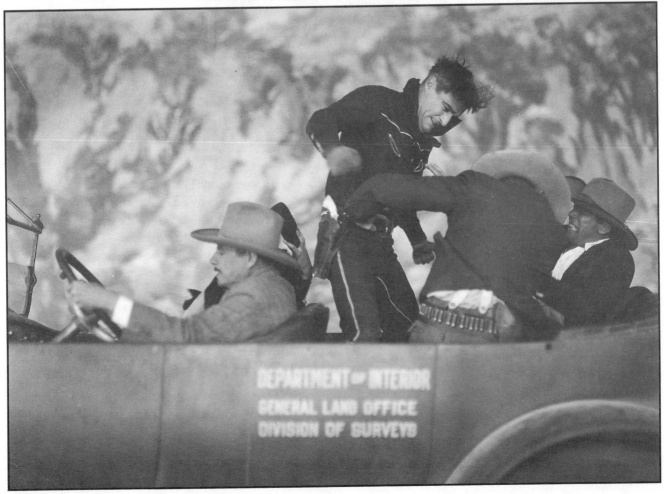

ingenuity and a certain elegance that raises it above the typical western to a punch melodramatic subject."

Rush. *Variety,* 1/25/28

1928 _____

DAREDEVIL'S REWARD

Fox Film Corporation. Released January 15, 1928. *Length:* 6 reels (5,484 feet).

Director: Eugene J. Forde. *Scenario:* John Stone, from his unpublished story titled "Wildcat Law." *Photography:* Daniel Clark.

Cast: Tom Mix (Tom Hardy), Natalie Joyce (Ena Powell), Lawford Davidson (Foster), Billy Bletcher (Slim), Harry Cording (Second heavy), William Welch (James Powell), Tony (a horse).

Note: This picture was copyrighted earlier under its working title, *The $5,000 Reward.* The film may have been re-edited before final release. The final gross domestic film rental for *Daredevil's Reward* was $227,200.00

Still Code: Forde-10

"Western in which Texas Ranger rounds up band of desperate highwaymen, headed by the uncle of the girl with whom he eventually falls in love. She is abducted by the bandits after her uncle is shot and is rescued by the hero in a mad plunge down the mountainside in an uncontrollable automobile."

Motion Picture News Booking Guide

"Many a manager's 'out' is Tom Mix. 'All I have to do is put Mix's name out front and they come back like prodigal sons,' he says. 'There's affection and trust in their eyes again when they lay down their dough. They take for granted that Mix will never go up against less than twenty guys. There's a man for 'em.'

"And here's another picture for the boys. It suffices that Mix outwits his not-less-than-20 men, rides his horse like a sedan, and turns out the lights by shooting across the room at a button. His necking is a little squeaky, but that's so with all rugged men.

"As usual, the plot is trimmed with novelties. Tom is a Texas Ranger, and gets a line on the thieves by appearing in various disguises, including two comedy portions as a medicine man and a waiter. The whole thing is done in that half satirical manner that makes Mix a favorite among some of

our best minds. Natalie Joyce is a determined but appealing heroine. Mix starts where the other westerns leave off. His pictures have some of the fastest footage to be found: his rescues are hotter, his shootings more numerous, his pursuers more multitudinous. Which is why he rates aces with 'the boys.'

Variety, 1/25/28

A HORSEMAN OF THE PLAINS

Fox Film Corporation. Released March 11, 1928. *Length:* 5 reels (4,399 feet).

Director: Benjamin Stoloff. *Scenario:* Fred Myton, from an unpublished story by Harry Sinclair Drago. *Photography:* Daniel Clark.

Cast: Tom Mix (Tom Swift), Sally Blane (Dawn O'Day), Heinie Conklin (Snowshoe), Charles Byer (J. Rutherford Gates), Lew Harvey (Flash Egan), Grace Marvin (Esmeralda), William Ryno (Michael O'Day), Tony (a horse).

Still Code: Sto-24

Note: The final gross domestic film rental for *A Horseman of the Plains* was $216,400.00

"Western in which Tom overcomes every obstacle in the grand sweepstakes obstacle race, saves the heavily mortgaged ranch of the girl and wins her for his bride."

Motion Picture News Booking Guide

"A western modernized in everything except plot. The plot is No. 666 about the family ranch that will be foreclosed unless the family nag wins the big race. But despite this hackneyed old yarn, the picture is entertaining.

"Explanation of paradox: good direction.

"Benjamin Stoloff has megaphoned life and breeze into the mortgage classic. The picture moves with zip and is distinctly better than the Tom Mix average for the last dozen or two.

"Stoloff even has Mix acting like a romantic juvenile, going into clinches with the heroine. That in itself is sort of revolutionary. Heretofore Mix's screen romances have been Bostonian in their neuter gender purity. The final fadeout generally showed Thomas patting the girl on the arm with a look of sheer brotherliness.

"A novelty too is the race, a combination affair started on foot, including laps in a chariot, hay wagon, speed car and ending with stage coaches.

"Only 45 minutes in the running and something popping every second. Great for western fans."

Land. *Variety,* 5/2/28

HELLO, CHEYENNE!

Fox Film Corporation. Released May 13, 1928. *Length:* 5 reels (4,618 feet).

Director: Eugene J. Forde. *Scenario:* Fred Kennedy Myton, from an unpublished story by Harry Sinclair Drago. *Titles:* Dudley Early. *Film Editor:* Robert W. Bischoff. *Photography:* Daniel Clark.

Cast: Tom Mix (Tom Remington), Caryl Lincoln (Diana Cody), Jack Baston (Buck Lassiter), Martin Faust (Jeff Bardeen), Joseph Girard (Fremont Cody), Al St. John (Zip Coon), William Caress (bus driver), Tony (a horse).

Still Code: Forde-11

Note: The final gross domestic film rental for *Hello, Cheyenne* was $211,100.00

"Two rival telephone crews race to be the first to make the wire connections with town of Cheyenne. Rival foreman steals daughter of construction crew foreman, but Tom rescues her and by dint of hard work makes wire connections ahead of his rival and winning the girl."

Motion Picture News Booking Guide

"One of Mix's typical westerns. Caryl Lincoln supports a gal who looks good and gets away from the dumbness of the usual plains heroines. Al St. John does not register so well for comedy, principally because of lack of material.

"One punch scene is where Mix hooks under a wagon and rides down a hill to evade a gang of gunmen trying to stop him from making a telephone connection. The stunt, whether trick or actually done, gets over strongly.

"Story is of rival telephone companies trying to be the first to complete a line between Cheyenne and Rawhide. Gal's father heading one of the companies, acquires the services of Tom and his funny pardner."

Mort. *Variety,* 6/20/28

PAINTED POST

Fox Film Corporation. Released July 1, 1928. *Length:* 5 reels (4,952 feet).

Director: Eugene J. Forde. *Scenario:* Buckleigh F. Oxford, from an unpublished story by Harry Sinclair Drago. *Titles:* Delos Sutherland. *Film Editor:* Robert W. Bischoff. *Photography:* Daniel Clark.

Cast: Tom Mix (Tom Blake), Natalie Kingston (Barbara Lane), Philo McCullough (Ben Tuttle), Al St. John (Joe Nimble), Fred Gamble (theatrical manager), Tony (a horse).

Still Code: Forde-12

Note: The final gross domestic film rental for *Painted Post* was $204,700.00

Not Up to Usual Mix Standard

"This latest Tom Mix vehicle for Fox is considerably slower than the Western star is accustomed to. It drags along through six reels [sic] of almost actionless stuff to a climax that is completely unconvincing. Mix pictures are usually synonymous with action. One can always depend upon a variety of thrills, but it is not so with this one.

"For the most part the story drags while the star and the villain vie for the attention of the newly arrived girl, who has come to sketch western types for a magazine. The scenes border more on light comedy than on hard-boiled Western stuff. The climax is too far fetched even for a Mix to get away with. Tom is battling a band of desperadoes who have made away with a payroll that was left in Tom's keeping. They are barricaded in a cabin and have the girl in their possession. The star mounts an adjoining high windmill and with the assistance of Tony succeeds in swaying the windmill until it falls through the roof of the cabin and precipitates Mix into the midst of the bandit gang. Single handed he battles them to a standstill until the arrival of Al St. John on a bicycle. The latter binds the bandits in a chain and leads them back to Painted Post while the star does a fadeout with the girl. Natalie Kingston is the Mix leading lady and she does her work well."

Chester J. Smith *Motion Picture News,* 6/23/28

THE DRIFTER

In the late '20s Tom Mix turned his hand to writing commentaries, reviews, and humorous observations—first for the show biz bible *Variety* for no pay, and later for popular magazines like *Photoplay, Cosmopolitan,* and *Liberty.* He also signed a contract with William Randolph Hearst's King Features Syndicate to write a regular newspaper column. The hope was that Tom Mix would prove to be another Will Rogers, and the cowboy star approached his new career with some enthusiasm.

"I used up about all my physical ability in making money and failed to be returned with any too much happiness as a reward," Tom wrote Victoria, "and I am now trying to harness up what mentality I have and see what results it can bring. It looks as if I can make around a hundred thousand a year from it, and the beautiful part is I can work in any country or climate without the help of horses—not that I am going back on my horses, but I would like to substitute them for a few lead pencils as a change and give the old body a chance to recondition itself."[1]

Tom's literary career was short-lived. He was a fair writer, but his humor was sometimes forced, and showed a slightly bitter edge. Where Will Rogers had the ability to make readers look at the world through new eyes, Tom Mix was just another guy with an opinion.

Fred Thomson and his horse Silver King. Thomson patterned his screen image in the Mix mold. As FBO's leading Western star from 1924 to 1927, he and Buck Jones ran a distant second to Tom Mix at the box-office.

When Tom's Fox contract came to an end, he signed with the Keith-Albee-Orpheum circuit for a vaudeville tour. His opening at the Hippodrome in New York was virtually ignored by Keith's publicity department, but even without much ballyhoo Tom Mix attracted a house record $32,500 at the K-A-O showplace. Receipts were $30,000 at the State-Lake in Chicago, and it was clear that Tom Mix was still a potent box-office attraction. Hollywood beckoned again. This time the offer came from FBO—the Film Booking Offices of America.

FBO was an outgrowth of the Robertson-Cole Company and produced and distributed its own pictures as well as the product of independent producers. The company struck paydirt in 1923 when Charles R. Rogers and Harry Joe Brown combined talents along with director Albert Rogell and a handsome minor leading man named Fred Thomson to produce a Western series.[2]

In twenty-one pictures over three years, Fred Thomson became a top cowboy star, rivaling Buck Jones and pretending to the throne of Tom Mix. The Thomson films were cast in the Mix mold—action, comedy, flashy costumes, and a horse with an I. Q. named Silver King. Fred Thomson was FBO's most successful star, but unfortunately for the studio, he left to make four big- budget specials for Paramount release.

Hoping to duplicate Thomson's success, FBO made cowboys of Vincent Markowski, Raymond Glenn and Robert N. Bradbury, Jr.—known to screen audiences as Tom Tyler, Bob Custer and Bob Steele. The company also turned out Westerns with pint-sized pre-teen "Buzz" Barton. These new Westerns were churned out quickly and cheaply and with some success, but they were not in the same league with the Thomson pictures. When Tom Mix became available, producer William LeBaron decided that the Mix name would add lustre to the FBO roster.

In many ways FBO was a come-down for Mix. The company was the leader of the low-rent competition that had diluted the market for Tom's Fox entertainments. But in 1928, there weren't many options. M-G-M was giving up its Tim McCoy series. Buck Jones and Rex Bell were out at Fox. After four straight losers, Fred Thomson's independent production contract with Paramount was not about to be renewed. They all planned to discontinue the production of Westerns. Universal still had Hoot Gibson, and First National released the Ken Maynard pictures. Columbia had not yet ventured into the series Western arena, and the poverty-row independents like William M. Pizor and Anthony J. Xydias produced whole features for less than Tom's weekly salary. So FBO was Tom's best, and perhaps only viable option. He signed a contract to make six silent Westerns for the studio.

Tom Mix, Sally Blane, Barney Furey, and Al Smith in *Outlawed* (1929). FBO's budgets for Westerns had been less than Tom's weekly salary, and, to compensate, the studio skimped on such expensive luxuries as going to distant location, giving the FBO Mix films a cheaper look than his Fox pictures.

Although Tom's marriage to Victoria was on the rocks by the late '20s, her brother, director Eugene Forde (right), joined the star at FBO. This photo was taken during production of *Daredevil's Reward* on September 22, 1927. Jodee Novak is behind the camera at left, and Dan Clark stands next to Forde.

Despite his problems with Vicky, Tom remained friendly with Eugene Forde, who directed three of the new series. The others were assigned to FBO house director Robert De Lacy. Cinematographer Dan Clark was still under contract to Fox and unavailable, so Mix promoted his assistant, Norman De Vol, to first cameraman. Many of Tom's stock company made the move to FBO as well, including Wynn Mace, Pat Chrisman, and Clyde Kinney; but Sid Jordan elected to remain at Fox.

As the cameras rolled on *Son of the Golden West* in July, 1928, negotiations were underway to merge FBO, DeMille-Pathe, and K-A-O Theatres with the Radio Corporation of America (RCA). By the time Tom Mix's first FBO film was ready for release in October, the credits read: An FBO Picture distributed by RKO Productions, Inc.[3]

It would be nearly a year before the FBO brand name gave way to the new RKO subsidiary, Radio Pictures, Inc., but it was clear that the company would concentrate on producing talkies. With primitive sound equipment, making outdoor pictures was difficult, and while rural theatres were still running silents well into 1930, they did not generate enough revenue to justify the continued production of silent films. The studios took to reissuing past successes, importing foreign films, and releasing mute sub-titled versions of their talkies to satisfy the ever-dwindling demand for silents.

Tom Mix was afraid that the primitive sound technology would drastically curtail the type of action sequences that were his specialty, and also worried that his voice would not register well on the microphone. He would complete only five of his scheduled pictures before it became clear the his concerns and the company's goals were not compatible. Although *The Dude Ranch* was announced as the sixth FBO Tom Mix film, the picture was never made and America's Champion Cowboy faded from the screen.

Only Tom's first FBO film received much attention in the trade. *Motion Picture News* was generally positive about *Son of the Golden West*, but *Harrison's Reports* said flat out that it was a terrible picture. Other films in the series were

"Is everybody Happy?" Tom Mix hits the Orpheum vaudeville circuit in 1928 with the "High-Hatted Tragedian of Song" Ted Lewis. Tom's still-potent box-office appeal led to his FBO contract.

criticized for being slow. The seven-reel lengths justified higher rentals, but reviewers complained that the films felt padded.

Of the five Mix FBO's, only one complete feature and a preview trailer for another are known to survive. *The Big Diamond Robbery* bears out the opinion of contemporary reviewers. It is slow, disjointed and not particularly interesting. The trailer for *King Cowboy* suggests a film with somewhat better production values, but it offers only a brief glimpse of the action.

Tom Mix fully expected that *The Big Diamond Robbery* would mark the end of his screen career. When the final scene was shot he had just turned forty-nine, and his battered body was feeling the effects of nearly twenty years of hard riding and rough and tumble stunts. He needed a rest.

NOTES

1. Letter from Tom Mix to Victoria Forde Mix, quoted in *Tom Mix Died For Your Sins*, Delacorte Press, 1975.
2. Production on the Thomson series began in 1923. His first FBO Western, *The Mask of Lopez*, was released January 27, 1924.
3. The initials RKO stand for Radio-Keith-Orpheum.

FBO PICTURES 1928—1929

SON OF THE GOLDEN WEST

FBO Pictures. Distributed by RKO Productions, Inc. Released October 1, 1928. *Length:* 6 reels (6,037 feet).

Production Started July 11, 1928. *Production Completed:* July 31, 1928.

Producer: William LeBaron. *Director:* Eugene J. Forde. Story and *Continuity:* George W. Pyper. *Titles:* Randolph Bartlett. *Assistant Director:* Charles Kerr. *Film Editor:* Henry Weber. *Photography:* Norman De Vol.

Cast: Tom Mix (Tom Hardy), Sharon Lynn (Alice Calhoun), Tom Lingham (Jim Calhoun), Duke R. Lee (Slade), Lee Shumway (Tennessee), Fritzi Ridgeway (Rita), Joie Ray (Keller), Mark Hamilton (Kane), Wynn Mace (Slade's henchman), Tony (a horse).

"If there is anyone in the western field who knows how to play the part of the dashing cowboy hero, it's Tom Mix, seen here in a whooping, whirlwind western, which gallops along at a hot pace, has all the necessary embellishments and is a good picture of its kind.

"Tom doesn't have to act. All he has to do is ride a horse, effect a thrilling rescue, pulverize the villains. You can bet he does all this, accomplishing it in a Mixian fashion. This cowboy veteran knows how to go through his paces with gusto and to carry any weak moments that may come along. There are a few of the latter that stand out in this production, but they are few and the good points are far in the majority.

Yes, you can say that this western comes home with a bang. A custom of Mr. Mix for a long time.

". . . THEME: Western drama telling of Pony Express rider's successful fight against lawless element, who are anxious to hold up the establishment of the telegraph. The Pony Express rider obtains the help of the militia, invades the stronghold of the villains, rescues the girl and lives happily ever afterwards with her."

Raymond Ganly—*Motion Picture News,* 9/29/28

"If Tom Mix (or FBO, whoever is responsible for this picture), cannot make better pictures than 'Son of the Golden West,' he had better give up producing to save himself from killing his reputation, and the exhibitors from being called down by their customers. It is not even a good program picture; it is the kind that any exhibitor can obtain from small independents at anywhere from five to seven and one-half dollars for the engagement. The picture is supposed to unfold in the Pony Express days, the purpose being to give Tom Mix to do good riding and the picture to offer excitement as a result of fights with Indians. But it is a tame affair at best.

"The main action revolves around the efforts of the pioneers to get a telegraph line laid out, and of the villains to prevent them from doing so, because they feared that an end would be put to their grafting game. Of course, the hero thwarts their plans and helps the pioneers get their telegraph.

"Some riding is done by Tom Mix, who takes the part of the Pony Express Rider; he is seen riding fast and changing horses at relay stations. . . ."

Harrison's Reports, 10/6/28

Tom Mix and Sharon Lynn in *Son of the Golden West*. Mix played a Pony Express rider, and although he wore his fancy Western shirt, he sported a flat crowned broad brim hat in keeping with the 1860 period of the story.

KING COWBOY

FBO Pictures. Distributed by RKO Productions, Inc. Released November 26, 1928. *Length:* 7 reels (6,269 feet).

Production Started August 9, 1928. Productions Completed: August 25, 1928.

Producer: William LeBaron. *Director:* Robert De Lacy. *Screenplay:* Frank Howard Clark. *Story:* S. E. V. Taylor. *Titles:* Helen Gregg and Randolph Bartlett. *Assistant Director:* James Dugan. Film Editors: Henry Weber and Tod Cheesman. *Photography:* Norman De Vol.

Cast: Tom Mix (Tex Rogers), Sally Blane (Polly Randall), Lew Meehan (Ralph Bennett), Barney Furey ("Shorty" Sims), Frank Leigh (Abdul El Hassan), Wynn Mace (Ben Suliman Ali), Robert Fleming (Jim Randall).

Working Title: *Drums of Araby*

Still Code: K.C.

Note: A preview trailer for *King Cowboy* was available in 16mm and 8mm film on the collectors' market some years ago.

"One of the best westerns seen recently and above the average Mix quality. A natural for any house that can stand westerns and strong enough to fill in on the split weeks.

"Conventional but appealing story of a band of cowboys on an expedition in Africa [sic] in search of their missing boss. Daughter of the missing man accompanies the outfit. Plans show the layout for oil fields involved and are responsible for the capture of the American by the African Amir. Resultant harem scenes carry a few laughs.

"Captured by the Amir and deprived of all firearms, the cowboys are virtually at the mercy of the African despot until they stage a midnight raid on the arsenal, recover their guns, and start a war following a rodeo given for the Amir's pleasure.

"Sally Blane is attractive as the heroine. Good support all around for Mix and scenic settings are lavish."

Mori. *Variety,* 12/26/28

OUTLAWED

FBO Pictures. Distributed by RKO Productions, Inc. Released January 21, 1929. *Length:* 7 reels (6,057 feet). 70 minutes.

Production Started September 7, 1928. *Production Completed:* September 29, 1928.

Producer: William LeBaron. *Director:* Eugene J. Forde. Story and *Continuity:* George W. Pyper. *Titles:* Helen Gregg. *Assistant Director:* James Dugan. *Film Editor:* Henry Weber. *Photography:* Norman De Vol.

Cast: Tom Mix (Tom Manning), Sally Blane (Anne), Frank M. Clark (Seth), Al Smith (Dervish), Ethan Laidlaw (McCasky), Barney Furey (Sagebrush), Al Ferguson (Sheriff).

"Falsely accused of murder and a bank robbery by the powerful leader of a robber gang, Tom Manning finds plenty of trouble clearing himself of the charge. He goes to jail and escapes before succeeding."

Motion Picture News Booking Guide, 3/15/30

"Cut down to 50 minutes this would be a fair Tom Mix offering. In present editing 'Outlawed' [is] painfully slow in first half. Then the other extreme is in so much effort for cramming action that the story is whirlwind of much used drug store rough stuff.

"Mix and Sally Blane are both poor on the love end. Galloping horsemen that might have been lifted from any indie western take up considerable footage. In this, however, the kids will get enough flashes of Mix to be happy.

"When Mix goes after the villains who would have swung the bank robbery and murder upon him is when the expected mix-up starts. After the dust clears and the bad lads have gotten theirs, Mix gets his—Miss Blane. She, incidentally, is a very blase little creature."

Waly. *Variety,* 2/13/29

THE DRIFTER

FBO Pictures. Distributed by RKO Productions, Inc. Released March 19, 1929. *Length:* 6 reels (5,896 feet). 68 minutes.

Production Started October 15, 1928. *Production Completed:* November 16, 1928.

Producer: William LeBaron. *Director:* Robert De Lacy. *Continuity:* George W. Pyper. *Story:* Oliver Drake and Robert De Lacy. *Assistant Director:* James Dugan. *Film Editor:* Tod Cheesman. *Photography:* Norman De Vol.

Cast: Tom Mix (Tom McCall), Dorothy Dwan (Ruth Martin), Barney Furey (Happy Hogan), Al Smith (Pete Lawson), Ernest Wilson (Uncle Abe), Frank Austin (Seth Martin), Joe Rickson (Hank), Wynn Mace (henchman).

Still Code: T.D.

"Tom Mix co-stars with a white mule here. A mystery angle about the value of the white mule partly bores and

Right: Mix and Kathryn McGuire in *The Big Diamond Robbery*, Tom's last silent and the only one of his FBO films known to survive.

Above-opposite: Tom and Dorothy Dwan in *The Drifter*. Norman De Vol took over as cameraman on the FBO series. This beautiful two-shot, achieved by back-lighting with the afternoon sun through a silk scrim and filling from the front with reflectors, is typical of the care taken with photography in the Mix films.

Below-opposite: Tom does his Wild West tricks for Arab Sheik Ben Suliman Ali (played by long-time Mix assistant director Wynn Mace) in *King Cowboy*.

Below: Visual symbolism in *Outlawed*. The hero in white hat, a portrait of Lincoln over his shoulder, unjustly arrested with hands cuffed and the shadow of jail bars on the wall.

arouses curiosity because it is not until half the footage has been projected that the animal's ability to lead to a gold mine is revealed. Last half, however, is crammed with action original for Mix and a battle in the air capitalizes some real thrills. A safe bet in the average house and especially good for the grinds since it is above par in both story and action.

"As the two-fisted government agent on the trail of dope smugglers Mix and his pal, Barney Furey, open with bugle practice. Action could be snapped up at the start were less footage devoted to landscapes.

"Al Smith, as the aviator dope runner and mystery man, is introduced attacking the daughter of a man who has been murdered, according to subtitles, after discovering a mine. The former role is played by Dorothy Dwan in the regular way.

"Key to the mine and the murderer is supposed to be vested in the mule which Mix has bought for 10 bucks. Interest is aroused when Mix socks the aviator and sky-high bidding is commenced by him for the animal.

"Going to work on the girl's ranch, Mix and his pal experience the usual foul play when bad man goes in for shooting after failing to get the mule. In the rush to get the animal headed for the mine gang double crosses each other. Highlight, particularly well done, is Mix's rush to take his claim in the same plane with the rival aviator. Series of loops and double exposures [is] more effective in pilot's effort to loose Mix out of the plane than usual hand-to-hand encounter on a wing.

"Story well knit and performances of cast average."

Waly. *Variety,* 3/20/29

THE BIG DIAMOND ROBBERY

FBO Pictures. Distributed by RKO Productions, Inc. Released May 13, 1929. *Length:* 7 reels (6,114 feet). 65 minutes.

Production Started December 10, 1928. *Production Completed:* January 10, 1929.

Producer: William LeBaron. *Director:* Eugene J. Forde. *Screenplay:* John Stuart Twist. *Story:* Frank Howard Clark. *Titles:* Randolph Bartlett. *Photography:* Norman De Vol.

Cast: Tom Mix (Tom Markham), Kathryn McGuire (Ellen Brooks), Frank Beal (George Brooks), Martha Mattox (Aunt Effie), Ernest Hilliard (Rodney Stevens), Barney Furey (Barney McGill), Ethan Laidlaw (Chick), Tony (a horse).

Still Code: T.B.D.R.

Note: A print of *The Big Diamond Robbery* is held by the Library of Congress.

"Underworld melodrama. Tom Markham, ranch foreman, fresh from the sage brush country, jumps right in the center of Metropolitan frenzy and wrestles with a wild taxicab which he finds more interesting than the wild broncos."

Motion Picture News Booking Guide, 3/15/30

"'The Great Diamond Robbery' could be edited into three short subjects. The production is so brought to the screen that, except for the titles and a few very thin directorial threads, the first two reels provide an old fashioned comedy; the second pair a fast society meller of the quickie school, while the last duet constitute a cowboy comedy-drama. A little realism just before the close as meller tonic.

"More has never been demanded of Tom Mix in any other picture. He is society man, ranch foreman, detective, bouncer and whatnot.

"While fans usually have the utmost cordiality for Tom, the guffaws of a grind audience were unmistakable when Tom leaped a street width from roof to roof. They were silent when, single-handed, he outwitted a gang of thugs who had stolen the jewels and laughed again when Tom, in a dark shot, hurled his lasso from the ground over a chimney perched three stories up.

"In this one, incidentally, autos beat trains and horses outsprinted autos. It's that way all through, with no regard for plausibility.

"Tom has to lean out of a taxi and pull a girl off her horse. Many film feet later on Tom's cab, breaking down, again halts the girl, this time in a car ducking the traffic cops.

"Were it not for the heavy's sly expression the picture could end there. But this bridges a gap to a night scene, burglars and a jewel robbery. Mix awakes and goes in for his first roof-jumping sequence. After trailing them to their den he overpowers the guy with the jewel and uses the bad man's chewing gum to secret it beneath a table. Mix delivers the stone to the girl on an outbound train inviting the taxi driver to the country.

"But the audience doesn't leave here. Following the train fade-out the bad men decide to take a short cut to the ranch and get back the jewel.

"The picture goes into a cowboy burlesque, the idea being to give the boss' daughter an idea of the old west. The outlaw gang arrives. Tom allows them to be received as guests, and more rough and tumble ensues."

Waly. *Variety,* 4/24/29

A pair of drug-store cowboys strut their stuff in the Mix manner.

With ill-fitting clothes and poorly-tooled leather work, these and the other poverty row cowboys were no match for Tom Mix in showmanship, but exhibitors found the ten dollar film rentals more attractive than the high stakes charged for the Mix pictures.

Right: Vincent Markowski tosses his loop around a trespasser. Markowski was better known to matinee fans as Tom Tyler.

Below: Another rubber-stamp hero was Raymond Glenn (right) who was given the name Bob Custer as the star of a series of low-budget oaters like *The Dead Line* (FBO, 1926) with Robert McKim (left) and Marianna Moya.

DESTRY RIDES AGAIN

When he finished at FBO in 1929, Tom Mix was convinced that his movie career was over. He was afraid that sound would bring an end to the type of extravagant outdoor action pictures he made, and that the added expense of the new technology would further erode the independence he had enjoyed during most of his tenure at Fox. He was also afraid that his voice would not register well, and concerned that the clicking sound of his dentures would further detract from his appeal as a talkie star.

Mix took his act on the road for another brief vaudeville tour before signing with the Sells-Floto Circus in May, 1929. The money was good, and the work was to Tom's liking. He relived childhood memories of Buffalo Bill's Wild West and Pawnee Bill's Far East Combined Show touring the nation as a circus headliner, and he thrilled at performing his feats of horsemanship and trick shooting before appreciative live audiences.

Also in May, the Federal Grand Jury in Los Angeles indicted Mix for trying to defraud the government of $175,967.65 in income taxes. The charges came down while Tom was appearing in Minneapolis, and the cowboy star said, "Really I don't know much about this income tax affair. I turned my income tax over to a woman expert, a Miss [J. Marjorie] Berger, some years ago, like I would turn an ailment over to a doctor. I thought I was paying the right amount of tax."

The major part of the case revolved around allegations of overstatement of deductions for the year 1925. One deduction in particular was cited as proof of a conspiracy to defraud the government. Tom's brother-in-law, Eugene J. Forde, was listed as business manager with a $12,000 annual salary. The government contended that Forde never received the salary, and instead was paid only $102.47 per quarter to cover the tax obligation on the phantom wages. Similar allegations were made against Mix's 1926 and 1927 returns as well. It did not help Mix's case that his tax consultant, Marjorie Berger, was under indictment for falsifying the tax returns of several other Hollywood celebrities as well. Finally in July, 1930 Mix paid the IRS $173,000 to settle the claim and avoided going to court.

After his first circus season Tom appeared in two entries of the Tiffany-Stahl *Voice of Hollywood* series, a pastiche of newsreel and publicity footage that gave the cowboy star his first exposure to the microphone. No Hollywood offers came from these brief talking screen appearances, but his Sells-Floto Circus contract remained in effect and Tom hit the sawdust trail again in 1930 and 1931.

When Victoria Mix left for Europe with Thomasina in late 1928, rumors were rampant that she planned a French divorce. Although Tom denied the stories, he could offer little to suggest that their marriage was still on solid ground.

"I haven't heard a word from her in some time," Mix was quoted as saying. "If she does return the door will be open to her an our daughter. I still insist that I do not want a divorce and I am quite positive Mrs. Mix will not seek one. But you can never tell.

"I write every week to her and our daughter but strangely I do not hear from them. Several of our mutual friends have told me that she has written plans to return but she hasn't written that fact to me."

Victoria finally returned to the States in July, 1929, after more than seven months on the Continent. She and Thomasina spent a week on the road with Tom, but Vicky made it clear that she had no intention of touring with her husband.

"His circus makes one-night stands and it would be too much of a strain on myself and daughter to remain with him," she told reporters. "I have no plans except to remain in Hollywood and I doubt that I will go back to Europe real soon."

In October, 1929 the stock market crashed, and the era of wonderful nonsense ended with it. While Tom could seemingly do no wrong in the roaring '20s, his luck went sour with the arrival of grim '30s.

In June, 1930 his seventeen-year-old daughter, Ruth, eloped to Yuma, Arizona with small-time actor Raymond Gilmore.

In October, Zack Miller filed a breach of contract suit against Mix charging that Tom had agreed to appear with the Miller Bros. 101 Ranch Show and instead had signed with Sells-Floto.

On November 1, 1930, only days after he returned to Hollywood at the

Tom Mix and an unidentified friend relax between shows on the grounds of the Sells-Floto Circus about 1930.

close of the circus season, newspapers reported that Mix had taken up separate residence at the Hollywood Roosevelt Hotel. A week later he was in the hospital for an operation to remove the wire supports from a now-healed shattered shoulder. Doctors also revealed that Mix was suffering from an old spinal injury compounded by the effects of arthritis.

In December, Victoria filed for divorce in Los Angeles Superior Court, charging mental cruelty and desertion.

"Mrs. Mix charged that her husband remained home only two days after returning last October from a circus tour," one newspaper reported, "then [he] left and did not communicate with her for nearly a month.

"He returned [home] November 20, [1930], she stated, after repeated requests by her to visit the bedside of their daughter, Thomasina, 9, who was ill.

"Mr. Mix frightened his wife at that time, she charged, by drawing a loaded gun from his pocket, twirling it on his finger, and in a 'loud and boisterous manner' announcing that he intended to leave her permanently."

Although Mix did not contest the suit, he did deny his wife's charges. On Christmas Eve the papers announced that Victoria Mix was granted a divorce.

1931 brought no end to Tom's run of bad luck. Zack Miller won the breach of contract suit and was awarded $90,000. Mix appealed, but when the final decision was handed down in February, 1933, Tom still came out the loser, forced to pay Miller some $66,000.

The Sells-Floto Circus fell victim to the depression and closed down after the 1931 season, however Tom received a film offer from Carl Laemmle of Universal Pictures to make a series of six all-talkie Westerns. Stanley Bergerman, who supervised the first six Tom Mix pictures for Universal, remembers that the contract called for Tom to receive $30,000 per picture, and that the star was actively involved in the creation of the films.

"Tom sat in on story conferences and had many suggestions, especially with regard to the action sequences," says Bergerman. "He was an expert, very knowledgeable in his field, and had many helpful ideas. He wanted to make good pictures."

Tom's first Universal picture was scheduled to start shooting during the last week of November, 1931, but the cameras never turned. On Monday November 23, Mix was stricken with a burst appendix. Dr. R. Nichol Smith performed emergency surgery. Although the operation was successful, peritonitis set in and the Western star hovered near death.

When Tom's cowboys came to Hollywood Hospital to visit their stricken boss, he was in no condition to see them. Pat Chrisman spoke for them all when he said, "It sure will be rough on a lot of western folks if Tom goes over the Big Divide."

Director Al Rogell, who directed *The Rider of Death Valley*, visits the star on the set of *The Texas Bad Man*.

On November 25th a supply of bacteriophage was flown to Los Angeles. It had little effect. A culture of Tom's infected cells was flown to Stanford University so that a new antitoxin could be concocted.

On Thursday, November 26th, Dr. Smith could only report that, "There is no improvement in Mr. Mix's condition. All I can hope for now is the best. We will be able to know definitely Friday night or Saturday morning the ultimate outcome.

"I do not want to appear gloomy about Mr. Mix's condition," Dr. Smith continued, "but he is in a precarious state and only time can tell. We are doing everything possible for him, and he has shown great courage and the value of this cannot be underestimated. He has a great constitution and a tendency to win, so we can still look forward to the best."

With modern medical technology, peritonitis is rarely a threat today, but in the early '30s it was serious indeed. Only five years earlier Rudolph Valentino died after a similar operation and infection. Mix did pull through however, and was soon recuperating at his Beverly Hills mansion. "Death isn't an accident," Mix reportedly told Relman Morin, who penned a colorful and largely bogus multi-part biography of the star for newspaper syndication in 1932, "It's figured out in advance, and calculated for the good of everybody concerned." The quote may or may not have been real, but in retrospect the words seemed to foreshadow Tom Mix's final race with death in 1940.

On January 4, 1932, Mabel Victoria Hannaford, known as Victoria Forde Mix, received her final divorce decree. A week later at the home of friends in Tuxedo Park, New York, she married Don Manuel A. De Olzabal, military attache to the Argentine embassy in Washington, D. C.

Rumors circulated that Tom was also planning to remarry. The woman was said to be circus aerialist Mabel Hubbell Ward, but Mix denied any romantic link. "I can't help what they're saying about me marrying," Tom told reporters, "but it isn't true. I'm going to free lance for the time being. Nobody would want me now anyway 'cause I'm broke. They'll all probably wait until I make another million."

For Tom's fifty-second birthday, Universal sent still photographer Ray Jones to shoot pictures of the cowboy star being visited by his famous horse, Tony, as the star rested on an outdoor chaise lounge at his home in Beverly Hills. Astute horse watchers noticed that Tony was not Tony at all, but another horse altogether. Tony had white stockings on his back legs. This horse had four white stockings and eventually became known as Tony, Jr., but the studio made no mention of the change of mounts. By late January, 1932 Tom was sufficiently recovered to go back to work, and on Monday the 25th the camera rolled on the first scenes of *Destry Rides Again*.

The film was clearly designed to introduce Tom Mix to a new generation of movie audiences. The opening sequence, devised by director Ben Stoloff, has a group of kids in the school yard waiting for Tom Destry to make his daily visit. They see the silhouette of a lone rider on a distant hill. Horse and rider charge headlong down the slope, jump the school fence, and ride up to greet the adoring youngsters. Tom demonstrates his skill with a six-shooter and gives one trickster a lesson in good citizenship. None of this has anything to do with the plot, which concerns Destry being framed for a shooting and sent to jail by his business partner, but it effectively erased Tom's three-year absence from the screen.

Universal made every effort to make him feel at home. The budget for *Destry* was about half of what Fox allotted for a Mix picture, but five times more than Columbia was spending on their Buck Jones series in the early '30s. The script was based on a novel by Max Brand, who had provided the source material for several of Tom's best films, and Universal borrowed Tom's favorite camera-man, Daniel Clark, to insure outstanding photography. Director Ben Stoloff, was another Mix alumnus from the '20s.

Opposite page: January 6, 1932. Tony visits Tom at his Beverly Hills home on Tom's birthday as the star recuperates from a burst appendix and a bout with peritonitis.

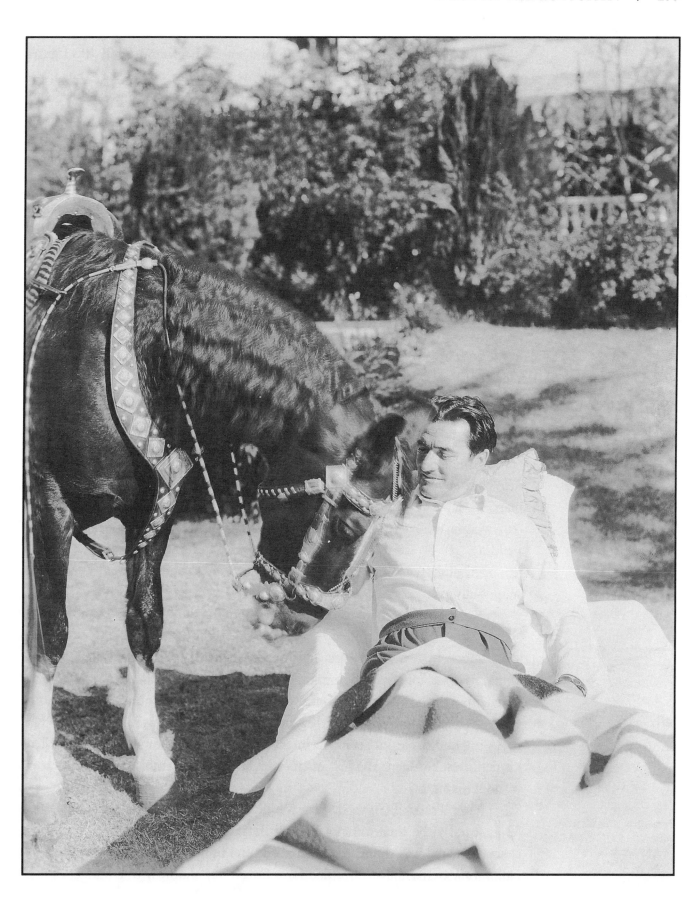

Even with his old associates around him, Mix found Hollywood more regimented than when he made his last silents. "Pictures sure have changed," he was quoted saying as *Destry* was going into production, "There's so many different new departments butting in on my work that I'm going to be lucky if any of these pictures get finished on time."

Clocking in at a brisk 53 minutes, *Destry Rides Again* left no time for subtlety or nuance. It was rather somber and offered Mix few opportunities to display any humor. Not surprisingly, given his recent operation, there was little physical action, either. However, on the crucial question the cowboy star proved to be an adequate actor in the talkies.

He was clearly uncomfortable with dialogue, but no more so than Ken Maynard or Buck Jones in their early talkies. Although he lacked John Wayne's naturalness, Mix spoke his lines with built-in pauses reminiscent of Wayne's purposely halting delivery. The one problem with Tom's voice was that it did not fit the sprightly screen image he developed on the silent screen. His flat, gravel-edged baritone was more suited to the serious persona he projected in *Destry* and most of his other Universal films. He became more adept with dialogue as he gained experience in the new medium and managed to show some of his old comic flair by the time he made *Flaming Guns* later in the year.

Immediately after *Destry* wrapped, Mix did a cameo in *The Cohens and Kellys in Hollywood;* and, despite his earlier denials, on February 15, 1932 Tom Mix married Mabel Ward.

Tom told reporters that his younger daughter was responsible for the wedding.

"Daddy, when are you going to get married?" the nine year old Thomasina supposedly asked.

"Well, honey," her father replied, "whom do you want me to marry?"

"Why, Mabel, of course."

Tom, Mabel, Thomasina and friends Mr. and Mrs. Monte Blue, drove to Yuma, Arizona for the wedding, then Tom, his new wife, and young daughter went across the border to Mexico for the briefest of honeymoons.

"I don't know why my father took me along," Thomasina remembered in 1968, "but he did. He got drunk one night and got in a bar room brawl and cracked his dentures. He spent the rest of the trip in his hotel, embarrassed to be seen without his teeth."

Tom's second Universal film was given the working title *Destry of Death Valley,* but by the time director Al Rogell called "Action!" in March, 1932, the character name was changed to Rigby, and the film was known as *The Rider of Death Valley.* Originally scheduled for a fifteen day shoot, with a budget of just

February 15, 1932, Tom with his new bride, Mabel Hubbell Ward. Mrs. Monte Blue, a friend and member of the wedding party sits on the arm of the chair, and Thomasina Mix, age nine, sits with Mabel.

above $100,000, the picture went past schedule and 20% over budget—however, the results were worth the effort.

The plot was the old wheeze about a map to a lost mine torn in three pieces and the efforts of the good, the bad, and (in this case) the beautiful to locate the gold. No matter. Writer Jack Cunningham, director Al Rogell, cameraman Dan Clark, and a strong cast combined to create a moody, atmospheric and disturbingly realistic parable of greed and misplaced trust.

Two national icons, Luis Trenker, king of German "mountain films," and Tom Mix, the king of American screen cowboys, meet during production of *The Rider of Death Valley*. Trenker was at Universal City to shoot the English language version *The Rebel*.

As Tom and his party bake in the Death Valley sun without water, their lips become parched, their eyes hollow, their movements listless and erratic. The convincing treatment of dehydration in the make-up and performances was unique for a series Western, and the results made the whole far greater than the sum of the parts. Even Tony's riderless return to the ranch to whinny and snort until the slow-witted cowboys realize the horse is trying to get them to follow takes on an urgency that erases the dramatic improbabilities.

"*The Rider of Death Valley* was a 'Super,' with a better than average budget," recalls Stanley Bergerman. "Thirst was the heavy. The two villains, Forrest Stanley and Fred Kohler, had a certain amount of charm, and even though they were killers and thieves you were concerned about their dying of thirst. It was a departure from the usual type of Western script, and it went over very well."

Mix had some problems with studio management on his third Universal picture, *The Texas Bad Man*. The direction was assigned to Edward Laemmle, nephew of studio head Carl Laemmle, and rumors circulated that Tom resented the interference from Laemmle's relatives.

The Texas Bad Man was a good picture, with beautiful outdoor photography by Dan Clark and a strong performance by Willard Robertson as a leading citizen who is also a bandit king. However, Tom looked more ill-at-ease than in either of his first two talkies.

"Edward Laemmle was a very willing and ambitious director," producer Stanley Bergerman remembers. "He had a great deal of experience in silent pictures, but limited experience in the talkies."

Edward Laemmle's lack of sound film experience showed. Although *The Texas Bad Man* was completed on its fifteen day schedule, dialogue director Gene Lewis was brought in to shoot two days of re-takes. During production of *My Pal, the King, Variety* reported:

> ## MIX WON'T PLAY FOR LAEMMLE RELATIVES
> ### Hollywood, May 30
> Tom Mix has given Universal 30 days' extension on its option for his services to enable Carl Laemmle in person to handle the negotiations.
>
> Mix was disinclined to discuss renewal terms with Stanley Bergerman, son-in-law of Laemmle and supervisor of the productions. Western star feels that his 24 years in the picture business entitle him to know the experience of the people he is to work with.
>
> In his negotiations Mix will insist that none of the Laemmle relatives be assigned to supervise or direct his pictures and also that hands be kept off by those unfamiliar with his type of pictures at the studio. He says that inexperience of executives associated with the pictures just made has been a handicap and an annoyance.

My Pal, the King was different from Tom's earlier Universal pictures. It was lighter in tone, and slighter in plot. Set in an imaginary European kingdom, Tom and his cowboys come to the aid of a boy-king played by Mickey Rooney. The story is pared to bare essentials and a good portion of the footage is given over to an extended Wild West Show staged for the exclusive pleasure of the king. As if to make up for the lack of plot complications, the film has a full musical under-score compiled from stock library music—very rare, indeed, for a 1932 film.

As Tom's fifth Universal picture was about to go into production, *Variety* reported that Mix had signed a new contract with the studio for an additional six films. The story reported that Universal executives promised that Mix "would get capable supervision and proper direction for the new slate."

While the contemporary trade stories suggest that there was a great deal of

P.E.635

friction between Mix and his producer, Stanley Bergerman has no memories of any such conflict.

"Tom was very friendly and professional," says Bergerman. "We became good personal friends and he gave me a prize revolver.

"Tom was an outstanding American," continues Bergerman. "He had courage and strength. He made history in motion pictures, and he deserves to be remembered with respect and admiration. He was a real Western star and a hero."

The Fourth Horseman turned out to be one of the best of Tom's Universal pictures, but it nearly proved to be a disaster. Hamilton MacFadden was signed as director, and he seemed to be an ideal choice for the job. The former director of the Theatre Guild School, he was also a stage producer and a Broadway actor, notably in *Beggar on Horseback.* MacFadden entered films in 1929, working first for Pathe Eastern Studio, before signing with Fox Film Corporation. Among his Fox pictures were two of the early Charlie Chan's, *Charlie Chan Carries On* and *The Black Camel* (both 1931), but he also directed a stylish version of Zane Grey's *Riders of the Purple Sage* (also 1931) with George O'Brien. With these credentials he was borrowed from Fox to direct *The Fourth Horseman.*

Budgeted at just over $92,000 and slated for a 10 day shoot, MacFadden brought *The Fourth Horseman* in on schedule and under budget—but the money he saved was no consolation, because the picture needed help if it was ever going to be released. Retakes were called by Universal, the budget was increased to $108,000, and Arthur Rosson was brought in to direct the new material. A little more than a month after the first version wrapped, Rosson shot five days of retakes, and over the following month an additional four days were spent re-shooting the picture.

The patch work on *The Fourth Horseman* is not immediately evident except in a scene where Tom saves Margaret Lindsay from a herd of stampeding horses. In the final version of the picture Tom changes costume from shot to shot. In some angles he is seen wearing a white shirt, and in others a dark shirt. Further evidence of "major surgery" comes in the credits which list Raymond Hatton as a member of the cast. Photos survive which clearly show Hatton working in scenes with Mix; but even though he receives screen credit, the character actor did not appear in release prints of *The Fourth Horseman.*

The last picture in Tom's first Universal series was *Hidden Gold,* an off-beat tale of three robbers who have made off with a small fortune. The criminals were captured, but the loot was never recovered, and deputy Tom Mix is sent to jail undercover to befriend the outlaws and find the hidden gold. The film includes a jail break, an extended car chase, and ends with a spectacular forest fire sequence. Cinematographer Dan Clark was not available, and Jerry Ash took over

Opposite page: From his collection of hats, Tom selects a Mexican sombrero to be used in the scenes in which he is disguised as a Mexican bandit in *The Texas Bad Man.*

behind the camera. A former actor with the Francis Ford-Grace Cunard serial unit during the Teens, Ash spent most of his career as a cameraman on low-budget action pictures.

Director Ray Taylor was assigned to *Hidden Gold,* but he only worked the first six days of the 12 day schedule. The official reason for Taylor's replacement was illness, and again Arthur Rosson was brought in to finish the picture. Ultimately, the film was 16 days in production, although not appreciably over budget.

Oh, Promise Me, a comic Western romance by Peter B. Kyne, was scheduled as the first picture in Tom's second series, but on October 4, 1932 *Variety* announced:

> ### TIFFS TAKE LAEMMLE KIN OFF MIX SERIES
> Hollywood, October 3.
>
> To prevent further bickering between Tom Mix and Stanley Bergerman, Universal has taken Carl Laemmle's son-in-law off the Mix series and will replace him with another supervisor. Bergerman will be assigned to other pictures. Pair had plenty of squabbles over direction.
>
> Henry MacRae will direct the next Mix feature, which will not be "Oh, Promise Me," which has been moved back so that a yarn with more hair on its chest can be substituted. . . .

Contrary to the trade reports, direction of *Terror Trail* was given to Western veteran Armand Schaeffer, who had a reputation for pinching pennies and turning out pictures on the cheap. Henry MacRae was assigned as producer, taking over Bergerman's chores on the rest of the second Universal series, but the change in supervisors offered a clue to Mix's status at Universal. MacRae was head of the studio's serial unit, and not generally assigned to prestigious projects.

Over all, *Terror Trail* was comparable to Tom's first six Universals. Although it was a more straightforward Western than his previous talkies, there were some opportunities for humor. In one scene Tom is awakened from a sound sleep by the gunfire of some drunks in the saloon below. He straps on his gun and puts an end to the disturbance, but when the dust is settled he realizes he's forgotten to put on his pants, much to the merriment of the saloon girls and his own embarrassment.

Oh, Promise Me finally made the schedule as *Flaming Guns.* Arthur Rosson was back in the director's chair for his third Mix Universal, and Dan Clark provided some spectacular visuals on the Lone Pine, California locations.

Opposite page: Tom signs autographs for fans along Vine Street in Hollywood in front of the world famous Brown Derby restaurant.

If one is expecting a hell-bent-for-leather action picture, *Flaming Guns* is disappointing. The "guns" of the title are not six-shooters but the stubborn, iron-willed characters in the story. Tom plays a cowboy back from World War I and not about to take any guff from anyone. Another former Fox Western star, William Farnum, plays a bull-headed ranch owner who hires Mix to stop rustling on his spread and then fires him because he thinks the cowboy is getting too familiar with his daughter. Ruth Hall plays the daughter as a free-spirited soul who defies her father's every wish.

Miss Hall got the role through her agent, Arthur Landau, and did not meet the cowboy star until she arrived on the set for her first day's work. Although she did not know him well, she remembers Mix with a great deal of affection.

"Tom was an absolute gentleman, wonderful to be with," she recalls. "Such a gentleman—more so than most of the other Western stars.

"He was very easy to work with. He generally got everything on the first take. He knew his lines, and he had every move planned. We would walk through a scene, but generally we rehearsed very little. The director catered to him, and said very little to me."

Veteran Universal serial producer-director Henry MacRae (left) took over production of the Mix films during the star's second series for the studio. This shot was taken on the set of *Flaming Guns*. William Farnum (right), another former Fox star, played a character role in the film.

Flaming Guns was more comedy than action picture, and the situations and dialogue were a bit racy, in keeping with other pre-code pictures. Despite the fact that prohibition was still the law of the land, Tom even takes Ruth Hall to a speakeasy, and rescues her when the Feds make a raid on the joint. By now, Tom was more comfortable with the microphone, and he played the humor for all it was worth.

In the one sustained action set piece, Tom rounds up a herd of stolen cattle and captures the rustlers single-handed. Beautifully photographed by Dan Clark, the sequence is a real treat for the eyes. While shooting the scene in the hills of Lone Pine, on October 21, 1932, Tom was injured when Tony, Jr. stepped in a hole, fell, and rolled over on the cowboy. He suffered three broken ribs, but he was back in the saddle less than a week later. After the fall, Universal finally announced the official retirement of Tony the Wonder Horse and his replacement by Tony, Jr. although the older animal had appeared in none of Tom's talkies.

Variety reported that Henry MacRae was ordered to "turn out a western of the old fashioned type . . . [with] nothing but time-tried range stuff, minus any of the non-sagebrush frills which have crept into recent horse operas," and *Rustlers Roundup* was the result. Frank Howard Clark, who wrote several of Mix's early Fox successes, was brought in to do the script, and it proved to be an entertaining Western with Tom again playing a masked crusader who is mistaken for an outlaw. The picture plowed old ground, however, and offered nothing out of the ordinary. The one element of interest was leading lady Diane Sinclair. Southern exhibitors would have been surprised to learn that the exotic looking actress who played Noah Beery, Jr.'s sister in *Rustler's Roundup* was a mulatto who managed to pass for white. If the fact had been known, the films would have been banned by circuits like Paramount-Richards Theaters, Inc., a New Orleans-based chain that preferred their pictures "lily white." Odd as it may seem, Sinclair appeared as leading lady to several of the screen's greatest Western stars, including Buck Jones and Tim McCoy.

Henry MacRae directed *Rustlers Roundup* himself, and the old serial hand did a creditable job—but ultimately the picture was just another Western. Whatever his differences with Stanley Bergerman, Mix benefited from the producer's ability to develop strong and off-beat screen properties.

On December 20, 1932 *Variety* noted that Tom Mix and Universal had agreed to part company by mutual consent. "Mix says recent accidents and influenza convinced him he needs a rest," the show-biz paper reported. "He'll go to Europe with Mrs. Mix for a delayed honeymoon and tour the world after a rest on the Continent. He may go out with a circus upon his return. . . He has suffered 26 broken bones and many wounds while at work in production. . ."

A wary Tom Mix offers a shooting lesson to leading lady Claudia Dell on the set of *Destry Rides Again*.

UNIVERSAL PICTURES 1931-1933

THE COHENS AND KELLYS IN HOLLYWOOD

A Universal Picture. Released March 28, 1932. *Length:* 75 minutes.

Director: John Francis Dillon. Supervisor: Stanley Bergerman. *Story:* Howard J. Green. Production Budget: $157,393.00. Production Schedule: 19 days. *Production Started* January 26, 1932.

Production Completed: February 18, 1932. 22 days principal photography. Final Negative Cost: $161,034.48.

Cast: George Sidney (Moe Cohen), Charlie Murray (Michael Kelly), June Clyde (Kitty Kelly), Norman Foster (Maurice Cohen), Emma Dunn (Mrs. Cohen), Esther Howard (Mrs. Kelly), Edwin Maxwell (Chauncey Chadwick), Dorothy Christie (Mrs. Chadwick), Luis Alberni (Solarsky), Tom Mix, Sidney Fox, Lew Ayres, Boris Karloff, Genevieve Tobin.

Note: Tom Mix and other Universal screen stars made cameo appearances in a sequence filmed at the Coconut Grove in the Ambassador Hotel.

Still Code: 328-1

"Number five of the series and still nothing new in thought, gesture, motion or mannerism. Four predecessors did pretty well at the b.o. in nabes and inland, and there's no reason why this one shouldn't follow along the same way. It's not the worst of the five.

"Sidney and Murray do their tricks in Hollywood this time. Kitty becomes a picture star in the silent days and the Kellys ozone the Cohens. Then come the talkers and the Kellys are out, but young Cohen lands big as a theme songwriter. Theme songs blow, and both families start on the long trek back to Hillboro.

"Throughout it is a meek attempt at satirizing picture business. But it's directors and actors that are burlesqued— not the makers of pictures. Which is almost a gag in itself.

"Sidney and Murray are as usual in their parts. June Clyde is surprisingly good as Kitty Kelly, especially in the takeoff of the actress gone Hollywood. And Norman Foster is a believable juve lead. All the laughs that the star team don't garner (and there are not too many) go to Luis Alberni doing his usual screwy business as a Russ director.

"At the Mayfair [Theater in New York] the biggest laugh came where it wasn't intended. Kitty Kelly as a lunchroom waitress had sent her picture to Hollywood asking for a picture chance. Week later telegram boy arrives asker her to come out pronto and become a star. The mob at the Mayfair thought that right here was a good place for a big, hearty laugh.

"And at the Mayfair the mob was equally unimpressed with the big scene at the Coconut Grove with cut-ins of famous movie stars. Stars were Tom Mix, Lew Ayres, Sidney Fox, Boris Karloff and Genevieve Tobin, all strangely enough working for Universal.

"But that's on Broadway. Where the customers are less exacting all that won't count."

Kauf. *Variety,* 4/26/32

Above: In *Destry Rides Again*, Tom is falsely accused of shooting an unarmed man, l-r: Edward Piel, Sr., [obscured], Robert "Clyde Kinney" Ruffner, Francis Ford, Mix, Frederic Howard.

Above-opposite: Although Tom Mix had already appeared in several promotional shorts in the *Voice of Hollywood* series, part of the campaign for *Destry Rides Again* revolved around the question: "What will his first two words be?"

Below-opposite: *Destry Rides Again* was Tom's first starring sound film, but it was not his first Universal talkie. He did a cameo in *The Cohens and Kellys in Hollywood*, produced after *Destry*, but released two weeks before. During a moment between scenes at the famed Coconut Grove nightclub, director John Francis Dillon sits with Tom and the new Mrs. Mix, the former Mabel Hubbell Ward.

Right: At the trial, after his conviction, Tom Destry swears vengeance on his accusers. Claudia Dell played Destry's lady friend Sally Dangerfield.

DESTRY RIDES AGAIN

A Universal Picture. Released April 17, 1932. 6 reels (53 minutes).

Associate Producer: Stanley Bergerman. *Director:* Benjamin Stoloff. *Continuity:* Isidore Bernstein. Dialogue: Robert Keith. Based on a novel by Max Brand. *Scenario Editor:* Richard Schayer. *Recording Engineer:* C. Roy Hunter. *Art Director:* Thomas F. O'Neill. *Film Editor:* Arthur Hilton. *Supervising Film Editor:* Maurice Pivar.

Production Budget: $108,300.00. Production Schedule: 17 days. *Production Started* January 25, 1932. Production completed: February 12, 1932. 17 days principal photography. Final Negative Cost: $109,503.86.

Cast: Tom Mix (Tom Destry), Claudia Dell (Sally Dangerfield), Earle Foxe (Brent), Stanley Fields (Sheriff Wendell), Frederick Howard (Clifton), Edward Piel, Sr. (Warren), Francis Ford (Judd Ogden), Robert "Clyde Kinney" Ruffner (Clyde), John Ince (Judge), Charles K. French (Jury Foreman), Edward J. Le Saint (Mr. Dangerfield), George Ernest (Willie), ZaSu Pitts (Temperance Worker), Ed Brady, Chris Pin Martin (coach passengers).

Still Code: 340-1

"The fears of some persons had lest Mr. Mix' voice should not record well will be dissipated by this picture, for the reproduction of it is excellent. The story material is very good; it is human, and the action keeps one's attention to the screen at all times. Mr. Mix again takes his old part, of being kindly and of setting no bad example for children. He shows attachment for little children. And the children show great affection for him and his horse. In the last one-third, George Ernest, a boy about eight years old, almost 'steals' the picture; Mix, slightly wounded, is supposed to be hunted by the outlaws. In his efforts to escape from them, he comes upon a farm house. Every one of the family is absent except George Ernest, who acts as a hero worshiper, the object of his worship being Mix (as Destry). At first the boy pretends he has not recognized him although he speaks admiringly of him. After washing his wound like an 'old-timer,' he advises Mix to sleep, undertaking to act as a guard, to notify him if any one should approach the house. These scenes will give much pleasure to those who will see the picture.

The story deals with a hero who is framed by his partner, secretly the leader of an outlaw gang, and sends him to jail for a year for murder. He vows to revenge the wrong done to him. When he comes out, he first pretends that he is a sick man and that he had given up his revenge plans. Suddenly he goes after the outlaws and gets every one of them. (He does not shoot any one of them himself.) He wins as a wife the heroine, who was coveted by this partner.

"Max Brand wrote the story; Ben Stoloff directed it. The direction could have been better. Claudia Dell is not so good a heroine. Earle Foxe is the villain.

"Good for children and for Sunday showing."

Harrison's Reports, 4/16/32

THE RIDER OF DEATH VALLEY

A Universal Picture. Released May 26, 1932. *Length:* 8 reels (78 minutes).

Associate *Producer:* Stanley Bergerman. *Director:* Albert Rogell. Story and *Screenplay:* Jack Cunningham. Dialogue Supervisor: Gene Lewis. Scenario Editor: Richard Schayer. Art *Director:* Thomas F. O'Neill. Recording Supervisor: C. Roy Hunter. *Film Editor:* Robert Carlisle. Supervising *Film Editor:* Maurice Pivar. *Photography:* Daniel B. Clark.

Production Budget: $104,670.00. Production Schedule: 15 days. *Production Started* March 4, 1932. *Production Completed:* March 22, 1932. 22 days principal photography, 7 days over schedule. Final Negative Cost: $129,549.09.

Note: Production dates copied from Universal records indicate a March 4 start date and a March 22 completion date with twenty-two days of principal photography. Obviously these dates do not add up. Since March 4, 1932 fell on a Friday, it seems likely that this is not the correct start date.

Cast: Tom Mix (Tom Rigby), Lois Wilson (Helen Joyce), Fred Kohler (Lew Grant), Forrest Stanley (Doctor Larribee), Edith Fellows (Betty Joyce), Willard Robertson (Bill Joyce), Mae Busch (Tillie), Otis Harlan (Peck), Francis Ford (Gabe Dillon), Tony, Jr.

Working *Titles:* DESTRY OF DEATH VALLEY, DEATH VALLEY

Still Code: 341-1

"Remember the good old days? They're back—with Tom Mix racing with death to rescue a pretty girl (Lois Wilson), swaggering fearlessly after dirty villains, lost on the desert with only Tony, his horse, to save him. Who can do that grand old hokum better than Tom and Tony? No one, we'll say! The kids will eat this up and Dad will be glad of the excuse to take Junior."

Photoplay Magazine, July, 1932

"Thirst was the villain in *The Rider of Death Valley*," says producer Stanley Bergerman.

Above: Doc Larribee (Forrest Stanley, left) is a respected citizen, but only as honest as he needs to be. His henchman is Lew Grant (Fred Kohler). Tom Rigby (Mix) intervenes to protect the secret of a murdered miner's claim for the rightful heirs. The odd vests that Mix wore in this and in *The Texas Bad Man* were reminiscent of his first Western costume cut down from an old coat when Tom was twelve years old and owe more to the circus than to the old West.

Right: Helen Joyce (Lois Wilson) takes a sip of precious water as Tom Rigby (Mix) is about to set out across Death Valley in search of help.

Right: Captain Carter of the Texas Rangers (Joseph Girard) helps create the subterfuge that Ranger Tom Bishop (Mix) is *The Texas Bad Man*. Tom stretched as an actor by playing a Mexican bandit, although his Latin accent was none too convincing. Overall, Mix seemed more ill at ease than in either of his first two talkies.

Below: In the outlaw lair. Typical of the movies, the bad men have a hidden settlement which the law has been unable to find. Tom is about to be sent on a mission by the bandit leader. Unknown to Tom, the others will follow and try to bushwhack him.

"A good Western; it holds one's interest to the very end. The situation in which the hero, the heroine, and two other men are in the desert without any water, is extremely realistic for they are shown as being parched and half mad with a desire for water. Mr. Mix's horse, Tony again displays fine intelligence. This is so especially in the situation in which he makes the hero's cowhands realize that he was trying to take them to his master, whose life was in danger. The closing situation in which the hero rescues the heroine from the mine just as it was to be blown up is exciting:—

"The hero knows that a certain doctor and his pal had killed the heroine's brother. The heroine's brother had found gold and the two men were desirous of getting the mine. He leaves a map to the doctor, but the hero, at the point of a gun, takes the map and tears it in three parts keeping the most important part for himself and giving the other two parts to the two men. When the heroine arrives in the town the doctor tries to poison her mind about the hero, and she believes him especially when she finds her young niece in a saloon to which the hero had brought her to buy her a soda. She demands the third part of the map from the hero but he refuses to give it to her telling her he will make the trip with her and the doctor and his pal. While riding in Death Valley the horses go wild and their outfit is smashed. They are left with very little water. The doctor's pal dies. The hero sends his horse back to the ranch for help. He leaves the heroine with the doctor so that he could look for his men if they were coming to him. The horse finally makes the men understand that they are to follow him. They find the hero, who had collapsed and h takes them to the heroine. He rescues the heroine from the mine just in time for the doctor had planned to dynamite it in the hope of getting water. The doctor is killed. The heroine is sorry for having doubted the hero. They are united. . . . "

Harrison's Reports, 5/28/32

THE TEXAS BAD MAN

A Universal Picture. Released June 30, 1932. *Length:* 7 reels (61 minutes).

Producer: Carl Laemmle, Jr. Associate *Producer:* Stanley Bergerman. *Director:* Edward Laemmle [and uncredited Gene Lewis]. Dialogue Supervisor: Gene Lewis. Story and *Screenplay:* Jack Cunningham. Scenario Editor: Richard Schayer. Art *Director:* Thomas F. O'Neill. Cinematographer: Daniel B. Clark. Recording Supervisor: C. Roy Hunt. Special Photographic Effects: John P. Fulton. *Film Editor:* Philip Cahn. Supervising *Film Editor:* Maurice Pivar.

Production Budget: $98,880.00. Production Schedule: 15 days. *Production Started* April 19, 1932. *Production Completed:* May 5, 1932. 15 days principal photography. Retakes: May 12-13, 1932, 2 days. Final Negative Cost: $99,257.05.

Cast: Tom Mix (Tom/Dan Bishop), Fred Kohler (Gore Hampton), Willard Robertson (Milton Keefe), Lucille Powers (Nancy Keefe), Joseph Girard (Captain Carter), Tetsu Komai (Yat Gow), Edward J. Le Saint (Chester Bigelow).

Working Title: THE GOOD BAD MAN

Still Code: 342-1

Note: Retakes were directed by dialogue supervisor Gene Lewis.

"A fast-moving Western with a story that holds the interest from beginning to end. The audience is held in suspense for fear lest the villain discover that the hero was a Texas Ranger and not a bandit as he purposely led him to believe he was. There are many exciting situations in which the hero is forced to make a hurried escape from the Rangers who think he is a bandit. The closing scenes are the most exciting; there the hero proves the guilt of the villain. There is a pleasant romance between the hero and the heroine:—

"The hero, a government marshal, is called on by the leader of the Texas Rangers to round up a gang of outlaws who had been terrorizing the countryside by bold holdups and murders. The hero poses as an outlaw and holds up a stage coach. In this way he gets in with the gang and meets the leader. He discovers that the leader is supposedly a law abiding citizen, respected by every one in the community. He accidentally meets the heroine, sister of the villain. She knows nothing of her brother's misdeeds. She tells the hero she will try to convert him from a bandit into a law abiding citizen. A holdup of the town bank is planned by the villain, in which the hero is made to participate. The villain receives the money from his henchmen and rushes to his ranch with it. The hero, with the captain of the Rangers, follows him and are forced to shoot him. The villain's sister is heartbroken when she learns the truth. The villain dies and the heroine is comforted by the hero."

Harrison's Reports, 10/1/32

MY PAL, THE KING

A Universal Picture. Released August 4, 1932. *Length:* 7 reels (74 minutes). Associate *Producer:* Stanley Bergerman. *Director:* Kurt Neumann. *Screenplay:* Jack Natteford and Tom J. Crizer. *Story:* Richard Schayer. *Photography:* Daniel B. Clark.

Left: Veteran character actor Paul Hurst is Tom's sidekick in *My Pal, The King*.

Above-opposite: A young Mickey Rooney played the boy-king in *My Pal, the King*. Here he introduces Tom to his older sister, the Princess Elsa (Noel Francis).

Below-opposite: To rescue the king from his evil ministers, Tom must storm a fortified castle by himself. At age fifty-two, Mix still performed many of his own stunts.

Below: In the film Tom brought his Wild West show to an imaginary European kingdom, giving Universal an opportunity to re-use the street set built for *All Quiet on the Western Front* in 1930.

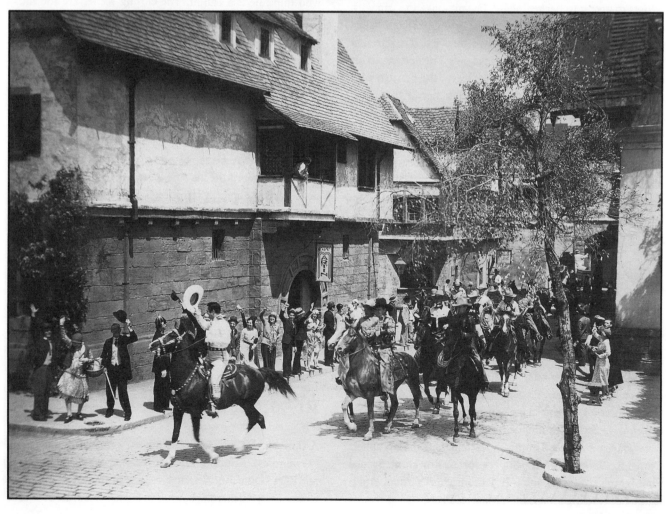

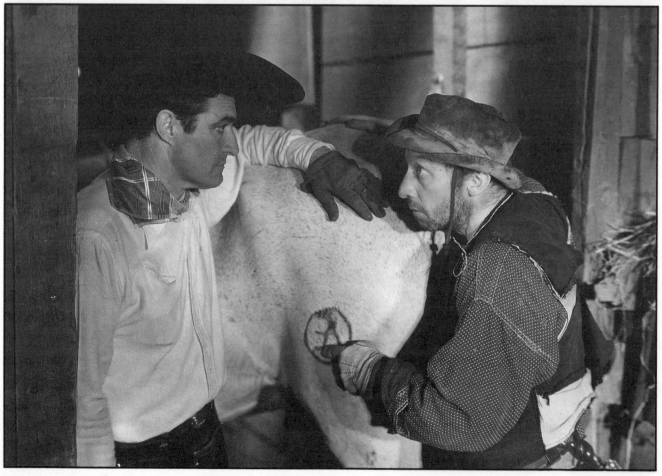

Right: Tom, with leading lady Margaret Lindsay is wearing the dark striped shirt he wore in most of the retake scenes in *The Fourth Horsemen*.

Above-opposite: Tom races to pay the back taxes on the heroine's town in *The Fourth Horseman*, which turned out to be one of the best of his Universal talkies.

Below-opposite: Raymond Hatton (right) receives screen credit as the character "Gabby" in *The Fourth Horseman*, and as this still indicates he worked with Mix in the film, but he is nowhere to be seem in the finished picture. *The Fourth Horseman* was beset by production problems and largely re-shot by director Arthur Rosson.

Below: Margaret Lindsay, Raymond Hatton, and Tom Mix in another scene cut from the final version of *The Fourth Horseman*. A stampede sequence in the finished film gives away the "major surgery" behind the scenes as Tom's shirt changes from dark to light from shot to shot.

Production Budget: $95,521.00. Production Schedule: 12 days. *Production Started* May 17, 1932. *Production Completed:* June 2, 1932. 14 days principal photography, 2 days over schedule. Final Negative Cost: $107,126.01.

Cast: Tom Mix (Tom Reed), Mickey Rooney (King Charles), James Kirkwood (Count De Mar), Wallis Clark (Professor Lorenz), Noel Francis (Princess Elsa), Finis Barton (Gretchen), Paul Hurst ("Red"), Stuart Holmes (Baron Kluckstein), James Thorpe (Black Cloud), Christian Frank (Etzel), Clarissa Selwynne (the dowager queen).

Working Title: KINGS UP

Still Code: 343-1

"Another sweet box office surprise from Universal, chock full of new and different entertainment elements that should mean busy times for the box office cashier. Richard Scahyer's story takes Tom Mix to the capital city of a mythical little European kingdom called Olvania. A happy idea, one that gives Mix the opportunity to retain all his western glamour and color, but transfers the settings to new and unusual places and makes possible a story and picture that not only promises a sensation with the youngsters, but more than that, has plenty of downright good entertainment for the grownups as well.

"The entire story centers around a boy king, little 10 or 11-year-old Mickey Rooney, who is going to be the envy of every boy in your town once they get a glimpse of him in 'My Pal, The King.' Like all small boys, even a king wants to see a wild west show when it comes to town. The manner in which the little king gives his counselors the slip, and unrecognized by the other urchins, manages to be picked up by Tom to ride in the parade, will stir the youngsters to wildest enthusiasm and give the adults many a laugh.

"The wild west show that is put on with the king and his aunt as special guests is a riot of thrills and excitement. Plenty of riding, roping, broncho busting, Indian fighting, the proverbial stage coach robbery. Then when the little kid and his party are treated to a ride in the stage coach, a run-away and a nerve tingling rescue by Tom follow.

"Villainy has its place as the false premier seizes the reins of government and puts the little king on the spot. Heroics with a punch as Tom and his cowboys and Indians rescue him. Then a touch of pathos as Tom and the circus move on to the next town and the little king is left wishing that he could change his kingdom for the career of a cowboy.

"There is but little romantic interest—no love making to dull the enthusiasm of the youngsters. Good, clean, wholesome entertainment without a vestige of anything that could stir objections from anyone. Primarily it is a kid's picture, but

if you can realize all the diverse entertainment that is contained in it, you certainly can whip up interest among the adults.

"Between the difference of its story construction, the personality and pull of Tom Mix at the box office, the added angle of the youthful appeal of Mickey Rooney (and that's a name that the kids will not easily forget), with the guarantee of entertainment, that has plenty of comedy, a little villainy and a lot of human interest, you have more than enough to lure the interest of all types of fans.

"Start on this one early. Do a little extra advertising. Don't be content to rest all your hopes on the name of Tom Mix, but play up the different atmosphere of the picture. . . . "
Motion Picture Herald, 7/9/32

THE FOURTH HORSEMAN

A Universal Picture. Released September 29, 1932. *Length:* 6 reels (63 minutes).

Director: Hamilton McFadden [and uncredited Art Rosson]. *Screenplay:* Jack Cunningham. *Story:* Nina Wilcox Putnam.

Production Budget: $92,400.00. Production Schedule: 10 days. *Production Started* June 20, 1932. *Production Completed:* July 1, 1932. 10 days principal photography. Final Production Cost: $85,034.29. Retakes Called and Budget Increased To: $108,000. Retakes: August 4-9, 1932; August 20, 1932; August 27, 1932; September 3, 1932; and September 10, 1932. 9 Days of retakes. Final Negative Cost: $107,078.21.

Cast: Tom Mix (Tom Martin), Margaret Lindsay (Molly O'Rourke), Raymond Hatton (Gabby), Fred Kohler (Softy Jones), Edmund Cobb (Slim), Buddy Roosevelt (Fancy), Richard Cramer (Thad), Harry Allen (Charlie), Herman Nowlin (Bill Thrasher), Paul Shawham (Billy the Kid), Duke Lee (Jim), Grace Cunard (Mrs. Elmer Brown), Frederic Howard (Elmer Brown), Helen Millard ("Baby Face"), Captain Anderson (Caleb Winters), Harry Allen (Charlie), Tony, Jr., also Walter Brennan, Martha Mattox.

Working Title: PONY BOY

Still Code: 344-1

"TOM MIX GOES OVER BIG WITH HIS ACTION STUFF IN FAST MOVING DRAMA THAT HAS THE STUFF.

"A typical Tom Mix opus that has all his old-time fire, with Tom in evidence most of the time and that means practically continuous action. An abandoned mining town is about to experience a boom, and Fred Kohler as head of the outlaw gang moves in with his henchmen and starts to take it over. He places all his men in the key spots, running the various games, gambling joints and dance halls. The girl in the case owns practically all the land in the town, but unknown to her it is about to be forfeited for taxes. So the heavy plans to keep her in ignorance and then pay the taxes and grab the property. It is in checkmating the gang leader in his scheme, and helping the incoming settlers fight the gang, that Tom Mix gets into plenty of fights, gun-play and fast riding. For the wind-up there is a fight in the town that involves all the settlers as they swoop down to clean out the gang. Tom takes care of the leader in a rough and tumble fight."

The Film Daily, 2/8/33

HIDDEN GOLD

A Universal Picture. Released November 3, 1932. *Length:* 6 reels (61 minutes).

Directors: Arthur Rosson [and uncredited Ray Taylor]. *Screenplay:* Jack Natteford and Jim Mulhauser. *Story:* Jack Natteford. *Photography:* Daniel B. Clark.

Production Budget: $87,000.00. Production Schedule: 12 days. *Production Started* August 15, 1932. *Production Completed:* September 1, 1932. 16 days principal photography, 4 days over schedule. Final Negative Cost: $89,660.39.

Cast: Tom Mix (Tom), Judith Barrie (Nora), Raymond Hatton (Spike), Eddie Gribbon (Big Ben), Donald Kirke (Doctor), Wallis Clark, Roy Moore.

Working Title: TOM'S IN TOWN

Still Code: 345-1

Note: Ray Taylor was the assigned director. He was replaced five days into production by Art Rosson due to illness.

"DIFFERENT WESTERN WITH GOOD PRISON ATMOSPHERE AND REALISTIC FOREST FIRE FOR CLIMAX.

"Most of the footage finds Tom Mix doing a big detective act trying to get the goods on a gang that has robbed a bank in a small western town. As the local fistic champ, the sheriff arranges to have him committed to prison where he can work himself into the confidences of the yeggs who robbed the bank. They consist of a prizefighter, his trainer and manager, who hid the gold before they were caught. As a pug himself, Tom in the cell gains their confidence. But they pull a surprise jail break, and force him to accompany them. The kick comes in the fact that the sheriff, the girl and all his pals in the

western town think Tom has betrayed them and thrown in his lot with the robbers. But he retrieves himself by capturing the gold cache after the gang uncovers it, with a strong climax in a very realistic forest fire scene in the midst of which the hero does his stuff with plenty of action, fights and thrill stuff."

The Film Daily, 3/22/33

TERROR TRAIL

A Universal Picture. Released February 2, 1933. *Length:* 6 reels (57 minutes).

Supervisor: Henry MacRae. *Director:* Armand Schaefer. *Screenplay:* Jack Cunningham. Based on "The Riders of Terror Trail by Grant Taylor. *Photography:* Dan Clark.

Cast: Tom Mix (Tom Munroe), Naomi Judge (Norma Laird), Arthur Rankin (Bernie Laird), John St. Polis (Ormsby), Frank Brownlee (Sheriff Judell), Raymond Hatton ("Lucky" Dawson), Francis McDonald (Tad McPherson), Robert Kortman (Tim McPherson), Lafe McKee (Shay), Henry Tenbrook (Deputy Sheriff), W. J. Holmes (Dr. Wilson), Hank Bell (Smith), Leonard Trainer (Jones), Jim Corey (Henry), Jay Wilsey (a prisoner), Tony, Jr. (a horse).

Still Code: 636

"Tom Mix comes to the talking screen once more, this time with Tony, Jr., able successor to the original Tony, in a western film cut to a pattern by no means new, with all the hard riding, the gun-popping, the majestic scenery, the villainy expected in a Mix western.

"It is necessary to say, however, that Mix was histrionically far more acceptable as a silent player than he is as an exponent of the art of the talking screen. When he is busily about his job of riding down desperadoes, dodging bullets and offering his own in return, or roping escaping thieves and flying through the mountain passes on the wing-footed Tony, he is the old Tom, very nearly as spry, that we all knew and thrilled to once on a time. But when he attempts to instill fear, confidence or command by the sound and manner of his voice, he is not quite convincing.

"However, where there is a market for the western, Mr. Mix and his activity should be found entertaining by the oldsters who still cotton to the fictional romance of the once rough West. And, without question, the lads of the community will rise in their chairs and cheer the rescuing riders, then go home and dream of cowboys, horses like Tony, and the next western picture.

" . . . It would be well, perhaps, not to indicate in any way that this is more than a western of ordinary type, featuring

Above: "Tom was such a gentleman," remembers Ruth Hall, his leading lady in the light-hearted *Flaming Guns*.

Above-opposite: Tom plays an undercover cop who poses as a boxer in *Hidden Gold*.

Below-opposite: Roping a bad guy in *Terror Trail*, the best of Tom's second Universal series.

Right: Tom gets the drop on Ernie Adams (center) and Bud Osborne in *Rustlers Roundup*, his last Universal picture.

Below: Douglas Dumbrille was the heavy in *Rustlers Roundup*, and the leading lady was Diane Sinclair, a mulatto who passed for white in a number of Hollywood films.

Tom poses with two Tonys. Tony (left) was retired before Tom made his first sound film. Just as Tony had many doubles, so did Tony, Jr. Note the horses Tom is riding in the photos from *My Pal, The King,* at the top of page 255 and *Terror Trail* at the bottom of page 260. Although these animals have similar markings, neither is Tony, Jr. The white blaise on the first does not extend to the lip, and the fore-stockings on the second do not go up to the knee.

the gang of horse thieves who are rounded up by Mix, thereby saving the boy who is entangled with them, winning the boy's sister, revealing the head of the local vigilante committee as the ringleader, all in expected fashion . . . ."

Aaronson, *New York Motion Picture Herald*, 2/18/33

FLAMING GUNS

A Universal Picture. Released June, 1933. *Length:* 6 reels (57 minutes).

Director: Arthur Rosson. *Scenario:* Jack Cunningham, from a story by Peter B. Kyne. *Film Editor:* Phil Cahn. *Photography:* Jerry Ash.

Cast: Tom Mix (Tom Malone), William Farnum (Ramsey), Ruth Hall (Mary Ramsey), Clarence H. Wilson (Mulford), George Hackathorne (Hugh), Duke Lee (Red McIntyre), Pee Wee Holmes (Pee Wee), Fred Burns (Sheriff), Jimmy Shannon, William Steele, Walter Patterson, Bud Osborne, Robert "Clyde Kinney" Ruffner.

Working Title: OH, PROMISE ME

Still Code: 635-1

"VERY GOOD WESTERN WITH PLENTY OF GOOD COMEDY PREDOMINATING IN THE STORY.

"Taken from the Peter B. Kyne story, 'Oh, Promise Me,' this one is way ahead of most westerns. A good story, well acted and directed with swell comedy touches all through it . Tom Mix plays the part of an ex- service man who comes back to the west and goes to work for his old employer. A friend of his old employer subsequently hires him and then fires him for being too friendly with the pretty daughter. Tom, however, gets a letter authorizing him to take over the ranch, so he goes ahead regardless of his sack. The old foreman has been robbing the place, so Tom gets rid of him. In the meantime the girl has fallen for Tom and goes to the ranch. The irate papa learns who is running the place, follows her and has Tom arrested for trespassing. The girl and the old employer

make the father turn a half interest in the ranch over to Tom to save his ears from being 'split' and Tom and the girl elope to Mexico despite being chased by the father. Good fun for everyone."

The Film Daily, 6/17/33

RUSTLERS ROUNDUP

A Universal Picture. Released September, 1933. *Length:* 6 reels (56 minutes).

Director: Henry MacRae. *Screenplay:* Frank Howard Clark. *Story:* Ella O'Neill. *Film Editors:* Albert Akst and Russell Schoenbarth. *Photography:* Daniel B. Clark.

Cast: Tom Mix (Tom Lawson), Diane Sinclair (Mary Brand), Noah Beery, Jr. (Danny Brand), Douglas Dumbrille (Bill Brett), Roy Stewart (Dave Winters), Nelson McDowell (Sheriff Brass), William Desmond (Sheriff Holden), Frank Lackteen (Bayhorse), Pee Wee Holmes (Husky), Bud Osborne (Sodden), William Wagner (Homer Jones).

Still Code: 637

"Typical Tom Mix meller has all the stuff the fans love in a routine western. This one follows the tried and true formula without any signs of originality in story, but it has been handled with a snap and punch, crowded with exciting incident, and of course with Tom Mix in evidence practically all the time, it is in the bag for thrill fans. Tom does the bandit act in order to save the girl's property, which the villainous foreman of her ranch is trying to take away from her. Later he comes to a showdown with the foreman, whose gang has been rustling the girl's cattle in order to force her to relinquish the ranch. There is also some exciting stuff with a rodeo, in which Mr. Mix does his well known equestrian stunts, taking all the honors from his rival who is also the villain. Works up to a slap- bag climax with plenty of meller action and all kinds of fighting and gun play."

The Film Daily, 9/16/33

THE MIRACLE RIDER

"The Tom Mix Ralston Straight Shooters are on the air . . . " On September 25, 1933 the Tom Mix radio show, sponsored by Ralston cereal, began what would become a 17 year run. By the late '30s the double handful of Mix talkies were generally out of distribution, and many latter-day fans only know the cowboy from his radio adventures. Yet, aside from lending his name and posing for occasional publicity pictures, Mix had nothing to do with the series. The program simply served to keep the Mix name before the public as he returned to the circus arena.[1]

Also in 1933, Mix announced a partnership with author Zane Grey for the production of Westerns. Scheduled to roll in November, the deal never got off the ground, and no explanations were ever offered.

After appearing with an act called the Tom Mix Roundup, he joined with circus showman Sam Dill for the 1934 season in the Tom Mix Wild West and Sam B. Dill Circus (Combined). The show was successful and Tom was set to go for the 1935 season when Sam Dill died suddenly of a heart attack. Tom loved circus life, and rather than give up the show, he bought it from Dill's estate.

"Tom Mix was the sole owner of the circus," recalled "Gypsy" Joe Bowers, a stage hand and clown who worked with Mix from his days with Sells-Floto to the end of the cowboy star's life. "There were no promoters or investors, although it would have been better for Tom to incorporate. When Tom took over he refitted the show. We had over 60 rolling pieces with more than 25 trailers for living quarters. It was, without doubt, the finest truck circus in the world."

Opposite page: Tom, in costume for *The Miracle Rider*, poses with a prototype of the Tom Mix watch.

Taking over a circus required no small investment, so Tom accepted an offer from producer Nat Levine of Mascot Pictures to make another movie comeback. The vehicle was an outlandish 15 episode serial called *The Miracle Rider.*

Serials were anything but prestige attractions in 1935—strictly kiddie and grind-house fare—but there were some compensations. The chapter play provided 15 weeks of continuous theatrical publicity and exposure, and with a late May release Tom's weekly screen adventures appeared throughout the height of the circus season. Even more to the point, however, was that Nat Levine was willing to pay Tom $10,000 a week for four week's work, and Tom needed the money for his tent show.

Although he turned out an occasional feature, Levine specialized in making serials. His two 1935 chapter plays, *The Phantom Empire* and *The Miracle Rider* represented a beginning for one extraordinary film career and a swan song for another. *The Phantom Empire* was the first starring vehicle for singing cowboy sensation Gene Autry, and *The Miracle Rider* proved to be the final screen role for Tom Mix.

The Mix serial presented special problems for Levine, who was accustomed to producing entire serials for under $200,000. Levine could not significantly cut production costs and still come up with an acceptable product, and he had little or no control over the rental fees a serial could generate in the market place.

His solution was ingenious. He increased the number of episodes from the usual 12 to 15, and padded the first chapter from three reels to five. This allowed for the first episode to be sold as a feature, with a traditionally higher rental fee, and also provided three weeks of additional of revenue.

The Miracle Rider proved to be one of Levine's better serials. Perhaps because of the additional length, more attention was paid to the plotting, and while it wasn't Shakespeare, the chapter play offered more to hold one's attention than was common for serials. There are two villains instead of one. Zaroff, played by Charles Middleton, is a standard serial bad guy, with an army of henchmen and nothing but evil on his mind. Zaroff's goal is to drive a tribe of Indians from their reservation so that he can mine a rare elemental explosive called X-94. The other evil- doer is Janss, played by Edward Hearn. Janss owns a tract of land he wants to unload on the government as a reservation site. At first Texas Ranger Tom Morgan (Mix) suspects Janss of trying to frighten the Indians from their land, and while this is not true, the land speculator finally comes to see that his interests and Zaroff's coincide and he allows himself to be drawn into Zaroff's plot

As with other Levine efforts of the period, there is a science fiction element. Zaroff has a radio controlled drone airplane called the Firebird, designed to play off the Indians superstitions. However, this aspect of the plot is dispensed with a third of the way into the serial when the Firebird crashes, and it is not allowed to become a tiresome intrusion throughout the fifteen chapters.

Direction on *The Miracle Rider* was assigned to Armand Scaeffer, who directed *Terror Trail* with Mix at Universal, and B. Reeves Eason, brother of Tom's secretary Teddy Eason. Known to his friends as "Breezy," Reeves Eason was considered a barely competent director of actors, but a brilliant second unit action director with the chariot race in *Ben-Hur* (1926) and *The Charge of the Light Brigade* (1937) among his best-known credits.

By now, Mix was comfortable with the microphone, and he delivered a solid performance, but at age 55 he looked wan and tired. It was evident that his jet-black hair came from a dye bottle, and for the first time it was obvious that he was being doubled in many of the action scenes.

Tom's double through most of *The Miracle Rider* was Cliff Lyons. He was a capable stunt performer, but he had the annoying habit of stuffing his hat down over his ears. This kept the hat on during a tussle, but it was always apparent that he was not the hero. Lyons later became a successful second unit director, and performed much better behind the camera than in front of it.

While Mix was still capable of doing his own stunts, the schedule and budget did not permit the star to do so, and much of Tom's screen appeal was lost. No longer was he the real thing in cowboys, he was just another Western star who fronted for the iodine squad, as Hollywood's stunt men were affectionately called.

None of this mattered at the time, however. Kids were thrilled by *The Miracle Rider,* and it proved to be a major hit. But it was Tom Mix's last.

NOTES

1. For accounts of the Tom Mix radio show and descriptions of the numerous Tom Mix radio premiums see: Norris, Merle G. "Bud," *The Tom Mix Book,* 1989, Waynesville, North Carolina, The World of Yesterday. and: Seiverling, Richard F., *Tom Mix - Portrait of a Superstar,* 1991, Hershey, Pennsylvania, Keystone Enterprises.

Left: Ranger Tom Morgan (Mix) fights with Longboat (Robert Kortman), in chapter eleven of *The Miracle Rider*.

Below: Yet another confrontation between Mix and Kortman.

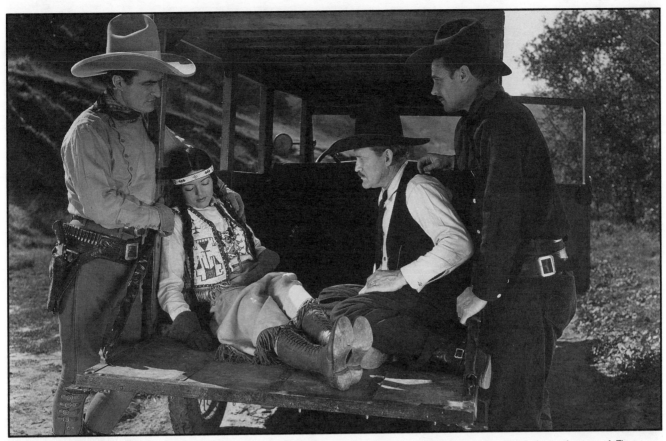

Above: Joan Gale is unconscious as Tom, Jack Rockwell, and Wally Wales (standing right) are caught "Between Two Fires" chapter fourteen of *The Miracle Rider*. Wales worked with Mix in the Teens under his real name, Floyd Alderson. He later became a screen villain under the name Hal Taliaferro (pronounced Tolifer).

THE MIRACLE RIDER

Mascot Pictures Corporation. A Mascot Master Serial. Released May 18, 1935. *Length:* 33 reels (309 Minutes).

Producer: Nat Levine. Supervisor: Victor Zobel. Directors: Armand Schaefer and B. Reeves Eason. Original *Story:* Barney Sarecky, Wellyn Totman, and Gerald Geraghty. *Screenplay:* John Rathmell. *Photography:* Ernest Miller and William Nobles. Supervising *Film Editor:* Joseph H. Lewis. *Film Editor:* Dick Fantl. Recording Engineer: Terry Kellum.

Cast: Tom Mix (Tom Morgan), Joan Gale (Ruth), Charles Middleton (Zaroff), Bob Fraser (Black Wing), Niles Welch (Metzger), Jason Robards, Sr. (Carlton), Bob Kortman (Longboat), Edward Earle (Adams), Edward Hearn (Janss), Tom London (Sewell), Edmund Cobb (Vining), Ernie Adams (Stelter), Max Wagner (Morley), Charles King (Hatton), George Chesebro (Crossman), Jack Rockwell (Rogers), Stanley Price (Chapman), George Burton (Mort).

Note: The name of Niles Welch was mis-spelled in the on-screen credits as Niles "Welsh." The five-reel first episode contains an "historical" prologue which uses scenes from previous Mascot serials, including *The Last of the Mohicans* (1932), and *Fighting With Kit Carson* (1933).

Chapter *Titles:*

1. The Vanishing Indian	9. The Silver Band
2. The Firebird Strikes	10. Signal Fires
3. The Flying Knife	11. A Traitor Dies
4. A Race With Death	12. Danger Rides With Death
5. Double Barreled Doom	13. The Secret of X-94
6. Thundering Hoofs	14. Between Two Fires
7. The Dragnet	15. Justice Rides The Plains
8. Guerrilla Warfare	

"Mix makes a big comeback as a Texas Ranger who seeks to prevent the crooked gang from chasing the folks out of a territory because of a secret explosive. First episode is filled with action and the whole thing looks like whirlwind stuff. Tom and Tony, Jr., come back strong and there is the Indian, western background to help. [Producer Nat] Levine has scored again. EXCELLENT."

The Philadelphia Exhibitor, 6/15/35

THE LAST TRAIL

The Tom Mix Circus was a source of satisfaction and frustration for Tom. He loved performing in front of a live audience, and he enjoyed sitting on the grounds between shows holding court for friends and adoring fans. The show was a great success—if success was measured by the number of playdates and the size of the crowds, but the circus was a cash-eating machine, and when there was a breakdown or a rain-out the costs kept multiplying and the money to bail out the show came from Tom's pocket.

The combined Mix-Dill Circus played 222 stands in 16 states during the 1934 season. Although it played 13 engagements in California, the show was largely a midwestern regional attraction. In 1935, when Mix took full control of the show he moved the winter quarters from Texas Fairgrounds in Dallas to Compton, California and refitted the show. He added three states to the tour, with 56 playdates in California, 11 in Oregon and 22 in Washington, but it was still largely a regional show. The balance of the season roughly followed the mid-west route established by Sam Dill in earlier years.

Business was good enough for Tom to expand the tour to 25 states for the 1936 season, and nearly as many for 1937 along with an appearance at the Canadian National Exposition in Toronto.

Things looked promising for the 1938 season, but it proved to be one long disaster. The economic depression that had gripped the country since the early '30s showed slow but steady improvement in the five years after Franklin Roosevelt's 1932 election, but the recovery hit the skids in 1937-38 and all circus

Opposite page: Tom Mix with Warrior (sometimes called Tony II) his show horse from 1935 to the end of his life.

"The Tom Mix Circus was the largest and finest truck show ever mounted," according to Gypsy Joe Bowers, who worked with Mix from 1931 through his final European tour. The show held its own for three seasons but sank in a sea of red ink during the disastrous 1938 season.

attractions took an unanticipated hit. Poor spring weather added to the woes of the Mix Circus. Even when Tom slashed ticket prices from 50 cents to 20 cents, audiences refused to brave the rain and cold just to see the show. Summer brought no improvement. Winds took down the big tent on July 10th in Neenah, Wisconsin, as 1,000 people watched the show. On several occasions, The Tom Mix Circus was forced to sneak out of town late in the night to avoid creditors. Through all of this Tom tried to keep his family of cowboys and friends together, but even here he found disappointment.

With the show's precarious finances, Tom's old associate Pat Chrisman took one of Tom's pistols and sold it to a fan for $100. Tom was devastated. He had risked everything he had to keep his people working, and this was how they repaid him. "Gypsy" Joe Bowers remembered Tom calling Chrisman into his private bus. With a lump in his throat Mix told his old friend, "If you'd only asked me I would have given you anything, Pat, you know that—but after all these years together you sneak in and just take it. You better pack your things and clear out."

By late summer it became obvious that the Tom Mix Circus needed a cash

237

MOTHERS!

here's a hot cereal children are *glad* to eat!

TEACHER TELLS ME YOU TWO WON MEDALS FOR ATTENDANCE AND GOOD WORK. I'M PROUD OF YOU.

RALSTON HELPED US, TOM.

SURE! WE'RE TRYING TO BE LIKE YOU. WE EAT RALSTON. IT MAKES US FEEL SO GOOD WE REALLY LIKE SCHOOL.

To get good marks in school—to win at games—your child needs boundless energy — abundant nourishment. Ralston provides both—in a delicious golden cereal which children and grown-ups, too, enjoy.

And it's "double-rich" in vitamin B, the element so essential to normal appetite

How LUCKY for you that children love Ralston Wheat Cereal— are eager for heaping bowls at breakfast time! For Ralston is so much *more* than just a delicious cereal with the natural color, the richer flavor and abundant food value of finest whole wheat! NOW Ralston also has the same effect as clear western air upon appetites and energy.

New Process Makes Ralston "Double-Rich" in Vitamin B

Within the last few years, scientists have discovered the tremendous influence of vitamin B upon the health of growing children. This factor, they say, is essential to normal development because, like western air, it helps them to have eager appetites.

Yet eminent authorities on child feeding declare that children's diets should be especially planned to include generous quantities of vitamin B, for this factor cannot be stored in the body and is found in very few of our modern, highly refined foods.

It remained for the Ralston Laboratories to end all doubt and uncertainty—to provide an easy, economical way to supply this vitamin. In these laboratories, a process has been perfected which makes it possible to *double* the normal quantity of vitamin B in Ralston Wheat Cereal.

Boys and Girls! Mothers and Fathers, too! Sure as my name's Tom Mix, I never saw anything takin' this country by storm like Ralston!

"Double-Rich" Ralston Does More for Your Child Than Ordinary Cereals

Think how much this can mean to the welfare of your child and children everywhere! Now—in one tempting food that children eat *gladly* you can provide all the value of whole wheat (only coarse bran is removed); MINERALS (phosphorous and iron); PROTEINS for firm flesh and rosy cheeks; CARBOHYDRATES for body heat and energy — and

twice the normal quantity of vitamin B—to keep them hungry for three full meals a day—so they'll gladly eat milk and vegetables, and other wholesome foods that growing bodies must have! Remember, too, that as a HOT cereal, Ralston is more satisfying—a richer source of quick energy!

Less Than One Cent a Dish!

For all its "double-richness," Ralston costs no more than ordinary cereals. And it takes only five minutes to prepare. Tell your grocer you want "double-rich" Ralston Wheat Cereal in the red and white checkerboard packages. It's a treat for the children and a wonderful way to give them the extra helps so many boys and girls need.

FREE SAMPLE: We will gladly send you a free sample of Ralston Wheat Cereal—enough to serve the whole family. Just write to Ralston Purina Company 57 Checkerboard Square Saint Louis, Missouri.

New Cereal for Babies!

BABY RALSTON—recommended by doctors as the ideal starting cereal — is specially prepared for baby's delicate digestion. Rich in vitamin B, palatable, quickly cooked—economical. Sample on request.

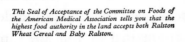

DOUBLE-RICH IN VITAMIN "B"

Ralston WHEAT CEREAL Whole Wheat

This Seal of Acceptance of the Committee on Foods of the American Medical Association tells you that the highest food authority in the land accepts both Ralston Wheat Cereal and Baby Ralston.

In using advertisements see page 6

Ralston cereal sponsored the *Tom Mix Ralston Straight Shooters* radio show and used the cowboy star as a spokesman in print ads. Tom never appeared on the show, other actors impersonated him in fictional adventures, but the program kept the Mix name alive with young fans while Tom was touring with his circus. The radio show also outlived Mix, remaining on the air until 1950.

Tom's touring bus was originally built for the president of General Motors and re-fitted by Mix to be his home on the road when he toured with the circus.

transfusion if it was to survive. Without telling anyone in the show, Mix signed a contract for a British vaudeville tour. Ruth Mix took over the management, but she could not hold the show together. The Tom Mix Circus played its final stand on September 10, 1938 in Pecos, Texas. The equipment and animals were divided among the troupe and creditors to settle outstanding obligations.

"We sneaked away from a small town outside of Kansas City and left for Southampton, England," said "Gypsy" Joe Bowers. "We opened about a week later at the Palladium Theatre in London. We toured the George Black theatres, and Tom sure was a big sensation. You've never seen such crowds. He had a beautiful almost white horse, seventeen and a half hands high, named Warrior. We billed the horse as Tony II for box-office purposes. In 1939 we went to Denmark and joined the Madam Belli one-ring circus."

Tom performed an array of roping and shooting tricks for his act, enhanced with numerous costume changes. One part of the act that remains vividly in the minds of those who saw Tom Mix in person was a stunt in which he set a meat cleaver and shot at the blade with such deadly accuracy that he split the bullet and hit two targets. Reviewers and fans all commented with awe at the sight, but none seemed to realize that trick marksmen routinely use bird shot in their shells to insure that their bullets hit the mark.

The success of Tom's European tour was tempered by the course of human events. He received several offers to return to Germany, including a personal call from Chancellor Adolph Hitler. He refused to lend any support to the Nazi regime, and in response to Hitler's invitation Tom told the interpreter, "I'll tour

Germany again to see my fans, but only over his dead body!" When war broke out in September, 1939, Mix and his small troupe, including Joe Bowers, Bud and Rosa Carlell, and Jack Knapp, returned to America.

Tom took to the road again with a "one horse" show playing arenas and theatres throughout the country, but the days of glory and big money were past. Thomasina Mix remembers seeing her father at his Compton, California ranch doing his best to keep up appearances. "He was used to having everything monogrammed," she looks back, "and when he could no longer afford to have the work done, he sat huddled over his work with his own monogramming machine wearing his newly acquired reading glasses. He put his initials on everything from his shirts to his underwear."

Despite his fondness for flashy appearances, however, Tom was not always consistent. "He had all sorts of fancy stationery made over the years," continues Thomasina, "but he almost never used it. He wrote most of his letters and notes on yellow legal size paper with a pencil."

Despite his age, Tom was still physically fit. In a local rodeo appearance on April 28, 1940 he challenged Buck Jones to an exhibition chariot race, and came out the winner. He gave some thought to returning to pictures in any capacity, and he visited George O'Brien at RKO to see if there might be anything for him. Tom had given O'Brien one of his first movie jobs back in 1920, and the younger star would have done what he could but his own contract with RKO was about to be canceled.

At 20th Century-Fox he visited with his old production manager "Lefty" Hough and director John Ford. The director could not see the former star lowering himself to take bit parts—a more or less polite way of saying there was no place in the Hollywood of 1940 for the star who built the studio.

On April 28, 1940, Tom Mix challenged Buck Jones to an exhibition chariot race at a rodeo near Los Angeles. As they round the turn, Buck is in the lead but Tom ultimately won the race.

While on the road in McNary, Texas, Tom chats with Deputy Sheriff Delaney when he stopped to gas up his 1937 Cord en route to Arizona in October, 1940.

There was talk with a friend from Argentina about a co-venture in horse training and the possibility of a new circus; but like his pal Sid Jordan, Tom never got to South America.

In the fall of 1940 Tom was on the road again, driving through the southwest and visiting with old friends. On October 10, Tom was in Tuscon, Arizona, at the Santa Rita Hotel. Western writer Walt Coburn was among those present.

"We met in the Santa Rita bar," wrote Coburn, "with Tom, Sheriff Ed Echols of Pima County, hotel manager Nick Hall, and a lot of our cattlemen and working cowhands. It was quite a gatherment and celebration, with Mix holding forth in his usual manner, swapping tall tales concerning Zack Miller's 101 Wild West Show and rodeo cowboys like his son-in-law Harry Knight and others too numerous to mention.

"During my career as a working cowhand in Montana and Arizona I had never entered professional rodeo contests," continued Coburn, "but I have personally known most of the world champion bronc riders, ropers and bulldoggers during the Tom Mix era, and Mix knew them all. So we had many friends in common among the old-time rodeo contestants and movie stars such as Hoot Gibson, Neal Hart, Bill Hart, Yakima Canutt, Buck Jones and all the rest, including the one and only Will Rogers and the great athlete Jim Thorpe. Thus was the talk that passed between us of cowboys, horses, rodeos, wild west shows, outlaws, the big cattle ranges of the old west that no longer exist."

Tom again joined Echols and Coburn at the writer's home the following evening, before returning to the Santa Rita Hotel. On Saturday morning, October 12, 1940, Tom Mix came down to the lobby and ran into Tuscon police officer Richard Lease. The two men talked for a little more than a half hour, and then Tom got into his yellow Cord roadster, and officer Lease went out to halt traffic as Tom got underway.

A half hour later, Dick Lease was on his motorcycle patrolling the north edge of Tuscon and he saw a 1937 Ford racing at nearly 80 miles an hour toward the city. Lease prepared to give chase, but he later recalled, "As soon as he saw me he headed right for me and nearly 'turtled' his little car to a stop then frantically told me: 'I've been looking for an officer. There's been an accident back there and it looks bad. It's a guy in a yellow Cord.

"I knew it was Tom Mix. No one else I had ever known had a yellow Cord."

Racing to the scene on the road to Florence, Arizona, Officer Lease found Tom's car overturned, the cowboy star dead in the wreckage.

Driving fast, as he always did, Tom Mix had come upon a work crew repairing the road. He cheated death so many times in performing his movie stunts, but this day his luck ran out. Swerving to avoid a collision he lost control of his car. As it overturned, a metal suitcase flew forward, clipped him, and snapped his neck. Tom was killed instantly. When his body was recovered there was not a mark on it, and his 1932 statement to Relman Morin came to mind: "Death isn't an accident. It's figured out in advance, and calculated for the good of everybody concerned."

Only in death did Tom's long-ago military desertion come to light. The hero of every boy in America was denied a flag for his coffin. Director John Ford intervened with the War Department, and Tom was buried with military honors.

Among the honorary pallbearers were his former studio bosses William Fox and Carl Laemmle; Jack Warner, Cecil B. DeMille, Hal Roach, Samuel Goldwyn and Louis B. Mayer. Western stars William S. Hart, George O'Brien, Gene Autry, Buck Jones, Harry Carey, Gary Cooper, and Hoot Gibson were also honorary pallbearers, as were Charlie Chaplin, Clark Gable, Mickey Rooney, and Sheriff Ed Echols.

Mourners file past Tom's coffin to pay final tribute at Forest Lawn Memorial Park, Glendale, California.

Tom's casket was carried by Los Angeles County Sheriff Eugene Biscailuz, actor Monte Blue, John Ford, Tom's attorney Ivon Parker, Colonel Monte Stone, Tom's old friend Herman Nowlin, director B. Reeves Eason, and cameraman Dan Clark. Services were held at the Little Church of the Flowers at Forest Lawn in Glendale, California on October 16, 1940, and he was laid to rest atop a hill in the Whispering Pines section of the cemetery.

What money there was in Tom's estate was willed to his wife Mabel and his daughter Thomasina. His saddles, guns, costumes, and other memorabilia were left to his attorney Ivon Parker. The citizens of Dewey, Oklahoma purchased the collection and opened the Tom Mix Museum in 1968. Today the museum is operated by the Oklahoma State Historical Society.

Although 20th Century-Fox had no use for Tom in 1940, after his death a sound stage was dedicated in his honor at the West Los Angeles studio. Sol Wurtzel presided over the unveiling of a bronze plaque to mark the occasion. Today, the plaque has disappeared, but a plaster cast of it is said to exist in a Hollywood prop house.

In December, 1947, the Florence, Arizona Chamber of Commerce dedicated a marker on the spot where Tom was killed. Gene Autry and Ed Echols dedicated the stone monument with an iron cut-out of a riderless horse and a

Western star Gene Autry and Pima County, Arizona Sheriff Ed Echols dedicate the Tom Mix memorial near Florence, Arizona, marking the site where Tom Mix lost his life. Echols competed in the 1912 Calgary Stampede promoted by Mix and Guy Weadick and was a life-long friend of Tom's.

bronze plaque, which reads: "In memory of Tom Mix whose spirit left his body on this spot and whose characterization and portrayals in life served to better fix memories of the Old West in the minds of living men." Several times over the years the iron horse has been removed by vandals, but the marker remains.

Tom once described his screen character as "a clean-minded an' right livin' cow puncher, always tryin' to do the right thing because it was the right thing to do. I decided to create a clean character. I tried to convey to the boys and girls a message of helpfulness. I tried to show them that it was the physically fit man who usually won out. . ."

Tom Mix spent his life creating that image, and if he did not always live up to his professed ideals off screen, he believed in them none the less. He was certainly no worse than the best of us.

Sometime, in a moment of reflection, Tom took a piece of his engraved stationery and sat down with pen in hand to write:

> *When the battle breaks against you*
> *And the crowd forgets to cheer*
> *When the anvil chorus echoes*
> *With the essence of a jeer*
> *When the knockers start their panning*
> *In the knockers' nimble way*
> *With a rap for all your errors*
> *And a josh upon your play*
> *There's a quick and ready answer*
> *That will nail them on the wing;*
> *There is one reply forthcoming*
> *That will wipe away the sting*
> *There is one elastic come back*
> *That will hold them as it should—*
> *Make Good.*

It has been nearly 60 years since Tom Mix made his last movie, more than 50 years since his death, so few today have seen "America's Champion Cowboy" on screen—yet the name Tom Mix still conjures up the image of a Cowboy star in fancy Western clothes and a real ten-gallon hat—not the puny six ounce variety favored by so many later screen cowboys.

Tom Mix remains a part of the American consciousness, and—though he may not have appreciated it in his own lifetime—he made good.

May you brand your biggest calf crop
May your range grass never fail,
May your water holes stay open,
May you ride an easy trail.

May you never reach for leather,
Nor your saddle horse go lame,
May you dab your loop on critters,
With your old unerring aim.

May your stack of chips grow taller,
May your shootin' e'er stay true,
May good luck plumb snow you under
Is always my wish for you.

Tom D. Mix

APPENDIX
DISPUTED CREDITS

In preparing this book, I used the following primary and secondary sources:

Scripts, synopses, continuities, release bulletins, and British release bulletins in the Selig Collection at the Academy of Motion Picture Arts and Sciences, and copyright deposit files at the Library of Congress.

Trade magazines, including: *The Nickelodeon, The Moving Picture World, Motion Picture News, Motography, The Film Daily, Variety, Motion Picture Herald, Harrison's Reports,* and *The Philadelphia Exhibitor.*

I also consulted several previously published listings of Tom Mix's film work:

Tom Mix Riding Up To Glory by John H. Nicholas, A Persimmon Hill Book, 1980.

The Tom Mix Book by M. G. "Bud" Norris, World of Yesterday, 1989.

Tom Mix, Portrait of a Superstar by Dr. Richard F. Seiverling, Keystone Enterprises, 1991.

The Life and Legend of Tom Mix, by Paul E. Mix, A. S. Barnes, 1972.

Of these four, Paul Mix's filmography was fragmentary and incomplete, and from the similarity of the listings it appears that both Richard Seiverling and Bud Norris based their listings on the basic index prepared by John Nicholas. Bud Norris, with help from Austrian Tom Mix fan Peter Schauer, added cast, author, copyright, and release information when it was available to him. Whether John Nicholas did original research or relied on earlier work by other investigators is unclear.

All four missed a number of Mix titles in compiling their filmographies. For example, none of the four lists *The Diamomd S Ranch,* a film which received a full page write-up in the February 10, 1912 issue of *The Moving Picture World.* While the four were conscientious in their efforts to compile a complete listing of the Mix pictures, they lacked access to basic research materials.

Just as they missed some titles, they also attributed films to Tom Mix which cannot be substantiated. Most of these disputed titles first appeared in the Nicholas filmography, and later researchers took Nicholas on faith, without questioning a number of dubious entries.

I could find no evidence that any of the following titles, appearing in previous Mix film listings, are in fact Tom Mix films. In offering this list of disputed titles, I have attempted to explain why I believe these films should not be credited to the cowboy star. If any readers are able to offer compelling evidence to the contrary, I would be pleased to hear from them.

———

The following are not real titles. No record has been found that any original films with these titles were ever made or released. However, it was common practice for later distributors to change the titles on reissue subjects, and it is possible that some of these are theatrical or home movie reissue titles.

IN THE DAYS OF DARING
(aka DAYS OF DARING)

Paul Mix lists this without a release date, while Bud Norris lists it as a 1909 Selig film, but I have found no record of any such title being released by any studio at any time during the years 1908 to 1920. It may be a reissue or home movie title.

PRIDE OF THE RANGE (1910)

No such title was released by any company in the years 1908-1920.

TAMING WILD ANIMALS (1910)

No such title was released by any company in the years 1908-1920.

RESCUED BY HER LIONS (1911)

No such title was released by any company in the years 1908-1920.

OUTLAW REWARD (1912)

No such title was released by any company in the years 1908-1920.

BUFFALO HUNTING (1914)

No such title was released by any company in the years 1908-1920. Possibly a home movie title for an abridged version of IN THE DAYS OF THE THUNDERING HERD. A film titled THE BUFFALO HUNT was released by 101 Bison in 1912.

———

The following are titles that have been mistakenly listed as Mix-Selig pictures. They are actually films produced by other compnaies.

THE PONY EXPRESS (1910)

The only films from this period with this title were released by Edison (1909) and Nestor (1911).

LOCAL COLOR (1913)

Norris lists the 1913 LOCAL COLOR as a "first version" of the Mix film of this title, but the 1913 film was a Kinemacolor production, and therefore not a Mix film.

LOCAL COLOR (1914)

Norris lists this as a "second version," but the 1914 film is a Vitagraph production, and therefore not a Mix film. Neither of these earlier films should be be confused with LOCAL COLOR ON THE A-1 RANCH (aka LOCAL COLOR), produced by Mix for Selig in 1916.

MAKING AN IMPRESSION (1916)

Paul E. Mix lists this without a release date, but the only film of this title was a Vitagraph production produced in 1916, and therefore not a Mix film.

THE SHERIFF'S GIRL (1914)

There is no record of a 1914 release with this title. There was a 1909 Centaur production of this name, but it was not a Mix film.

WESTERN JUSTICE (1915)

This may have been used as a reissue or home movie title for a Mix picture, but the only original films released with this title were made by Lubin (1910), Bison (1910), and Yankee (1910).

THE LONG TRAIL (1916)

Norris lists this, but the 1916 film of this title is a Paramount picture, and therefore not a Mix film.

WAY OF THE RED MAN (1916)

Norris lists a "second version" of this title produced in 1916, but no such film was produced or released. Not to be confused with the 1914 film of this title.

YOUR GIRL AND MINE (1914)

Nicholas and Norris list this, but it is a World Films production and therefore not a Tom Mix film.

———

The following films are not original productions, but are reissue titles of earlier Tom Mix films.

SINGLE SHOT PARKER

Norris lists this as a 1914 film, but it is the reissue title of the 1917 Mix feature THE HEART OF TEXAS RYAN.

THE STAGE COACH DRIVER

This is an Aywon Film Corporation reissue title, and may have been used for reissues of THE STAGE COACH DRIVER AND THE GIRL (1915) or THE STAGE COACH GUARD (also 1915).

MR. HAYWOOD PRODUCER (1915)

This is the reissue title of BILL HAYWOOD, PRODUCER.

THE WAGON TRAIL (1916)

There was no such 1916 title released by any company. This is the 1920's Aywon reissue title for IN THE DAYS OF THE THUNDERING HERD (1914).

The following are Selig West Coast productions, made before Tom Mix came to California and before he entered films.

**ON THE LITTLE BIG HORN,
or CUSTER'S LAST STAND (1909)**

UP SAN JUAN HILL (1909)

————

The following films were produced before Tom Mix entered pictures in 1910.

BRITON AND BOER (1909)

WHEELS OF JUSTICE (1909)

THE COWBOY MILLIONAIRE (1909)

AN INDIAN WIFE'S DEVOTION (1909)

————

The following are Selig West Coast productions, made before Tom Mix came to California in 1914.

THE SCHOOLMASTER OF MARIPOSA (1910)

THE COWBOY AND THE SHREW (1911)

IN OLD CALIFORNIA, WHEN THE GRINGOES CAME (1911)
Erroneously listed as a Mix film in *American Film Index 1908-1915*

IN THE DAYS OF GOLD (1911)

KIT CARSON'S WOOING (1911)
Erroneously listed as a Mix film in *American Film Index 1908-1915*

A RECONSTRUCTED REBEL (1912)

ME AND BILL (1912)

THE NOISY SIX (1913)
Erroneously listed as a Mix film in *American Film Index 1908-1915*

THE WORDLESS MESSAGE (1913)

SONGS OF TRUCE (1913)
Erroneously listed as a Mix film in *American Film Index 1908-1915*

BUDD DOBLE COMES BACK (1913)

A PRISONER OF THE CABANAS (1913)

————

The following are Selig films produced by the Francis J. Grandon unit after Tom Mix became a star/director heading his own unit. Mix was not involved in their production, nor did he appear in them.

WIGGS TAKES THE REST CURE (1914)

TO BE CALLED FOR (1914)

JIM (1914)

THE LIVID FLAME (1914)

FOUR MINUTES LATE (1914)

GARRISON'S FINISH (1914)

OUT OF PETTICOAT LANE (1914)

IF I WERE YOUNG AGAIN (1914)

THE SOUL MATE (1914)

THE LURE O' THE WINDIGO (1914)

WADE BRENT PAYS (1914)

FLOWER OF FAITH (1914)

HEART'S DESIRE (1915)

HEARTS OF THE JUNGLE (1915)

JACK'S PALS (1915)

THE PUNY SOUL OF PETER RAND (1915)

THE FACE AT THE WINDOW (1915)

————

The following was produced by the Oscar Eagle unit after Tom Mix became a star/director heading his own unit. Mix was not involved in its production, nor did he appear in it.

LURE OF THE LADIES (1914)

The following was produced by the Burton King unit after Tom Mix became a star/director heading his own unit. Mix was not involved in its production, nor did he appear in it.

THE PARSON WHO FLED WEST (1915)

––––––

The following pictures were produced by the William Duncan unit in Prescott, Arizona, in late 1912 while Tom Mix was away from the picture business.

HOW IT HAPPENED (1913)

THE RANGE LAW (1913)

––––––

The following first appeared on a filmography published in Italy a number of years ago, but Tom Mix is not listed in contemporary credit lists, and there is no evidence that he appeared in these films.

TOBIAS WANTS OUT (1913)
   (aka TOBIAS WINS OUT)
This was part of a brief Selig comedy series, and Mix was not in any of the "Tobias" films.

PAULINE CUSHMAN, THE FEDERAL SPY (1913)
Mix is not listed in the cast of this film, which was produced either in Chicago or California at a time when Tom Mix was in Prescott, Arizona.

Mix is not listed in contemporary credit lists for these films, and there is no other evidence that he appeared in them. He was not involved in their production.

THE LONG TRAIL (1910)
This is a 1910 Selig release, but there is no evidence that Tom Mix appeared in it.

LOST IN THE JUNGLE (1911)
Long attributed to Mix, it appears that this film was made in Florida sometime after Tom Mix left to join another Selig unit at Prescott, Arizona.

THE TOTEM MARK (1911)

LOST IN THE ARCTIC (1911)

WHEELS OF JUSTICE (1911 remake)

THE MILLIONAIRE COWBOY (1913)

SHOTGUN JONES (1914)

ME AND BILL (1914 remake)

THE LEOPARD'S FOUNDLING (1914)

HIS FIGHT (1914)

THE REVELER (1914)

THE FIFTH MAN (1914)

THE LONESOME TRAIL (1914)

HEARTS AND MASKS (1914)

––––––

The following title was announced by FBO as the sixth film in the Mix-FBO series, but it was never produced or released.

THE DUDE RANCH (1929)

INDEX OF TITLES